# A GUIDE TO
# THE HISTORY OF
# FLORIDA

**Recent Titles in**
**Reference Guides to State History and Research**

A Guide to the History of Louisiana
*Light Townsend Cummins and Glen Jeansonne, editors*

A Guide to the History of Massachusetts
*Martin Kaufman, John W. Ifkovic, and Joseph Carvalho III, editors*

A Guide to the History of Texas
*Light Townsend Cummins and Alvin R. Bailey, Jr., editors*

A Guide to the History of California
*Doyce B. Nunis, Jr., and Gloria Ricci Lothrop, editors*

# A GUIDE TO
# THE HISTORY OF
# FLORIDA

*Edited by* Paul S. George
*Foreword by* Samuel Proctor

REFERENCE GUIDES TO STATE HISTORY AND RESEARCH
*LIGHT T. CUMMINS AND GLEN JEANSONNE, SERIES EDITORS*

**GP**

**GREENWOOD PRESS**
New York • Westport, Connecticut • London

**Library of Congress Cataloging-in-Publication Data**

A Guide to the history of Florida / edited by Paul S. George ;
   foreword by Samuel Proctor.
      p.  cm. — (Reference guides to state history and research)
      Bibliography: p.
      Includes index.
      ISBN 0–313–24911–3 (lib. bdg. : alk. paper)
      1. Florida—History—Bibliography.  2. Florida—History—Sources—
Bibliography.  I. George, Paul S.  II. Series.
  Z1271.G85  1989
   [F311]
  016.9759—dc 19       88–38080

British Library Cataloguing in Publication Data is available.

Copyright © 1989 by Paul S. George

Library of Congress Catalog Card Number: 88–38080
ISBN: 0–313–24911–3

First published in 1989

Greenwood Press, Inc.
88 Post Road West, Westport, Connecticut 06881

Printed in the United States of America

∞

The paper used in this book complies with the
Permanent Paper Standard issued by the National
Information Standards Organization (Z39.48–1984).

10 9 8 7 6 5 4 3 2 1

# CONTENTS

# FOREWORD

FLORIDA'S RICH AND colorful history stretches back through time for more than half a millennium. The libraries are filled with accounts of Indian life, Spanish discovery and exploration, British settlement, and American growth and development. Thousands of books, monographs, articles, newspaper accounts, diaries, journals, memoirs, and letters recount the exploits, adventures, and the daily life experiences of the celebrated and not so famous folks who have walked across the stage of Florida history. There are also sizeable collections of photographs, archaeological artifacts, video and audio tapes, art works, and a vast array of material culture objects.

The vast assemblage of Florida primary and secondary source material is in the libraries and archives of universities and colleges, historical societies, governmental agencies, museums, and public and private collections throughout the state. Research scholars, academics, graduate students, teachers, genealogists, and the interested public often have difficulty determining where to find a desired item. *A Guide to the History of Florida* will provide the information on what is available for research and study and where it may be found. Paul S.

George, editor of this volume, has wisely selected Florida's best-known historians, archivists, and librarians to write the essays. The *Guide* will fill a need for the historical and general community.

                                                            Samuel Proctor

# PREFACE

IN THE LATE 1980s, Florida's population soared to twelve million, moving it ahead of Pennsylvania as the nation's fourth most populous state. Although many observers think of the Sunshine State as young because its most significant development has come in recent decades, it was actually the first part of today's United States discovered and settled by Europeans. The Spanish established St. Augustine, the first permanent settlement in the United States in 1565, or forty-two years before England planted its colony of Jamestown. The flags of five nations have flown over Florida, creating, in the process, an historical tapestry as colorful, rich, and unique as that of any state.

This work focuses on Florida's historical record and includes information on the lengthy era that preceded its discovery by Europeans. Many of Florida's leading historians, archivists, and librarians and an archaeologist have contributed illuminating essays on the state's chronological development, topical themes, and its most important historical collections and repositories. The first study of its kind, *A Guide to the History of Florida* represents an undertaking that is long overdue.

The *Guide* consists of two sections. The first contains historiographical essays examining the major works and key interpretations for each period of Florida history, as well as several topical themes. The second section provides an overview of the most important archives in Florida and several outside of the state that contain major collections in Florida history. The study also includes information on smaller, more specialized collections, which contain rich nuggets of information on one or more facets of Florida's history.

Each essay reflects the unique style and work of its creator. Occasionally, two or more contributors have cited the same bibliographic entry but in a context pertinent to their study. Sir Jack D. L. Holmes's essay (with a bibliographic section by William Coker) speaks to both sections of the book, since it contains detailed information on sources as well as an annotated bibliography. A careful examination of the essays will yield valuable information for scholar and layman alike.

The editor's heaviest debt in preparing this work rests with the talented essayists who unselfishly gave of their time and expertise so that students of the subject could embark upon an illuminating trail of discovery. I am especially indebted to Samuel Proctor, a dean of Florida history, for his guidance and direction from the project's inception to its completion. Dr. Proctor has rendered inestimable assistance to me and scores of others working in Florida history for more years than we—and he—would care to admit. Other persons instrumental in the completion of this project include Light T. Cummins and Glen Jeansonne, the series editors who first approached me about it, Serge Martinez, Gerald McSwiggan, Jean Kaufman, Joan Welch, Laura Gamon, Gina Lipianin, Gary Mormino, Sandy Mesics, Valerie Dorsett, James Cortada, and, of course, *my* long-suffering editor, Cynthia Harris. On a more personal note, I wish to acknowledge an immense debt to my parents, Sargis and Alice George, for their unflagging support of all of their son's endeavors. It is to them that I dedicate this work.

## PART ONE

---

# THE HISTORICAL LITERATURE

# 1

## ABORIGINAL FLORIDA

### JERALD T. MILANICH

THE HISTORIOGRAPHY PRESENTED here is intended to provide the student of Florida aborigines with an overview of the various cultures who have resided in the state from about 10,000 B.C. to the demise of native cultures early in the eighteenth century. The first section introduces Florida and its distinctive environments, which through time have helped to shape the cultures of the many aboriginal groups who have lived here. Other sections refer to those peoples known only from archaeological research.

Europeans first reached Florida early in the sixteenth century, bringing many changes to the aboriginal cultures. Ultimately European contact led to the total destruction of the native cultures and populations. The last section of the essay reviews the aborigines at the time of this contact and during the first Spanish period.

### FLORIDA, A LAND OF ENVIRONMENTAL AND
### CULTURAL DIVERSITY

In order to understand the Florida aborigines, their origins, and their development we must have some knowledge of the various present-day environmental zones as well as changes that have occurred in the past and their effects on humans. Robert S. Chauvin's article "The Natural Setting: Geography and Geology," in *Florida from Indian Trail to Space Age,* vol. 1, ed. Charlton W. Tebeau and Ruby Leach Carson (Delray Beach, Fla., 1965) (hereafter cited as *Indian Trail*) gives a concise and readable geological history of the state and serves to introduce the reader to its various physiographic zones.

An excellent collection of papers on environmental changes in South Florida during the period of human habitation is Patrick J. Gleason, ed., "Environments of South Florida, Present and Past," *Miami Geological Society Memoir* (Miami, 1974) (hereafter cited as *MGSM*), and in a new, revised edition, also edited by Gleason, *Environments of South Florida, Present and Past II* (Coral Gables, 1984) (hereafter cited as *Environments II*).

Through time the Florida Indians adapted to their changing environments. The resulting changes, along with growing human populations and increasing social complexity, led to the development of many different lifestyles reflected in different archaeologically definable cultures. The first attempt to present an areal and chronological ordering of those cultures is M. W. Stirling, "Florida Cultural Affiliations in Relation to Adjacent Areas," in *Essays in Anthropology in Honor of Alfred Louis Kroeber*, ed. R. H. Lowie (Berkeley, 1936). John M. Goggin's "A Preliminary Definition of Archaeological Areas and Periods in Florida," *American Antiquity*, 13 (October 1947) built on Stirling's taxonomy and set forth the basic spatial framework for Florida archaeological studies still in use today. However, as with all studies published prior to the early 1950s and the advent of radiocarbon dating, Goggin's chronological framework has been revised.

In a subsequent paper by Goggin, "Cultural Traditions in Florida Prehistory," in *The Florida Indian and His Neighbors*, ed. John W. Griffin (Winter Park, Fla., 1949), the different lifestyles of the prehistoric peoples living within the various regions of the state are further defined. A more popular summary is Ripley P. Bullen's "Florida Prehistory," in *Indian Trail*, which provides a more up-to-date chronology to go with Goggin's earlier studies. A similar overview can be found in chapter 1 of the revised edition of Charlton W. Tebeau's *A History of Florida* (Coral Gables, 1980).

The most comprehensive overview of Florida's aborigines is by Jerald T. Milanich and Charles H. Fairbanks. *Florida Archaeology* (New York, 1980) serves as a basic introduction to the subject and includes information on the archaeology of the historic period aborigines and the Seminole.

## Paleoindian and Archaic Period

In Florida the Paleoindian period, dating from 10,000 B.C. or earlier to 7000 B.C., is recognized largely by the presence of lanceolate-shaped stone projectile points or knives. Ripley P. Bullen's *A Guide to the Identification of Florida*

*Projectile Points* (Gainesville, 1975), describes these artifacts and also serves as a guide to points from later time periods.

Many Paleoindian tools have been found in river and spring deposits with the bones of now extinct animals. A summary of such finds and their importance can be found in Wilfred T. Neill, "The Association of Suwannee Points and Extinct Animals in Florida," *Florida Anthropologist* (hereafter cited as *F.A.*), 17 (March 1964). Some of these bones have been worked by humans, as described in Ripley P. Bullen, S. David Webb, and Benjamin I. Waller, "A Worked Mammoth Bone from Florida," *American Antiquity* (hereafter cited as *A.A.*), 35 (April 1970). Several articles document the correlation between Paleoindian points and karst geologic areas of the state; these include Benjamin I. Waller, "Some Occurences of Paleo-Indian Projectile Points in Florida Waters" *F.A.*, 23 (December 1970); Waller and James Dunbar, "Distribution of Paleo-Indian Projectiles in Florida," *F.A.*, 30 (June 1977); and Dunbar and Waller, "A Distribution Analysis of the Clovis/Suwannee Paleo-Indian Sites of Florida—A Geographical Approach," *F.A.*, 36 (March–June 1983).

Dramatic proof of the contemporaneity of humans and Pleistocene fauna in Florida is offered in S. David Webb, et al., "A *Bison Antiquus* Kill Site, Wacissa River, Jefferson County, Florida," *A.A.*, 49 (April 1984).

Underwater excavations in limestone sink holes (cenotes) have revealed animal bones, artifacts, and human remains, including tissue, which date from the Paleoindian and early Archaic periods. The first recognition of such extraordinary finds was made by William Royal and Eugenie Clark in "Natural Preservation of Human Brain, Warm Mineral Springs, Florida," *A.A.*, 26 (October 1960). Two technical reports on the same site are by Carl J. Clausen, H. K. Brooks, and A. B. Wesolowsky, "Florida Spring Confirmed as 10,000-Year-Old Early Man Site," *Florida Anthropological Society Publications* (hereafter cited as *FASP*), 7 (1975), and W. A. Cockrell and Larry Murphy, "Pleistocene Man in Florida," *Archaeology of Eastern North America*, 6 (Summer 1978). Another excellent report on a similar site is Clausen, et al., "Little Salt Spring: A Unique Underwater Site," *Science*, 203, no. 4381 (February 1979), which also summarizes local climatic changes occurring during Paleoindian and early and middle Archaic times.

Between 7000 B.C. and 5000 B.C., the early Archaic period, people made new types of stone tools and established numerous camps, especially in the forests of northern Florida where their hunting, collecting, and fishing lifestyle continued for thousands of years. Several reports on Archaic sites are Ripley P. Bullen and Laurence E. Beilman, "The Nalcrest Site, Lake Weohyapka, Florida," *F.A.*, 26 (June 1973); Bullen and Edward M. Dolan, "The Johnsons Lake Site, Marion County, Florida," *F.A.*, 12 (December 1959); E. Thomas Hemmings and Timothy A. Kohler, "The Lake Kanapaha Site in North Central Florida," *Florida Bureau of Historic Sites and Properties Bulletin* (hereafter cited as *FBHSP Bulletin*), 4 (1974); and Barbara A. Purdy, "The Senator Edwards Chipped Stone Workshop Site (Mr–122), Marion County, Florida: A Preliminary Report of Investigations," *F.A.*, 28 (December 1978).

Two thorough studies of Archaic lithic artifacts are Barbara A. Purdy and Laurie M. Beach, "The Chipped Stone Tool Industry of Florida's Preceramic Archaic," *Archaeology of Eastern North America*, 8 (1980) and Purdy, *Florida's Prehistoric Stone Technology, a Study of the Flintworking Techniques of Early Florida Stone Implement Makers* (Gainesville, 1981).

During the Middle Archaic period human burials continued to be placed in sinkholes where, under certain conditions, the remains and artifacts with them were preserved. Two such discoveries in southern Florida are John Beriault, et al., "The Archeological Salvage of the Bay West Site, Collier County, Florida," and Barry R. Wharton, George R. Ballo, and Mitchell Hope, "The Republic Groves Site, Hardee County, Florida," both in *F.A.*, 34 (June 1981).

Sometime before 4000 B.C., Archaic peoples began to settle in large numbers along the St. Johns River and its tributaries. Many of the same riverine sites continued to be occupied over thousands of years by the descendants of these Archaic populations. Gradually huge piles of discarded debris, mostly the remains of shellfish used for food, accumulated. Jeffries Wyman's *Freshwater Mounds of the St. Johns River, Florida* (New York, 1973), originally published in 1875, provides an interesting firsthand description of these extensive shell deposits, some thirty feet high.

Another nineteenth century Florida visitor excavated in several shell middens spanning the Archaic and later periods. Clarence B. Moore's "Certain Shell Heaps of the St. Johns River, Florida, Hitherto Unexplored," *American Naturalist*, 27 (1893) describes the contents of a number of sites. Stephen Cumbaa's "A Reconsideration of Freshwater Shell Exploitation in the Florida Archaic," *F.A.*, 29 (June 1976), employs zooarchaeological techniques to quantify the meat diet of the early Indian inhabitants of these Archaic shell middens. Illustrations of many of the artifacts recovered from one Archaic site can be found in Otto L. Jahn and Ripley P. Bullen, "The Tick Island Site, St. Johns River, Florida," *FASP*, 10 (1978).

Shortly after 2000 B.C., the shellmound Archaic peoples began to make fired clay pottery. An excellent description of this early pottery and its distribution and cultural significance are included in Ripley P. Bullen, "The Orange Period of Peninsular Florida," *FASP*, 6 (1972). Two reports on excavations at Orange period fiber-tempered pottery sites are John W. Griffin and Hale G. Smith, "The Cotton Site: An Archaeological Site of Early Ceramic Times in Volusia County, Florida," *Florida State University Studies*, 16 (1954), and Ripley P. Bullen, "Stratigraphic Tests at Bluffton, Volusia County, Florida," *F.A.*, 8 (March 1955).

## GROWTH AND FLORESCENCE OF REGIONAL CULTURES

During the period 2000 B.C. to 500 B.C. the Florida Indians continued to increase in population, occupying nearly all of the inhabitable areas within the state except the Keys. Contact between the Florida peoples and prehistoric societies to the north was occurring throughout this millennium and a half, and it continued unabated into the nineteenth century. These contacts and their effects on Florida cultures are examined in two articles by Ripley P. Bullen: "Regionalism in Florida during the Christian Era," *F.A.*, 23 (June 1970); and "The Origins of the Gulf Tradition as Seen from Florida," *F.A.*, 27 (March 1974).

## Northwest and North Florida

The basic culture sequence for Northwest Florida was established by Gordon R. Willey and Richard B. Woodbury in "A Chronological Outline for the Northwest Florida Coast," *A.A.*, 7 (January 1942).

Working in the early twentieth century, archaeologist Clarence B. Moore dug tens of mound sites in Northwest Florida as well as along the peninsular Gulf Coast. His reports include "Certain Aboriginal Remains of the Northwest Florida Coast (Part 1)," *Journal of the Academy of Natural Sciences of Philadelphia* (hereafter cited as *JANSP*), 11 (1901); "Certain Aboriginal Remains of the Northwest Florida Coast (Part 2)" *JANSP*, 12 (1902); "Certain Aboriginal Mounds of the Apalachicola River," *JANSP*, 12 (1903); "Certain Aboriginal Mounds of the Florida Central West Coast," *JANSP*, 12 (1903); and "The Northwestern Florida Coast Revisited," *JANSP*, 16 (1918). Without Moore's work and his reports, crude by today's scientific standards, many sites would surely have been looted and any knowledge of them lost forever.

Utilizing Moore's information as well as new data, Gordon R. Willey's "Archeology of the Florida Gulf Coast," *Smithsonian Miscellaneous Collections*, 113 (Washington, D.C., 1949) was issued as a detailed overview of each of the successive post–500 B.C. cultures found in the panhandle (Deptford, Swift Creek and Santa Rosa, Weeden Island, and Fort Walton historic Indians) and the related cultures of the peninsular Gulf Coast north of Charlotte Harbor. The book remains a mainstay of Florida and southeastern archaeology.

Three articles by William H. Sears, "The Sociopolitical Organization of Precolumbian Cultures on the Gulf Coastal Plain," *American Anthropologist*, 56 (June 1954); "Burial Mounds on the Gulf Coastal Plain," *A.A.*, 23 (January 1958); and "Hopewellian Affiliations of Certain Sites on the Gulf Coast of Florida," *A.A.*, 28 (July 1962), discuss aspects of the political and social organization and the religious life of Northwest Florida aborigines. A compilation by period of dietary information for various panhandle cultures can be found in George Percy, "A Review of Evidence for Prehistoric Indian Use of Animals in Northwest Florida," *FBHSP Bulletin*, 4 (1974). Dietary information is also the focus of Mabel K. Stockdale and Sally E. Bryenton's "Indian Plant Foods of the Florida Panhandle," *F.A.*, 31 (September 1978).

Other publications provide information on specific cultures. The Deptford culture, circa 500 B.C. to A.D. 1, is described in Jerald T. Milanich, "The Southeastern Deptford Culture: A Preliminary Definition," *FBHSP Bulletin*, 3

(1973), and the evolution of Deptford into later cultures is considered in William H. Sears, "The Tucker Site on Alligator Harbor, Florida," *Contributions of the Florida State Museum, Social Sciences*, 9 (1963).

Somewhat less information is available on the succeeding Swift Creek culture. David S. Phelps's "Swift Creek and Santa Rosa in Northwest Florida," *University of South Carolina Institute of Archeology and Anthropology Notebook*, 1, nos. 6–9 (1969), differentiates the Swift Creek culture from the more westerly Santa Rosa culture and gives brief descriptions of excavations at several Swift Creek sites. A more detailed report is Daniel T. Penton, "Excavations in the Early Swift Creek Component at Bird Hammock" (M.A. thesis, Florida State University, 1970).

A summary of archaeological traits of the Weeden Island culture in Northwest Florida, A.D. 250–950, is provided in Gordon R. Willey's pioneering study "The Weeden Island Culture: A Preliminary Definition," *A.A.*, 10 (July 1945). Detailed information on the activities of a single, late Weeden Island period family can be found in Jerald T. Milanich, "Life in a Ninth-Century Indian Household, a Weeden Island Fall-Winter Site on the Upper Apalachicola River, Florida," *FBHSP Bulletin*, 4 (1974). Descriptions of materials from a village site and interpretations on inland Weeden Island lifestyles are also offered in George W. Percy's "Salvage Investigations at the Scholz Steam Plant Site, a Middle Weeden Island Habitation Site in Jackson County, Florida," *FBHSP Bulletin*, 35 (1976).

In North Florida a project was begun in the mid–1970s to investigate the Weeden Island culture which inhabited that region after A.D. 200. Brenda J. Sigler-Lavelle's "The Political and Economic Implications of the Distribution of Period Sites in North Florida" (Ph.D. diss., New School for Social Research, 1980) generates an explanatory model for the settlement-economic-political system. Detailed information on the McKeithen village site, an Early Weeden Island mound-village complex in Columbia County is found in Tim A. Kohler, "The Social and Chronological Dimensions of Village Occupation at a North Florida Weeden Island Village Site" (Ph.D. diss., University of Florida, 1978). Ann S. Cordell's "Ceramic Technology at a Weeden Island Period Archaeological Site in North Florida," *Ceramic Notes 2, Occasional Publications of the Ceramic Technology Laboratory, Florida State Museum* (1984) is a detailed, scientific analysis of the pottery from that same site. An overview of the North Florida project also containing information on other Weeden Island cultures in Florida and the Southeast is Jerald T. Milanich, et al., *McKeithen Weeden Island, the Culture of Northern Florida, A.D. 200–900* (New York, 1974).

In Northwest Florida after A.D. 950 the development of more complex forms of social organization and the increased importance of horticulture are reflected in the appearance of the Mississippian-related Fort Walton culture. Two important articles examining the chronological development of the culture are John F. Scarry, "The Chronology of Fort Walton Development in the Upper Apalachicola Valley, Florida," *Southeastern Archaeological Conference Bulletin* (hereafter cited as *SEAC Bulletin*), 22 (1980), and Scarry, "Fort Walton Culture: A Redefinition," *SEAC Bulletin*, 24 (1981). David S. Brose and George W. Percy's "Fort Walton Settlement Patterns," in *Mississippian Settlement Patterns*, ed. Bruce D. Smith (New York, 1980), focuses on the interrelationships between sites and the natural environment.

The three most comprehensive and up-to-date Fort Walton studies are Nancy Marie White, "The Curlee Site and Fort Walton Development in the Upper Apalachicola–Lower Chattahochee Valley" (Ph.D. diss., Case Western Reserve University, 1982); David S. Brose, "Mississippian Period Cultures in Northwestern Florida," in *Perspectives on Gulf Coast Prehistory* (hereafter cited as *Perspectives*), ed. Dave D. Davis (Gainesville, 1984); and John F. Scarry, "Fort Walton Development: Mississippian Chiefdoms in the Lower Southeast" (Ph.D. diss., Case Western Reserve University, 1984).

The best known and largest Fort Walton site is described in B. Calvin Jones's "Southern Cult Manifestations at the Lake Jackson Site, Leon County, Florida: Salvage Excavation of Mound 3," *Midcontinental Journal of Archaeology*, 7 (1982). William M. Morgan's *Prehistoric Architecture in the Eastern United States* (Cambridge, Mass., 1980) provides a scale drawing of the site and its plazas. A cogent overview of the Pensacola culture and its temporal and spatial relationships is Vernon J. Knight, Jr., "Late Prehistoric Adaptation in the Mobile Bay Region," in *Perspectives*.

## Peninsular Gulf Coast

The post–500 B.C. cultures of the peninsular Gulf Coast north of Charlotte Harbor are related to those of Northwest Florida with some distinct differences. In general, the student of archaeology will find that many of the articles on Northwest Florida topics contain information also pertinent to the more southerly Gulf Coast. A brief overview of at least a portion of that coast is found in Ripley P. Bullen's "Archaeology of the Tampa Bay Area," *Florida Historical Quarterly* (hereafter cited as *FHQ*), 34 (January 1955).

Perhaps the most famous of the peninsular sites is the mound-village complex of Crystal River, which is a designated State Archaeological Site. Descriptions and interpretations of the site and artifacts found there include Gordon R. Willey's "Crystal River Florida: A 1949 Visit," *F.A.*, 2 (September–December 1949); Hale G. Smith's "Crystal River Revisited, Revisited, Revisited," *A.A.*, 17 (October 1951); Ripley P. Bullen's "The Famous Crystal River Site," *F.A.*, 6 (March 1953); and Bullen's "Stelae at the Crystal River Site, Florida," *A.A.*, 31 (October 1966).

Between A.D. 200 and 1000 or later, the culture of the coastal inhabitants was related to the more northerly Weeden Island culture. Tim A. Kohler's "The Garden Patch Site: A Minor Ceremonial Center on the North Peninsular Florida Gulf Coast" (M.A. thesis, University of Florida, 1975) describes a Weeden Island-related site, focusing on subsistence. Another view of a mound-village complex, one south of Tampa Bay, is Ripley P. Bullen and Adelaide D. Bullen, "The Palmer Site," *FASP*, 8 (1976). George M. Luer and Marion M. Almy's "A Definition of the Manasota Culture," *F.A.*, 35 (March 1982), synthesizes updated information regarding the Tampa Bay region aborigines during the period 500 B.C. to A.D. 800.

Perhaps influenced by the Northwest Florida Fort Walton culture and other southeastern Mississippian societies, the Safety Harbor culture developed in the greater Tampa Bay region by about A.D. 1000. Several excavations have been carried out at these mound-village complexes as well as at other sites. Reports include John W. Griffin and Ripley P. Bullen, "The Safety Harbor Site, Pinellas County, Florida," *FASP*, 2 (1950); Ripley P. Bullen, "The Terra Ceia Site, Manatee County, Florida," *FASP*, 3 (1951); Bullen, "Eleven Archaeological Sites in Hillsborough County, Florida," *Florida Geological Survey, Report of Investigations*, 8 (1952); and William H. Sears, "The Tierra Verde Burial Mound," *F.A.*, 20 (March–June 1967). An excellent summary statement is George M. Luer and Marion M. Almy, "Temple Mounds of the Tampa Bay Area," *F.A.*, 34 (September 1981).

The Pánfilo de Nárvaez (1528) and Hernando de Soto (1538) expeditions both landed at Tampa Bay and traveled northward through Safety Harbor territory. Artifact evidence for contact between Spaniards and the Safety Harbor culture comes from a number of mounds and villages. Two new sources of such evidence north of Tampa Bay are described in Jeffrey M. Mitchem, et al., "Early Spanish Contact on the Florida Gulf Coast: The Weeki Wachee and Ruth Smith Mounds," *FASP*, 4 (1985).

### North-Central Florida

The geographical region between the Santa Fe River and southern Marion County was only sparsely occupied from late Archaic times until about A.D. 100. Beginning then, Deptford peoples began to practice a more sedentary lifestyle. By A.D. 200 the Cades Pond culture, year-round inhabitants, had evolved from their Deptford predecessors. A popularly written account of the aboriginal history of the area is Jerald T. Milanich, "Indians of North-Central Florida," *F.A.*, 31 (December 1978).

Archaeologists have devoted a relatively large amount of attention to the development and nature of the Cades Pond culture. E. Thomas Hemmings's "Cades Pond Subsistence, Settlement, and Ceremonialism," *F.A.*, 31 (December 1978), defines and describes archaeological traits and places the culture in time and space. Further information on culture history and environmental and political factors determining Cades Pond settlement patterns are presented in that same issue by Jerald T. Milanich in "Two Cades Pond Sites in North-Central Florida—The Occupational Nexus as a Model of Settlement." One of the finest subsistence studies for any Florida aboriginal culture involved a Cades Pond site; the analyses are presented in Stephen L. Cumbaa, "An Intensive Harvest

Economy in North Central Florida" (M.A. thesis, University of Florida, 1972). However, the identification of domesticated beans cited by Cumbaa is now known to be an error.

By A.D. 800 the Cades Pond population was apparently pushed eastward out of North-Central Florida by agriculturalists moving southward from south-central and southeastern Georgia. An overview of this new culture is found in Jerald T. Milanich, "The Alachua Tradition of North-Central Florida," *Contributions of the Florida State Museum, Anthropology and History*, 17 (1971). Evidence for this southerly movement of Georgia aborigines is documented in Milanich, et al., "Georgia Origins of the Alachua Tradition," *FBHSP Bulletin*, 5 (1976).

The Alachua tradition population is ancestral to the Potano and Ocale Indians who occupied Alachua and western Marion counties in the historic period. An archaeological account of life in an early-seventeenth-century Potano village is found in Jerald T. Milanich, "Excavations at the Richardson Site, Alachua County, Florida," *FBHSP Bulletin* 2 (1972), which also examines evidence for Potano cultural changes in the historic period.

Our knowledge of burial ceremonialism in the Alachua tradition is based largely on two mound excavation reports: Ripley P. Bullen's "The Woodward Site," *F.A.*, 2 (September–December 1949), and L. Jill Loucks's "Early Alachua Tradition Burial Ceremonialism: The Henerson Mound, Alachua County, Florida" (M.A. thesis, University of Florida, 1976).

## East and Central Florida

From the late Archaic period into historic times the St. Johns River Valley, the Atlantic coastal strand south to below Cape Canaveral, and the lake district of Central Florida constituted a distinct culture region. A synthesis of the St. Johns region north of Cape Canaveral excluding the central lake district was published by John M. Goggin in "Space and Time Perspective in Northern St. John Archaeology, Florida," *Yale University Publications in Anthropology* (hereafter cited as *YUPA*), 47 (New Haven, 1952). A similar overview, including excavation descriptions, is Irving Rouse's "A Survey of Indian River Archaeology, Florida," *YUPA*, 44 (1951), which covers the coast from Cape Canaveral south to St. Lucie Inlet.

Several thorough reports on excavations in various St. Johns mounds and villages have been written. See Jesse D. Jennings, Gordon R. Willey, and Marshall T. Newman, "The Ormond Beach Mound, East Central Florida," *Smithsonian Institution, Bureau of American Ethnology Bulletin*, 164, *Anthropological Papers* (hereafter cited as *BAE Bulletin*), 149 (Washington, D.C., 1957). Ripley P. Bullen, Adelaide D. Bullen, and William J. Bryant's "Archaeological Investigations at the Ross Hammock Site, Florida," *William L. Bryant Foundation, American Studies Report* (hereafter cited as *BFASR*) (1967), reports findings at a circa A.D. 1 eastern Volusia County village with two adjacent burial mounds.

Two reports on excavations of large coastal shell heaps in the Daytona and New Smyrna area provide definitive information on the St. Johns people from well before A.D. 800 up to at least late prehistoric times. Ripley P. Bullen and Frederick W. Sleight, "Archaeological Investigation of the Castle Windy Midden, Florida," *BFASR*, 1 (1959), and Bullen and Sleight, "Archaeological Investigations of Green Mound, Florida," *BFASR*, 2 (1960), also illustrate a large number of St. Johns artifacts and provide some information on coastal subsistence. Additional information on subsistence is presented in Arlene Fradkin, "Faunal Remains from the Alderman Site, Volusia County, Florida," *F.A.*, 32 (June 1979); Marilyn C. Stewart, "Subsistence in the St. Johns Region: The Alderman Site," in the same issue; and James J. Miller, "Coquina Middens of the Florida East Coast," *F.A.*, 33 (March 1980).

Burial and platform or temple mounds, especially from the post–A.D. 800 period, dot East and Central Florida. Several large mound complexes similar to those of the panhandle and the Tampa Bay region are found along the St. Johns River. Clarence B. Moore's "Certain Sand Mounds of the St. Johns River, Florida, Parts 1 and 2," *JANSP*, 10 (1984), gives an account of excavations and artifacts from two such sites. Ripley P. Bullen's "Carved Owl Totem, Deland, Florida," *F.A.*, 8 (September 1955), describes a unique two-meter-tall wooden owl recovered from the St. Johns River near the Thursby site that dates to A.D. 1300. A nearby midden with well-preserved organic remains, the Hontoon Island site, has been reported in Barbara A. Purdy and Lee A. Newsom, "Significance of Archaeological Wet Sites: A Florida Example," *National Geographic Research*, 1, no. 4 (1985). An account of a late St. Johns period burial mound is E. Thomas Hemmings and Kathleen A. Deagan, "Excavation on Amelia Island in Northeast Florida," *Contributions of the Florida State Museum, Anthropology and History*, 18 (1973).

## South Florida

The southern part of peninsular Florida, the region below a line drawn from Charlotte Harbor east to just north of St. Lucie Inlet on the Atlantic coast, can be divided into three subregions. John W. Griffin's "Archaeology and Environment in South Florida," *MGSM*, 1, explains the basis for these divisions. See also John M. Goggin's *Indian and Spanish Selected Writings* (Coral Gables, 1964). Goggin and Frank H. Sommer III's "Excavations on Upper Matecumbe Key, Florida," *YUPA*, 41 (1949) focuses on the northern Keys and contains ethnohistoric description of the Keys Indians.

A recent report on a large archaeological project in Miami is John W. Griffin, et al., *Excavations at the Granada Site: Archaeology and History of the Granada Site*, vol. 1 (Tallahassee, 1984). The paleoethnobotanical data is particularly interesting. More information on regional plant use is presented in Daniel F. Austin, "Historically Important Plants of Southeastern Florida," *F.A.*, 33 (March 1980).

Since the late 1970s the Southeastern Archeological Center of the National Park Service has performed systematic surveys of Big Cypress Swamp in southern Florida. Summaries of results are found in Robert Taylor, "Archeological Survey of Big Cypress National Preserve," *SEAC Bulletin*, 23 (1980), and Robert S. Carr and John Beriault, "Prehistoric Man in South Florida," *Environments II*.

An important research topic in Southwest Florida is the evolution of the Calusa Indians who lived along the coast. An excellent study is Randolph J. Widmer's *The Evolution of the Calusa, a Non-agricultural Chiefdom on the Southwest Florida Coast* (Tuscaloosa, 1988).

A spectacular archaeological find of preserved organic materials was made in the late nineteenth century at the Key Marco site. Frank H. Cushing's "Exploration of Ancient Key-Dweller Remains on the Gulf Coast of Florida," *Proceedings of the American Philosophical Society*, 25 (1897), is a fascinating account of his recovery of wood, fiber, and other artifacts preserved in muck. An illustrated catalogue of the Key Marco collection is published in Marion Spjut Gilliland's *The Material Culture of Key Marco Florida* (Gainesville, 1975).

A more recent study of one of the large shellworks sites is William H. Marquardt's "The Josslyn Island Mound and Its Role in the Investigation of Southwest Florida's Past," *Florida State Museum Anthropology Miscellaneous Project Report Series*, 22 (1984).

Similar large complex sites, but with mounds and other works made of earth rather than shell, are found in the Lake Okeechobee Basin. Gordon R. Willey's "Excavations in Southeast Florida," *YUPA*, 42 (1949) describes two such sites in the eastern basin. Two articles providing information on the site of the Belle Glade culture at Fort Center west of Lake Okeechobee are William H. Sears, "Food Production and Village Life in Prehistoric Southeastern United States," *Archaeology*, 24 (October 1971), and Sears, "Archaeological Perspectives on Prehistoric Environment in the Okeechobee Basin Savannah," *MGSM*, 1. Sears's final report on the Fort Center excavations, including many illustrations and descriptions of the prehistoric wooden carvings found there, is *Fort Center, an Archaeological Site in the Lake Okeechobee Basin* (Gainesville, 1982). For a detailed analysis of Belle Glade subsistence patterns based on faunal remains from Fort Center, see H. Stephen Hale's "Prehistoric Environmental Exploitations around Lake Okeechobee," *Southeastern Archaeology*, 3 (Winter 1984).

## ABORIGINES OF THE HISTORIC PERIOD

Archaeological evidence for contact is summarized in Hale G. Smith's "The European and the Indian," *FASP*, 4 (1956), his "The Spanish Gulf Coast Cultural Assemblage, 1500–1763," *Spain and Her Rivals*, ed. Ernest F. Dibble and Earle W. Newton (Pensacola, 1971), and in Smith and Mark Gottlob's "Spanish-Indian Relationships: Synoptic History and Archaeological Evidence, 1500–1763," in

*Tacachale, Essays on the Indians of Florida and Southeastern Georgia During the Historic Period*, ed. Jerald T. Milanich and Samuel Proctor (Gainesville, 1978).

Summary articles on the Florida aborigines during the historic period can be found in John R. Swanton, "Early History of the Creek Indians and Their Neighbors," *BAE Bulletin*, 73 (Washington, D.C., 1922), and in Milanich and Proctor, eds., *Tacachale*. Sources whose coverage includes the Florida aborigines are John R. Swanton, "The Indians of the Southeastern United States," *BAE Bulletin*, 137 (1946), and Charles M. Hudson, *The Southeastern Indians* (Knoxville, 1976).


## Apalachee

The Apalachee Indians, historic descendents of the Fort Walton population in Northwest Florida, were first encountered by the Pánfilo de Nárvaez (1528) and Hernando de Soto (1539) expeditions. In the seventeenth century the Franciscans established missions in Apalachee territory. The missions were destroyed by the English in 1702–1704. Archaeological studies have focused on the missions themselves. A large number of pertinent documents along with reports on the excavation of two missions are available in Mark F. Boyd, Hale G. Smith, and John W. Griffin, *Here They Once Stood, the Tragic End of the Apalachee Missions* (Gainesville, 1951). James W. Covington's "Apalachee Indians, 1704–1763," *FHQ*, 50 (April 1972), recounts the history of the Apalachee from the missions' destruction until the last of the dispersed population was completely wiped out.

The most comprehensive historical study of the Apalachee and their relationships with the Spanish is John H. Hann, *Apalachee, the Land between the Rivers* (Gainesville, 1988). Hann's work provides a basis for all Apalachee and Spanish mission studies.

The layout and a reconstruction of a typical Apalachee mission complex based on archaeological data are pictured in L. Ross Morrell and B. Calvin Jones, "San Juan de Aspalaga, a Preliminary Architectural Study," *FBHSP Bulletin*, 1 (1970). Rochelle A. Marrinain's "The Archaeology of the Spanish Mission of Florida: 1565–1704," *FASP*, 4 (1985), reviews all of the work done on Apalachee and other Florida missions; its bibliography is indispensable to any student of the Spanish missions.

Charles W. Spellman's "The Agriculture of the Early North Florida Indians," *F.A.*, 1 (September–December 1948), is pertinent to the Apalachee as well as to the Timucua and other Florida groups. A source of information on the southeastern stick-ball game as it was played among the Apalachee is Amy Turner Bushnell's "That Demonic Game: The Campaign to Outlaw Indian *Pelota* Playing in Spanish Florida, 1675–1684," *The Americas*, 35 (1978). Bushnell has immortalized an Apalachee chief in "Patricio de Hinachuba: Defender of the Word of God, the Crown of the King, and the Little Children of Ivitachuco," *American Indian Culture and Research Journal*, 3 (1979).

Apalachee was a Muskhogean language. A summary of available information, including a bibliography of known sources, is discussed in James W. Crawford's "Southeastern Indian Languages," in *Studies in Southeastern Indian Languages*, ed. James W. Crawford (Athens, Ga., 1975).

## Timucuans

The Timucuans of North, North-Central, and East Florida were actually composed of at least fourteen separate groups which spoke several dialects of the Timucuan language. Two articles, those by Kathleen A. Deagan, "Cultures in Transition: Fusion and Assimilation among the Eastern Timucua," and by Jerald T. Milanich, "The Western Timucua: Patterns of Acculturation and Change," both in *Tacachale*, delineate the various Timucuan groups and histories of the groups vis-à-vis the colonial powers. James W. Covington's "Relationships between the Eastern Timucuan Indians and the French and Spanish, 1564–1567," *Four Centuries of Southern Indians*, ed. Charles M. Hudson (Athens, Ga., 1975) summarizes a brief, though intense period of contact.

Secondary sources for general ethnographic information include W. W. Ehrmann, "The Timucua Indians of Sixteenth-Century Florida," *FHQ*, 18 (January 1940), and Lillian M. Seaberg, "The Zetrouer Site: Indian and Spaniard in Central Florida" (M.A. thesis, University of Florida, 1955). Ethnographic information is also contained in three Spanish documents translated into English: Luís Gerónimo de Or, "The Martyrs of Florida (1513–1616)," *Franciscan Studies*, 18 (New York, 1936); James W. Covington, ed., *Pirates, Indians, and Spaniards; Father Escobedo's "La Florida"* (St. Petersburg, 1963); and Lucy L. Wenhold, "A Seventeenth Century Letter of Gabriel Díaz Vara Calderón, Bishop of Cuba," *Smithsonian Miscellaneous Collections*, 95, no. 16 (Washington, D.C., 1936).

Jerald T. Milanich and William C. Sturtevant's *Francisco Pareja's 1613 Confessionario: A Documentary Source for Timucuan Ethnography* (Tallahassee, 1972), contains ethnographic information and describes the known primary and secondary sources for the Timucuan language. Only two modern linguistic studies have been published: John R. Swanton's "Terms of Relationship in Timucua," in *Holmes Anniversary Volume, Anthropological Essays Presented to William Henry Holmes*, ed. F. W. Hodge (Washington, D.C., 1916), and Julian Granberry's "Timucua I: Prosodics and Phonemics of the Mocama Dialect," *International Journal of American Linguistics* 11 (1956). Woodcuts portraying Timucuans, copies of watercolors based on observations made by a Frenchman in 1564, are reproduced in Stefan Lorant, *The New World, the First Pictures of America* (New York, 1946).

Archaeological investigations have been carried out at several Spanish Franciscan Timucuan missions. Materials recovered from the mission of San Francisco de Potano northwest of Gainesville are described in M. I. Symes and

M. E. Stephens, "A–272: The Fox Pond Site," *F.A.*, 18 (June 1965), while Kathleen A. Deagan, "Fig Springs: The Mid-Seventeenth Century in North-Central Florida," *Florida Archaeology*, 6 (1972), examines the mission of Santa Catalina de Afuerica located near the Ichetucknee River. A Timucuan *visita* or mission in southern Suwannee County was the focus of excavations reported in L. Jill Loucks, "Political and Economic Interactions between Spaniards and Indians: Archaeological and Ethnohistorical Perspectives of the Mission System in Florida" (Ph.D. diss., University of Florida, 1979). John H. Hann's "Demographic Patterns and Changes in Mid-Seventeenth-Century Timucua and Apalachee," *FHQ*, 64 (1986), describes Spanish-initiated movements of peoples in North Florida.

Archaeological investigations have also been carried out in St. Augustine at the Fountain of Youth site, a settlement of Christian Timucuans adjacent to the Spanish mission at the north end of Spanish St. Augustine. Results of several excavations at the site are detailed in J. Donald Merritt's "Beyond the Town Walls: The Indian Element in Colonial St. Augustine," in *Spanish St. Augustine, the Archaeology of a Colonial Creole Community*, by Kathleen A. Deagan (New York, 1983). Deagan's excellent archaeological and historical study documents the lifestyle of the Spanish inhabitants of St. Augustine and the Indian and mestizo populations who also resided within and adjacent to the town. An earlier paper by Deagan, "*Mestizaje* in Colonial St. Augustine," *Ethnohistory*, 20 (Winter 1973), examines the documentary and archaeological evidence for Spanish-Indian cultural mixing. Additional information on the archaeology of Spanish St. Augustine and the processes of interaction between the Florida aborigines and the Spanish has been edited by Deagan for "Sixteenth Century St. Augustine Issue" *F.A.*, 38 (March–June 1985).

### Tocobaga

The Tocobaga Indians and the related Mococo, Ucita, and other groups oc-cupied a region centered on Tampa Bay but extending northward into Citrus and perhaps Levy County, southward at least to Charlotte Harbor, and eastward into the interior of Florida well into Polk County. Both the Nárvaez and de Soto expeditions landed among the Tampa Bay Indians, and the narratives from those excursions provide a great deal of information on the various chiefdoms of that region. On the Nárvaez *entrada* see Adolph F. Bandelier, ed., and Fanny R. Bandelier, trans., *The Journey of Alvar Nuñez Cabeza de Vaca and His Companions from Florida to the Pacific, 1528–1536* (New York, 1904; reprinted Chicago, 1964; and reprinted and reedited Barre, Mass., 1972); another translation is Buckingham Smith, trans., *Relation of Alvar Nuñez Cabeza de Vaca* (New York, 1871).

The three firsthand accounts of the de Soto expedition are found in Buckingham Smith, ed., and Edward Gaylord Bourne, trans., *Narratives of the Career of Hernando de Soto in the Conquest of Florida*, vol. 1 and 2 (New York, 1904;

reprinted New York, 1922). The account of Garcilaso de la Vega, written several decades after the *entrada* and based on interviews with survivors, is found in John and Jeanette Varner, eds. and trans., *The Florida of the Inca* (Austin, 1951). John R. Swanton, ed., "Final Report of the United States de Soto Expedition Commission," *76th Congress, 1st Session, House Document 71* (1939; reprinted Washington, D.C., 1985), is a mainstay for de Soto researchers.

A controversy has always raged concerning the exact location of the de Soto landing. Rolf F. Schell's *De Soto Didn't Land at Tampa* (Fort Myers Beach, Fla., 1966), and Warren H. Wilinson's "Opening the Case against the U.S. de Soto Commission's Report and Other de Soto Papers," *Alliance for the Preservation of Florida Antiquities*, 1 (1954), and his "The de Soto Expedition in Florida," *American Eagle*, 45 (1966), argue for a landing near Fort Myers among the Calusa Indians, but examination of Schell's and Wilkinson's interpretations indicates that their arguments should not be believed.

Attempts also have been made to correlate Safety Harbor archaeological sites with the Indian village of Uita where de Soto established his Tampa Bay camp. Ripley P. Bullen's "De Soto's Uita and the Terra Ceia Site," *FHQ*, 30 (March 1952), and John R. Swanton's "De Soto and Terra Ceia," *FHQ*, 31 (January 1953), debate the evidence and arrive at different conclusions.

Ripley P. Bullen's article "Tocobaga Indians and the Safety Harbor Culture," in Jerald T. Milanich and Samuel Proctor, eds., *Tacachale: Essays on the Indians of Florida and Southeastern Georgia During the Historic Period* (Gainesville, 1978), correlates the ethnohistorical evidence with the archaeological data in a concise overview. His "Southern Limit of Timucuan Territory," *FHQ*, 47 (April 1969), clarifies the geographical relationships between the Tocobaga and the Calusa to the south.

### Tequesta

During the colonial period modern Dade County was the home of the Tequesta (Tekesta) Indians. For several years during the late 1560s and early 1570s the Spanish maintained a Jesuit mission and a military garrison among the Tequesta on the Miami River. John M. Goggin's "The Tekesta Indians of South Florida," *FHQ*, 18 (April 1940); Robert E. McNicoll's "The Caloosa Village Tequesta, a Miami of the Sixteenth Century," *Tequesta*, 1 (March 1941); and Arva Moore Parks's *Where the River Found the Bay, Historical Study of the Granada Site, Miami, Florida; Archaeology and History of the Granada Site*, vol. 2 (Tallahassee, 1984), provide information on the Tequesta, who were nonagriculturalists, as were other South Florida aborigines.

A pertinent source on a 1740s settlement of South Florida aboriginal groups gathered at a village on the Miami River is William C. Sturtevant's "The Last of the South Florida Aborigines," in Jerald T. Milanich and Samuel Proctor, eds., *Tacachale: Essays on the Indians of Florida and Southeastern Georgia During the Historic Period* (Gainesville, 1978).

### Calusa

The largest and most politically powerful group in South Florida was the Calusa, whose main village in the sixteenth century was on the Gulf Coast near Fort Myers. A very informative firsthand account of the Calusa is David O. True, ed., and Buckingham Smith, trans., *Memoir of Do. d' Escalante Fontaneda Respecting Florida, Written in Spain, about the Year 1575* (Coral Gables, 1945; reprinted Miami, 1973). Fontaneda was shipwrecked in southern Florida about 1545 and rescued almost 20 years later. Many letters related to the Spanish Jesuit mission and Spanish garrison among the Calusa have been published in Felix Zubillaga, "Monumenta Antiquae Floridae (1566–1572)," *Monumenta Historica Societatis Iesu* 69: *Monumenta Missionum Societatis Iesu* 3 (Rome, 1946). Those documents are the best source of Calusa ethnographic data.

See also John M. Goggin and William C. Sturtevant, "The Calusa: A Stratified Nonagricultural Society (with Notes on Sibling Marriage)," *Explorations in Cultural Anthropology: Essays in Honor of George Peter Murdock*, ed. Ward H. Goodenough (New York, 1964); Clifford M. Lewis's "The Calusa," *Tacachale*; Charles J. Wilson's *The Indian Presence, Archeology of Sanibel, Captiva, and Adjacent Islands in Pine Island Sound* (Sanibel Island, Fla., 1982).

Like their neighbors to the north, the Calusa population died out in the eighteenth century as a result of disease epidemics. A topic of current interest in New World aboriginal studies is the magnitude and form of this disaster that killed millions of New World natives. Henry F. Dobyns's *Their Number Become Thinned, Native American Population Dynamics in Eastern North America* (Knoxville, 1983), attempts to reconstruct the level of the Florida Indian population at the time of first contact before the disease epidemics took place. Dobyns's use of sources cited as evidence for epidemics has been questioned by David Henige in "Primary Source by Primary Source? On the Role of Epidemics in New World Depopulation," *Ethnohistory*, 33 (1986); Jerald T. Milanich in "Corn and Calusa; de Soto and Demography," *Arizona State University Anthropological Research Papers* (1986), refutes Dobyns's evidence for Calusa farming and questions other interpretations.

### Other Groups

On other aboriginal groups, John M. Goggin's "The Indians and History of the Matecumbe Region," *Tequesta*, 10 (1950), describes the Indians of the northern Keys. A diary which graphically describes the adventures of the survivors of a late–seventeenth-century shipwreck on the Southeast Florida coast and also provides information on the Ais Indians who lived in the vicinity of Hobe Sound is reproduced in Evangeline W. Andrews and Charles McLean Andrews, *Jonathan Dickinson's Journal, or, God's Protecting Province* (New Haven, 1945; reprinted Stuart, Fla., 1975).

Many other groups are mentioned in documents. Two sources of information on these groups are Frederick Webb Hodge, "Handbook of North American Indians, Parts I and II," *BAE Bulletin*, 30 (Washington, D.C., 1907, 1910), and John R. Swanton, "The Indian Tribes of North America," *BAE Bulletin*, 145 (1952, reprinted Washington, D.C., 1968).

A great deal is known about the Florida aborigines, but even more remains to be discovered. Archaeologists, anthropologists, and historians are continuing to work to piece together the heritage of Native Americans.

**2**

# THE EARLY CONTACT
# PERIOD, 1513–1565

## MICHAEL V. GANNON

THERE IS AN abundant literature for students of the half-century long period of Spanish discovery and exploration of Florida prior to its permanent settlement at St. Augustine in 1565. Most of it dates from earlier periods than our own. With few exceptions the most important original work has not been done in the last quarter century. Almost every one of the titles listed is in the collection of the University of Florida Libraries, in Gainesville, specifically in either the P. K. Yonge Library of Florida History or the Latin American Collection.

In any examination of sources for the early contact period, one should turn first to the existing documentary collections, among which the following are indispensable: Martín Fernández de Navarrete, *Colección de los viajes y descubrimientos que hicieron por mar los españoles desde fines del siglo XV con varios documentos ineditos concernientes a la historia de la marina castellana y de los establecimientos españoles en Indias*, 5 vols. (Madrid, 1825–37); Navarrete, *Colección de documentos y manuscritos; prólogo del Almirante Julio Guillén Tato*, 32 vols. (Nendeln, Liechtenstein, 1971); Manuel Serrano y Sanz, *Documentos históricos de la Florida y la Luisiana, siglos XVI al XVIII* (Madrid,

1912); Buckingham Smith, *Colección de varios documentos para la historia de la Florida y tierras adyacentes* (London, 1857); Benjamin Franklin French, *Historical Collections of Louisiana and Florida, Including Translations of Original Manuscripts Relating to Their Discovery and Settlement, With Numerous Historical and Biographical Notes* (New York, 1869); and *Colección de documentos inéditos relativos al descubrimiento, conquista y organización de las antiguas posesiones españolas de America y Oceanía; sacados de los archivos del reino, y muy especialmente del de Indias*, 42 vols. (Madrid, 1864–84). Also valuable are selected documents in Woodbury Lowery, "Manuscripts of Florida," transcripts on microfilm, P. K. Yonge Library of Florida History; Buckingham Smith, "Buckingham Smith Collection," transcripts on microfilm, P. K. Yonge Library of Florida History; and John B. Stetson, "John B. Stetson Collection," photostat cards and microfilm, P. K. Yonge Library of Florida History. Almost two million microfilm images from Spanish archives have been added to the P. K. Yonge collection in the past ten years, but most, like the majority of the Lowery, Smith, and Stetson collections, come from the post-Menendez period. One should also consult: Archivo Histórico Nacional, *Colección de reales cédulas del Archivo Histórico Nacional: catálogo* (Madrid, 1977); and Santiago Montoto, comp., *Colección de documentos inéditos para la historia de Ibero-América* (Madrid, 1927).

Direction to additional materials is available in: James A. Robertson, *List of Documents in Spanish Archives Relating to the History of the United States, Which Have Been Printed or of Which Transcripts Are Preserved in American Libraries* (Washington, D.C., 1910); Robertson, *The Spanish Manuscripts of the Florida State Historical Society* (Worcester, Mass. 1929); Luis Rubio Moreno, *Inventarios del Archivo General de Indias* (Madrid, 1924-); Rubio Moreno, *Inventario general de registros cedularios del Archivo General de Indias de Sevilla* (Madrid, 1928?). There are two more recent guides to manuscript holdings of the Archivo General de Indias (hereafter cited A.G.I.): José María de la Peña y Cámara, *Archivo General de Indias de Sevilla: Guia del Visitante* (Madrid, 1958); and Peña y Cámara, *A List of Administrative Judicial Reviews of Colonial Officials in the American Indies, Philippines, and Canary Islands* (Washington, D.C., 1955). UNESCO funded a guide to all known archives for Spanish-American materials in Spain, both public and private: *Guía de Fuentes para la Historia de Ibero-America, conservadas en España* (Madrid, vol. 1, 1966, vol. 2, 1969). Other useful guides are: Luis Mariano Perez, *Guide to the Materials for American History in Cuban Archives* (Washington, D.C., 1907); *Spain and Spanish America in the Libraries of the University of California: A Catalogue of Books* (Berkeley, 1928–30); and David B. Quinn, ed., *New American World: A Documentary History of North America to 1612*, 5 vols., edited with commentary by D. B. Quinn, with the assistance of Alison M. Quinn and Susan Hillier (New York, 1979).

The following works on maps and charts are important for the period: Woodbury Lowery, *The Lowery Collection: A Descriptive List of Maps of the*

*Spanish Possessions within the Present Limits of the United States, 1502–1820*, edited with notes by Philip Lee Majors (Washington, D.C., 1912). Pedro Torres Lanzas, *Relación descriptiva de los mapas, planos, etc. de México y Florida existente en el Archivo General de Indias* (Seville, 1900); Jacobo María Duque de Berwick, *Mapas españoles de América, siglos XV-XVII* (Madrid, 1951); and Francisco Vindel, *Mapas de América en los libros españoles de los siglos XVI al XVIII (1503–1798). Con 241 facsímiles.* (Madrid, 1955).

The general histories of the period from the Spanish side tend to embrace, as one might expect, the entire Spanish enterprise in the Americas. La Florida has its proper, though minor, role in these accounts. The López de Gómara, Oviedo, and Herrera chronicles are the most notable: Francísco López de Gómara, *Historia general de las Indias* (first published sometime before 1560; first part reprinted Madrid, 1932); Gonzalo Fernández de Oviedo y Valdés, *Historia general y natural de las Indias, islas y tierra firme del mar océano, por el Capitán Gonzalo Fernández de Oviedo y Valdés, primer cronista del Nuevo Mondo*, (the first part originally published in 1535; Madrid, 1851–55); and Antonio de Herrera y Tordesillas, *Historia general de los hechos de los castellanos en las islas y tierra firme del mar océano. Escrita por Antonio de Herrera cronista mayor de su majestad de las Indias y su cronista de Castilla. En cuatro Decadas desde el año de 1492 hasta el de [1]531. Decada primera al rey nuestro señor*, 9 vols., (first published in 1601 and 1615; reprinted Madrid, 1726–27). A translation is available of the famous *Décadas del Nuevo Mundo*, or "Decades," of Pedro Mártir de Anglería (Peter Martyr): Richard Eden, ed. and trans., *The Decades of the Newe Worlde of West India, conteyning the navigations and conquests of the Spanyardes...Wrytten in the Latine tounge by Peter Martyr of...Angleria* (London, 1555). Two recent versions of the famous *Histora de Indias* by Bartolomé de las Casas are: *Historia de las Indias*, edición de Agustín Millares Carlo y estudio preliminar de Lewis Hanke (Mexico City, 1951); and *History of the Indies*, trans. André Collard (New York, 1971). A commentary on four of the general chroniclers is available in: Edmundo O'Gorman, *Cuatro historiadores de Indias, siglo XVI: Pedro Martir de Anglería, Gonzalo Fernández de Oviedo y Valdés, Bartolomé de las Casas, Joseph de Acosta* (Mexico City, 1972).

Important material for understanding the place of La Florida in the context of early empire appears in the following works: Edmundo O'Gorman, *The Invention of America: An Inquiry into the Historical Nature of the New World and the Meaning of Its History* (Bloomington, Ind., 1961); John Horace Parry, *The Spanish Seaborne Empire* (New York, 1966); Kenneth R. Andrews, *The Spanish Caribbean: Trade and Plunder, 1530–1630* (New Haven, 1978); Edward Gaylord Bourne, *Spain in America, 1450–1580, with a New Introduction and Supplementary Bibliography by Benjamin Keen* (New York, 1968); Henry Folmer, *Franco-Spanish Rivalry in North America, 1524–1763* (Glendale, Calif., 1953); Clarence H. Haring, *Trade and Navigation between Spain and the Indies in the Time of the Hapsburgs*, 2nd ed., (Gloucester, Mass., 1964); Haring, *Las instituciones coloniales de hispano-américa (siglos XVI a*

*XVIII)* (San Juan, P.R., 1957); Haring, *The Spanish Empire in America* (New York, 1963); Charles Gibson, *Spain in America* (New York, 1967); Francisco Morales Padrón, *Historia del descubrimiento y conquista de America* (Madrid, 1973); Lyle N. McAlister, *Spain and Portugal in the New World 1492–1700* (Minneapolis, 1984); Consejo de Indias, *Recopilación de leyes de los reinos de las Indias, mandadas imprimir y publicar por la Magestad Católica del rey don Carlos II, nuestro señor*, 4 vols. (Madrid, 1756); *The New Laws for the Government of the Indies and for the Preservation of the Indians, 1542–1543* (Amsterdam, 1968).

For the role of the *conquistadores*, important especially for Hernando de Soto in Florida (1539–40), a select bibliography would include the following: Mario Mateo, *La leyenda negra contra España: una compañía de calumnias que dura cuatro siglos* (Mexico City, 1949); Francisco Morales Padrón, *Historia negativa de España en América* (Ateneo, 1956); Mario Góngora, *Los grupos de conquistadores en Tierra Firme, 1509–1530; fisonomía histórica de un tipo de conquista* (Santiago, Chile, 1962); Paul Horgan, *Conquistadors in North American History* (New York, 1963); Charles Gibson, *The Black Legend: Anti-Spanish Attitudes in the Old World and the New* (New York, 1971); and Morales Padrón, *Los conquistadores de América* (Madrid, 1974).

The first serious historical study of Florida, including its proto-Spanish period, contained a number of sources no longer extant in any form: Barcía Carballido y Zúñiga, Andrés González de (pseudonym Gabriel de Cardensa z Cano) *Ensayo cronológico para la historia general de la Florida, 1512–1722* (Madrid, 1723); trans. Anthony Kerrigan (Gainesville, 1951). The classic modern English language study of the early contact period in Florida is still Woodbury Lowery, *The Spanish Settlements within the Present Limits of the United States, Volume 1, 1513–1561* (New York and London, 1901). It is expected that parts of this work will be superceded by a forthcoming history of the period by Paul E. Hoffman (see below). A publication that has had a substantial influence on attempts to define landing sites of such expedition leaders as Lucas Vásquez de Ayllón (see below) and de Soto appeared in 1983: Paulino Castañeda Delgado, *Alonso de Chaves, Quatri partitu en cosmografía práctica y por otro nombre Espejo de navegantes* (Madrid, 1983). A recent work that features Florida's Gulf Coast during the period is Robert S. Weddle, *The Spanish Sea: The Gulf of Mexico in North American Discovery, 1500–1685* (College Station, Tex., 1985).

Students of the period will also want to see: Paul Quattlebaum, *The Land Called Chicora: The Carolinas Under Spanish Rule, with French Intrusions, 1520–1670* (Gainesville, 1956); and the first two chapters of J. Leitch Wright, Jr., *The Only Land They Knew: The Tragic Story of the American Indians in the Old South* (New York, 1981). Perhaps the most provocative book ever published on Florida's native peoples is by Henry F. Dobyns, *Their Number Become Thinned: Native American Population Dynamics in Eastern North America* (Knoxville, 1983).

The recent literature on Juan Ponce de León, discoverer of Florida in 1513, is not as strong as students of the early contact period would prefer. One reason is a paucity of documentary sources for the discoverer's two Florida voyages. Another, apparently, is the greater attraction for students of the period of the later Narváez and de Soto expeditions. The normative study at this date is: Vicente Murga Sanz, *Juan Ponce de León, fundador y primer gobernador del pueblo Puertorriqueño, descubridor de la Florida y el Estrecho de las Bahamas* (San Juan, P.R., 1959). From Spain there is the relatively recent Manuel Vallve, *Juan Ponce de León, descubridor de la Florida "en busca de la fuente maravillosa de la juventud perenne," por Manuel Vallvé, illustraciones de J. de la Helguera* (Barcelona, 1956).

The latest attempts in the United States to piece together the various findings and interpretations relating to Ponce de León appear in Carl O. Sauer, *Sixteenth-Century North America: The Land and the People as Seen by the Europeans* (Berkeley, 1971); Samuel Eliot Morison, *The European Discovery of America: The Southern Voyages, A.D. 1492–1616* (New York, 1974); Weddle, *Spanish Sea*, and Lindsey Wilger Williams, *Boldly Onward: A True History Mystery...The Incredible Adventures of America's "Adelantados" and Clues to Their Landing Places in Florida, Ponce de León, Pánfilo Narváez, Hernando de Soto* (Charlotte Harbor, Fla., 1986). An attempt to identify the first landing site is presented in Edward W. Lawson, *Determination of the First Landing Place of Juan Ponce de León on the North American Continent in the Year 1513* (St. Augustine, Fla., 1954). Additional interpretative material is available in Jack D. L. Holmes, "The Historical Contribution of Juan Ponce de León in the Age of Discovery" (n.p., 1983?).

The oft-overlooked settlement of Lucas Vásquez de Ayllón and six hundred companions at San Miguel de Gualdape, probably on the coast of Georgia, in 1526 has as yet no book-length chronicler despite the fact that San Miguel was the first European settlement in what is now the United States. To augment the fragmentary accounts in Martyr, Herrera, and López de Gómara we soon shall have Paul E. Hoffman's account in his forthcoming *A New Andalucía and a Way to the Orient: A History of the American Southeast During the Sixteenth Century* (tentative title, Baton Rouge).

The expedition to Florida's Gulf by Pánfilo de Narváez in 1528 has been described by his treasurer and high sheriff Alvar Núñez Cabeza de Vaca, one of only four survivors. There are various versions, of which the following two provide a comparison: *The Narrative of Alvar Núñez Cabeza de Vaca*, translated by Fanny Bandelier (Barre, Mass., 1972), introduction by John Francis Bannon, with Oviedo's version of the Joint Report presented to the Audiencia of Santo Domingo translated by Gerald Theisen (Barre, Mass., 1972); and *The Narrative of Alvar Núñez Cabeza de Vaca*, translated by Buckingham Smith (Washington, D.C., 1851). The most recent secondary accounts are by Jose B. Fernández, *Alvar Núñez Cabeza de Vaca, the Forgotten Chronicler* (Miami, 1975); and

Fernández, *Contributions of Alvar Núñez Cabeza de Vaca to History and Literature in the Southern United States* (Ann Arbor, 1976). A frequently read popular work is Morris Bishop, *The Odyssey of Cabeza de Vaca* (Westport, Conn., 1933, 1971).

The most voluminous list of book titles for any single exploration, as one might expect, treats the Hernando de Soto *entrada* of 1539–40. Four original narratives exist, three from the hands of participants in the ill-fated march and one from an interviewer of the survivors. There is a brief account by the King's *factor* that was written immediately after the event, Luis Hernández DeBiedma, "Relación de la isla de la Florida," in *Colección de varios Documentos para la Historia de la Florida y Tierras adyacentes (1516–1794)*, ed. Buckingham Smith (London, 1857). Several translations are available: *The Discovery and Conquest of Terra Florida by Don Fernando de Soto and Six Hundred Spaniards*, ed. Luis H. DeBiedma (New York, 1966); "A Narrative of the Conquest of Florida by Hernando de Soto" in *Narratives of the Career of Hernando de Soto in the Conquest of Florida...*, ed. Edward G. Bourne (London, 1905); and "A Translation of a Recently Discovered Manuscript Journal of the Expedition of Hernando de Soto into Florida," in Benjamin F. French, *Historical Collections of Louisiana and Florida* (Philadelphia, New York, 1846–1853).

Another eyewitness account, from de Soto's private secretary Rodrigo Rangel, appears in condensed form and without its concluding chapters in our only extant source for it, Oviedo's *Historia General y Natural de las Indias* (1851–1855). The earliest narrative in time of publication is by an anonymous Portuguese companion of de Soto's, the "Gentleman of Elvas," *Relaçam verdadeira dos trabalhos que ho governador Don Fernando de Souto y certos fidalgos portugueses passarom no descobrimento de provinçia de Florida. Agora nouamente feita per hun fidalgo de Eluas* (Evora, Portugal, 1557). Numerous translations exist of which the following is representative: James Alexander Robertson, trans. and ed., *True Relation of the Hardships Suffered by Governor Fernando de Soto and Certain Portuguese Gentlemen during the Discovery of the Province of Florida. Now Newly Set Forth by a Gentleman of Elvas* (Deland, Fla., 1932).

The longest narrative, romantic in character and of doubtful accuracy, was written by Garcilaso de la Vega, "The Inca," *La Florida del Ynca. Historia del Adelantado, Hernando de Soto, Gouernador, y Capitain General del Reyno de la Florida y de otros Caualleros, Españoles e Indios* (Lisbon, 1601). The most recent translation of "The Inca" is John Grier Varner and Jeannette Johnson Varner, trans. and eds., *The Florida of the Inca* (Austin, 1951). An important recent addition to the body of original material is found in Eugene Lyon, "The Cañete Fragment: Another Narrative of Hernando de Soto" (n.p., 1982).

The major modern study of the route of de Soto through Florida and the other southern states was written by ethnohistorian John R. Swanton, *Final Report of the United States de Soto Expedition Commission* (Washington, D.C., 1939). This still valuable work was recently republished with an introduction and presentation of new data by Jeffrey P. Brain and a foreword by William C. Sturtevant (Washington, D.C., 1985). Two notable dissenters from the Swanton route are Warren H. Wilkinson, *Opening the Case against the U.S. de Soto Commission's Report...*, Papers of the Alliance for the Preservation of Florida Antiquities, vol. 1, no. 1, (Jacksonville Beach, Fla., 1960); and Rolfe F. Schell, *de Soto Didn't Land at Tampa* (Ft. Myers Beach, Fla., 1966). De Soto buffs will also want to see the theories advanced in Williams, *Boldly Onward*. A more up-to-date account of the de Soto march through Florida, based on new historical and archaeological discoveries, is emerging from the work of the state-supported de Soto Trail Committee. The data will be published soon by Jerald T. Milanich and Charles M. Hudson. There are provocative interpretations of the effect of the de Soto expedition on native populations in several of the essays appearing in R. Reid Badger and Lawrence A. Clayton, eds., *Alabama and the Borderlands: From Prehistory to Statehood* (University, Ala., 1985).

An original source for the Fray Luis Cáncer de Barbastro expedition in 1549 is "Relación de la Florida para el Ilmo. Señor Visorrei de la Nueva España la qual trajo Fr. Gregorio de Beteta," in Smith, ed., *Colección de varios Documentos*; the best secondary account is in Victor Francis O'Daniel, O.P., *Dominicans in Early Florida* (New York, 1930). For the Tristán de Luna settlement at Pensacola there are Agustin Dávila y Padilla, O.P., *Historia de la Fundación y Discurso de la Provincia de Santiago de México* (México, 1596), and two works by Herbert Ingram Priestly, trans. and ed., *The Luna Papers: Documents Relating to the Expedition of Don Tristán de Luna y Arellano for the Conquest of la Florida in 1559–1561*, 2 vols. (DeLand, Fla., 1928); and *Tristán de Luna, Conquistador of the Old South: A Study of Spanish Imperial Strategy* (Glendale, Calif., 1936).

For the immediate pre-Menendez period there is the curious and unreliable account of the native Floridians by Hernando de Escalante Fontaneda who after being shipwrecked on the southern coast as a thirteen-year-old in 1548 spent eighteen years on the peninsula before being rescued by Menendez de Aviles: *Memoir of D° d'Escalente Fontaneda respecting Florida. Written in Spain, about the Year 1575. Translated from the Spanish with notes by Buckingham Smith* (Washington, D.C., 1854), reprinted, ed. David O. True (Miami, 1944).

# 3

# SPANISH FLORIDA, 1565–1763, AND SPANISH EAST FLORIDA, 1784–1821

AMY TURNER BUSHNELL

SPANISH FLORIDA WAS a military jurisdiction marked by changing borders and inconstant allegiances. For the purposes of this historiographical essay, it is limited to those parts of the Southeast which from 1565 to 1763 fell within the captaincy general of Florida and from 1784 to 1821 within the governorship of East Florida, which came under the captaincy general of Cuba. Setting aside the sixteenth-century period of discovery, Spanish Florida thus begins with the founding of St. Augustine in 1565 and ends with the United States takeover in 1821—two and a half centuries interrupted by the twenty-one-year British period

(1763–1784) which for Florida historians separates the first Spanish period from the second. Spanish Florida history differs from southeastern in being restricted at any point in time to the places where there were people of Hispanic descent or allegiance. In studies of the seventeenth-century mission provinces or of eighteenth-century fugitive slaves it merges with ethnohistory.

For a colony whose capital was the earliest permanent European settlement in North America, Florida is markedly missing from colonial North American historiography. James Axtell analyzes the reasons for this in "Europeans,

Indians, and the Age of Discovery in American History Textbooks," *The American Historical Review* 92 (June 1987). Others who discuss the problem are Michael G. Kammen, "The Unique and the Universal in the History of New World Colonization," in Samuel Proctor, ed., *Eighteenth-Century Florida and Its Borderlands* (Gainesville, 1975); Wilcomb E. Washburn, "The Southeast in the Age of Conflict and Revolution," and Michael C. Scardaville, "Approaches to the Study of the Southeastern Borderlands," both in R. Reid Badger and Lawrence A. Clayton, eds., *Alabama and the Borderlands from Prehistory to Statehood* (Tuscaloosa, Ala., 1985).

Latin American colonialists pay little more attention to Florida than North American colonialists do. As a result, much of the research on Spanish Florida is done by scholars without academic affiliation, working as consultants to historical archaeology or on the staffs of museums or governmental agencies, subject to the needs of historic preservation and to the cycles of commemoration noted by Charles W. Arnade in "Recent Problems of Florida History," *Florida Historical Quarterly (FHQ)*, 42 (July 1963).

The literature, nevertheless, is sufficiently vast that in order to treat it comprehensively in a short essay one can only identify earlier reviews and survey what has been published since. For the first Spanish period, historiography of a traditional kind begins promisingly with Luís Rafael Arana, "The Exploration of Florida and Sources on the Founding of St. Augustine," *FHQ*, 44 (July 1965), and Lyle N. McAlister, introduction to the facsimile edition (Gainesville, 1964) of the *Pedro Menndez de Avils Memorial* by Gonzalo Solís de Merás (1567), trans. Jeanette Thurber Connor, only to drop off sharply at the end of the age of discovery.

Second Spanish Period historiography, on the other hand, was brought to a high level in the early 1970s at a series of Gulf Coast history and humanities conferences. Subsequently published reviews of the literature include Samuel Proctor, "Bibliographical Resources in the United States for Gulf Coast Studies," in Ernest F. Dibble and Earle W. Newton, eds., *In Search of Gulf Coast Colonial History* (Pensacola, 1970); William S. Coker and Jack D. L. Holmes, "Sources for the History of the Spanish Borderlands," *FHQ*, 49 (April 1971); and Proctor, "Research Opportunities in the Spanish Borderlands: East Florida, 1763–1821," published with a composite bibliography in *Latin American Research Review* 7 (Summer 1972). These merely need to be brought up to date.

The state of historiography for Florida's First Spanish Period was similarly improved in the 1980s with the appearance, in the American Indian Bibliographical Series of the Indiana University Press, sponsored by the D'Arcy McNickle Center for the History of the American Indian at the Newberry Library in Chicago, of two critical reviews of the ethnohistorical literature: James Howlett O'Donnell III, *Southeastern Frontiers: Europeans, Africans and American Indians, 1513–1840. A Critical Bibliography* (Bloomington, Ind., 1982), and W. R. Swagerty, ed., *Scholars and the Indian Experience: Critical Reviews of Recent Writing in the Social Sciences* (Bloomington, Ind.,

1984), in particular his chapter on "Spanish-Indian Relations, 1513–1821."

These critical reviews serve the interests of Spanish as well as Indian history for they include many of the standard Florida sources and studies. At the same time, sweeping across the entire Southeast or the whole of Spanish-Indian relations in North America, they draw Spanish Florida out of a provincialism that is frequently self-imposed.

The colonial Florida historian also finds much that is of interest in archaeological reports, for which there are two comprehensive bibliographies: Thomas Ray Shurbutt and Janet Lois Gritzner, *Historical Archaeology of the Colonial Southeastern Atlantic Coast: A Bibliography* (Gainesville, 1979); and Gregory Toole, Nelson Rowen Comer-Tesar, and Mary LePoer, comps., "Bibliography of Florida Archaeology through 1980," indexed by James J. Miller, Yvonne Gsteiger, and David Bradley in *Florida Archaeology* 1 (1986).

Looking over what has been published in the field of Spanish Florida history since the early 1970s, one is struck by the shortage of synthesis. There is still no history of the colony as a whole. The closest alternative is Jean Parker Waterbury, ed., *The Oldest City. St. Augustine, Saga of Survival* (St. Augustine, 1983). Its lack of a bibliography can be remedied with the exhaustive one by Paul L. Weaver in his *Historic Properties Survey of St. Johns County, Florida* (St. Augustine, 1985).

Few of the writers on Spanish Florida attempt to follow their subjects out of one period into another, or beyond the confines of the captaincy or governorship. An exception in both regards is Kathleen Deagan, whose "Spanish-Indian Interaction in Sixteenth-Century Florida and Hispaniola," in William W. Fitzhugh, ed., *Cultures in Contact: The Impact of European Contacts on Native American Cultural Institutions A.D. 1000–1800* (Washington, D.C., 1985), 281–318, and *Artifacts of the Spanish Colonies of Florida and the Caribbean, 1500–1800*, vol. 1: *Ceramics, Glassware, and Beads* (Washington, D.C., 1987), establish Florida as part of the Caribbean.

Sixteenth-century exploration and settlement continue to invite interest, with Paul E. Hoffman, "The Chicora Legend and Franco-Spanish Rivalry in *La Florida*," *FHQ*, 59 (January 1981); and Chester B. DePratter, Charles M. Hudson, and Marvin T. Smith, "The Route of Juan Pardo's Explorations in the Interior Southeast, 1566–1568," *FHQ*, 62 (October 1983). Since 1979 the South Carolina Institute of Archaeology and Anthropology has published yearly reports on Stanley South's excavations at Santa Elena, including Eugene Lyon's *Santa Elena: A Brief History of the Colony, 1566–1587* (Columbia, S.C., 1984).

Subsistence has received increasing attention, including that of Elizabeth J. Reitz and C. Margaret Scarry, *Reconstructing Historic Subsistence with an Example from Sixteenth-Century Spanish Florida*, Society for Historical Archaeology Special Publications Series 3 (Glassborg, N.J., 1985); Lewis H. Larson, *Aboriginal Subsistence Technology on the Southeastern Coastal Plain During the Late Prehistoric Period* (Gainesville, 1980); and the methodologically controversial Henry F. Dobyns, *Their Number Become Thinned: Essays on Native*

*American Population Dynamics in Eastern North America* (Knoxville, 1983).

Religious history of a traditional kind has not maintained its earlier momentum. Since the publication of Gregory Joseph Keegan and Leandro Tormo Sanz's *Experiencia misionera en la Florida (siglos xvi y xvii)* (Madrid, 1957), with its incomparable bibliography, little has been added beyond Frank Marotti, Jr., "Juan Baptista de Segura and the Failure of the Florida Jesuit Mission, 1566–1572," *FHQ*, 58 (January 1985).

On the other hand, interest has been growing in mission towns as frontier settlements and scenes of cultural interaction. Summaries of information to date include David Hurst Thomas and Lorann S. A. Pendleton, "What *Do* the Missions of *La Florida* Look Like? An Archaeological Perspective," in Thomas, *The Archaeology of Mission Santa Catalina de Guale: 1. Search and Discovery*, American Museum of Natural History Anthropological Papers 63 (1987); Thomas's "Saints and Savages at Santa Catalina: An Alternative Hispanic Design for Colonial America," in Mark P. Leone and Parker B. Potter, Jr., *The Recovery of Meaning in Historical Archaeology* (Washington, D.C., in press); and Rochelle A. Marrinan's "The Archaeology of the Spanish Missions of Florida: 1565–1704," in Kenneth W. Johnson, Jonathan M. Leader, and Robert C. Wilson, eds., *Indians, Colonists, and Slaves: Essays in Memory of Charles H. Fairbanks*, *Florida Journal of Anthropology* Special Publication 4 (Gainsville, 1985).

John Hann, historian at the San Luis Archaeological Site, has begun to publish the results of years of work on the mission provinces: "Demographic Patterns and Changes in Mid-Seventeenth Century Timucua and Apalachee," *FHQ*, 66 (July 1987), a full issue of *Florida Archaeology* 2 (1986) devoted to edited translations, and *Apalachee: The Land between the Rivers* (Gainesville, in press). The book on the Apalachees is especially welcome as it fills a gap in an otherwise excellent survey of historic period Indian groups: Jerald T. Milanich and Samuel Proctor, eds., *Tacachale: Essays on the Indians of Florida and Southeastern Georgia During the Historic Period* (Gainesville, 1978).

Amy Turner Bushnell has continued her work on Indian-Spanish society in the provinces with "The Menndez Marquez Cattle Barony at La Chua and the Determinants of Economic Expansion in Seventeenth-Century Florida," *FHQ*, 56 (April 1978); "Patricio de Hinachuba: Defender of the Word of God, the Crown of the King, and the Little Children of Ivitachuco," *American Indian Culture and Research Journal* 3 (July 1979); "Ruling the Republic of Indians in Seventeenth-Century Florida," in Peter Wood, M. Thomas Hatley, and Gregory A. Waselkov, eds., *Powhatan's Mantle: Ethnohistory of Indians in the Colonial Southeast* (Lincoln, Nebr., in press); and *Material Culture of the Franciscan Doctrinas in Spanish Florida*, forthcoming with the American Museum of Natural History in the Santa Catalina series which reports the David Hurst Thomas excavations at St. Catherine's Island.

Fred Lamar Pearson, Jr., has been turning the institution of the *visita* to good account with "The Florencia Investigation of Spanish Timucua," *FHQ*, 51

(October 1972); "Spanish-Indian Relations in Florida, 1602–1675: Some Aspects of Selected *Visitas*," *FHQ*, 52 (January 1974); and "Timucuan Rebellion of 1656: The Rebolledo Investigation and the Civil-Religious Controversy," *FHQ* 61 (January 1983).

St. Augustine, the jurisdiction's one Spanish municipality after 1587, receives a steady share of attention. The St. Augustine Foundation research project described in *El Escribano* 14 (1977) by Eugene Lyon, "St. Augustine 1580: The Living Community," and Paul Hoffman, "St. Augustine 1580: The Research Project" has resulted in two historical films: *Dream of Empire* (1984) and *Struggle to Survive* (1983). Some of the research has also seen publication in sections of Kathleen Deagan, *Spanish St. Augustine: The Archaeology of a Colonial Creole Community* (New York, 1983), and in Albert Manucy, "Building Materials in Sixteenth-Century St. Augustine," *El Escribano* 20 (1983), which supplements his "Changing Traditions in St. Augustine Architecture," in Samuel Proctor, ed., *Eighteenth-Century Florida: The Impact of the American Revolution* (Gainesville, 1978).

Between 1968 and 1973 Luís Rafael Arana published a series of articles in *El Escribano*, journal of the St. Augustine Historical Society, while he was its editor. Among them are "Documents about Fort Apalachicola (1689–1691)," "Military Organization in Florida, 1671–1702," "Private Coquina Construction in St. Augustine, 1689–1702," "Fort San Diego," "Aid to St. Augustine after the Pirate Attack, 1668–1670," and "The Mose Site." Arana, historian for Castillo de San Marcos, has since written "The Fort at Matanzas Inlet," *El Escribano* 17 (1980), and with Albert Manucy, *The Building of Castillo de San Marcos* (Philadelphia, 1977). With Arana's aid, Ricardo Torres-Reyes of the National Park Service has prepared a set of *Historical Base Maps: Castillo de San Marcos National Monument* (St. Augustine, Fla., 1972) of the city and environs.

Colonial government and finances have been treated by Amy Turner Bushnell, *The King's Coffer: Proprietors of the Spanish Florida Treasury, 1565–1702* (Gainesville, 1981); William R. Gillaspie, "Survival of a Frontier Presidio: St. Augustine and the Subsidy and Private Contract Systems, 1680–1702," *FHQ* 62 (January 1984); and Engel Sluiter, in a separately published book, *The Florida Situado: Quantifying the First Eighty Years, 1571–1651* (Gainesville, 1985).

Maritime history is integral to the field of Spanish Florida. Paul Hoffman sets the stage with *The Spanish Crown and the Defense of the Caribbean, 1535–1585: Precedent, Patrimonialism, and Royal Parsimony* (Baton Rouge, 1980); Eugene Lyon describes the colony's maritime beginnings in *The Enterprise of Florida: Pedro Menndez de Avils and the Spanish Conquest of 1565–1568* (Gainesville, 1976). In *The Search for the Atocha* (Port Salerno, Fla., 1985), Lyon tells a tale of seventeenth-century shipwreck and twentieth-century salvagers.

Robert S. Weddle continues the maritime history of Florida in sections of *The Spanish Sea: The Gulf of Mexico in North American Discovery, 1500–1685* (College Station, Tex., 1985), and *Wilderness Manhunt: The Spanish Search for La Salle* (Austin, 1973), placing in context the late seventeenth-century buccaneers who swarmed into Florida waters and the Florida-based expeditions into the Gulf.

A large share of the contributions to a knowledge of the seventeenth-century First Spanish Period has been made by historical archaeologists. Charles H. Fairbanks summarized their work to date and outlined their research goals in "From Missionary to Mestizo: Changing Culture of Eighteenth-Century St. Augustine," in Samuel Proctor, ed., *Eighteenth-Century Florida and the Carribbean* (Gainesville, 1976). Kathleen Deagan's aforementioned *Spanish St. Augustine: The Archaeology of a Colonial Creole Community*, documents the fulfilling of this promise.

Historians no longer treat as a unit the time between the loss of the mission provinces during the Queen Anne's War and the cession of the colony to Great Britain in 1763. Juan Marchena Fernández disregards traditional periodization altogether in his "Guarniciones y población militar en Florida Oriental (1700–1820)," *Revista de Indias* (January–June 1981): 163–64.

The question of fugitive slavery is taken outside of political time frames by John J. TePaske, "The Fugitive Slave: Intercolonial Rivalry and Spanish Slave Policy, 1687–1764," in Proctor, ed., *Eighteenth-Century Florida and Its Borderlands*, and Jane Landers, "Spanish Sanctuary: Fugitives in Florida, 1687–1790," *FHQ*, 62 (January 1984).

Historians have become more conscious of the cultural exchange between blacks and Indians. A groundbreaking study of this type is J. Leitch Wright, Jr., *The Only Land They Knew: The Tragic Story of the American Indians in the Old South* (New York, 1981).

Peter H. Wood's "The Changing Population of the Colonial Southeast: An Overview, by Race and Region, from 1685 to 1790," in Wood, Hatley and Waselkov, eds., *Powhatan's Mantle*, provides a long overdue demographic base on which to build. In the same work, Helen Hornbeck Tanner creates a similar starting point for geography in "The Land and Communication Systems of the Southeastern Indians."

The reader should be aware of a bicentennial series edited by Samuel Proctor on eighteenth-century Florida borderlands, frontier life, the Caribbean, the revolutionary South, and the impact of the American Revolution, published by the University Presses of Florida between 1975 and 1978. Its five volumes contain significant articles on Spanish Florida.

The Bicentennial Floridiana Facsimile Series of the University of Florida Press, also edited by Proctor, is valuable for its new historical introductions. Those that concern Spanish Florida are the aforementioned introductions by Lyle N. McAlister, to the Gonzalo Solií de Merás *Memorial* (Gainesville, 1964); by Aileen Moore Topping, to *An Impartial Account of the Late Expedition against St. Augustine under General Oglethorpe* [1742] (Gainesville, 1978); by John W. Griffin, to *Narrative of a Voyage to the Spanish Main* [1819] (Gainesville, 1978); and by William S. Coker, to Daniel Coxe, *A Description of the English Province of Carolina, by the Spaniards call'd Florida, and by the French La Louisiane* [1722] (Gainesville, 1976).

William Coker is editor and publisher of *John Forbes's Description of the Spanish Floridas, 1804* (Pensacola, 1979). His introduction to the Forbes description supplies a summary of events in the Floridas from 1792 to 1821, in Proctor, ed., *Eighteenth-Century Florida and the Caribbean*, and could double as an introduction to his and Thomas D. Watson's impressive *Indian Traders of the Southeastern Spanish Borderlands: Panton, Leslie & Company and John Forbes & Company, 1783–1847* (Pensacola, 1986).

The first East Florida census has attracted the attention of historians, among them Philip D. Rasico, "The Minorcan Population of St. Augustine in the Spanish Census of 1786," *FHQ*, 65 (October 1987); Theodore G. Corbett, "The Problem of the Household in the Second Spanish Period," in Proctor, ed., *Eighteenth-Century Florida: The Impact of the American Revolution*; and Pablo Tornero Tinajero, "Sociedad y población en San Agustín de la Florida (1786)," *Annuario de Estudios Americanos* 35 (1978). Ann P. Emerson makes use of military diet orders to evaluate "Standards of Nutrition in a St. Augustine Hospital, 1783–1821," *FHQ*, 65 (October 1986).

An example of the trend toward increased attention on Anglo-Americans and Indians is Helen Hornbeck Tanner, "Pipesmoke and Muskets: Florida Indian Intrigues of the Revolutionary Era," in Proctor, ed., *Eighteenth-Century Florida and Its Borderlands*. Frank Lawrence Owsley, Jr., in *Struggle for the Gulf Borderlands: The Creek War and the Battle of New Orleans, 1812–1815* (Gainesville, 1981), shows how the Creek War of 1813–1814 leads to the First Seminole War of 1817–1818. J. Leitch Wright, Jr., takes a more culturally oriented view of the same events in *Creeks and Seminoles: Destruction and Regeneration of the Muscogulge People* (Lincoln, Nebr., 1987).

A rare description of the typical Anglo-American backwoodsman seeking land in Florida is presented by James A. Lewis in *"Cracker*—Spanish Florida Style," *FHQ*, 63 (October 1984). Burke G. Vanderhill traces a route of settlers into the peninsula in "The Alachua Trail: A Reconstruction," *FHQ*, 55 (April 1977), and "The Alachua-St. Marys Road," *FHQ*, 66 (July 1987).

East Florida history, as told by local authorities, was a sequence of settlers' rebellions punctuated by fillibusterers. First there was the adventurer William Augustus Bowles, a part of whose story is retold by Lawrence Kinnaird and Lucia B. Kinnaird in "War Comes to San Marcos," *FHQ*, 62 (July 1983). Then came the 1795 Patriots' Rebellion. In *Juan Nepomuceno de Quesada: Governor of Spanish East Florida, 1790–1795* (Washington, D.C., 1981), Janice Borton Miller shows the centrality of the free trade issue to this uprising. A number of pertinent documents have been published in Charles E. Bennett, trans. and ed., *Florida's "French" Revolution, 1793–1795* (Gainesville, 1981).

East Florida in the early 1800s saw two republics declared and overthrown. Events of the first have been reviewed in J. H. Alexander, "The Ambush of Captain John Williams, U.S.M.C.: Failure of the East Florida Invasion, 1812–1813," *FHQ*, 56 (January 1978).

The second republic receives serious attention in David Bushnell, comp., *La República de las Floridas: Texts and Documents* (Mexico City, 1986), with chapters by David Bushnell, "The Florida Republic: An Overview"; L. David Norris, "Failure Unfolds: The Loss of Amelia Island"; Gerald E. Poyo, "La Republica de las Floridas: The Mexican Connection, 1814–1817"; and Charles H. Bowman, Jr., "Amelia Island and Vicente Pazos of Upper Peru."

Two books by Spanish historians are essential to an understanding of the Floridas in the late Second Spanish Period. Elena Sánchez-Fabres Mirat's *Situación histórica de las Floridas en la segunda mitad del siglo XVIII (1782–1819)* (Madrid, 1977) explains the political economy of the Floridas within the dissolving Spanish Empire. Pablo Tornero Tinajero, in *Relaciones de dependencia entre Florida y Estados Unidos, 1783–1820* (Madrid, 1979), discusses the colonies' growing economic dependence on the United States.

The history of Spanish Florida began in the sixteenth century with entrepreneurial contracts and distant wars of religion. Indebtedness and wars of independence were what in the early nineteenth century brought it to a business-like conclusion.

# 4

# BRITISH FLORIDA, 1763–1784

ROBIN F. A. FABEL

BRITISH RULE IN Florida lasted but two decades. British East Florida corresponded roughly with the modern state of Florida, but British West Florida comprised part of what is now Florida, half of what is now Alabama, some of what is now the state of Louisiana and a large part of modern Mississippi. This lack of geographical neatness has often resulted in chapter- or even paragraph-length treatments of West Florida in works focused more broadly elsewhere. With Mississippi an honorable exception, the historians of the Floridas have, until recent decades, tended to come from outside the area of the original provinces, and the classic syntheses emanated from the university presses of California, Oklahoma, and Yale.

Neither colony had more than a few thousand, mostly illiterate, inhabitants; naturally they wrote very few journals, diaries and letterbooks. Even fewer have survived. The rudimentary ecclesiastical life in the provinces produced minimal church records. Government officials filed returns, but surviving customs reports are fragmentary, while court minutes have all but disappeared. The most extensive existing manuscripts concerning the Floridas are military.

The first writing on the British Floridas was penned soon after their acquisition. The military needed accurate information about them, while the curiosity of potential settlers and the interests of those hoping to attract them resulted in several works. Much of it was ephemera, which Charles L. Mowat discussed, with emphasis on East Florida, in "The First Campaign of Publicity for Florida," *Mississippi Valley Historical Review* (hereafter cited as *MVHR*) 30 (December 1943), but some of the contemporary works had a primitive historical dimension. During the Second World War appeared the first comprehensive book-length studies of the provinces as British colonies. A third tide of publications coincided with the celebration of the bicentennial of the American Revolution in the 1970s. It still flows, thanks to the currently flourishing schools of Gulf Coast and Spanish Borderlands history and a renewed interest by Spanish historians.

One of the earliest descriptions was William Stork's *An Account of East Florida with a Journal kept by John Bartram of Philadelphia, Botanist to His Majesty for the Floridas upon a Journey from St. Augustine up the River St. Johns* (London, 1766), which included a detailed estimate of the expenses of a would-be immigrant. Much more comprehensive was Bernard Romans's *A Concise Natural History of East and West Florida* (New York, 1775; reprinted Gainesville, 1973), which contains a wealth of information on Indians, diseases, navigational directions, and much else. William Bartram's *Travels through North and South Carolina, Georgia, East and West Florida* (Philadelphia, 1791; reprinted New York, 1928), is fascinating for the historian of natural science but frustrating for those interested in people and geographical precision. An army engineer, Lieutenant Philip Pittman, published, with useful maps, *The Present State of the European Settlements on the Mississippi* in London in 1770. The strength of the better of two reprinted editions (Gainesville, 1973) is Robert R. Rea's excellent introduction, which adds valuable historical perspective. Thomas Hutchins, another sapper officer, knew West Florida well. He published *An Historical Narrative and Topographical Description of Louisiana and West Florida* in Philadelphia in 1784 (reprinted Gainesville, 1962). Although poorly written, James Adair's *History of the American Indians* (London, 1775; reprinted Johnson City, Tenn., 1932) gives unique insights into Indians of the Southeast and life in the forest.

None of these useful primary sources was reprinted in the nineteenth century. Lorenzo Sabine was unusual in finding losers worthy of study. His *Biographical Sketches of Loyalists of the American Revolution* (Boston, 1864), has material relating to the Floridas, which were both loyalist asylums. Part of John Francis Hamtranck Claiborne's *Mississippi as a Province, Territory and State* (Jackson, Miss., 1981), deals with West Florida.

The Floridas were featured too in Max von Eelking's *Die Deutschen Hulfenstruppen im Nord Amerikanischen Befreiungskriege, 1776 bis 1783* (Hanover, Germany, 1863). Thirty years later, J. G. Rosengarten translated the work into English (Albany, N.Y., 1893) for American readers, among whom there was an appetite for more scientific history in the admired German mode. A vague, sometimes inaccurate, work, Richard Campbell's *Historical Sketches of Colonial Florida* (Cleveland, Ohio, 1892), did not qualify, but Peter J. Hamilton's *Colonial Mobile: An Historical Study* (Boston, 1897), did. Consciously honoring the German school of history, it was less concerned with incidents than institutions and embodied the then fashionable belief that history was essentially about racial and national conflict. *Colonial Mobile*, the first sound work specifically on British West Florida, sold well, and an enlarged edition was published in New York in 1910 (reprinted University, Ala., 1976). Hamilton also wrote a more general survey, "British West Florida," Mississippi Historical Society *Publications* 7 (1903). At twenty-seven pages, it was a summary, but for long the best available study.

Following Claiborne, Mississippians continued to provide worthwhile works on West Florida. Dunbar Rowland, Director of the Mississippi Department of Archives and something of a historian, was a pioneer in ransacking European archives for colonial materials, some of which he reproduced in 1911 in Volume I of *Mississippi Provincial Archives: English Dominion* (Nashville, 1911). His wife, Eron Opha Rowland, made significant contributions to Floridian studies with "Peter Chester, Third Governor of the Province of West Florida under British Dominion, 1770–1781," Mississippi Historical Society *Publications*, Centenary Series 5 (1923), and with *Life, Letters and Papers of William Dunbar of Elgin, Morayshire, Scotland and Natchez, Mississippi* (Jackson, Miss., 1930).

In the 1920s began the first serious consideration of non-Britons in the Floridas. In *The Early History of the Creek Indians and Their Neighbors* (Washington, D.C., 1923), John Reed Swanton studied their most important tribe. It was the first of Swanton's several sympathetic and scholarly contributions to a subject still under investigation. The Spanish connection with the British Floridas was explored by Kathryn Abbey in "The Efforts of Spain to Maintain Sources of Information in the British Colonies before 1779," *MVHR*, 14 (June 1928), and by Alberto Risco in two articles on "Don Francisco de Saavedra y la Guerra de la Independencía de los Estados Unidos," in *Razón y Fe* 85 (October and November 1928).

Biography predominated in the lean 1920s. In addition to previously noted works on Chester, Dunbar and Saavedra, Sir Frederick Haldimand, an erstwhile resident of Pensacola, was studied by Francis-J Audet in Royal Society of Canada *Transactions*, series 3, volume 17, section 1 (May 1923). In 1926 the Oxford University Press (New York) reprinted Jean Mullwraith's fuller 1904 biography, *Sir Frederick Haldimand*. Philip Lee Phillips wrote *Notes on the Work and Life of Bernard Romans* (DeLand, Fla., 1924), and Edgar Legare Pennington published a brief pioneer study, "The Reverend James Seymour, S.P.G. Missionary in Florida," in *Florida Historical Quarterly (FHQ)*, 5 (April 1927). In 1930 Alastair M. Grant published a life of East Florida's first governor, *General James Grant of Ballindalloch, 1720–1806* (London), and Harry Miller Lydenburg edited *Archibald Robertson, Lieutenant-General R. E.: His Diaries and Sketches in America, 1762–1780* (New York). Robertson was one of the many engineer officers who helped establish British rule in Florida.

The early 1930s saw further and more ambitious exploration of Indian and Spanish themes. An important contribution was Helen Louise Shaw, *British Administration of the Southern Indians* (Lancaster, Pa., 1931). A major historian, Arthur Preston Whitaker, edited *Documents Relating to the Commercial Policy of Spain in the Floridas* (DeLand, Fla., 1931), and another, John W. Caughey, published "Bernardo de Gálvez and the English Smugglers on the Mississippi, 1778," *Hispanic-American Historical Review* 12 (1932), one of several significant articles which would culminate in his excellent *Bernardo de Gálvez in Louisiana, 1776–1783* (Berkeley, 1934). In the following year appeared a classic on an economic aspect of the region in Peter Alexander Brannon's *The Southern Indian Trade, Being a Study of Material from the Tallapoosa River Valley of Alabama* (Montgomery, 1935). It was followed by a traditional biography of a Mississippi trader, James A. James's *Oliver Pollock: The Life and Times of an Unknown Patriot* (New York and London, 1937).

From 1939 there was renewed interest in the British in the Floridas. Clinton N. Howard contributed profusely. He wrote "The Military Occupation of British West Florida, 1863," *FHQ*, 17 (January 1939), and "The Interval of Military Government in West Florida," *Louisiana Historical Quarterly* (hereafter cited as *LHQ*), 22 (January 1939). Later in the year he published "Governor Johnstone in West Florida," *FHQ*, 17 (April 1939), to be followed by "Some Economic Aspects of British West Florida, 1763–1768," *Journal of Southern History* (hereafter cited as *JSH*), 6 (May 1940), and "Colonial Pensacola: The British Period," *FHQ*, 19 (October 1940). His careful scholarship and judicious conclusions about West Florida were matched by Charles Loch Mowat, a Briton resident in the United States, who concerned himself with the sister province at Howard's suggestion. He published "Material relating to British East Florida in the Gage papers and other Manuscript Collections in the William L. Clements Library," *FHQ*, 18 (July 1939), a useful contribution, since the outbreak of the war two months later precluded research trips to England. James A. Padgett also helped by reproducing minutes of the early sessions of West Florida's legislative assembly in *LHQ*, 22 (April and October 1939), 23 (January 1940), and selected minutes of its provincial council, *LHQ*, 23 (April 1940). Only decades later would Robert R. Rea and Milo B. Howard, Jr., make available a superior printed version of the assembly's work in *The Minutes, Journals, and Acts of the General Assembly of British West Florida* (University, Ala., 1979).

Mark F. Boyd contributed information and commentary on part of the Gulf Coast with "From a Remote Frontier: Letters and Documents pertaining to San Marcos de Apalache, 1763–1769, during the British Occupation of Florida," *FHQ*, 19 (January, April, and July 1941), 20 (October 1941; January, April, and July, 1942), 21 (October 1942). Forts also interested Moreau Browne Congleton Chambers, who in 1942 finished a master's thesis at Duke University, "The History of Fort Panmure at Natchez, 1763–1779," and Stanley Faye, who published "British and Spanish Fortifications of Pensacola, 1781–1821," *FHQ*, 20 (January 1942).

The culmination of this wartime interest in British imperial administration was the appearance of the two foremost general studies of the British Floridas. These were Cecil Johnson's *British West Florida, 1763–1783* (New Haven, 1943), and Mowat's *East Florida as a British Province, 1763–1784* (Berkeley and Los Angeles, 1943). Both were comprehensive without prolixity, and models of sound research and cool judgment. Clinton Howard's *The British Development of West Florida, 1763–1769* (Berkeley, 1947) supplemented Johnson usefully with detailed maps and with tables of all land grants to 1769. While discussing general treatments, mention may be made here of Lawrence H. Gipson, who summarized the early history of the British Floridas in chapters 8 and 9 of *The Triumphant Empire: New Responsibilities within the Enlarged Empire, 1763–1766* (New York, 1968).

Since the days of Mowat, Johnson, and Howard, work on the British Floridas has been less concerned with reinterpretation than with detailing topics outlined by those writers. Among such subjects have been economic life, the work of individual royal officers, Indians, and military affairs, especially during the Revolution.

Marion Bragg looked very briefly at land distribution in "British Land Grants in Warren County, Mississippi," *Journal of Mississippi History* (hereafter cited as *JMH*), 26 (1964), as did Gordon M. Wells at greater length in "British Land Grants-William Wilton Map, 1774," *JMH*, 28 (1966). Robert L. Gold examined "Politics and Property during the Transfer of Florida from Spanish to English Rule, 1763–1764," *FHQ*, 42 (July 1963), and Daniel L. Schafer examined what use was made of land grants in his "Plantation Development in British East Florida: A Case Study of the Earl of Egmont," *FHQ*, 63 (October 1984). A broader similar survey for the companion province was Robert R. Rea's "Planters and Plantations in British West Florida," *Alabama Review* (hereafter cited as *AR*), 29 (July 1976). So far the only substantial articles on those who worked the land have been Wilbur H. Siebert's "Slavery and White Servitude in East Florida, 1726 to 1776," *FHQ*, 10 (July 1931), and J. Leitch Wright, Jr., "Blacks in British East Florida," *FHQ*, 54 (April 1976).

Another comparatively neglected aspect of economic life is the trade in peltry. The best background information is in Paul Chrisler Phillips, *The Fur Trade*, 2 vols. (Norman, Okla., 1961): Chapters 27, 30, 37 and 38 concern the Floridas. Deerskins loom large in "British West Florida Trade and Commerce in the Customs Records," *AR*, 37 (April 1986), in which Robert Rea draws sensible conclusions from incomplete documents.

David R. Chesnutt discusses trade in "South Carolina's Impact upon East Florida, 1763–1776," in Samuel Proctor, ed., *Eighteenth-Century Florida and the Revolutionary South* (Gainesville, 1978). John D. Born's *Governor Johnstone and Trade in British West Florida, 1764–1767* (Wichita, 1968), is not a thorough exploration, but his "Charles Strachan in Mobile: The Frontier Ordeal of a Scottish Factor, 1764–1768," *AHQ*, 27 (Spring and Summer 1965), is useful. Traders of a later era are examined by William S. Coker in

"Entrepreneurs in the British and Spanish Floridas, 1775–1821," in Samuel Proctor, ed., *Eighteenth-Century Florida and the Caribbean* (Gainesville, 1976).

After 1766, the Spanish in New Orleans could theoretically throttle Britain's trade with its hinterland settlements. Douglas S. Brown examined a scheme to remove this possibility in "The Iberville Canal: Its Relation to Anglo-French Commercial Rivalry, 1763–1775," *MVHR*, 32 (March 1946). John Preston Moore, in his paradoxically titled "Anglo-Spanish Rivalry on the Louisiana Frontier," in John Francis McDermott, ed., *The Spanish in the Mississippi Valley, 1762–1804* (Urbana, 1974), concluded that actually, for a time, cooperation was characteristic of Anglo-Spanish relations. Jack Holmes in "Some Economic Problems of Spanish Governors of Louisiana," *Hispanic American Historical Review* 42 (1962); John G. Clark in *New Orleans, 1718–1812: An Economic History* (Baton Rouge, 1970); and Robin Fabel in "Anglo-Spanish Commerce in New Orleans during the American Revolutionary Era," in William S. Coker and Robert R. Rea, eds., *Anglo-Spanish Confrontation on the Gulf Coast during the American Revolution* (Pensacola, 1982) demonstrate how Floridians achieved a favorable trade balance with Louisiana. Margaret Fisher Dalrymple illumines one of them in *The Merchant of Manchac: The Letterbooks of John Fitzpatrick, 1768–1790* (Baton Rouge, 1978).

Without settlers, the economies of the Floridas would have failed. East Floridian immigration early attracted attention with Carl Rosenberger's "The Settlement of Charlotia (Rolles Town), 1765," *FHQ*, 4 (July 1925) and Carita Doggett's "Denys Rolle and Rollestown," *FHQ*, 7 (October 1928). Following a short account of an experiment with Mediterranean immigrants in Kenneth H. Beeson's "Janas [Strangers] in British East Florida," *FHQ*, 44 (July and October 1965), appeared E. P. Panagopoulos, *New Smyrna: An Eighteenth-Century Greek Odyssey* (Gainesville, 1966).

A number of longer studies have considered immigration to West Florida, including Jeannette M. Long's unpublished University of Kansas master's thesis, "Immigration to British West Florida, 1763–1781," (1969). W. M. Drake's "A Note on the Jersey Settlers of Adams Country," *JMH*, 15 (1953) and J. Barton Starr's "Campbell Town: French Huguenots in British West Florida," *FHQ*, 54 (April 1976) were more specialized.

Among the very best of recent studies of royal servants is John D. Ware and Robert R. Rea, *George Gauld, Surveyor and Cartographer of the Gulf Coast* (Gainesville, Tampa, 1982). Of similar quality is Louis de Vorsey, ed. and intro., *De Brahm's Report of the General Survey in the Southern District of North America* (Columbia, S.C., 1971), which looks thoroughly at a royal surveyor general. A royal agent for West Florida has received attention in two good articles, Robert R. Rea, "The King's Agent for British West Florida," *AR* 16 (April 1963), and Roy A. Rauschenberg, "John Ellis, Royal Agent for West Florida," *FHQ*, 62 (July 1983). Governors and their lieutenants are obvious subjects. With older studies of Grant and Chester, already mentioned, should be included Mary Durnford's *Recollections of Lieutenant General Elias Walker Durnford* (Montreal, 1863), on a former lieutenant governor of West Florida. Eleanor W. Townshend wrote on "John Moultrie Junior, M.D., 1729–1798, Royal Lieutenant Governor of East Florida," *Annals of Medical History*, 3rd series, 2 (March 1940), but Governor Patrick Tonyn of East Florida still awaits a biographer. Aspects of a governorship are seen in Robin Fabel's "Governor George Johnstone of British West Florida," *FHQ*, 54 (April 1976), while Robert R. Rea looked at his successor in "John Eliot, Second Governor of British West Florida," *AR*, (October 1977).

Important both as a study of a royal official and of the Indians in the Floridas was John R. Alden, *John Stuart and the Southern Colonial Frontier: A Study of Indian Relations, War, Trade, and Land Problems in the Southern Wilderness, 1754–1775* (Ann Arbor, 1944). A deputy superintendent of Indians is discussed in Robert R. Rea's "Redcoats and Redskins on the Lower Mississippi, 1763–1776; the Career of Lieutenant John Thomas," *LHQ*, 11 (Winter 1970). John Caughey wrote of a tribal leader in *McGillivray of the Creeks* (Norman, Okla., 1938), a study usefully supplemented by James H. O'Donnell III's "Alexander McGillivray: Training for Leadership, 1777–1783," *Georgia Historical Quarterly* (hereafter cited as *GHQ*), 49 (June 1965). An indispensable classic of McGillivray's nation is David H. Corkran, *The Creek Frontier, 1540–1783* (Norman, Okla., 1967). Other substantial works on the Indians appeared in the 1960s. The introduction of Milo B. Howard, Jr., and Robert R. Rea, trans. and ed., *The Memoire Justicatif of the Chevalier Montault de Monberaut* (University, Ala., 1965) gives important insights into British Indian diplomacy, and a geographer, Louis De Vorsey, clarified an important subject in *The Indian Boundary in the Southern Colonies, 1763–1775* (Chapel Hill, 1966). The Indians of East Florida received special attention in Edwin C. Reynolds, *The Seminoles* (Norman, Okla., 1957), and in Robert L. Gold, "The East Florida Indians under Spanish and English Control, 1763–1765," *FHQ*, 44 (July 1965). A more general consideration may be found in Howard F. Cline's *Florida Indians: Notes on Colonial Indians and Communities in Florida, 1700–1821*, in two volumes, or in James Fletcher Doster's *The Creek Indians and Their Florida Lands*, all published in New York in 1974.

John Shy put the large peacetime garrisons of the Floridas in proper perspective in *Toward Lexington: The Role of the British Army in the Coming of the American Revolution* (Princeton, 1965). Robert R. Rea details their activities in West Florida, ably using the Gage Papers, the Haldimand Papers and War Office records. He began with "Outpost of Empire: David Wedderburn at Mobile," *AR*, 7 (July 1954), and followed with "Military Deserters from British West Florida," *LHQ*, 9 (Spring 1968); "The Trouble at Tombeckby," *AR*, 26 (July 1973); "Lieutenant Colonel James Robertson's Mission to the Floridas, 1763," *FHQ*, 53 (July 1974); "Brigadier Frederick Haldimand—The Florida Years," *FHQ*, 54 (April 1976); and "Life, Death and Little Glory: The British Soldier on the Gulf Coast, 1763–1781," in

William S. Coker, ed., *The Military Presence on the Gulf Coast* (Pensacola, 1978).

The subject of Rea's "Graveyard for Britons: West Florida, 1763–1781," *FHQ*, 47 (April 1969), is disease among soldiers. In this connection three other articles are relevant. In "Medical Practice in the Lower Mississippi during the Spanish Period," *Alabama Journal of Medical Sciences* 1 (July 1964), Sir Jack D. L. Holmes considered the Natchez District of West Florida, Laura S. Harrel wrote on "Colonial Medical Practice in British West Florida, 1763–1781," in *Bulletin of the History of Medicine* 40 (1967), and William M. Straight on "Doctors and Disease in the British Floridas," Florida Medical Association *Journal* 63 (August 1976).

Other significant articles about the peacetime redcoat army are Charles L. Mowat, "St. Francis Barracks, St. Augustine: A Link with the British Regime," *FHQ*, 21 (January 1943); his "The Southern Brigade: A Sidelight on the British Military Establishment in America, 1769–1775," *JSH* 10 (February 1944); and Bettie Jones Conover, "British West Florida's Mississippi Frontier Posts, 1763–1779," *AR* 29 (July 1976).

Robert Rea's interest in the British Army is at least matched by Jack Holmes's scholarly enthusiasm for the Spanish troops who would overwhelm the redcoats in the campaigns of 1779 through 1781. An important book is his *Honor and Fidelity: The Louisiana Infantry Regiment and the Louisiana Militia Companies, 1766–1821* (Birmingham, Ala., 1965). A related study is W. James Miller, "The Militia System of Spanish Louisiana, 1769–1783," in William S. Coker, ed., *The Military Presence on the Gulf Coast* (Pensacola, 1978).

The American Revolution has generated more writing on the British Floridas than any other aspect, partly, but not only because of the excellent symposia organized by the Florida Bicentennial Commission in the 1970s and the Gulf Coast History and Humanities conferences, particularly that of 1981, which coincided with the Gálvez Bicentennial Celebration.

Building on work pioneered by Sabine, Wilbur H. Siebert wrote several articles on loyalists culminating in two volumes, the *Loyalists in East Florida, 1774 to 1785: The Most Important Documents Pertaining Thereto* (DeLand, Fla., 1929), which is much more than a mere document collection. Despite minor inaccuracies, his "The Loyalists of West Florida and the Natchez District," *MVHR*, 2 (March 1916), is still the best overview of loyalists in West Florida, where they have been less studied than in its sister province. Thelma Peters published "The American Loyalists in the Bahama Islands: Who They Were," *FHQ*, 40 (January 1961), one of several articles on the exodus from East Florida, which Carole W. Troxler also addressed in her well-researched "Loyalist Refugees and the British Evacuation of East Florida, 1783–1785," *FHQ*, 60 (July 1981). Some years before, J. Leitch Wright had written more generally on them in "Lord Dunmore's Loyalist Asylum in the Floridas," *FHQ*, 49 (April 1971), following it with "British East Florida: Loyalist Bastion," in Samuel Proctor, ed., *Eighteenth-Century Florida: The Impact of the American*

*Revolution* (Gainesville, 1978). Wright is the only historian to attempt a comprehensive monograph on the Revolution embracing both provinces, in *Florida in the American Revolution* (Gainesville, 1975).

He was also one of the first historians to study the international dimension to the British Floridas in his *Anglo-Spanish Rivalry in North America* (Athens, Ga., 1971), although another more detailed study had appeared two years before, Robert L. Gold's *Borderland Empires in Transition: The Triple-Nation Transfer of Florida* (Carbondale, Ill., 1969). Articles about international interest in the Floridas, chiefly with military intent, after they became British include Katherine S. Lawson, "Luciano de Herrera, Spanish Spy in British St. Augustine," *FHQ*, 23 (January 1945); Mark F. Boyd and José Navarro Latorre, "Spanish Interest in British Florida and in the Progress of the American Revolution," *FHQ*, 32 (October 1953); and Joseph G. Tregle's "British Spy along the Mississippi: Thomas Hutchins and the Defenses of New Orleans, 1773," *Louisiana History* 8 (1967). Other than Wright's comprehensive treatment of the Floridas during the Revolution, attempts at synthesis include his student, J. Barton Starr's *Dons, Tories and Rebels: The American Revolution in British West Florida* (Gainesville, 1976), and Robert V. Haynes' *The Natchez District and the American Revolution* (Jackson, Miss., 1976). Burton Barrs's early companion study, *East Florida in the American Revolution*, (Jacksonville, 1932), was to some extent superseded by Martha Condray Searcy's *The Georgia-Florida Contest in The American Revolution, 1776–1778* (Tuscaloosa, Ala. 1985). East Florida stayed British, largely because of naval operations. Harvey H. Jackson wrote about them in "The Battle of the Riceboats: Georgia Joins the Revolution," *Georgia Historical Quarterly* (hereafter cited as *GHQ*), 68 (Summer 1974), as, more broadly, did George E. Buker and Richard A. Martin in "Governor Tonyn's Brown-Water Navy: East Florida during the American Revolution, 1775–1778," *FHQ*, 58 (July 1979).

Edward G. Williams wrote of the senior British officer in East Florida in "The Provosts of the Royal Americans," *Western Pennsylvania Historical Magazine* 16 (January 1973), but Gary D. Olson considered a more dashing commander in "Thomas Brown, Loyalist Partisan, and the Revolutionary War in Georgia, 1777–1782," *GHQ*, 14 (Spring 1970). Mowat considered the relations between the civil and military authorities as important as military aspects of the Revolutionary War. W. Calvin Smith assesses them in "Mermaids Riding Alligators: Divided Command on the Southern Frontier, 1776–1778," *FHQ*, 54 (April 1976).

Twenty-three years after he wrote his classic study, Cecil Johnson was still uncertain that Spanish conquest of West Florida affected the decision to return it to Spain; see "West Florida Revisited," *JMH*, 28 (1966). Participants in the campaign included Britons, Spaniards, Germans, and French. The sole manifestation of American patriot involvement, the raid in 1778 of Captain James Willing, has been considered by several authors, including John W. Caughey, "Willing's Expedition down the Mississippi, 1778," *LHQ*, 15 (January 1932) and Robert V. Haynes, "James Willing and the Planters of Natchez: The American

Revolution Comes to the Southwest," *JMH*, 37 (1975). Americans serving the British in West Florida have been neglected, but there is an article on one of the two loyalist units sent there, P. R. N. Katcher's "The First Pennsylvania Loyalist Battalion, 1777–1783," Society for Army Historical Research *Journal* 48 (Winter 1970). From Germany the Waldeck regiment also served in West Florida. The major articles about it are by Albert W. Haarmann, "The 3rd Waldeck Regiment in British Service, 1776–1783," Society for Army Historical Research *Journal* 48 (Autumn 1970) and by Jack Holmes, who usually writes from the other side of the parapet, in "German Troops in Alabama during the American Revolution: The Battle of January 7, 1781," *Alabama Historical Quarterly* 38 (Spring 1976), which is broader than its title suggests.

The naval aspect of the campaign for West Florida is discussed in Robert Rea's introduction to James D. Servies, ed., *The Log of H.M.S. Mentor: A New Account of the British Navy at Pensacola* (Pensacola, 1982), and Robin Fabel has something to say on the navy in "West Florida and British Strategy in the American Revolution" in Proctor, ed., *Eighteenth-Century Florida and the Revolutionary South*. The commander of the province's land forces was studied by G. C. Osborn in "Major-General John Campbell in British West Florida, 1778–1781," *FHQ*, 27 (April 1949), but other than in Kathryn T. Abbey's "Peter Chester's Defense of the Mississippi after the Willing Raid," *MVHR*, 22 (June 1935), Chester's military role has been neglected.

The British looked for allies with some success among the Indians, a subject discussed by Helen Hornbeck Tanner in "Pipesmoke and Muskets: Florida Indian Intrigues of the Revolutionary Era," in Samuel Proctor, ed., *Eighteenth-Century Florida and Its Borderlands* (Gainesville, 1975). Michael D. Green examined part of the same subject in detail in "The Creek Confederacy in the American Revolution: Cautious Participants," in William S. Coker and Robert R. Rea, ed., *Anglo-Spanish Confrontation on the Gulf Coast during the American Revolution* (Pensacola, 1982). So far the best overview is James H. O'Donnell III, *Southern Indians in the American Revolution* (Knoxville, 1973).

From Spain in recent years have come a number of publications illuminating West Florida. Naturally many of them concern Bernardo de Gálvez, and in particular his conquest of Pensacola. The best work on Gálvez, however, is still John D. Caughey's, and despite its errors, the most useful single work on the siege, thanks in part to its excellent maps, is N. Orwin Rush, *The Battle of Pensacola: Spain's Final Triumph over Great Britain in the Gulf of Mexico* (Tallahassee, 1966). Those particularly interested in this subject should consult *The Siege of Pensacola: A Bibliography* (Pensacola, 1981), by James D. Servies. Using hitherto unexplored Spanish resources, Eric Beerman, a resident of Spain, wrote particularly noteworthy articles on the siege: " 'Yo Solo' not 'Solo': Juan Antonio de Riaño," *FHQ*, 58 (1979) and "Jose Solano and the Spanish Navy at the Siege of Pensacola" in William S. Coker and Robert R. Rea, eds., *Anglo-Spanish Confrontation on the Gulf Coast during the American Revolution* (Pensacola, 1982). A Spanish Jesuit scholar, Father Francisco de Borja Medina Rojas, in

*Jose de Ezpeleta, Gobernador de la Mobila, 1780–1781* (Seville, Spain, 1980) deals thoroughly with a neglected topic. Jack D. L. Holmes has a deep acquaintance with the archives of Spain. Of his many significant contributions to the Spanish role in the conquest of West Florida may be mentioned here "Juan de la Villebeuvre: Spain's Commandant of Natchez during the American Revolution," *JMH*, 37 (1975), and *The 1779 'Marcha de Gálvez': Louisiana's Giant Step Forward in the American Revolution* (Baton Rouge, 1975). Two articles relate to the slight French role in the conquest of Pensacola: Rene Quatrefages, "La Participación Militar de Francia en la Toma de Pensacola," *Revista de Historia Militar* 42 (1977) and Jack D. L. Holmes, "French and Spanish Military Units in the 1781 Pensacola Campaign," in Coker and Rea, eds., *Anglo-Spanish Confrontation on the Gulf Coast during the American Revolution.*

The history of the British Floridas remains incomplete. Major controversies over interpretation have not emerged. No iconoclast has questioned the high reputation of Gálvez; no apologist has restored Governor Johnstone's low one. The tradition that the Floridas remained loyal in the Revolution remains intact. An analysis of the disloyal elements has never been attempted. That West Florida was not a total economic liability to the mother country is the thesis of a forthcoming book, but the traditional view that Britain gained little and lost little by the acquisition and cession of both the Floridas still prevails. Social and political analyses, which in other colonies have given rise to much debate, could be revealing. The field has been lightly plowed rather than dug deeply.

# 5

# WEST FLORIDA (THE SPANISH PRESIDIOS OF PENSACOLA), 1686–1763

WILLIAM S. COKER

IN THIS CHAPTER, I refer the reader to specific numbers in the bibliography. I shall make one exception to the use of numbers in referring to bibliographic entries. James A. Servies, formerly director of libraries at the University of West Florida, has compiled one of the best bibliographies of Florida, and especially West Florida (75 and 76). I utilized those four volumes extensively in preparing this study. I have also taken the liberty of inserting in brackets immediately following each entry the number for that citation given in Servies's bibliographies. If brackets do not follow an entry, then it is not in the published bibliographies, which extend only through 1976.

The published histories, when properly documented, will indicate in the notes or bibliographies the specific primary sources utilized and where they were obtained. With those words of advice, let us now turn to our topic. First, a chronological review of the period, including bibliographic numbers as appropriate, followed by an overview of the major archives and libraries where much of the resource material is located.

For the purpose of this study the history of Pensacola and its presidios is divided into six periods: 1686–1698, 1698–1719, 1719–1721, 1722–1753, 1753–1763, and 1763.

I. The years 1686 to 1698 include: (1) The search for La Salle, which led to the rediscovery of Pensacola Bay in 1686. (2) The several expeditions to the bay capped by the Pez-Sigüenza survey of 1693. (3) Plans to occupy Pensacola (1693–1698) and New Spain's (Mexico's) failure to carry out the crown's orders for the occupation of the bay to the summer of 1698. (4) Orders by the Spanish Crown to occupy the *Bahía Santa María de Galve*, the name for Pensacola Bay, in 1698. These orders followed British and French efforts to establish a settlement on the Gulf Coast following the disastrous La Salle expedition.

Two expeditions set forth to carry out the occupation: Juan Jordán de Reina from Havana and Andrés de Arriola from Veracruz. Jordán de Reina reached the bay on 17 November 1698, four days ahead of Arriola.

See 3, 14, 16, 26, 28, 29, 33, 39, 40, 42, 48, 54, 59, 63, 64, 65, 85, 86, 91.

II. From the establishment of the *Presidio Santa María de Galve* in 1698 to 1719 (excluding its surrender to the French in 1719).

This era includes construction of Fort San Carlos de Austria under the supervision of Capt. Jaime Franck and the creation of the village, or *población*, nearby, 1698–99; the arrival of the French expedition led by Iberville, its reception at Pensacola, and the interaction of the Spanish and French, 1699–1719; the establishment of a settlement at Darien by the Scots and its effect upon supplies and troops for Pensacola, 1698–1701; Arriola's displeasure with the site and his controversy with Sigüenza, 1699–1700; the quality of the soldiers and the *presidiarios* sent there (Was it a penal colony?); the unhealthy location and large numbers of sick personnel, 1698–1719; the War of the Spanish Succession, 1702–1713, and the periodic Indian attacks on the presidio; the French Fort Crevècoeur on St. Joseph's Bay, 1718.

See 3, 7, 8, 9, 14, 17, 21, 23, 25, 26, 30, 31, 32, 33, 34, 35, 40, 43, 46, 59, 61, 65, 72, 74, 79, 80, 86.

III. The War of the Quadruple Alliance and Pensacola, 1719–1721.

These years include the capture of Pensacola by French forces from Mobile and Dauphin Island and its recapture by Spanish forces from Havana, summer 1719; the construction of the battery on Santa Rosa Island *(Fuerte Señor Príncipe de Asturias)* and Pensacola's fall to the French a second time, summer 1719; disposition of the Spanish prisoners of war; the French occupation, 1719–1722; Spanish plans to send a squadron to recapture Pensacola; and the Treaty of Alliance between Spain and France and the secret articles by which Pensacola was returned to Spain, 1721.

See 3, 17, 26, 27, 30, 31, 32, 33, 35, 40, 43, 49, 57, 59, 61, 71, 79, 80, 81, 87.

IV. The Presidio Isla de Santa Rosa, or Presidio Punta de Siguenza, 1722–1753. In this era the French burned all but a building or two at the site of the old presidio, 1722, and Alexander Wauchope arrived to take command for the Spaniards, 26 November 1722. Other events include the move to Santa Rosa Island and the construction of the fort and buildings there, 1722–24; the development of the presidio about one mile east of Punta de Sigüenza; Dominic Serres's drawing of the presidio, 1743; Pedro de Rivera's report on the presidio, 1744; construction of a small fort, San Miguel, on the mainland, 1740s; the hurricane of November, 1752, which destroyed the presidio and decided the Spaniards to move back to the mainland.

See 13, 14, 17, 18, 23, 27, 30, 31, 33, 35, 37, 38, 43, 45, 59, 61, 65, 71, 77, 79, 80, 81, 82.

V. The move to the mainland and the new presidio there, 1753–1763.

Developments in this era include the movement to the vicinity of Fort San Miguel; the name change to Presidio San Miguel de las Amarillas, 1756; the name change by the Crown to the Presidio San Miguel de Panzacola, 1757; illicit trade with French and English; the arrival of Col. Miguel Román de Castilla y Lugo as governor, 1759–1761; the attack on Yamasee villages, *Escambe* and *Punta Rasa*, by British Indian allies and the movement of the Yamasees to the vicinity of the presidio; and Col. Diego Ortiz Parrilla's governorship, 1761–1763.

See 17, 23, 35, 59, 61, 65, 73, 77, 81, 90.

VI. Transfer of Pensacola (and the rest of Florida) to Great Britain in 1763.

This period includes the Spaniards' preparation for the move to Veracruz; the arrival of land speculator James Noble and the purchase of Yamasee lands; the sale of Noble's ship *Jupiter* to the Spaniards for thirteen thousand pesos worth of goods; the purchase of lands from departing Spaniards by other Englishmen; the arrival of Lt. Col. Augustin Prevost (August 1763) to take command of Pensacola and West Florida until the governor reached there; Prevost's efforts to hurry the Spaniards on their way; the departure of the Spaniards and their Indian allies, September 1763; the arrival of the Spaniards and Yamasee at Veracruz; and the final settlement of the Yamasee at San Carlos de Chachalacas, 1765; and the Yamasee move to Nautla in 1776.

See 17, 27, 41, 43, 50, 51, 52, 61, 65, 78, 81, 84, 89, 90.

There are several ways for discovering what archives and libraries contain the documents for the subject under consideration. The first is to review the guides to those depositories. However, in many instances the guides, particulary the very excellent Carnegie guides, were published some years ago. Although still useful, they should be consulted principally for a general orientation to the depositories. Since the publication of the Carnegie guides, some depositories have moved to new locations, have acquired additional materials, or have discovered new documents among their holdings. Each depository has unpublished guides, finding aids, calendars, and other means for getting to the desired subject matter. Many such checklists have been prepared or updated since the publication of the Carnegie guides, and that work continues. Also, many libraries and archives in the United States have acquired thousands of pages of documents on microfilm, xerox copies, etc., from foreign archives in recent years, thus making almost all published guides outdated but still useful. A letter to the particular archive or library is in order before making the trip. Specialists in the archives and libraries have an intimate knowledge of the materials there and can be counted upon within certain limits to assist the researcher. Those archives and libraries where Pensacola and West Florida material may be found include the following:

John C. Pace Library, University of West Florida, Pensacola. The Collection is vast, but there is no calendar of its documents. There are, however, two ways for determining what is available. Several files among the papers of Panton, Leslie and Company contain the lists of microfilm requests to the various archives and libraries. There is also a general guide to the more than 515 reels of microfilm in the Papers of Panton, Leslie and Company.

Ann Ruebush Greybiel and others screened all of the volumes published in French indicated in the bibliography, plus some not included there, and made a note card on each document cited, a summary of its contents and its location. This card file is a gold mine of French sources for Pensacola history. Many of these documents have been acquired on microfilm.

*Archivo General de la Nación*, Mexico City. I believe that this archive may well have more documents on our subject than any other depository including all of the Spanish archives (see 6). Many of these documents have been copied and are either in the Library of Congress, the Newberry Library, Chicago, or the University of West Florida.

The Spanish archives and libraries in general (see 2, 10, 15, 19, 20, 22, 68, 77).

*Archivo General de Indias*, Seville, Spain (see 2, 10, 47, 66). Many of the pertinent documents have been copied and are in the Stetson Collection in the P. K. Yonge Library of Florida History, Gainesville, or are at the Library of Congress, the University of Texas at Austin, or the University of West Florida.

*Archivo Histórico Nacional*, Madrid (see 2). There are very few documents for our period here; one exception, however, is in *Estado, legajo* 3882.

*Biblioteca Nacional*, Madrid (see 2, 64). The only documents I found here were in Manuscripts 19508.

*Archivo General de Simancas*, Valladolid, Spain (see 59, 67). The documentation here for the early history of Pensacola is minimal but important for the titles and rank of some of the officers.

*Archivo General Militar*, Segovia, Spain. Although some documents for military officers at Pensacola after 1781 are there, I did not find any service records for the military officers at Pensacola before 1763.

The archives and libraries of France (2, 5, 40, 53, 61, 68, 79). Many documents were obtained from the *Archives Nationales de France* and the *Bibliotheque Nationale de Paris*. See the preceding note (John C. Pace Library) on French documents at the University of West Florida.

The archives and libraries of Great Britain. There is very little in the British depositories until 1763. One item in the British Museum (see 37) was helpful.

Of course, the Public Record Office has a number of scattered documents in Colonial Office 5/574–635 for West Florida that pertain to the Spanish exodus from Pensacola in 1763. All of these documents are available on microfilm at several locations including the University of West Florida.

The archives in Havana, Cuba (see 2, 62). From all I can determine there are very few documents noted in the guides that bear directly upon our subject.

The Library of Congress, Manuscripts Division (see 2, 58). There are thousands of pages of documents there from the Spanish, French, and Mexican archives. The typed guide to the Manuscripts Division lists several hundred pages of material on this subject. See also Servies [1912–18] for the Woodbury Lowery Collection of maps there.

P. K. Yonge Library of Florida History, University of Florida, Gainesville (see 1, 2, 70, 81). In addition to the entries in the bibliography, there is a typed guide to the manuscript collections there. The collection that holds the most promise for our period is the Stetson Collection. It has recently been calendared, and the calendar has been microfilmed and is available for purchase. Many documents have recently been acquired from Spain.

The Clements Library, University of Michigan, Ann Arbor (see 2). This repository contains several post-1763 documents about Pensacola, but little before then. The Karpinski Collection does have two maps, nos. 167 and 208, that were in some way connected with Col. Diego Ortiz Parrilla.

The Newberry Library, Chicago, Illinois (See 2, 11, 30, 31). This library may have one of the largest collections for our period anywhere in the United States. The documents came from Spain, France and Mexico.

Center for Louisiana Studies, University of Southwestern Louisiana, Lafayette (see 24). This center has been aggressively collecting French and Spanish documents for several years. Some of these documents are vital to Pensacola history.

Other Louisiana libraries and depositories. Each of the following has extensive documentary collections: the Louisiana State Archives and Records Service and the Library at Louisiana State University, both in Baton Rouge; the Howard-Tilton Library, Tulane University; the Louisiana Historical Center, Louisiana State Museum; the New Orleans Public Library; and the New Orleans Historic Collection; all in New Orleans.

The Libraries, University of Texas at Austin (see 12, 28, 29, 68, 84, 85). Several of the officers who served at Pensacola pre-1763 had been active in the *Provincias Internas* before coming to Pensacola. Several manuscript collections there have much information about Diego Ortiz Parrilla, and a lesser amount about Colonel Miguel Román de Castilla y Lugo and Gervasio Cruzat y Góngora. Of course, the Dunn transcripts from Seville are there too, and are especially useful for the years 1686–1700.

The John Carter Brown Library, Brown University, Providence, Rhode Island (see 2, 82, 87). This library contains several pertinent documents including a copy of the Rivera report on Pensacola of 1744.

State of New York (see 88). There may be a few documents in the Buckingham Smith Papers in the New York Historical Society and the Obadiah Rich Collection at the New York Public Library regarding Pensacola. The Bancroft Manuscripts at this library contain a copy of the Siguenza report about Pensacola published in Mexico City in 1694. The French Papers in the New York State Library (Albany) contain a few documents about Iberville and the French on the Gulf Coast.

There is much yet to be written about the history of Pensacola and its Spanish presidios, 1686–1763, and the documents are plentiful and available.

## REFERENCES

1. Arnade, Charles W. "Florida History in Spanish Archives. Reproductions at the University of Florida." *Florida Historical Quarterly (FHQ)*, 34 (1955): 36–50 [1955–1]. Arnade provides a history of the Stetson Collection, its use by early scholars, and a description of the richness of the collection for Florida history.

2. ———. "A Guide to Spanish Florida Source Material." *FHQ*, 35 (1957): 320–25 [1957–4]. See Servies bibliography, pages 322–25, for histories of Florida and guides to various archives and libraries.

3. Barcia Carballido y Zúñiga, Andres González de. *Ensayo cronológico para la historia general de la Florida*. By Don Gabriel de Cardenas z Cano [pseud.] Madrid; *En la Oficina Real, y Costa de Nicolas Rodriquez Franco. Impresor de Libros*, 1723. Translated with introduction by Anthony Kerrigan. Gainesville: 1951 [1723–1 and 1951–1]. This may be the first published book on the history of Pensacola Bay, 1686–1719. It has a few errors.

4. Barlow, R. H. "A Hitherto Unknown Map of the Pensacola Coastal Region, 1762." *FHQ* 22 (1943), 41 [1943–1]. The State Museum of Jalisco in Guadalajara reported that the map could not be located.

5. Beers, Henry Putney. *The French in North America: A Bibliographical Guide to French Archives, Reproductions, and Research Missions*. Baton Rouge, 1957 [1957–7]. For a bibliography of French activities on the Gulf Coast see pages 174–76.

6. Bolton, Herbert Eugene. *Guide to the Materials for the History of the United States in the Principal Archives of Mexico*. Washington, D.C., 1913 [1913–2]. Although dated, it is a good place to begin.

7. Boyd, Mark F. "The Fortifications at San Marcos de Apalache." *FHQ*, 15 (1936): 3–34 [1936–2].

8. ———. *Here They Once Stood: The Tragic End of the Apalachee Missions*. Gainesville, 1951 [1951–3].

9. ———. "Mission Sites in Florida." *FHQ*, 17 (1939): 254–80 [1939–3]. Boyd's studies show some interaction between Pensacola and the Apalachee area. The name of the Indian village Escambe near Pensacola may have originated in Apalachee. See "Mission Sites" map, page 254.

10. Burrus, Ernest J., S.J. "An Introduction to Bibliographical Tools in Spanish Archives and Manuscript Collections Relating to Hispanic America." *Hispanic American Historical Review*, 35 (1955): 443–83 [1955–3]. Guides and inventories to Florida documents are found throughout the article. Mentions fire in the *Archivo General de Indias* which destroyed some *legajos* and damaged others. At least one of these *legajos* contained Pensacola documents.

11. Butler, Ruth Lapham. *A Check List of Manuscripts in the Edward E. Ayer Collection*. Chicago, 1937. Many transcripts of Pensacola material are in the Ayer Collection.

12. Castañeda, Carlos Eduardo and Dabbs, Jack Aubrey, eds. *Guide to the Latin American Manuscripts in the University of Texas Library*. Cambridge, Mass., 1939. Still the only published guide to the vast holdings there, although a new guide is under preparation.

13. Charlevois, Rev. Pierre Francois Xavier de. *History and General Description of New France*. Trans. with notes by John Gilmary Shea. 6 vols. New York, 1872; reprint Chicago, 1962. Refers to Alexander Wauchope (variously spelled), who arrived in Pensacola in November 1722 to reclaim the area from France.

14. Chatelain, Verne E. *The Defenses of Spanish Florida, 1565 to 1763*. Washington, D.C., 1941 [1941–4; see also 1941–5]. Gives reasons for Spanish occupation of Pensacola Bay in 1698. Stresses Spanish-French cooperation after 1700.

15. Coker, William S. "Documentos relativos a la independencia de norte america existentes en archivos españoles." *Hispanic American Historical Review*, 59 (1979): 702–5. Review of the five published volumes on this subject.

16. ———. "The English Reaction to La Salle." In *La Salle and His Legacy: Frenchmen and Indians in the Lower Mississippi Valley*, edited by Patricia K. Galloway, 129–35. Jackson, Miss., 1982. Brief discussion of Spanish, French, and British rivalry for a settlement on the Gulf Coast, 1686–1698.

17. ———. "The Financial History of Pensacola's Spanish Presidios, 1698–1763," *Pensacola Historical Society Quarterly* 9 (Spring 1979), 1–20. Contains *situado* (annual subsidy) and other data on Pensacola's financial history, pictures of coins recovered from presidio site on Santa Rosa Island and a brief biography of Dominic Serres who drew the only known sketch of that Presidio in 1743.

18. ———. "Pedro de Rivera's Report on the Presidio of Punta de Sigüenza, Alias Panzacola, 1744," *Pensacola Historical Society Quarterly*, 8 (Winter 1975), 1–22 [1975–90]. Revised edition 1980. Rivera's evaluation of the presidio at Pensacola and whether it should be retained or abandoned.

19. ———. "Research in the Spanish Borderlands." *Latin American Research Review* 7 (1972) 3–94 [1972–87]. A series of articles coordinated by Coker about resources for a study of the Southeastern Spanish Borderlands, most post–1781. Extensive bibliography, pages 55–94.

20. ———. "Research Possibilities and Resources for a Study of Spanish Mississippi." *Journal of Mississippi History* 34 (1972): 117–28 [1972–15]. Pertains primarily to the years 1779–1798.

21. ———. "The Village on the Red Cliffs." *Pensacola History Illustrated* 1 (1984): 22–26. Describes the first village *(población)* on the *barrancas coloradas*, 1698, including 1699 plan with legend, and so forth, translated.

22. Coker, William S., and Holmes, Jack D. L. "Sources for the History of the Spanish Borderlands." *FHQ*, 49 (1971): 380–93 [1971–26]. While devoted primarily to the post-1779 history of West Florida including Natchez, Mobile, Pensacola, and so forth, there are references to earlier materials.

23. Coleman, James C., and Coleman, Irene S. *Guardians on the Gulf: Pensacola Fortifications, 1698–1980*. Pensacola, 1982. A convenient summary based upon published sources.

24. Conrad, Glenn R., and Brasseaux, Carl A. *A Selected Bibliography of Scholarly Literature on Colonial Louisiana and New France*. Lafayette, La., 1982. Reviews

manuscript and published material available in the extensive French and Spanish holdings of the Center for Louisiana Studies at University of Southwestern Louisiana, some of it pertinent to Pensacola history, 1686–1763.

25. Cox, Isaac Joslin. "Florida, Frontier Outpost of New Spain." In *Hispanic Essays, a Memorial to James Alexander Robertson*, edited by A Curtis Wilgus, 150–166. Chapel Hill, 1942. Previously published in Spanish: "Florida, avanzada fronteriza de Nueva España." Translated by Román Giménez. In *Il Congreso internacional de America. . .* , 6 vols. Buenos Aires, 1938. Credits Pensacola with thwarting the eastward expansion of France, thus turning the French westward toward Texas.

26. Coxe, Daniel. *A Description of the English Province of Carolana, By the Spaniards call'd Florida, And by the French La Louisiane*. A facsimile reproduction of the 1722 edition with an introduction by William S. Coker. Gainesville, 1976 [1722–1]. Coxe described Pensacola ca. 1719 and classified it as a colony of "malefactors."

27. Davenport, Frances Gardiner, ed., *European Treaties Bearing on the History of the United States and Its Dependencies*. 4 vols. Washington, D.C., 1917–37 [1917–13]. Includes the secret articles by which France agreed to return Pensacola to Spain in 1721, the Convention of *El Pardo*, 1739, and the Treaty of 1763.

28. Dunn, William Edward. "The Occupation of Pensacola Bay, 1689–1698," 3 parts. *FHQ*, 4 (1925–26), 3–14, 76–89, 140–54 [1925–7; 1926–7]. The account really extends to the spring of 1700.

29. ———. *Spanish and French Rivalry in the Gulf Region of the United States, 1678–1702: The Beginnings of Texas and Pensacola*. Bulletin No. 1705. Austin, Texas, 1917 [1917–15]. In-depth study of the background and founding of Pensacola with emphasis upon Spanish-French rivalry. The Dunn transcripts, copied from the Spanish archives, used in this study are calendared on pages 219–27, and copies are at the University of Texas Library.

30. Faye, Stanley. "The Contest for Pensacola Bay and Other Gulf Ports, 1698–1722." 2 parts. *FHQ*, 24 (1946): 167–95; 302–28 [1946–7.]

31. ———. "Spanish Fortifications of Pensacola, 1698–1763." *FHQ*, 20 (1941): 151–68 [1941–9]. Faye's studies plowed much new ground utilizing the Spanish transcripts at the Newberry Library, Chicago.

32. Folmer, Henry. *Franco-Spanish Rivalry in North America, 1524–1763*. Glendale, Calif., 1953 [1953–12]. Traces interaction of French and Spanish on the Gulf Coast, 1699–1721, and the diplomacy involving the return of Pensacola to Spain in 1721.

33. Ford, Lawrence Carroll. *Triangular Struggle for Spanish Pensacola, 1689–1739*. Washington, D.C., 1939 [1939–10]. Covers the years to the *El Pardo* convention of 1739 which provided for a frontier *status quo*, a milestone in the history of the triangular struggle for Pensacola Bay. Contains a calendar of the documents used.

34. French, Benjamin Franklin, ed. *Historical Collections of Louisiana and Florida, including translations of original manuscripts relating to their discovery and settlement, with numerous historical and biographical notes. . . .* New Series. New York, 1869 [1869–5]. Among others he included the narrative of the arrival of the French at Pensacola in 1699. About French's works James A. Servies warns, "some documents . . . have been silently abridged."

35. Galloway, Patricia K. *Mississippi Provincial Archives:*
*French Dominion*. 2 vols. Collected, edited and translated by Dunbar Rowland and A. G. Sanders; revised and edited by Patricia K. Galloway. Baton Rouge, 1984. Some documents pertain to French-Spanish relations on the Gulf Coast, 1699–1763.

36. ———. *La Salle and His Legacy: Frenchmen and Indians in the Lower Mississippi Valley*. Jackson, Miss., 1982. See Coker (16) and Holmes (48).

37. Gayangos, Pasqual de. *Catalogue of the Manuscripts in the Spanish Language in the British Museum*. London, 1877. See ms. Add. 17,637 on communication of Capt. Don José Primo de Ribera.

38. Geiger, Maynard. *Biographical Dictionary of the Franciscans in Spanish Florida and Cuba (1528–1841)*. Paterson, N.J., 1940 [1940–16]. Refers to the secondary convent of St. Mary de Galves [*sic*] at Pensacola in 1736.

39. Gil Munilla, Roberto, "Politica española en el Golfo Mexicano; expediciones por la entrada del Caballero La Salle (1685–1707)." *Anuario de Estudios Americanos* 12 (1955): 467–611 [1955–27]. Contains data on reconnaissance and occupation of Pensacola Bay, 1693–98.

40. Giraud, Marcel. *Histoire de la Louisiane Française 1698–1720*. 3 vols. Paris, 1953–66. Vol. 1 translated by Joseph C. Lambert, *A History of French Louisiana: The Reign of Louis XIV, 1698–1715*. Baton Rouge, 1974 [1974–56]. Detailed study of French on the Gulf Coast and relationship of French and Spanish.

41. Gold, Robert L. *Borderland Empires in Transition: The Triple-Nation Transfer of Florida*. Carbondale, Ill., 1969 [1969–14]. Details Spanish and Yamasee Indian exodus from Pensacola in 1763, and tells something about James Noble, the British land speculator. For the Yamasee move to Nautla see 89.

42. Gómez Raposo, Luis. "Diario del descubrimiento que hizo el Capitán Don Andres del [sic] Pex." In *Colección de diarios y relaciones para la historia de los viajes y descubrimientos*. Vol. 4:114–30. Madrid, Spain, *Instituto Histórico de Marina*, 1943- . Pez's 1687 voyage along the Gulf Coast (and Pensacola Bay).

43. Griffen, William B. "Spanish Pensacola, 1700–1763." *FHQ*, 37 (1959): 242–62 [1959–16]. An overview of the era.

44. Griffith, Connie G. "Collections in the Manuscript Section of the Howard-Tilton Memorial Library." *Louisiana History* 1 (1960), 320–27. Lists several collections (Favrot, Kuntz and Peters-Le Monnier-Lastrapes) that date from 1695.

45. Hackett, Charles Wilson. "Policy of the Spanish Crown Regarding French Encroachments from Louisiana, 1721–1762." In *New Spain and the Anglo-American West*, edited by Charles W. Hackett, George P. Hammond, and J. Lloyd Mecham, 107–45 Lancaster, Pa., 1932 [1932–18]. Discusses French trade with Pensacola and efforts of officials in Spain and New Spain to stop this illicit business.

46. Hart, Francis Russell. *The Disaster of Darien: The Story of the Scots Settlement and the Causes of Its Failure, 1699–1701*. Boston, 1929 (see 82). The Scots at Darien were of far greater concern to Spain than the French at Biloxi.

47. Hill, Roscoe R. *Descriptive Catalogue of the Documents Relating to the History of the United States in the Papeles Procedentes de Cuba Deposited in the Archivo General de Indias at Seville*. Washington, D.C., 1916 [1916–8]. Only a few *legajos* contain documents pertinent to the pre-1763 era; see *legs*. 480 and 548.

48. Holmes, Jack D. L. "Andres de Pez and Spanish Reaction to French Expansion into the Gulf of Mexico." In Galloway (36), pp. 106–28. Includes Pez's 1686 and 1693 expeditions to Pensacola Bay and his continuing interest in the area.

49. ———. "Dauphin Island in the Franco-Spanish War, 1719–22." In *Frenchmen and French Ways in the Mississippi Valley*, edited by John Francis McDermott, 103–25.

Urbana, Ill., 1969 [1969–20]. Renders full account of the attacks and counterattacks at Pensacola and Dauphin Island during the war.

50. Howard, Clinton N. "Alleged Spanish Grants in British West Florida." *FHQ*, 22 (1943): 74–85 [1943–12]. Relates James Noble's purchase of Yamasee lands and sixteen other land purchases all disapproved by West Florida council in 1765.

51. ———. "The Military Occupation of British West Florida, 1763." *FHQ*, 17 (1939): 181–99 [1939–17]. Provides a brief survey of port and city of Pensacola, its reliance upon Mobile for beef, and the delay in the Spanish departure.

52. Johnson, Cecil. *British West Florida, 1763–1783*. New Haven, 1943; reprint, Hamden, Conn., 1971 [1943–14]. A lack of transports and problems in loading the ships delayed the Spanish departure for nearly a month after British officials arrived in August 1763.

53. Leland, Waldo G., John J. Meng, and Abel Dossie, eds., *Guide to Materials for American History in the Libraries and Archives of Paris*. 2 vols. Washington, D.C., 1932, 1943. Much on Pensacola in vol. 2.

54. Leonard, Irving Albert. "Don Andres de Arriola and the Occupation of Pensacola Bay." In *New Spain and the Anglo-American West*, edited by Charles W. Hackett, George P. Hammond, and J. Lloyd Mecham. Vol 1:81–106. Lancaster, Pa., 1932 [1932–18]. Biographical sketch of Arriola, his expedition to occupy Pensacola, and his controversy with Carlos de Sigüenza in 1699–1700.

55. ———. *Spanish Approach to Pensacola, 1689–1693*. Albuquerque, 1939 [1939–20]. The introduction provides an overall account of the expeditions to Pensacola and is followed by the translated documents extensively noted as to source, and so forth.

56. ———. "The Spanish Re-Exploration of the Gulf Coast in 1686." *Mississippi Valley Historical Review*, 22 (1936): 547–57 [1936–18]. A translation of Juan Jordán de Reina's diary, the only one to survive, of this voyage to Pensacola Bay.

57. Le Page du Pratz, Antoine Simon. *Histoire de la Louisiane*. . . . 3 vols. Paris, 1758 [1763–7]. Recounts French capture and eventual destruction of Pensacola, 1719–22.

58. Library of Congress. "Spanish and Spanish-American Reproductions [in the] Manuscript Division—Library of Congress." 38-page typed guide. See pages 30–32 for documents from *Archivo General de la Nación* (Mexico City).

59. Magdaleno Redondo, Ricardo, José Maria de la Peña y Cámara, Miguel Bordonau, and Angel de la Plaza. *Catalogo XX del Archivo General de Simancas. Títulos de Indias*. Valladolid, Spain, 1954. Includes at least seven of Pensacola's governors, 1698–1763.

60. Manucy, Albert. "The Founding of Pensacola—Reasons and Reality." *FHQ*, 37 (1959): 223–41 [1959–27]. Provides translations of two important documents: Arriola's report of December 1, 1698, and Jaime Franck's letter of February 19, 1699.

61. Margry, Pierre. *Découvertes et Etablissements des Français dans L'Ouest et dans le Sud de L'Amérique Septentrionale, 1614–1754*. 6 vols. Paris, 1876–1886 [1876–5]. Contains many documents relating to the establishment of the French on the Gulf Coast and their relations with Pensacola. See especially volumes 3–5.

62. Marino Pérez, Luis. *Guide to the Materials for American History in Cuban Archives*. Washington, D.C., 1907. Some material on Florida commerce with Veracruz, Havana, and Campeche, ca. 1760, but most pre-1763 records are for St. Augustine. See Burrus (10, p. 458) for a supplement to this guide.

63. Morfi, Fray Juan Agustín. *History of Texas, 1673–1779,* translated by Carlos Eduardo Castañeda. 2 parts. Albuquerque, 1935. Some material on the rediscovery of Pensacola Bay, exploration by Barroto and Sigüenza, and Iberville's stop there.

64. Muñoz, Juan Bautista. *Catálogo de la Colleción de Don Juan Bautista Muñoz.* 3 vols. Madrid, 1954. Contains references to Andrés de Pez and the 1693 expedition to Pensacola. On the Muñoz collection, see Burrus (10, p. 470).

65. Parks, Virginia. *Pensacola: Spaniards to Space Age.* Pensacola, 1986.

66. Peña y Cámara, Jośe María de la. *Archivo General de Indias de Sevilla: Guia del Visitante.* Seville, 1958. See especially Appendix 2, "Orientación Bibliográfica" (pp. 149–63) for a review of the guides to the various archives and libraries in Cuidad Real, Madrid, Segovia, Seville, and Simancas.

67. Plaza Bores, Angel de la. *Archivo General de Simancas: Guia del Investigador.* Valladolid, Spain, 1962. For the four previously published guides see pages cv-cvi.

68. Robertson, James Alexander. "The Archival Distribution of Florida Manuscripts," *FHQ*, 10 (1931): 35–50 [1931–32]. Among others, he surveys Spanish and French archives, the Rich Collection at the New York Public Library, Buckingham Smith Papers at the New York Historical Society, and the García Collection at the University of Texas at Austin.

69. ———. *List of Documents in Spanish Archives relating to the History of the United States, which Have Been Printed or of which Transcripts are Preserved in American Libraries.* Washington, D.C., 1910 [1910–9]. Pinpoints a series of Pensacola documents for the years 1689–1728: Nos. 1874–75, 1883–86, and 1939–40.

70. ———. "The Spanish Manuscripts of the Florida State Historical Society." *American Antiquarian Society* n.s. 39 (1929): 16–37 [1929–15]. Provides an overview of the material there in 1929: 100,000 photostats, thousands of typewritten and handwritten transcripts from Spanish Archives, hundreds of maps. Includes a brief history of the Stetson Collection (now at Gainesville. See 81).

71. Rowland, Dunbar. *Fifth Annual Report of the Director of the Department of Archives and History of the State of Mississippi.* Nashville, 1907 [1907–29]. Refers to a number of Pensacola-related documents from 1708–1723.

72. Rubio Mañe, J. Ignacio, ed. *Introducción al estudio de los virreyes de Nueva España, 1535–1746.* 4 vols. Mexico City, 1959. Comments upon the Arriola-Sigüenza controversy of 1699–1700 in 3:65–66.

73. Sarrablo Aguareles, Eugenio. *El Conde de Fuenclara, Embajador y Virrey de Nueva España (1687–1752).* Seville, 1955. Contains much information about Miguel Román de Castilla y Lugo at Pueblo before he came to Pensacola in 1759.

74. Serrano y Sanz, Manuel. *Documentos históricos de la Florida y la Luisiana, Siglos XVI al XVIII.* Madrid, 1912 [1912–16]. Contains two letters from Gregorio de Salinas Varona at Pensacola in 1717 concerning problems of the Spanish Indians.

75. Servies, James A. *A Bibliography of West Florida.* 3 vols. Revised ed. Pensacola, 1978. A comprehensive guide to the literature of the ten westernmost counties of Florida from the first known printed work in 1535 through 1971.

76. Servies, James A.; Eubank, Frances A.; and Perdue, Robert W. *A Bibliography of West Florida, First Supplement.* Pensacola, 1978. This volume extends the coverage through 1976. The two Servies bibliographies describe in varying detail over six thousand titles. For the purpose of this study the following additional entries should be consulted: 1720–1, 1720–3, 1728–1, 1728–2, 1753–1, 1755–1, 1761–1, 1763–2, 1766–1, 1762–2, 1762–6, 1768–3, 1768–4, 1770–2, 1900–2.

77. Shepherd, William R. *Guide to the Materials for the History of the United States in Spanish Archives (Simancas, the Archivo Histórico Nacional, and Seville).* Washington, D.C., 1907. Some Florida documents, 1740–1763, are noted.

78. Siebert, Wilbur H. "How the Spaniards Evacuated Pensacola in 1763." *FHQ*, 11 (1932): 48–57 [1932–22]. This represents a detailed account of the evacuation.

79. Surrey, N. M. Miller, ed. *Calendar of Manuscripts in Paris Archives and Libraries relating to the History of the Mississippi Valley to 1803*. 2 vols. Washington, D.C., 1926. Identifies many documents concerning Pensacola, 1698–1763. For the most part, these documents have been microfilmed and are at the John C. Pace Library, University of West Florida.

80. TePaske, John Jay. *The Governorship of Spanish Florida, 1700–1763*. Durham, N.C., 1964. Contains several references to Pensacola between 1704 and 1747.

81. University of Florida, the P. K. Yonge Library of Florida History. *The Calendars of the Spanish Borderlands Collection*. Microfilm. The calendar of the Stetson Collection (3 reels) is very valuable for the period under consideration.

82. Van den Eynde, Damian. "Calendar of Spanish Documents in John Carter Brown Library." *Hispanic American Historical Review* 16 (1936): 564–607 [1936–35]. Calendars 3 volumes of Mexican or Spanish archival material. For Pensacola documents see pages 574, 581, 586, 589, 599–601.

83. Velásquez, María del Carmen. *Establecimiento y Perdido del Septentrion de Nueva España. Centro de Estudios Históricos, Nueva Serie 17*. Mexico, D. F., 1974. While it contains only a few references to *Panzacola*, the sources for her data noted in the bibliographic review (pp. 4–21) are very important.

84. Weddle, Robert S. *The San Sabá Mission: Spanish Pivot in Texas*. Austin, 1964. Provides much information about the career of Diego Ortiz Parrilla before coming to Pensacola in 1761.

85. ———. *Wilderness Manhunt: The Spanish Search for La Salle*. Austin, Texas, 1973 [1973–117]. Weddle reviews the history of Pensacola Bay from its rediscovery in 1686 to its settlement in 1698.

86. Wilson, Samuel L. "Architecture in Eighteenth-Century West Florida." In *Eighteenth-Century Florida and Its Borderlands*, edited by Samuel Proctor, 102–39, Gainesville, 1975 [1975–85]. Briefly describes the construction of Fort San Carlos de Austria (1698–99) and the materials used (pp. 105–107).

87. Wroth, Lawrence C. "Some Materials of Florida History in the John Carter Brown Library of Brown University." *FHQ*, 20 (1941): 3–46 [1941–31]. Describes a group of materials relating to Pensacola, 1692–1744, in the library there.

88. Owen, Thomas McAdory, ed. *Report of the Alabama History Commission to the Governor of Alabama. December 1, 1900*. Vol. 1. Montgomery, Ala., 1901 [1901–1]. Although dated, this comprehensive review of resources for Alabama (and northwest Florida) history is still useful. Included is a calendar of the Buckingham Smith Papers in the New York Historical Society, and notes, and so forth, on the Obadiah Rich and George Chalmers Papers and the Bancroft Manuscripts in the New York Public Library. The Bancroft Manuscripts contain a copy of the 1694 published report of Sigüenza.

89. Szewczyk, David M. (compiler and editor) with Barnes, Catherine A. *The Viceroyalty of New Spain and Early Independent Mexico: A Guide to Original Manuscripts in the Collections of the Rosenbach Museum and Library*. Philadelphia, 1980, p. 91. Refers to Yamasee Indians of Pensacola who moved to San Carlos de Chachalacas, Mexico, in 1765. In the document cited here the Indians, who once numbered 121 families, had been reduced to ten families because of disease. They wanted to move to Nautla and Viceroy Bucareli approved their request.

90. Griffith, Wendell L. "The Royal Spanish Presidio of San Miguel de Panzacola, 1753–1763." MA Thesis, University of West Florida, 1988. Concentrates on the governorships of Colonels Román de Castilla and Diego Ortiz Parrilla, 1759–63.
91. Hann, John H. *Apalachee: The Land Between the Rivers*. Gainesville, 1988. Two Indian villages in present-day Tallahassee area used the name Panzacola, 1657 and 1677. First mention of the name at Pensacola was in 1686. (See 56.)

# 6

# WEST FLORIDA, 1779–1821

## SIR JACK D. L. HOLMES

FLORIDA IN THE early years following its "discovery" by the Spanish was immense: it stretched from the Atlantic Ocean to Soto la Marina (Rio de las Palmas) in Mexico, and from the Florida Keys to Labrador. See Robert Weddle, *The Spanish Sea: The Gulf of Mexico in North American Discovery, 1500–1685* (College Station, Tex., 1985). The section later referred to as "West Florida" was the result of Spanish conquests over British West Florida during the 1779–1783 war, contemporary with the American Revolution. The hero of those conquests was the youthful governor of Louisiana and commander in chief of the allied armies (French and Spanish), Bernardo de Gálvez (1746–1786), whose exploits in the capture of Pensacola earned him promotion, the creation of the Province of West Florida, and a special coat of arms, as described in Jack D. L.

William S. Coker contributed the bibliographic survey which comprises the final segment of this chapter.

Holmes, *Gálvez* (Birmingham, Ala., 1980); and Holmes, "Bernardo de Gálvez: Spain's 'Man of the Hour' During the American Revolution," in *Cardinales de dos independencias (Noreste de México—Sureste de los Estados Unidos)*, ed. Beatriz Ruiz Gaytán, et al. (Mexico City, 1978).

West Florida begins as a French colony in the early eighteenth century. It was not called Florida at all. Based on the controversial, but accepted, claims of Robert Cavelier, Sieur de La Salle, in 1682, the coastal colonies of Mobile and Biloxi were known as "Louisiana." This remained true until the Seven Years War settled by the Treaty of Paris (1763), when France's claim to all of Louisiana *east* of the Mississippi River, excepting New Orleans, was permanently extinguished. In 1762 France ceded "Louisiana," including New Orleans, to Spain, a secret treaty affirmed the following year. Great Britain and Spain were neighbors, with the Mississippi River shared—a point destined to place West Florida in a state of conflict between Spain and the United States.

When the British occupied what had been French Louisiana and Spanish Florida (Mobile, Pensacola, Baton Rouge, Natchez) during 1763–1764, they realized that the best land along the Mississippi at Natchez was *north* of the 31st parallel. Therefore, in 1764 the British moved the northern boundary to the confluence of the Yazoo and Mississippi Rivers. By the Proclamation of 1763, which created the two provinces of East and West Florida, lands were opened in both East and West Florida to settlers. From 1763 to 1783, then, both East Florida (with its capital at St. Augustine) and West Florida (with its capital at Pensacola), were British colonies, conquered by Spanish arms in the campaigns of 1779–1781.

What were these areas, and how did Spain incorporate them into the Spanish-American Empire? When Spain created the Province of West Florida from conquered British territory, she added a post which had, during early Florida history, been subordinate to East Florida's capital of St. Augustine: San Marcos de Apalache. It was Bernardo de Gálvez who decreed the joining of St. Marks to Pensacola rather than to St. Augustine due to difficulty in supplying and defending it as related by Vizente Manuel Céspedes (Zéspedes) to José de Gálvez, No. 86, San Agustín de Florida, June 20, 1785; and Zéspedes to Marqués de Sonora (José de Gálvez), No. 16, *reservado*, San Agustín de la Florida, March 30, 1787 (both in *Archivo Histórico Nacional*, Madrid, *Sección de Estado, legajo* 3901). Until the evacuation of Spanish troops following the Adams-Onís Treaty (1819–1821), Fort San Marcos de Apalache was under the jurisdiction of the commandant (later governor) of Pensacola.

Following the Camino Real westward (U.S. 90 and I–10), the next major post in Spanish West Florida was Pensacola. But for Spanish haste, the French might have been in possession of Pensacola in 1699 when Pierre Le Moyne, Sieur d'Iberville, established settlements near Ocean Springs and on Dauphin Island, as discussed in Jack D. L. Holmes, "Dauphin Island in the Franco-Spanish War, 1719–1722," in *Frenchmen and French Ways in the Mississippi Valley*, ed. John

Francis McDermott (Urbana, 1969). Because of its location on a plain, Pensacola would become an easy conquest.

Mobile was an easy mark, too. British Mobile fell to Bernardo de Gálvez in 1780, and much easier from Spain to the Americans under General James Wilkinson in 1813, as related in Jack D. L. Holmes, "The Mobile *Gazette* and the American Occupation of Mobile in 1813: A Lesson in Historical Detective Work," *Journal of the Alabama Academy of Science* 47 (April 1976). During the Spanish period from 1780 to 1813, the Mobile District included the Port City as well as the settlements along the Tombigbee and Tensaw Rivers, as discussed by Jack D. L. Holmes, in "Notes on the Spanish Fort San Esteban de Tombecbe," *The Alabama Review* 18 (October 1965); "Alabama's Forgotten Settlers: Notes on the Spanish Mobile District, 1780–1813," *Alabama Historical Quarterly* 33 (Summer, 1971); "The Role of Blacks in Spanish Alabama: The Mobile District, 1780–1813," *Alabama Historical Quarterly* 37 (Spring 1975); and "Up the Tombigbee with the Spaniards: Juan de la Villebeuvre and the Treaty of Boucfouca (1793)," *Alabama Historical Quarterly* 40 (Spring and Summer 1978).

The coastal settlements Spain maintained along the Gulf of Mexico from Mobile to the Mississippi River included Pascagoula, Pass Christian, Biloxi, and Bay St. Louis. Although not major centers of population, they were among the earliest European colonies, and during the West Florida Controversy, 1803–1821, they were of great importance.

As organized in 1763, British West Florida extended from the Apalachicola River in the east to, but not including, the "Isle of Orleans": that bit of New Orleans and environs surrounded by the Mississippi River, Lake Pontchartrain and the Iberville River (today's Bayou Manchac). Although the northern boundary was set initially at the 31st parallel of north latitude, British administrators realized that much of the good land along the Mississippi would not be included, so in 1764 the northern boundary extended by treaty with the Choctaws to the confluence of the Yazoo and Mississippi Rivers in latitude 32° 28'. This northern boundary was won by Spain as a result of the 1779 conquests at Baton Rouge and Manchac and was recognized as such in the Treaty of San Lorenzo (Pinckney's Treaty of 1795) by the United States and Spain. Brief Choctaw resistance to the cession of the strategic Walnut Hills (present-day Vicksburg) due to nonpayment by Great Britain was overcome by strategy and some $2,000 in "presents" at the Natchez Treaty between Spain and the Indians in May 1792, as explained in Jack D. L. Holmes, *Gayoso: The Life of a Spanish Governor in the Mississippi Valley, 1789–1799* (Baton Rouge, 1965).

Spain's Natchez Governor Manuel Gayoso de Lemos capped years of Spanish-American rivalry over the Chickasaw Bluffs (present-day Memphis) in 1795 with the Chickasaw Cession of a small strip of land on which the Spaniards constructed the most strategic fort protecting all of lower Louisiana and West Florida: Fort San Fernando de las Barrancas. Before its evacuation in 1797, in keeping with the Treaty of San Lorenzo ceding lands north of the 31st parallel to the United States, the fort made sure that non-Spanish flatboats would obey the restrictive rules Spain enforced from 1784 to the said treaty in 1795, by which the United States gained equal rights to navigate the Mississippi and to establish a right of deposit at New Orleans or some other site nearby. The treaty of San Lorenzo contained a clause permitting the Spaniards to cancel the right of deposit if it proved prejudicial to Spanish interests, and in 1802 Intendant Juan Ventura Morales, as related in Jack D. L. Holmes, *"Dramatis Personae* in Spanish Louisiana," *Louisiana Studies* 6 (Summer 1967), did just that, provoking such a vigorous reaction from the United States and Thomas Jefferson that it led the following year to the Louisiana Purchase and subsequent "annexation" of West Florida east of New Orleans. In a very real sense, therefore, the story of Spanish West Florida is the story of America's first steps in territorial expansion.

The major population centers of West Florida, in summary, were (1) Pensacola and St. Marks; (2) Mobile District, including coastal Alabama and Mississippi and the Tombigbee and Tensaw river basins; (3) Natchez District, stretching from the Thompson Creek settlement at New Fleciana north to Memphis and east as far as Choctaw and Chickasaw Indians would permit; (4) Baton Rouge, which assumed strategic importance following the March 1798 evacuation of the Natchez District and San Fernando de las Barrancas and was the focus for armed rebellion during the West Florida Controversy in 1810. For accounts of these developments, see Isaac Joslin Cox, *The West Florida Controversy, 1798–1813: A Study in American Diplomacy* (Baltimore, 1918), and two "classics" by Arthur P. Whitaker: *The Spanish-American Frontier, 1783–1795: The Westward Movement and the Spanish Retreat in the Mississippi Valley* (Boston, 1927), and *The Mississippi Question, 1795–1803* (New York, 1934).

When I began in this field in 1957 there were but a few major documentary collections of Spanish documents. The most valuable, I discovered, for Louisiana and West Florida was the three-volume translation with superb introductions by Lawrence Kinnaird, *Spain in the Mississippi Valley, 1765–1794*, vols. 2–4, *Annual Report of the American Historical Association for 1945* (Washington, D.C., 1946–1949). Documents from Spain, Cuba, and the fabulously rich Bancroft Collection at the University of California in Berkeley make up this classic, which has been reprinted with justification.

For West Florida, another valuable compilation (not translated) is Manuel Serrano y Sanz, *Documentos históricos de la Florida y la Luisiana, siglos xvi al xviii* (Madrid, 1912), who also did two combination monograph-documentary collections: *El brigadier Jaime Wilkinson y sus tratos con España para la independencia del Kentucky (Años 1787 á 1797)* (Madrid, 1915); and *España y los indios Cherokis y Chactas en la segunda mitad del siglo xviii* (Seville, 1916). Another magnificent combination of guide, documents, illustrations and narrative, which I have used with great advantage, is Miguel Gómez del Campillo, *Relaciones diplomáticas entre España y los Estados Unidos según los documentos del Archivo Histórico Nacional*, 2 vols. (Madrid, 1944, 1945).

Whitaker also published translated documents on West Florida: *Documents Relating to the Commercial Policy of Spain in the Floridas, with Incidental Reference to Louisiana* (DeLand, Fla., 1931). Since Fort San Fernando de las Barrancas lay on the Upper Mississippi, documents concerned with its founding and close relationship with St. Louis and New Madrid are important for West Florida. Louis Houck produced a three-volume narrative, *History of Missouri from the Earliest Explorations and Settlements until the Admission of the State into the Union* (Chicago, 1908), and a two-volume translated group of documents: *The Spanish Regime in Missouri* (Chicago, 1909). Major volumes dealing with Spanish West Florida (particularly the upper Mississippi portions) are Abraham P. Nasatir's *Before Lewis and Clark: Documents Illustrating the History of the Missouri, 1785–1804*, two vols. (St. Louis, 1952) and Nasatir's *Spanish War Vessels on the Mississippi, 1792–1796* (New Haven, 1968). See also Holmes, *Documentos inéditos para la historia de la Luisiana, 1792–1810* which appeared as vol. 15 of the Colección Chimalistac de Libros y Documentos Acerca de la Nueva España, published by Sr. José Porrúa Turanzas, brother of the famous Porrúa-Robredo booksellers of Mexico City.

My relationship with Don José and his son, Jose Porrúa Venero ("Pepe") led to two additional volumes in Spanish: vol. 26 in the Chimalistac series, *José de Evia y sus reconocimientos del Golfo de México, 1783–1796* (Madrid, 1968); and the introduction to Luis de Onís, *Memoria sobre las negociaciones entre España y los Estados Unidos de América* (Madrid, 1969). Evia (known as Hevia in Spanish Louisiana and West Florida) conducted an extremely valuable reconnaissance of the Gulf of Mexico between 1783 and 1786 and in 1792 led the expedition which succeeded in capturing the adventurer William Augustus Bowles, a major figure in West Florida history between 1780 and 1804, at Fort San Marcos de Apalache. Luis de Onís was the Spanish diplomat assigned "Mission Impossible," and whose signature on the Adams-Onís Treaty of 1819 and 1821 resulted in his incarceration back in Spain as a sell-out.

Except for the narrow-minded, jingoistic "local historians" and reliance on heavily biased accounts such as that of Andrew Ellicott, discussed in Jack D. L. Holmes, "Interpretations and Trends in the Study of the Spanish Borderlands: The Old Southwest," *Southwestern Historical Quarterly* (hereafter cited as *SHQ*) 74 (April 1971), most recent historians have used Spanish sources. Most significant on the American Revolution in West Florida are J. Leitch Wright, Jr., *Florida in the American Revolution* (Gainesville, 1975) and J. Barton Starr, *Tories, Dons, and Rebels: The American Revolution in British West Florida* (Gainesville, 1976), and I ask your pardon for including my own Bicentennial contribution, *The 1779 "Marcha de Gálvez:" Louisiana's Giant Step Forward in the American Revolution* (Baton Rouge, 1974), which tells of the Spanish conquest of British West Florida along the Mississippi River and around Lake Pontchartrain. As for immigration to Spanish West Florida and studies of changing Spanish policy toward that province, the most recent studies of Gilbert C. Din merit perusal: "The Immigration Policy of Governor

Esteban Miró in Spanish Louisiana [1785–1791]," *SHQ* 73 (October, 1969); and "Proposals and Plans for Colonization in Spanish Louisiana, 1787–1790," *Louisiana History* 11 (Summer 1970).

Still useful are some classic studies from the early decades of this century completed under the auspices of the Carnegie Institution of Washington, D.C., for they included major archives in Spain, France, England, Cuba, and Mexico. These include William R. Shepherd, *Guide to the Materials for the History of the United States in Spanish Archives (Simancas, the Archivo Histórico Nacional, and Seville)* (Washington, D.C., 1907); Roscoe R. Hill, *Descriptive Catalogue of the Documents Relating to the History of the United States in the Papeles Procedentes de Cuba Deposited in the Archivo General de Indias at Seville* (Washington D.C., 1916); James Alexander Robertson, *List of Documents in Spanish Archives Relating to the History of The United States, Which Have Been Printed or of Which Transcripts are Preserved in American Libraries* (Washington, D.C., 1910); Waldo G. Leland, et al., *Guide to Materials for American History in the Libraries and Archives of Paris*, 2 vols.(Washington, D.C., 1932 and 1943); Charles Oscar Paullin and Frederick L. Paxson, *Materials in London Archives for the History of the United States since 1783* (Washington, D.C., 1914); Luis Marino Perez, *Guide to the Materials for American History in Cuban Archives* (Washington, D.C., 1907); and Herbert Eugene Bolton, *Guide to the Materials for the History of the United States in the Principal Archives of Mexico* (Washington, D.C., 1913).

Among the time-honored guides to historical documents I had occasion to use in my research, most have been cited in my various articles and books. My earliest contribution in this regard was "Research Opportunities in the Spanish Borderlands: Louisiana and the Old Southwest," *Louisiana Studies* 1 (Winter 1962). I tried to place various historical works and their authors in perspective in my "Interpretations and Trends in the Study of the Spanish Borderlands: The Old Southwest," *SHQ* 74 (April 1971). During the American Revolution Bicentennial I tried to call attention to the need to tell Louisiana's (and West Florida's) story of two-hundred years ago in "The Historiography of the American Revolution in Louisiana," *Louisiana History* 19 (Summer 1978). William S. Coker and I teamed up on a major "survey" project: "Sources for the History of the Spanish Borderlands," *Florida Historical Quarterly*, *(FHQ)* 49 (April 1971), reprinted in *Spain and Her Rivals on the Gulf Coast* (Pensacola, 1971).

Coker also supervised a major tour de force concerning the subject, joined by various historians specializing in the field. "Research in the Spanish Borderlands," *Latin American Research Review* 7 (Summer 1972), combined the work of J. Leitch Wright, Jr. (for West Florida), Samuel Proctor (East Florida), Coker (Spanish Mississippi, or the Natchez District) and Jack D. L. Holmes (Spanish Louisiana and the Mobile District in West Florida). In the works cited above are innumerable references to Spanish documents and the guides to them.

Among the most useful recent additions are a series of volumes I call the "red books," because they are bound in scarlet leather. As a result of the United States-Spanish Treaty of January 24, 1976, thousands of pesetas funded the organization and publication of two series of works. The "blue books" (bound in dark blue as above) featured solid monographs produced on the Spanish Borderlands of the southeast by a new generation of Spanish historians trained in new techniques of quantitative history. But it is the set of "red books" which promises us new fields of research in the "Big Three" Spanish archives: Archivo General de Simancas, Archivo Histórico Nacional, and Archivo General de Indias (A.G.I.). María Francisca Represa Fernández, Carlos Álvarez García, and Miguel Represa Fernández joined forces to cover Simancas in two volumes of the general series entitled *Documentos relativos a la independencia de Norteamerica existentes en archivos espãnoles* (Madrid, 1976). The inclusive dates are 1750–1820. These volumes are most useful for a wide range of topics involving West Florida.

In the same series are Volumes I, II, VII, and IX, each of which has more than one part in most cases and which covers the A.G.I. For example, vol. I, part 2, includes the section of "Gobierno" in the A.G.I., compiled by Purificación Medina Encina. The "Cuban Papers" (so named because they were shipped from Havana to Spain at the end of the nineteenth century, but which cover the Spanish Borderlands in the Southeast) are covered by Reyes Siles Saturnino in Volume II (Madrid, 1980). The Archivo Histórico Nacional in Madrid is treated in several volumes: III, Parts 1 and 2 by Pilar León Tello; and IV by the same archivist (with excellent help by Concepción Menédez and Carmen Torroja (1980).

The UNESCO guide to Spanish archives picks up where the "Big Three" leave off. State and local archives throughout the Iberian peninsula are included in the two-volume *Guía de fuentes para la historia de Ibero-América conservadas en España* (Madrid, 1966, 1969).

Historians sometimes ignore what may be the most useful of all primary source materials: maps, charts and *planos*. In the case of West Florida, where historical boundaries have been disputed, accurate charts are essential. The following may be considered useful in this regard: Henry Edward Chambers, *West Florida and its Relation to the Historical Cartography of the United States* (Baltimore, 1898). The University of Michigan's William L. Clements Library may be the world's foremost repository of early maps of America, and the holdings on West Florida are particularly good. See D. W. Marshall, *Research Catalog of Maps of America to 1860 in the William L. Clements Library of the United States, 1502–1820* (Boston, 1972). Another useful guide is edited by Philip Lee Phillips: *The [Woodbury] Lowery Collection: A Descriptive List of Maps of the Spanish Possessions Within the Present Limits of the United States, 1502–1821* (Washington, D.C., 1912).

Two rarely consulted archival treasuries in Spain are located in Madrid. The Servicio Histórico Militar and its Geográfico counterpart are archives of the army and include stupendous holdings of cartographical treasures, some of which have been published in "coffee table" size books under the general title of *Cartografía de Ultramar*. In the two-volume (one for maps, one for text) *Carpeta II: Estados*

*Unidos y Canada* (Madrid, 1953) are some great *planos*, including some by Juan María Perchet of Fort San Marcos de Apalache (St. Marks, Florida). Following the 1953 publication of United States and Canada, the two military services issued the two-volume *Carpeta III: Mexico* (Madrid, 1955), which contains Francisco de Paula Gelabert's "Plano de la Batería de San Antonio y Fuerte Provisional de San Carlos."

I have also published several guides and studies of maps as historical documents: "Maps, Plans and Charts of Colonial Alabama in French and Spanish Archives," *Alabama Historical Quarterly* 27 (Spring and Summer, 1965); "Maps, Plans and Charts of Louisiana in Spanish and Cuban Archives: A Checklist," *Louisiana Studies* 2 (Winter 1963); "Maps, Plans and Charts of Louisiana in Paris Archives: A Checklist," *Louisiana Studies* 4 (Fall 1965); and "A Mystery Map of West Florida: A Cartographical Puzzle," in *Threads of Tradition and Culture along the Gulf Coast* (Pensacola, 1986).

Among the other guides to maps and charts, I have indicated here the ones which are most useful: Servicio Histórico Militar, *Catálogo de la Biblioteca Central Militar*, Part II: *Mapas y planos* (Madrid, 1945); *Atlantic Neptune* (London, 1777–1780), which includes in vol. 2 plates of Pensacola by George Gauld and the Iberville-Mississippi-Yazoo Rivers; William P. Cumming, *The Southeast in Early Maps* (Princeton, 1958); Servicio Historia Militar, Depósito de la Guerra, *Catálogo general del archivo de mapas, planos, y memorias del depósito de la guerra*, 2 vols. (Madrid, 1900); Hank T. Holmes, "Pre–1830 Cartographic Holdings: Special Title Listing as of February 27, 1987," unpublished typed list of eighteen pages in the Mississippi Department of Archives and History, Jackson; Pilar León Tello, *Mapas, planos y dibujos de la Sección de Estado del Archivo Histórico Nacional* (Madrid, 1969); and Pedro Torres Lanzas, *Relación descriptiva de los mapas, planos, etc., de México y Floridas, existentes en el Archivo General de Indias*, 2 vols. (Seville, 1900).

A fascinating "inventario" of charts delivered to the French prefect Laussat in 1804 (AGI, PC, legajo 142-A) lists the following: General map of the province, chart of the city and its environs, three plans of Plaquemines, pilot station of Balize, City of Natchez, District of Natchez, two charts showing the course of the Mississippi River, an English chart of the Mississippi as far north as Manchac, six plans showing fortifications at Los Nogales (Vicksburg), town of St. Bernard, New Orleans, Pointe Coupée, Avoyelles, New Madrid, three plans of Natchez, chart on the entrance to Barataria, and two plans of Tombecbe (Fort Confederation at Epes, Alabama). Others, however, such as the famous charts of Philip Nolan and Aaron Burr, are missing.

Spain was reluctant for many years following the 1898 catastrophe to allow its historic treasures to be copied by foreigners. Great progress resulted from the activities of Father Ernest Burrus, S.J., with an agreement to organize and copy pertinent documents from a section known as Audiencia de Santo Domingo in the A.G.I. in Seville. For the guide to Section 5 of the Audiencia de Santo Domingo, see *(Catálogo de documentos del Archivo General de Indias:*

*Sección V: Gobierño (Audiencia de Santo Domingo) sobre la época española de Luisiana*, 2 vols. (Madrid and New Orleans, 1968). The director of the A.G.I. then, José de la Peña y Cámara, directed the cooperative project and helped smooth the way for wholesale copying of documents, something the archives had forbidden to that time.

I reviewed these guides in *Louisiana History* 12 (Spring 1971), when I wrote, "Considering the time and expense involved in the preparation of archival catalogs, it is readily apparent why they are published 'few and far between,'" and I added that the catalog was *not* a replacement for actual research in the documents being catalogued.

For researchers unable or unwilling to subsidize a research trip to Spain, New Orleans offers a viable alternative with a few additional benefits! There are copies of the so-called "Loyola Project" at Loyola University on St. Charles Avenue, as well as at International House and the Historic New Orleans Collection. Once you learn how to use these sources, it is a "piece of cake," so to speak.

My first microfilms came from the Archivo General de la Nación of Mexico City, obtained in 1959 after I had completed my "Gayoso" dissertation and before I was awarded the Ph.D. degree from the University of Texas. The subjects of my Mexican research were the activities of Philip Nolan, America's premier filibusterer who met his fate near Waco in 1801. I was also interested in the activities of Spanish Louisiana and José de Evia, and due consideration was paid my research in C. Harvey Gardiner, "The Mexican Archives and the Historiography of the Mississippi Valley, in the Spanish Period," in *The Spanish in the Mississippi Valley, 1762–1804* (Urbana, 1974).

Dr. Eugene Watson, head of the Northwestern State University library, arranged with me to have copied a large group of microfilms dealing primarily with southwestern and northwestern Louisiana, but also including several important documents on the Natchez District. In January 1987, while I was scholar-in-residence for the Mississippi Department of Archives and History, I borrowed the twelve reels, had them copied for the department, and paid for a copy for my own ninety-six-reel Louisiana Collection Series. The twelve reels deal with a wide number of topics, many of which are centered in West Florida. For example, Reel No. 3, with documents from A.G.I., PC, leg. 2353, recalls the attempt by José de Hevia (nee Evia) to capture William Augustus Bowles at St. Marks.

The Holmes Collection at the University of Northwestern Louisiana also includes documents from the Ministerio de Asuntos de Exteriores in Madrid as well as some pertinent maps and charts of the Natchitoches area. The microfilm in the Holmes Collection deals primarily with Louisiana west of the Mississippi, but notable exceptions include the 1792 description of the Natchez District in West Florida.

At least since 1959 I have been trying without success to visit the archives of Cuba, inasmuch as several important bundles detail Cuban documents connected with West Florida. The personal (marriage, birth, death) records of the

Louisiana Infantry Regiment are there waiting for me to follow up my *Honor and Fidelity: The Louisiana Infantry Regiment and the Louisiana Militia Companies, 1766–1821* (Birmingham, 1965).

The late Duvon C. Corbitt first utilized Cuban archives to the fullest when he combined missionary activity with research for his doctoral dissertation on the Spanish administrative system in Florida. He brought back to the United States a solid block of documents concerned with West Florida and the Old Southwest, and in 1937 translated and edited documents in the *East Tennessee Historical Society Publications*. He explained his ideas for this in "Exploring the Southwest Territory in the Spanish Records," in *East Tennessee Historical Society Publications* 38 (1966). Corbitt also contributed a similar series, "Papers Relating to the Georgia-Florida Frontier, 1784–1800," *Georgia Historical Quarterly*, beginning with 20 (December 1936) and following through 25 (June 1941). Since many of the documents deal with such West Florida notables as Alexander McGillivray and William Augustus Bowles, they are of great importance to researchers looking for primary sources.

West Florida sources are also in Joaquín Llaverías, *Historia de los archivos de Cuba* (Havana, 1912), and Duvon C. Corbitt, "Señor Joaquín Llaverías and the Archivo Nacional de Cuba," *Hispanic American Historical Review* 20 (May 1940). What Corbitt did, of course, was to translate and edit the many thousands of pages of documents found at the Lawson McGhee Library at the Knoxville Public Library, some of which were obtained by Whitaker in the late 1920's.

For researchers in West Florida history, a convenient set of guides is the *Catálogo de los mapas, planos, croquis y árboles genealógicos existentes en el Archivo Nacional de Cuba*, 4 vols. (Havana, 1951–1956). Another source is the *Catálogo de los fondos de las Floridas* (Havana, 1944), while a complete guide to the Archivo Nacional de Cuba holdings on West Florida might include *Documents Pertaining to the Floridas Which Are Kept in Different Archives of Cuba*: Appendix No. 1: Official List of Documentary Funds of THE FLORIDAS—Now Territories of the States of Louisiana, Alabama, Mississippi, Georgia and Florida—Kept in the National Archives (Havana, 1945). No discussion of Cuban sources for West Florida should fail to include the biographical and genealogical data contained in Francisco Zavier de Santa Cruz (Conde de San Juan de Jaruco), *Historia de las familias cubanas*, 6 vols. (Havana, 1940–1950). These last four titles were compiled by The Cuban National Archives.

An early pioneer in the study of Florida history, Buckingham Smith, has left a legacy of document collections as well as a combination of fact and myth. The Buckingham Smith documents in the New York Public Library are among the relatively unsung sources of West Florida history. Two major guides to this repository are the *Dictionary Catalog of the History of the Americas*, 37 vols. (Boston, 1961) and *Dictionary Catalog of the Rare Book Division*, 22 vols. (Boston, 1971). Lawrence C. Wroth has furnished us with a guide to a Rhode Island source of Florida History in "Source Materials of Florida History in the John Carter Brown Library of Brown University," 20 (July 1941). A "must" is also James Alexander Robertson, "The Archival Distribution of Florida Manuscripts," *FHQ*, 10 (July 1931), which tells of the early Florida material at the New York Public Library and in the Genaro García Collection of the University of Texas.

The fabulous Louisiana Collection of the Bancroft Library in Berkeley includes five boxes and sixteen volumes, and some documents contained therein are unique. Many have been translated and included in Lawrence Kinnaird's *Spain in the Mississippi Valley* set mentioned above, but not all. For example, the census of the Choctaw Indians in Alabama and Mississippi during 1795 was published by Jack D. L. Holmes "The Choctaws in 1795," *Alabama Historical Quarterly* 30 (Spring 1968). The Southern Historical Collection at Chapel Hill also has some interesting documents, including records of Natchez "jack of all trades" William Dunbar, who may be considered West Florida's earliest great scientist, discussed in Jack D. L. Holmes, "William Dunbar," in *Lives of Mississippi Authors, 1817–1967*, ed. James B. Lloyd (Jackson, Miss., 1981).

Another ideal place for research on Spanish West Florida is the John C. Pace Library at the University of West Florida outside Pensacola. Two men are responsible for making this the best single repository of copies of Spanish documents on West Florida: history professor William S. Coker and former library director James Servies. In 1974, Coker began to collect microfilm copies of materials relating to the southeast's first megafirm, Panton, Leslie and Co.; see William S. Coker, "The Papers of Panton, Leslie and Company," *Ex Libris* 2 (Fall 1978). For many years Servies has been compiling a computerized listing of all works on West Florida, and his forthcoming publication should make it easier for scholars working in this field.

For the Natchez District, scholars are urged to consult Frederick S. Allis, Jr., *Guide to the Microfilm Edition of the Winthrop Sargent Papers* (Boston, 1965); William S. Coker, "Research Possibilities and Resources for a Study of Spanish Mississippi," *Journal of Mississippi History* 34 (May 1972); and the various guides cited above.

We should not omit the holdings of the Mississippi Valley Collection at Memphis State University, for which a guide has been published by Eleanor McKay: *The West Tennessee Historical Society: Guide to Archives and Collections* (Memphis, 1979).

Occasionally, in doing research on specific individuals, scholars should seek such sources in Louisiana as the Notarial Archives in New Orleans; see Rudolph H. Waldo, *Notarial Archives of Orleans Parish, 1731–1953* (New Orleans, 1957). In similar ways, Eric Beerman, an "expatriate" Californian living in Madrid, has used the Spanish Archivo de Protocolos to obtain accurate biographical data on early figures in West Florida history. He has also examined the dossiers submitted when an important government official was knighted in several Spanish orders, as Santiago, Calatrava, and Carlos III. See *Indice de prubas de los caballeros de la real y distinguida órden española de Carlos III* (Madrid, 1904); Vicente Vignau, *Indice de pruebas de los caballeros que han vestido el hábito de Calatrava, Alcántara y Montesi desde el siglo xvi hasta la fecha* (Madrid, 1903).

In my research into West Florida history, I have found important documents in the Huntington Library in San Marino and the Department of Archives and History in Raleigh, North Carolina. Still, in the United States the best research centers for documents on West Florida are at Jackson, Mississippi, and at the University of Alabama in Birmingham.

The Mississippi Department of Archives and History (Jackson) has a wide range of important documentary sources on West Florida. One of the planned, organized "collections" was the 1966–1968 survey of the Mobile District, 1780–1813. Known as the "Holmes Collection," this features the Port City during the final era of Spanish control, as well as coastal Alabama and Mississippi. A rough description of the archival data is my "Genealogical and Historical Sources for Spanish Alabama, 1780–1813," *Deep South Genealogical Quarterly* 5 (February, 1968). In addition, this writer's own Louisiana Collection Series of Books and Documents on Colonial Louisiana includes West Florida as well as Louisiana. In addition to the publication of five major books, the Louisiana Collection Series has organized thousands of slides, photos, original maps and charts, as well as about 100 reels of microfilm, and thousands of pages of typescript gathered in ten research trips to Mexico, Spain and Paris between 1961 and 1988. Some of these "treasures" are in Jackson (copies) and also at the University of Northwestern Louisiana in Natchitoches—lying there to lure students into the still wide-open field of West Florida history. Perhaps the guides I have indicated above will help serious researchers find new and fascinating information on the early history of the region.

For additional bibliography, see James A. Servies, *A Bibliography of West Florida* (Pensacola, 1982). Servies's three-volume study includes publications by year as follows: Volume I (1535–1915) and Volume II (1916–1971); Volume III consists of the index. *A Bibliography of West Florida, 1981 Supplement* (Pensacola, 1982), brings the bibliography through 1981 and includes titles through the entire colonial period not in the previous volumes. There is also an unpublished "Bibliography of West Florida: 1985 Supplement," in the Special Collection Department, University of West Florida, which includes ninety-three pages of titles for the years 1767 through 1945 that are not in the printed bibliographies.

See also William S. Coker, "Research Possibilities and Resources for the Study of Spanish Mississippi," *Journal of Mississippi History* 34 (May 1972), and Coker, et al., "Research in the Spanish Borderlands," *Latin American Research Review* 7 (Summer 1972). This volume includes five bibliographic essays: Jack D. L. Holmes, "Spanish Alabama" and "Spanish Louisiana"; Samuel Proctor, "East Florida, 1763–1821"; J. Leitch Wright, Jr., "Spanish West Florida"; and William S. Coker, "Spanish Mississippi." Additionally, a bibliography by Michael H. Harris, which contains eight hundred titles, *Florida History: A Bibliography* (Metuchen, N.J., 1977), is helpful. James A. Servies,

*The Siege of Pensacola, 1781: A Bibliography* (Pensacola, 1981), includes a substantial bibliography.

Eric Beerman has written on several important officials and soldiers in Spanish West Florida. See "Arturo O'Neill: First Governor of West Florida During the Second Spanish Period," *FHQ*, 60 (July 1980); "Baron de Carondelet (1747–1807): A Biographical Portrait of a Flemish Governor of Spain in Louisiana," *Louisiana Genealogical Register* 29 (March 1982); "Jose Solano (I Marques de Socorro) y la Batalla de Pensacola," *Revista General de Marina* (June 1983).

On military events, see William S. Coker and Hazel P. Coker, *The Seige of Mobile, 1780, in Maps with Data on Troop Strength, Military Units, Ships, Casualties, and Prisoners of War Including a Brief History of Fort Charlotte (Conde)*, Vol. 3, Spanish Borderlands Series (Pensacola, 1982); Coker and Coker, *The Siege of Pensacola, 1781, in Maps: with Data on Troop Strength, Military Units, Ships, Casualties and Related Statistics*, vol. 8, Spanish Borderlands Series (Pensacola, 1981); William S. Coker and Robert Rea, eds., *Anglo-Spanish Confrontation on the Gulf Coast during the American Revolution* (Pensacola, 1982). See Mario Hernandez Sanchez-Barba, "Bernardo de Gálvez, militar y politico en la Florida acidental (un bicentenario y una reparacion historica)," *ARBOR* no. 425 (May 1982) for an overview and evaluation of the career of Bernardo de Gálvez, Spanish Governor of Louisiana and conqueror of Pensacola during the American Revolutionary War. Carmen de Reparaz, *Yo Solo: Bernardo de Gálvez y la Toma de Panzacola en 1781* (Barcelona, 1986), is a well-illustrated and scholarly history of the conquest of Pensacola in 1781. Thomas Fleming, "Bernardo de Gálvez, the Forgotten Revolutionary Conquistador who saved Louisiana," *American Heritage* 33 (April-May 1982), contains information on campaigns of Gálvez in West Florida.

The people of the region are examined in Winston DeVille, "Mobile in 1786," *Deep South Genealogical Quarterly* 19 (February 1982); Winston DeVille, "Some Anglo-American residents of Spanish Alabama in 1753," *The Genealogical and Historical Magazine of the South* 4 (February 1987); William S. Coker, "Religious Census of Pensacola, 1786–1801," *FHQ*, 61 (July 1982); Albert Tate, "Spanish Census of the Baton Rouge District for 1786," *Louisiana History* 24 (Winter 1983); William S. Coker and Douglas G. Inglis, *The Spanish Censuses of Pensacola 1784–1820: A Genealogical Guide to Spanish Pensacola*, vol. 3, Spanish Borderlands Series (Pensacola, 1980).

On a major enterprise of the region, see William S. Coker and Thomas D. Watson, *Indian Traders of the Southeastern Spanish Borderlands: Panton, Leslie and Company and John Forbes and Company, 1783–1847* (Pensacola, 1986). Additional aspects of the region's Indians are treated in John Sugden, "The Southern Indians in the War of 1812: The Closing Phase," *FHQ*, 60 (January 1982) and Jack D. L. Holmes, "Benjamin Hawkins and United States Attempts to Teach Farming to Southeastern Indians," *Agricultural History* 60 (Spring 1986).

Other works of interest on a variety of topics include Gilbert C. Din, "War Clouds on the Mississippi: Spain's 1785 Crisis in West Florida," *FHQ*, 60 (July 1981); Jack D. L. Holmes "Educational Opportunities in Spanish West Florida, 1781–1821," *FHQ*, 60 (July 1981); and Ángel Del Rio, *La Mision de Don Luis de Onís en Los Estados Unidos (1809–1819)* (New York and Barcelona, 1981). The last citation examines the life of Onís and his diplomatic mission including the negotiations for the cession of the Floridas to the United States.

# 7

# TERRITORIAL FLORIDA, 1821–1845

## HERBERT J. DOHERTY, JR.

ON FEBRUARY 22, 1819, the Adams-Onís treaty between Spain and the United States was signed in Washington ceding to the United States East and West Florida and defining the western boundary of the Louisiana Purchase. After ratification by the United States Senate, arrangements for the transfer were then set in motion. President James Monroe named a reluctant Andrew Jackson as the provisional governor with vague, poorly understood powers to receive the Floridas from Spain and to establish local government. On July 17, 1821, the formal transfer took place in Pensacola and Jackson was in charge. Florida remained a territory until it was granted statehood in 1845.

There are a number of general histories of Florida which deal more or less satisfactorily with the territorial era. Comprehensive histories compiled as commercial ventures have not been impressive either for accuracy or felicity of style, but Junius E. Dovell, *Florida: Historic, Dramatic, Contemporary* (New York, 1952), and Rowland H. Rerick, *Memoirs of Florida* (Atlanta, 1902) have mined much valuable information from scattered sources. Each should be used with much caution. More scholarly works of value include Kathryn Abbey Hanna,

*Florida, Land of Change* (Chapel Hill, N.C., 1948) and Caroline Brevard, *A History of Florida* (DeLand, Fla., 1925). The latter received the benefit of careful editing and indexing by historian James A. Robertson. Best of all the general histories of Florida is Charlton W. Tebeau, *A History of Florida* (Miami, 1971). The four chapters covering the territorial period have been called the best in the book.

The only scholarly history which focuses on the territorial period alone is Sidney Walter Martin, *Florida during the Territorial Days* (Athens, Ga., 1944). Developed from a doctoral dissertation, the number of errors suggest that if it is used as a reference it should be checked against other sources. Its usefulness lies in the fact that it covers the major problems and events of the period and is helpful in giving a broad general impression of the period. Two old works which have been reprinted in the *Floridiana Facsimile and Reprint Series* of the University of Florida Press, both written by John Lee Williams, are *The Territory of Florida* (Gainesville, 1962) and *A View of West Florida* (Gainesville, 1976). Neither should be accepted as faithful historical chronicles, but rather as reflections of life in the territory and of how little Floridians of that day knew either about the history or geography of the peninsula.

Immediate post-transfer problems centered around the transfer itself, the establishment of local governments, and the flood of settlers into the area. Early studies have perpetrated two myths which have persisted: that Florida was "purchased" from Spain and that Jackson was a "military" governor. Both are false. The United States paid Spain nothing but agreed to settle certain claims which American citizens had against Spain up to a limit of five million dollars. The best account is Philip C. Brooks, *Diplomacy and the Borderlands—the Adams-Onís Treaty of 1819* (Berkeley, 1939). The "purchase" notion has received detailed analysis and refutation in Harris G. Warren, "Textbook Writers and the Florida 'Purchase' Myth," *Florida Historical Quarterly* (*FHQ*) 41 (April 1963). The impression that Jackson was a military governor comes from David Y. Thomas, *A History of Military Government in Newly Acquired Territory of the United States* (New York, 1904). Jackson had left the army before assuming the governorship, and the regime he established was a provisional civilian government treating Florida as one province divided into two counties. Two articles by this writer help explain the temporary arrangements: "The Governorship of Andrew Jackson," *FHQ*, 33 (July 1954), and "Andrew Jackson vs. the Spanish Governor, Pensacola, 1821," *FHQ*, 34 (October 1955). Also valuable is the concluding chapter of Robert Remini, *Andrew Jackson and the Course of American Empire, 1767–1821* (New York, 1977), as well as Allen Morris and Amelia Rea Maguire, "Beginnings of Popular Government in Florida," *FHQ*, 57 (July 1978) and Charles D. Ferris, "The Courts of Territorial Florida," *FHQ*, 19 (April 1941).

Though very productive of documents, Jackson's stay in Florida lasted only eleven weeks. He departed in October 1821, and was succeeded by Virginian William P. DuVal. One of the early projects of the DuVal administration was to plant a centrally located capital in place of the alternate uses of Pensacola and St. Augustine for legislative meetings. In 1823 Dr. William H. Simmons and John Lee Williams were commissioned to explore and select a site. Portions of Williams's *View of West Florida* was based on material gathered on that journey. His journal was reprinted in *FHQ*, 1 (April 1908) as "The Selection of Tallahassee as the Capital."

Difficult travel in the large, thinly populated peninsula necessitated a new capital. Roads were virtually non-existent, railroads were yet to come, and rivers, for the most part, facilitated only north-south travel. Some detail of the actual construction of the new capital can be found in Lee H. Warner, "Florida's Capitols," *Florida Historical Quarterly* 61 (January 1983).

A number of articles and monographs are available on government and politics in the territorial period as well as some biographical treatments of leading politicians. The factional strife which characterized much of territorial politics has been sketched in this writer's articles in the *FHQ*: "Political Factions in Territorial Florida," 28 (October 1949) and "Andrew Jackson's Cronies in Florida Territorial Politics," 34 (July 1955). The Democrats were the first full-fledged party to organize in Florida, at the Constitutional Convention of 1838. Arthur W. Thompson has described the organization and early development of that party in his perceptive *Jacksonian Democracy on the Florida Frontier* (Gainesville, 1961). The territorial roots of the opposition Whig party have been traced in this writer's *The Whigs of Florida, 1845–1854* (Gainesville, 1959).

Two leaders quite prominent in shaping the early Democratic party in Florida were David Levy Yulee and Robert Raymond Reid. Neither has received adequate biographical treatment, though several graduate theses have been done on Yulee, whose original name Levy was changed to Yulee in 1845. The standout study is Arthur W. Thompson, "David Yulee: A Study of Nineteenth Century American Thought and Enterprise" (Ph.D. diss., Columbia University, 1954). Other theses include Mills M. Lord, "David Levy Yulee, Statesman and Railroad Builder" (M.A. thesis, University of Florida, 1940); James L. Alderman, "David Levy Yulee, Antebellum Florida Leader, 1810–1886" (M.A. thesis, University of North Carolina, 1946), and Leslie R. Stein, "David Levy and Florida Territorial Politics" (M.A. thesis, University of South Florida, 1973). Leon Huhner wrote "David L. Yulee, Florida's First Senator," American Jewish Historical Society *Publications* 25 (1917), and provided some background on family in "Moses Elias Levy, Florida Pioneer," *FHQ*, 19 (April 1941).

Except for Andrew Jackson, only two territorial governors have received extensive biographical study. Herbert J. Doherty, *Richard Keith Call, Southern Unionist* (Gainesville, 1961), is a thoroughly researched work which sheds much light on various aspects of territorial history. The last territorial governor, John Branch, was the subject of Marshall D. Haywood, *John Branch, 1782–1883* (Raleigh, N.C., 1915), but he was only peripherally a participant in Florida politics. William P. DuVal, who served longest as governor and led a colorful life, has received only poorly documented notice in James Owen Knauss, "William Pope DuVal, Pioneer and State Builder," *FHQ* 11 (January 1933). The only "Van Buren Democrat" to sit in the gubernatorial chair was Georgia's Robert Raymond Reid. A different kind of frontier politician—reflective, gentle, bookish—Reid deserves more study than he has received: Warren G. Fouraker, "The Administration of Robert Raymond Reid" (M.A. thesis, Florida State University, 1949). The term of John H. Eaton, a period of virtual exile, was uneventful and has received little notice.

Joseph M. White had the longest term of service as delegate from Florida in Congress but, like DuVal, he has attracted little study. The only significant work is Dorothy E. Hill, "Joseph M. White, Florida Territorial Delegate, 1825–1837" (M.A. thesis, University of Florida, 1950). Joseph M. Hernandez, the first delegate, and Charles Downing, who followed White for two terms, have had no study.

The Second Seminole War (1835–1842) would probably have been ranked by contemporary residents as the most important event in Florida territorial history. Though the contemporary history by John T. Sprague, *Origin, Progress, and Conclusion of the Florida War* (New York, 1848), is still valuable as a source, the definitive work is now John K. Mahon, *History of the Second Seminole War, 1835–1842* (Gainesville, 1967). His work is solid, judicious, and based on extensive research in primary and secondary sources. The most persistent researcher into the role of blacks in the war, however, has been Kenneth Wiggins Porter. For a quarter century he has written articles on that theme: "Florida Slaves and Free Negroes in the Second Seminole War, 1835–1842," *Journal of Negro History* 28 (October 1943); "The Negro Abraham," *FHQ*, 25 (July 1946); "The Episode of Osceola's Wife: Fact or Fiction," *FHQ*, 26 (July 1947); "Billy Bowlegs (Holata Micco) in the Seminole Wars," *FHQ*, 45 (January 1967); and "Negroes and the Seminole War, 1835–1842," *Journal of Southern History* 30 (November 1964). A few of his articles are highly speculative, but he has brought out a facet of the Seminole Wars often minimized in conventional textbooks. He judges the blacks to have been a powerful influence in rallying resistance and, ultimately, in persuading Indians to agree to removal.

Though the role of the navy in the Second Seminole War has often gone unnoticed, the authority on the topic is clearly George E. Buker, whose *Swamp Sailors: Riverine Warfare in the Everglades, 1835–1842* (Gainesville, 1975), clarifies the innovative tactics that conflict demanded of navy men and illuminates the specialized form of combat required in shallow inland streams. See also his articles "Lieutenant Levin M. Powell, U.S.N., Pioneer of Riverine Warfare," *FHQ*, 47 (January 1969), and "The Mosquito Fleet's Guides and the Second Seminole War," *FHQ*, 57 (January 1979).

Glimpses into army life in wartime Florida may be gained from Jacob Rhett Motte, *Journey into Wilderness*, ed. James F. Sunderman (Gainesville, 1963) and John Bemrose, *Reminiscences of the Second Seminole War*, ed. John K. Mahon (Gainesville, 1966). Gripping, novelistic, but well-documented stories of two battles of the war have been told by Frank Laumer in *Massacre!* (Gainesville, 1968), and "Encounter by the River," *FHQ*, 46 (April 1968).

The most famous Indian leader of the war was doubtless the flamboyant Osceola. Sources on his life are rare, but much that is fanciful, inventive, and romantic has been written about him. In 1955, however, the *FHQ*, 33 (January-April 1955), published a double number containing articles, portraits, and illustrations of his dress which shed light on his parentage, life, capture, death in prison, and subsequent decapitation.

Virtually all the leaders on the side of the whites came out of the war with tarnished reputations. Most have received full biographical study: Rembert W. Patrick, *Aristocrat in Uniform: General Duncan L. Clinch* (Gainesville, 1963); James W. Silver, *Edmund Pendleton Gaines: Frontier General* (Baton Rouge, 1949); Chester L. Keiffer, *Maligned General: Thomas S. Jessup* (San Rafael, Calif., 1979); Charles W. Elliott, *Winifield Scott, the Soldier and the Man* (New York, 1937); and Brainerd Dyer, *Zachary Taylor* (Baton Rouge, 1964).

Despite all its costs in life, property destruction, and outlays of money, the Second Seminole War did leave a legacy of improved transportation. In 1935, Mark Boyd brought together documents which told the story of "The First American Road in Florida: Pensacola-St. Augustine Highway, 1824," *FHQ*, 14 (October 1935 and January 1936). Alice Whitman soon after wrote "Transportation in Territorial Florida," *FHQ* 17 (July 1938), which is helpful for dealing with taverns, waterways, railroads, and mail service as well as roads.

The authority on steamboat travel is Edward A. Mueller, who has amassed much information, some of which has appeared in three articles in *FHQ*: "East Coast Florida Steamboating, 1831–1861," 40 (January 1962); "Suwannee River Steamboating," 45 (January 1967); and "Steamboat Activity in Florida During the Second Seminole Indian War," 64 (April 1986). Despite the initiation of steamboat travel and the cutting of new roads, communication remained difficult. Postal service was disrupted by bad weather, Indian raids, incompetent and dishonest postal contractors, and the lack of public transportation. The cynical view that it was easier to visit London, the Great Lakes, or New Orleans than it was to send a letter from Tallahassee to Pensacola was reported by Richard J. Stanaback in "Postal Operations in Territorial Florida, 1821–1845," *FHQ*, 52 (October 1973), and in the same journal, "Florida's Disrupted Mail Service, 1821–1845," 52 (July 1974).

Railroads were to come, but not extensively enough to improve transportation and communications in the territorial era. Though many projects were proposed and lines chartered, only two came to fruition, and they were designed to give commerce and agriculture access to seaports. Dorothy Dodd has surveyed the abortive projects as well as those which were built in "Railroad Projects in Territorial Florida" (M.A. thesis, Florida State College for Women, 1929). An interesting account of tracing the physical remains of the first railroad, the Lake Wimico and St. Joseph (soon reorganized as the St. Joseph and Iola) is Robert R. Hurst, "Mapping Old St. Joseph, Its Railroads, and Environs," *FHQ*, 39

(April 1961). The ambitious but abortive projects undertaken in Pensacola are described in Charles W. Hildreth, "Railroads Out of Pensacola, 1833–1883," *FHQ*, 37 (January-April 1959).

Though newspaper editors complained as loudly as any about poor roads and postal service, it was through the newspapers that territorial Floridians received whatever communication they received about the outside world. The comprehensive study on journalism is still James Own Knauss, *Territorial Florida Journalism* (DeLand, Fla., 1926). Considered to be a model history in its day, the work summarizes territorial history, describes forty-five papers in detail, and contains biographical sketches of most of the newspapermen.

Life in the territory was primarily rural and agricultural and land was the major attraction for new settlers. In earlier years, both Spain and England had given residents and absentee owners large tracts. Years of litigation over the validity of a number of those grants delayed settlement in some areas. Some of the problems of contested land claims have been sketched by Sidney Walter Martin, "The Public Domain in Territorial Florida," *Journal of Southern History* 10 (May 1944), and by George Whatley and Sylvia Cook, "The East Florida Land Commission: A Study in Frustrations," *FHQ*, 50 (July 1971). The largest and the most litigated grant was that made west of Tallahassee to John Forbes and Company. John C. Upchurch, a geographer, in "Aspects of the Development and Exploration of the Forbes Purchase," *FHQ*, 48 (October 1969), has described the quality and character of the land and its resources and summarized the legal disputes.

In 1824, a grateful Congress gave the Marquis de Lafayette a township of land near Tallahassee as a reward for Revolutionary War services, but he apparently never derived much income from it. Kathryn Abbey Hanna has described the grant in "The Story of the Lafayette Lands in Florida," *FHQ*, 10 (January 1932). See also Lucretia R. Bishko, "A French Would-Be Settler on Lafayette's Township," *FHQ*, 62 (July 1983). Clearing titles to old grants was complicated by the fact that the Spanish removed land records to Havana at the change of flags. That problem is described in two articles in A. Curtis Wilgus, ed., *Hispanic American Essays, A Memorial to James Alexander Robertson* (Chapel Hill, N.C., 1942): A. J. Hanna, "Diplomatic Missions of the United States to Cuba to Secure the Spanish Archives of Florida," and Irene A. Wright, "The Odyssey of the Spanish Archives of Florida."

Most territorial Floridians derived their livelihood from the land, and only a minority were planters with vast acreages and slaves. It has been the life-styles of the elite, however, which has been honored in written history virtually to the exclusion of the dirt farmers. What we know of slavery is also inevitably wrapped up in the chronicles of plantation life, and the free black, mostly located in the towns, is rarely noted. A thorough documentation of the slave and plantation economy is found in Julia Floyd Smith, *Slavery and Plantation Growth in Antebellum Florida, 1821–1860* (Gainesville, 1973). This work makes good use of probate records and official documents but uses few plantation records.

Included are slave narratives and lists of major planters and their holdings. Two graduate theses worth notice are Katherine Chatham, "Plantation Slavery in Middle Florida" (M.A. thesis, University of North Carolina, 1938), and Lula D. Appleyard, "Plantation Life in Middle Florida, 1821–1845" (M.A. thesis, Florida State College for Women, 1940).

A romanticized view of territorial social life written by one who was part of it is Ellen Call Long, *Florida Breezes; or, Florida New and Old*, (Floridiana Facsimile and Reprint Series (Gainesville, 1962). Mrs. Long was the daughter of Richard Keith Call. Another governor's daughter, offspring of Thomas Brown, left similar reminiscences in Bertram H. Groene, ed., "Lizzie Brown's Tallahassee," *FHQ*, 48 (October 1969). A scholarly view of life among the elite is Alfred J. Hanna, *A Prince in Their Midst: The Adventurous Life of Achille Murat on the American Frontier* (Norman, Okla., 1946). The prince was an eccentric, but frontiers often breed eccentrics, and two others are worth note. George J. F. Clarke and Zephaniah Kingsley have both been recorded in the *FHQ*: Louise Bates Hill, "George J. F. Clarke, 1774–1836," 21 (January 1943); Philip S. May, "Zephaniah Kingsley, Nonconformist, 1765–1843," 23 (January 1945). Kingsley has also rated a thesis by Faye L. Glover, "Zephania Kingsley, Nonconformist, Slave Trader, Patriarch" (M.A. thesis, Atlanta University, 1970). Kingsley was appointed by President Monroe to the first legislative council, and Clarke had been a trusted agent of the Spanish government before the transfer.

For the most part, free black people were concentrated in the small urban centers of Key West, Pensacola, and St. Augustine. Julie Ann Lisenby, "The Free Negro in Antebellum Florida, 1821–1861" (M.A. thesis, Florida State University, 1947) is one of the few studies of this group. Overwhelmingly, the black slave population was in rural areas. The three urban centers mentioned were the centers of commerce and handcraft industries. Both Key West and Pensacola were centers of federal military activity and those relationships have been described by Ernest F. Dibble, *Antebellum Pensacola and the Military Presence* (Pensacola, 1974), and Clayton D. Roth, "The Military Utilization of Key West and the Dry Tortugas from 1822–1900" (M.A. thesis, University of Miami, 1970). A double number of the *FHQ*, 37 (January-April 1959) was devoted to varied aspects of Pensacola history. E. Ashby Hammond, "Notes on the Medical History of Key West, 1822–1832," *FHQ*, 46 (October 1967) gives some insights on life in the island city. A well researched history of St. Augustine that describes the community through the lives of its most significant family is Thomas Graham, *The Awakening of St. Augustine: The Anderson Family and the Oldest City, 1821–1924* (St. Augustine, 1978).

The three urban centers noted above were the centers of banking in Florida. The Bank of Pensacola, the Union Bank in Tallahassee, and the Southern Life Insurance and Trust Company in St. Augustine provided financial facilities for planter and businessman alike. Three chapters in Junius E. Dovell, *History of Banking in Florida, 1828–1924* (Orlando, 1955), tell their stories succinctly.

Though pedestrian in style, the work brings together important sources difficult to find. Valuable information about the Panic of 1837 and its impacts may be found in a chapter on Florida in Reginald C. McGrane, *Foreign Bondholders and American State Debts* (New York, 1935). An article pointing up the weaknesses and collapse of the banks is Kathryn Abbey Hanna, "The Union Bank of Tallahassee," *FHQ*, 15 (April 1937).

Catholicism was the deeply rooted religion in Spanish Florida, but the territorial days were dark ones for Catholics. Michael V. Gannon in *The Cross in the Sand, the Early Catholic Church in Florida, 1513–1870* (Gainesville, 1965), in two chapters relates troubles stemming from the Church's separation from government, lack of priests, attempts at lay control, and schism within. Protestant denominations are adequately treated in Joseph D. Cushman, Jr., *A Goodly Heritage: The Episcopal Church in Florida* (Gainesville, 1965); John L. Rosser, *History of Florida Baptists* (Nashville, 1949); and Charles T. Thrift, *The Trail of the Florida Circuit Rider, An Introduction to the Rise of Methodism in Middle and East Florida* (Lakeland, Fla., 1944).

The transition from territorial status to statehood began as early as 1838, when a constitutional convention was held in St. Joseph. Important information about the convention is in F. W. Hoskins, "The St. Joseph Convention: The Making of Florida's First Constitution," *FHQ*, 16 (July 1937, October 1937, April 1938). The most valuable single work on the coming of statehood, however, is Dorothy Dodd, *Florida Becomes a State* (Tallahassee, 1945). The volume includes the complete journal of the St. Joseph Convention, the full text of the Constitution of 1838, and scores of other pertinent documents, including the text of the Adams-Onís treaty of 1819.

No researcher into the territorial period of Florida's history can ever afford to bypass the single most important collection of source materials now in print. Between 1956 and 1960 the federal government published in five hefty volumes selections from the files of the original records of the Territory of Florida in the National Archives. The papers are arranged chronologically with an index for each volume. The background of many documents is explained, persons and places referred to are identified, and the materials are cross-referenced. This massive work of extreme importance is Clarence Edwin Carter, ed., *Territorial Papers of the United States*, vols. 22–26, *The Territory of Florida* (Washington, D.C., 1956–1960).

# 8

# FLORIDA, FROM STATEHOOD THROUGH RECONSTRUCTION, 1845–1877

PAUL S. GEORGE

IN A SINGLE generation in the mid-1800s, Florida entered the Union as a new state, seceded, joined the Confederate States of America, and reentered the United States following its "reconstruction." The literature devoted to Florida during the period of early statehood, Civil War, and Reconstruction, an eventful and momentous period, is vast and varied. It is especially rich in scholarly articles, master's theses, and doctoral dissertations, but includes relatively few books. While the *Florida Historical Quarterly* (FHQ) represents the single most important source for scholarship, local, regional, and even national journals offer plenty of material on the era. Because of space constraints this essay will cite only the most pertinent publications. Moreover, since the literature on blacks, a key element in the history of the period, as well as Florida's Indians and women, are covered in other essays, little mention will be made of them here.

## EARLY STATEHOOD, 1845–1861

Florida's preparation for statehood began with its acquisition by the United States in 1821. Delayed by the politics of sectionalism and slavery, statehood finally came in 1845. Several articles chronicle elements of the process. See Franklin A. Doty, "Florida, Iowa, and the National 'Balance of Power,' 1845," *FHQ*, 35 (July 1956), for a comprehensive survey of the complications attendant to the admission of two states at the same time. See also T. Frederick Davis, "Pioneer Florida, Admission to Statehood, 1845," *FHQ*, 22 (January, 1944); Benjamin D. Wright, "Contemporaneous Reactions To Statehood," *FHQ*, 23 (April 1945); "Inaugural Address of Governor Mosely," *FHQ*, 23 (April 1945); and Daisy Parker, "The Inauguration of the First Governor of the State of Florida," *Apalachee* 2 (1946).

Edwin L. Williams, Jr., provided an overview of the period in "Florida in the Union, 1845–1861" (Ph.D. diss., University of North Carolina, 1951). Dorothy Dodd focused on the state during the first year of statehood in "Florida in 1845" and "Florida's Population in 1845," *FHQ*, 24 (July 1945). Several contemporary observers, as well as historians, have assessed the Florida of this period. Olin Norwood, ed., "Letters From Florida in 1851," *FHQ*, 29 (April 1951), offers fascinating, insightful letters on the raw but beautiful state, as do those of a prominent historian of the era in Patricia P. Clark, " 'A Tale to Tell From Paradise Itself,' George Bancroft's Letters From Florida, March 1855," *FHQ*, 48 (January 1970). Virginia Steele Wood, "Elizah Swift's Travel Journal From Massachusetts to Florida, 1857," *FHQ*, 55 (October 1976) contains an interesting picture of Tallahassee, the bustling capital. Writing in the *FHQ*, 35 (July 1956), Herbert J. Doherty, Jr., explored "Florida in 1856," and found that year fruitful for the young state. Rodney E. Dillon, Jr., sketched the demographic, geographic, and economic picture of the sparsely settled southern sector of the state in "South Florida in 1860," *FHQ*, 60 (April 1982).

Despite the overwhelmingly rural character of antebellum Florida, several of its cities were emerging as important centers. In the past decade, numerous book-length studies of Florida cities have appeared with portions devoted to the state's early years. They are discussed in Raymond Mohl's essay elsewhere in this study.

One of Florida's most important cities in the decade before the Civil War was the subject of William W. Rogers, "A Great Stirring in the Land: Tallahassee and Leon County in 1860," *FHQ*, 64 (October 1985). Rogers focused on one aspect of the capital area in "The Way They Went: Death in Leon County in 1860," *Apalachee* 9 (1980–1983). Clifton Paisley has authored a fascinating economic and social study of the capital city: "Tallahassee through the Storebooks, 1843–1863: Antebellum Cotton Prosperity," *FHQ*, 50 (October 1971).

Richard Martin has written extensively on Jacksonville, including "It Was a Tough Town in 1850," *Jacksonville* 18 (March/April 1981), and "Jacksonville of the 1850s Wasn't All Brawls and Shootouts," *Jacksonville* 16 (July/August 1979). In "Hillsborough County (1850): A Community in the South Florida Flatwoods," *FHQ*, 62 (October 1983), John S. Otto examined the origins of open-range livestock herding in Hillsboro County.

In many ways, antebellum Florida was a thoroughly southern state. Its economy was dominated by cotton production and the plantation system. Virtually no industry existed. Middle Florida, the rich lands between the Apalachicola and Suwannee rivers, represented its cotton belt. Julia Floyd Smith, *Slavery and Plantation Growth in Antebellum Florida, 1821–1860* (Gainesville, 1973), examined the subject in great detail. Margaret T. Ordonez, "Plantation Self-Sufficiency in Leon County, Florida: 1824–1860," *FHQ*, 60 (April 1982), outlined the efforts of one county to achieve self-sufficiency.

Smith elaborated on the marketing and selling of cotton in "Cotton and the Factorage System in Antebellum Florida," *FHQ*, 49 (July 1970). In "Slavetrading in Antebellum Florida," *FHQ*, 50 (January 1972), she observed the rapid growth of Florida's slave population, along with skyrocketing prices for human chattel.

The open-range cattle industry was important to the economy of nineteenth-century Florida, prompting several historical studies. John S. Otto's articles on cattle raising in south and central Florida have appeared in the *FHQ*, 63–65 (July 1984, July 1985, January 1987), and in the *Journal of American Folklore* (July-September 1984). See also William Mealor, Jr., "The Open-Range Ranch in South Florida and Its Contemporary Successor," (Ph.D. Diss., University of Georgia, 1972). Joe A. Akerman, Jr., provided a comprehensive overview of the industry in *Florida Cowmen: A History of Florida Cattle Raising* (Kissimmee, Fla., 1976).

Florida in the pre-Civil War era offered a variety of economic endeavors. Michael G. Schene has examined a large sugar plantation worked by slaves in "Sugar along the Manatee: Major Robert Gamble, Jr. and the Development of Gamble Plantation," *Tequesta* 41 (1981), and "Robert and John Grattan Gamble: Middle Florida Entrepreneurs," *FHQ*, 54 (July 1975). Lucius Ellsworth studied the brick industry in "Raiford and Abercrombie: Pensacola's Premier Antebellum Manufacturer," *FHQ*, 52 (January 1974). In "Lumber and Trade in Pensacola and West Florida: 1800–1860," *FHQ*, 51 (June 1973), John A. Eisterhold surveyed the leading lumberers in a major lumber exporting center. Pensacola was also the focus for Charles R. McNeil, "The Red Snapper Industry in Pensacola, 1845–1865: An Historical Perspective" (M.A. thesis, University of West Florida, 1977). Twenty-five miles from Pensacola were two interesting industrial complexes described in Brian Rucker, "Arcadia and Bagdad: Industrial Parks of Antebellum Florida," *FHQ*, 67 (October 1988). Junius E. Dovell, *History of Banking in Florida, 1828–1854* (Orlando, 1955), examined a troubled industry in that era.

Politics provided a lively forum for debate in the young state. James B. Mool offered an early overview of the state and the national scene in "Florida in Federal Politics: Statehood to Secession," (M.A. thesis, Duke University, 1940). Thomas S. Graham followed its politics through two of the capital's newspapers in "Florida Politics and the Tallahassee Press, 1845–1861," *FHQ*, 46 (January 1968). Herbert J. Doherty, Jr., has produced several studies of the politics of the era. In "Union Nationalism in Florida," *FHQ*, 29 (October 1950), Doherty examined the unyielding beliefs in the preservation of the Union on the part of the state's Whig leaders. Doherty studied a former territorial governor and his steadfast devotion to the Union in *Richard Keith Call: Southern Unionist* (Gainesville, 1961). Doherty's *The Whigs of Florida, 1845–1854* (Gainesville, 1955), further illuminates the nationalist sentiment in the state.

The Compromise of 1850 split the Whig Party into northern and southern factions. Four years later, the party ceased to exist. John Meador, "Florida and the Compromise of 1850," *FHQ*, 39 (July 1960), is a detailed account of the agreement and its deleterious effects on the Whigs.

David Yulee (nee Levy) was one of Florida's first two United States senators and the first Jew to serve in that body. An important figure in the periods of territorial and early statehood, Yulee's career was examined in two important works: Arthur W. Thompson, "David Yulee: A Study of Nineteenth-Century Thought and Enterprise" (Ph.D. diss., Columbia University, 1954), and Joseph Adler, "The Public Career of Senator David Levy Yulee" (Ph.D. diss., Case Western Reserve University, 1973).

## THE CIVIL WAR ERA

Florida was the third state to secede from the Union, formalizing this momentous decision amid widespread rejoicing on January 11, 1861. General studies of the event include Donald R. Hadd, "The Secession Movement in Florida, 1850–1861" (M.A. thesis, Florida State University, 1972). Ralph A. Wooster, "The Florida Secession Convention," *FHQ*, 36 (April 1958), investigated the background of convention delegates and explained the two major factions among them. John F. Reiger, "Secession of Florida from the Union—A Minority Decision?" *FHQ*, 46 (April 1968), focused on the spirited role of Unionists who attempted to stem the tide of rebellion. In "The Irony of Secession," *FHQ*, 41 (July 1962), Donald Hadd argued that secession resulted from the belief by convention delegates that the "sanctity of property was worth every sacrifice that such a radical measure . . . might entail."

While most of the fighting in the Civil War occurred outside of Florida, the state witnessed numerous raids and hosted one significant military encounter. Several forts in Florida became objects of hostile fighting between the rival forces, and the Union blockade wrapped itself around Florida's lengthy coastline. Florida also played a critical role as a supplier of troops, food, and other goods and materials to the Confederacy. Fifteen thousand Floridians fought in the Civil War, while untold numbers of farmers provided corn, peas, potatoes, and citrus; the state also contributed sugar, syrup, fish, and salt to the southern war effort. Its production of beef cattle and hogs was an important source of supply; by 1864, Florida was virtually the only supplier of beef for Confederate armies in the East.

In addition to the multivolume official records of the war published by the federal government, general studies of the conflict include John E. Johns,

*Florida during the Civil War* (Gainesville, 1963), a comprehensive treatment of the subject. Rodney Dillon, Jr., examines "The Civil War in South Florida" (M.A. thesis, University of Florida, 1980). A valuable bibliographic guide is Edward Smith, "Researching the Civil War in Florida: An Introduction to the Southern Historical Collection," *El Escribano* 23 (1986).

Ernest F. Dibble, "War Averters: Seward, Mallory, and Fort Pickens," *FHQ*, 49 (January 1971), reviews the attempt of these two high-ranking officials on opposite sides to avoid war. George C. Bettle, "Florida Prepares For War, 1860–1861," *FHQ*, 51 (October 1972), detailed the myriad obstacles that accompanied the state's preparation for war. When war came, the Confederacy failed to provide adequate defenses for Florida, argued John F. Reiger in "Florida after Secession: Abandonment by the Confederacy and Its Consequences," *FHQ*, 50 (October 1971).

On the Union naval blockade, see Church E. Barnard, "The Federal Blockade of Florida during the Civil War" (M.A. thesis, University of Miami, 1966), and Stanley L. Itkin, "Operations of the East Coast Blockade Squadron in the Blockade of Florida, 1862–1865" (M.A. thesis, Florida State University, 1962). Alice Strickland and Thelma Peters have studied efforts to circumvent the blockade, which yielded mixed results, in, respectively, "Blockade Runners," *FHQ*, 36 (October 1957), and "Blockade Running in the Bahamas during the Civil War," *Tequesta* 51 (1945). See also Joseph D. Cushman, Jr., "Blockade and Fall of Apalachicola, 1861–1862," *FHQ*, 41 (July 1962).

The most important military engagement in Florida took place at Olustee near Lake City in February 1864, when Confederate forces halted a Federal attempt to reach and destroy a crucial supply line between Florida and Georgia in a fierce battle. David J. Coles, "A Fight, a Licking, and a Fortune: The 1864 Florida Campaign and the Battle of Olustee" (M.A. thesis, University of Florida, 1985), examined the Union invasion, the role of black soldiers in the battle, and its political results. Allen W. Jones, "Military Events in Florida during the Civil War, 1861–1865," *FHQ*, 39 (July 1960), briefly surveys the fighting in the state. William Nulty, "The 1864 Florida Expedition: Blundering into Modern Warfare" (Ph.D. diss., University of Florida, 1986), provides important information on the Union military presence in northeast Florida. See also Mark F. Boyd, "The Federal Campaign of 1864 in East Florida," *FHQ*, 29 (July 1950).

For accounts of other military action see Katherine J. Willis and William W. Rogers, "Encounter at the Ancilla, 1962," *FHQ*, 61 (October 1982); Rodney E. Dillon, Jr., " 'The Little Affair': The Southwest Florida Campaign, 1863–64," *FHQ*, 62 (January 1984); Rodney Dillion, Jr., "The Battle of Fort Myers," *Tampa Bay History* 5 (Fall/Winter 1983); and Edwin C. Bearss, "Federal Expedition against Saint Marks Ends at Natural Bridge," *FHQ*, 45 (April 1967).

Economic aspects of the war are the focus of Robert L. Clarke, "Northern Plans for the Economic Invasion of Florida, 1862–1865," *FHQ*, 28 (April 1950); C. A. Haulman, "Changes in the Economic Power Structure in Duval County, Florida, during the Civil War and Reconstruction," *FHQ*, 52 (October

1973); Robert Taylor, "Cattle and the Confederacy" (M.A. thesis, University of South Florida, 1985) and "Cow Cavalry: Mannerlyn's Battalion in Florida, 1864–1865," *FHQ* 55 (October 1986), and "Rebel Beef: Florida Cattle and the Confederate Army, 1862–1864," *FHQ*, 57 (July 1988); and Ellen H. Patterson, "The Stephens Family in East Florida: A Profile of Plantation Life along the St. Johns River, 1859–1864," (M.A. thesis, University of Florida, 1979).

Numerous studies focus on the importance of the Civil War on Florida urban centers. Federal troops occupied Jacksonville on four occasions, destroying large portions of the city. Richard Martin and Daniel Schafer have provided a highly readable account of that city's struggle in *Jacksonville's Ordeal by Fire: A Civil War History* (Jacksonville, 1984). See also Samuel Proctor, "Jacksonville During the Civil War," *FHQ*, 41 (April 1963). St. Augustine is the subject of several articles in *El Escribano* 23 (1986). The collection includes an overview by Thomas Graham, " 'The Home Front': Civil War Time in St. Augustine." See also Edwin L. Bearss, "Civil War Operations in and around Pensacola, Part I," *FHQ*, 36 (October 1957), "Part II," "Part III," *FHQ*, 39 (January, April 1961); Virginia Parks, Alan Rick, and Norman Simons, "Pensacola in the Civil War," *Pensacola Historical Society Quarterly* (Spring 1978); and Clifton Paisley, "Tallahassee through the Storebooks: War Clouds and War, 1860–1863," *FHQ*, 51 (July 1972).

The publication of collections of correspondence has enriched the literature on the Civil War in Florida. Ellen Hodges and Stephen Kerber, "Children of Honor: Letters of Winston and Octavia Stephens, 1861–1862," *FHQ*, 56 (July 1977), provides a rare view of civilian and military conditions in Florida in the early months of the Civil War. Thomas Graham, ed., "Letters From a Journey through the Federal Blockade, 1861–1862," *FHQ*, 55 (April 1977), describes the events at Cedar Key, site of the first major raid on Florida's shores by the Union navy. See also Hodges and Kerber, "'Rogues and Black Hearted Scamps,' Civil War Letters of Winston and Octavia Stephens, 1862–1863," *FHQ*, 57 (July 1978); Bertram H. Groene, ed., "Civil War Letters of Colonel David Long," *FHQ*, 54 (January 1976); Margaret Anderson Uhler, ed., "Civil War Letters of Major General James Patton Anderson," *FHQ*, 56 (October 1977); and Clifton Paisley, ed., "How to Escape the Yankees: Major Scott's Letter to His Wife at Tallahassee, March 1864," *FHQ*, 50 (July 1971).

For studies of military leaders in wartime Florida, see Larry Rayburn, " 'When the Fight Is Thickest': General James Patton Anderson of Florida," *FHQ*, 60 (January 1982), and Marion B. Lucas, "Civil War Career of Colonel George Washington Scott," *FHQ*, 58 (October 1979).

On other elements of the war, see John F. Reiger, "Antiwar and Pro-Union Sentiment in Confederate Florida" (M.A. thesis, University of Florida, 1966), and "Deprivation, Disaffection, and Desertion in Confederate Florida," *FHQ*, 48 (January 1970); Ovid L. Futch, "Salmon P. Chase and Radical Politics in Florida, 1862–1863" (M.A. thesis, University of Florida, 1952). James C. Clark, *Last Train South: The Flight of the Confederate Government from*

*Richmond* (Jefferson, N.C., 1984) recalled Florida's role as a way station and temporary haven for high-ranking Confederate fugitives.


## RECONSTRUCTION

Since Florida's losses in real and personal property reached $42 million in the Civil War, "Reconstruction" meant not only the political reconstitution of the state but also the rebuilding of its shattered economic base and its natural and man-made assets. Florida met this daunting challenge with energy and persistence, realizing success over a period of years.

After complying with the Radical Republican or Congressional plan for reconstruction, Florida returned to the United States in 1868. However, the Republican Party, anathema to Floridians and Southerners, remained in power, with the help of a large black vote, until 1877, when Democrats returned to rule, marking the end of Reconstruction. Joe Richardson and Maxine Jones have covered the story of Florida's freedmen, an essential component of the bibliography of this rancorous era, in their essay on black Floridians.

For decades, the standard work on the era was William Watson Davis, *The Civil War and Reconstruction in Florida* (New York, 1913, facsimile edition, Gainesville, 1954). Davis shared the view of his mentor, William Dunning, an early twentieth-century historian, who characterized blacks as lazy and inferior, Republicans as evil, and the entire episode shameful. Jerrell Shofner, *Nor Is It Over Yet: Florida in the Era of Reconstruction, 1863–1877* (Gainesville, 1974), rejected the Dunning school and has since replaced Davis's work as the standard study on Reconstruction in Florida. Shofner's revisionist work argued that Florida was beginning to revive economically during Reconstruction. See also Philip D. Ackerman, Jr., "Florida Reconstruction from Walker through Reed, 1865–1873" (M.A. thesis, University of Florida, 1948).

The stormy politics of the era, with its carpetbaggers, scalawags, and newly enfranchised freedmen, has drawn close attention from historians. See Jerrell H. Shofner, "Political Reconstruction in Florida," *FHQ*, 45 (October 1966), for an overview, as well as his "A New Jersey Carpetbagger in Reconstruction Florida," *FHQ*, 52 (January 1974), which depicts the career of Captain George B. Carse, a Republican politician who provided inestimable assistance to blacks while associated with the Freedman's Bureau. Mildred L. Fryman, "Career of A 'Carpetbagger': Malachi Martin in Florida," *FHQ*, 51 (January 1978) examines a controversial state official. Chapter 2 of Thelma Peters, *Biscayne Country, 1870–1926* (Miami, 1981), and Lewis H. Cresse, Jr., "A Study of William Henry Gleason: Carpetbagger, Politician, Land Developer" (Ph.D. diss., University of South Carolina, ca. 1977), examine the rambunctious political boss of Dade County, who also served as lieutenant governor of Florida. Merlin Cox, "Military Reconstruction in Florida," *FHQ*, 46 (January 1968), recounted the period of military rule (1867–1868) following adoption of the Radical Republican plan of

Reconstruction. Cox's revisionist interpretation argued that military power was exercised with reason and restraint.

On Florida's Constitution of 1868, the document that heralded Florida's return to the United States, see "Constitution of Florida," U.S. House of Representatives, 40th Cong., 2nd Sess., miscellaneous document no. 109, which contains, in addition to a copy of the Constitution, an essay on the history of the convention that crafted it. Jerrell H. Shofner, "The Constitution of 1868," *FHQ*, 41 (April 1963), argued that the Constitution was not a radical document imposed on a helpless white population by carpetbaggers and their allies, but the result of compromises between men of widely divergent views, with the Moderates winning out. See also Richard L. Hume, "Membership of the Florida Constitutional Convention of 1868: A Case Study of Republican Factionalism and the Reconstruction South," *FHQ*, 51 (July 1972).

Ralph L. Peek, "Aftermath of Military Reconstruction, 1868–1869," *FHQ*, 43 (October 1964), examines the period following the withdrawal of federal troops from Florida, one marked by an increase in violence. In "Election of 1870 and the End of Reconstruction in Florida," *FHQ*, 45 (April 1967), Peek argued that the election of a Democrat to the office of lieutenant governor in 1870 marked the end of Reconstruction in Florida. Peek's "Curbing Voter Intimidation in Florida, 1871," *FHQ*, 53 (April 1965), suggested that the Enforcement Acts of 1870 and 1871, ostensibly designed to protect black voting rights, were also used as a device to maintain the slim Republican majority in Reconstruction Florida. Derrell Roberts, "Social Legislation in Reconstruction Florida," *FHQ*, 53 (April 1965), suggested that the state did not solve its social problems or meet the needs of the time, but it did lay the foundation for stronger public welfare programs in the following century.

Clearly the most important political event of the later years of the era was the disputed presidential election of 1876, which ultimately brought Reconstruction to an end. As one of three states with disputed votes, Florida played a pivotal role in the drama. Several studies have focused on the election. Jerrell H. Shofner has contributed three incisive articles on the contest. In "Fraud And Intimidation in the Florida Election of 1876," *FHQ*, 42 (April 1964), Shofner argued that fraudulent activities in the state during the election were "most notable for their mildness." See also his "Florida Courts and the Disputed Election of 1876," *FHQ*, 48 (July 1969), and "Florida in the Balance: The Electoral Count of 1876," *FHQ*, 47 (October 1968). Karen Guenther and Derrell Roberts focused on the "Potter Commission Investigation of the Disputed Election of 1876," *FHQ*, 61 (January 1983), which, they maintained, failed to reach a clear verdict over which of the political parties was most guilty of misconduct in Florida. See also Lee S. Theisen, " 'Fair Count' in Florida: General Lew Wallace and the Contested Presidential Election of 1876," *Hayes Historical Journal* 3 (Spring 1978).

While Florida remained a hotbed of political chicanery and machinations in the era, its economy began to recover from wartime destruction and move in new directions. Tourism, a future growth industry, was examined in Paul S. George, "Passage to the New Eden: Tourism in Miami, from Flagler through Everest G. Sewell," *FHQ*, 59 (April 1981), and Elliott Mackle, "The Eden of the South: Florida's Image in American Travel Literature and Painting, 1865–1900," (Ph.D. Diss., Emory University, 1977).

Clifton Paisley has contributed several important studies on economic themes in that era. See *From Cotton to Quail: An Agricultural Chronicle of Leon County, Florida, 1860–1967* (Gainesville, 1968), and "Madison County's Sea Island Cotton Industry, 1870–1916," *FHQ*, 54 (January 1976), which detailed the development of Florida's most productive postwar cotton crop. See also Jerrell H. Shofner, "A Merchant-Planter in the Reconstruction South," *Agriculture History* (April 1972).

Reconstruction era cities are profiled in Elizabeth Vickers and Virginia Parks, "The Golden Dream: Life in Pensacola in the 1870s," *Pensacola Historical Society Quarterly* (Spring 1974); Arva M. Parks, "Miami in 1876," *Tequesta* 35 (1975); Clifton Paisley, "Tallahassee through the Storebooks: Era of Radical Reconstruction, 1867–1877," *FHQ*, 53 (July 1974); Gerald E. Poyo, "Cuban Revolutionaries and Monroe County Reconstruction Politics, 1868–1876," *FHQ*, 60 (April 1977); and Gustavo J. Godoy, "Jose Aljandro: A Cuban Patriot in Jacksonville Politics," *FHQ*, 54 (October 1975).

For the observations of visitors in Reconstruction-era Florida, see Patricia P. Clark, "Florida, 'Our Own Italy': James F. B. Marshall's Post-Civil War Letters to Edward Everett Hale," *FHQ*, 59 (July 1980); "A New England Emigrant Aid Company Agent in Postwar Florida: Selected Letters of James F. B. Marshall, 1867," *FHQ*, 55 (April 1977); and Joe M. Richardson, ed., "A Northerner Reports on Florida: 1866," *FHQ*, 40 (April 1962).

A critical and even remarkable era in Florida's history, the middle decades of the 1800s gave rise to issues and events that influenced the state's direction and development for many decades. The era continues to invite close historical scrutiny, adding further illumination to its multifaceted nature and character.

# 9

---

# FLORIDA IN THE GILDED AGE AND PROGRESSIVE ERA, 1877–1917

---

JAMES B. CROOKS

WITH JUST 187,748 residents in 1870, Florida was the least populated of the southeastern states. Ninety-two percent of Florida's population was rural. In an era of rapid national growth, Florida clearly was an underdeveloped part of the country.

No single source describes conditions throughout the state at the beginning of the Gilded Age, but many articles and books report pieces. Exploration of the wilderness parts of Florida attracted considerable attention during the Gilded Age. The New Orleans *Times-Democrat* sponsored two treks into the Everglades in the 1880s, reported in Morgan Dewey Peoples and Edwin Adams Davis, eds., "Across South-Central Florida in 1882: The Account of the First New Orleans *Times-Democrat* Exploring Expedition," *Tequesta* 10 and 11 (1950 and 1951), and Mary K. Worthington, ed., "North and South Through the Glades in 1883: The Account of the Second Expedition into the Florida Everglades by the New Orleans *Times-Democrat*," *Tequesta* 23 and 24 (1963 and 1964). Walt P. Marchman edited "The Ingraham Everglades Exploring Expedition, 1892," *Tequesta* 7 (1948), which is supplemented by Alonzo Church's memoir, "A Dash through the Everglades," *Tequesta* 9 (1949).

Charles William Pierce, *Pioneer Life in Southeast Florida* (Coral Gables, 1970) is a memoir of the period. Thelma Peters's two volumes, *Lemon City: Pioneering on Biscayne Bay, 1850–1925* (Miami, 1976), and *Biscayne Country, 1870–1926* (Miami, 1981), are part memoir and part history. William T. Cash describes Brevard, Dade, and Monroe Counties before development in "The Lower East Coast, 1870–1890," *Tequesta* 8 (1948), while Mary Douthit Conrad, "Homesteading in Florida during the 1890s," *Tequesta* 17 (1957), is another memoir of early Dade County. Floyd and Marion Rinehart, *Victorian Florida: America's Last Frontier* (Atlanta, 1986), is a pictorial history of the era.

Traditional law and order was not characteristic of much of frontier Florida. William Warren Rogers, Jr., portrays one part in the 1880s in "Rube Burrows, 'King of the Outlaws' and His Florida Adventures," *Florida Historical Quarterly* (*FHQ*) 59 (October 1980). Janet Snyder Matthews, " 'He Has Carried His Life in His Hands': The Sarasota Assassination Society of 1884," *FHQ*, 58 (July 1979), describes another aspect of frontier vigilantism. Robert P. Ingalls, "General Joseph B. Wall and Lynch Law in Tampa," *FHQ*, 63 (July 1984), examines the popular support for vigilante justice in 1882 for whites and blacks.

Yet more than wilderness and frontier, rural conditions characterized Florida in Gilded Age America. Barbara F. Agresti describes the preurban, preindustrial climate of DeFuniak Springs and Walton County from the 1885 census in "Town and Country in a Florida Rural County in the Late Nineteenth Century: Some Population and Household Comparisons," *Rural Sociology* 42 (Winter 1977). Judy R. Nichols, "The Middle Florida Agricultural Fair, 1879–1885," *Apalachee* 7 (1970), portrays the recreational and educational nature of the Leon County fair. Though Clifton L. Paisley's description of a country store in "Van Brunt's Store, Iamonia, Florida, 1902–1911," *FHQ*, 48 (April 1970), is a generation later, it doubtless had its counterparts in the Gilded Age.

Yet if the predominant condition of Florida at the beginning of the Gilded Age was wilderness, frontier, or rural, the dynamic of the era became development, a force that characterized much of the next one hundred years. An overview of the thrust to develop Florida may be seen in the standard history text, Charlton W. Tebeau, *A History of Florida* (Coral Gables, 1980 edition), especially chapter 17. Earlier texts, as well as the many descriptions of contemporary travelers promoting the state, are listed in Michael H. Harris, ed., *Florida History: A Bibliography* (Metuchen, N.J., 1972).

To date no historians have approached the developmental theme comprehensively. Monographs and articles, however, do examine parts of it. Wallace Martin Nelson, "The Economic Development of Florida, 1870–1930" (Ph.D. diss., University of Florida, 1962), provides a statistical analysis of growth decade by decade. More promising are studies of various developers. Edward N. Akin, *Flagler, Rockefeller Partner and Florida Baron* (Kent, Ohio, 1988), describes the vast industrial and business network that Florida's preeminent entrepreneur developed on the state's eastern seaboard. Another recent biography, David Leon Chandler, *Henry Flagler: The Astonishing Life and Times of the Visionary*

*Robber Baron Who Founded Florida* (New York, 1986), is disappointing and often inaccurate. An older biography, Sidney Walter Martin, *Florida's Flagler* (Athens, Ga., 1949), though dated, is useful. Martin's "Flagler's Associates in East Florida Development," *FHQ*, 26 (January 1948); Akin, "The Sly Foxes: Henry Flagler, George Miles and Florida's Public Domain," *FHQ*, 58 (July 1979); and Nathan D. Shappee, "Flagler's Undertakings in Miami in 1897," *Tequesta* 19 (1959), examine still other aspects.

For the other great entrepreneur of the Gilded Age, Henry Plant, no modern biography exists. G. Hutchinson Smyth, *The Life of Henry Bradley Plant* (New York, 1898), is useful but clearly dated. Dudley S. Johnson, "Henry Bradley Plant and Florida," *FHQ*, 45 (October 1966), describes the development of his railroad links to Tampa in the 1880s. James W. Covington, "The Tampa Bay Hotel," *Tequesta* 26 (1966), looks at Plant's construction of his major resort hotel there. S. Walter Martin, "Henry Bradley Plant," *Georgians in Profile* (Athens, Ga. 1959), is a brief biographical sketch. Edward C. Williamson touches on a third important railroad entrepreneur in "William D. Chipley, West Florida's Mr. Railroad," *FHQ*, 25 (April 1947).

Joseph A. Fry, *Henry S. Sanford: Diplomacy and Business in Nineteenth-Century America* (Reno, 1982), describes another speculator's efforts in land, town, and citrus development. Richard J. Amundson, "The Florida Land and Colonization Company," *FHQ*, 44 (January 1966), covers similar turf as does Amundson's dissertation at Florida State University in 1963.

For other speculators, exploiters, entrepreneurs, and developers, see T. Frederick Davis, "The Disston Land Purchase," *FHQ*, 17 (January 1939), an attempt at land development beginning in 1881–82; Helen R. Sharp, "Samuel A. Swann and the Development of Florida, 1855–1900," *FHQ*, 20 (October 1941); Lewis H. Cresse, Jr., "A Study of William Henry Gleason: Carpetbagger, Politician, Land Developer" (Ph.D. Diss., University of South Carolina, 1975); and J. E. Dovell, "Thomas Elmer Will, Twentieth-Century Pioneer," *Tequesta* 8 (1949). More comprehensive in examining development in a specific area is Alfred Jackson Hanna and Kathryn Abbey Hanna, *Lake Okeechobee: Wellspring of the Everglades,* (Indianapolis, 1948), which provides insight into the Disston land purchase and later development in south central Florida.

Key to development in Gilded Age Florida were the railroads. Many writings examine aspects of railroading. Unfortunately, most are of marginal value. George W. Pettengill, Jr., *The Story of Florida Railroads, 1834–1903* (Boston, 1952), is a superficial study. Dudley S. Johnson, "The Railroads of Florida, 1865–1900" (Ph.D. diss., Florida State University, 1965), identifies the five great systems established by 1900. Ralph G. Hill and James H. Pledges compile a list, *The Railroads of Florida* (Tallahassee, 1939). Howard D. Dozier, *A History of the Atlantic Coast Line Railroad* (Boston, 1920), is of limited use as is William Harry Jourbet, "A History of the Seaboard Air Line Railway Company" (Ph.D. diss., University of Florida, 1935). J. E. Dovell, "The Railroads and the Public Lands of Florida, 1879–1905," *FHQ*, 34 (January 1956), shows the state largess to railroad developers. Of less significance are David L. Willing, "Florida's Overseas Railroad," *FHQ*, 35 (April 1957); O. Burton Adams, "Construction of Florida's Overseas Railway," *Apalachee* 7 (1970); Herbert J. Doherty, "Jacksonville as a Nineteenth-Century Railroad Center," *FHQ*, 58 (April 1980); Paul Fenlon, "The Struggle for the Control of the Florida Central Railroad, 1867–1882," *FHQ*, 34 (January 1956); Dudley S. Johnson, "The Florida Railroad after the Civil War," *FHQ*, 47 (January 1969); Nathan D. Shappee, "The Celestial Railroad to Juno," *FHQ*, 40 (April 1962); and Vernon E. Peeples, "Charlotte Harbor Division of the Florida Southern Railroad," *FHQ*, 56 (January 1980).

Railroads linked cities, and urban development became increasingly important to Florida history. Raymond A. Mohl has written the bibliographical chapter on this experience.

In addition to railroads and cities, Floridians saw late nineteenth-century growth include industrial, commercial and agricultural development. Arch Frederic Blakey describes *The Florida Phosphate Industry: A History of the Development and Use of a Vital Mineral* (Cambridge, Mass., 1973). William Nathaniel Thurston, "A Study of Maritime Activity in Florida in the Nineteenth Century" (Ph.D. diss., Florida State University, 1972), covers Gilded Age expansion of lumber and phosphate shipping. Richard W. Massey, Jr., "A History of the Lumber Industry in Alabama and West Florida, 1880–1914" (Ph.D. diss., Vanderbilt University, 1960), looks at pine timber as a new industry of the era. Other developments are reported in Joe A. Akerman, *Florida Cowmen: A History of Florida Cattle Raising* (Kissimmee, Fla., 1976); Jerry Woods Weeks, "Florida Gold: The Emergence of the Florida Citrus Industry, 1865–1895" (Ph.D. diss., University of North Carolina at Chapel Hill, 1977); Clifton Paisley, "Madison County's Sea Island Cotton Industry, 1870–1916," *FHQ*, 57 (January 1976); Caroline Johnson Commenos, "Florida's Sponge Industry: A Cultural and Economic History" (Ph.D. diss., University of Florida, 1982); Pat Dodson, "Hamilton Disston's St. Cloud Sugar Plantation, 1887–1901," *FHQ*, 49 (April 1971); Harold W. Dorn, "Mango Growing Around Early Miami," *Tequesta* 16 (1956); Edward F. Keuchel, "A Purely Business Motive: German-American Lumber Company, 1901–1918," *FHQ*, 52 (April 1974); Drew Harrington, "Burton-Swartz Cypress Company of Florida," *FHQ*, 63 (April 1985); and Alfred P. Tischendorf, "Florida and the British Investor, 1880–1914," *FHQ*, 33 (October 1954). Michael L. Sanders, "The Great Freeze of 1894–95 in Pinellas County," *Tampa Bay History* 2 (Spring–Summer 1980), describes the impact upon the citrus industry. James Hopkins, *Fifty Years of Citrus: The Florida Citrus Exchange, 1909–1954* (Gainesville, 1960), is promotional, but so was much of the writing about Florida in the era, as John M. Spivack observes in "Paradise Awaits: A Sampling and Brief Analysis of Late Nineteenth-Century Promotional Pamphlets in Florida," *Southern Studies* 21 (Winter 1982). Maurice M. Vance, "Northerners in Late Nineteenth-Century Florida: Carpetbaggers or Settlers?" *FHQ*, 38 (January 1959), concludes from census data that the

Yankee migration was predominantly business and professional, contributing to the state's growth.

While development became a major theme in Florida history in the Gilded Age and Progressive Era, politics also attracted historical attention. Again Tebeau's *History*, chapters 18, 19, and 21 offer an overview. So does C. Vann Woodward, *Origins of the New South, 1877–1913* (Baton Rouge, 1951), in the context of regional history. Edward C. Williamson, *Florida Politics in the Gilded Age, 1855–1893* (Gainesville, 1976), examines sixteen years of political history. His "Independentism: A Challenge to the Florida Democracy of 1884," *FHQ*, 27 (October 1948), looks at a third party effort. His "The Constitutional Convention of 1885," *FHQ*, 41 (October 1962), follows an attempt by Democrats to ensure hegemony. The resulting document is analyzed by Manning Dauer and William C. Havard, "The Florida Constitution of 1885—A Critique," *University of Florida Law Review*, 7 (Spring 1955). The impact of the constitution for Florida politics is seen in J. Morgan Kousser, *The Shaping of Southern Politics: Suffrage Restriction and the Establishment of the One-Party South, 1880–1910* (New Haven, Ct., 1974). One result was the weakness of the Farmers Alliance and Populist Party in the state, as chronicled by James Owen Knauss, "The Farmers Alliance in Florida," *South Atlantic Quarterly* 25 (July 1926); Samuel Proctor, "The National Farmers Alliance Convention in 1890 and its 'Ocala Demands'," *FHQ*, 28 (January 1950); and Kathryn T. Abbey, "Florida versus the Principles of Populism, 1896–1911," *Journal of Southern History* 4 (November 1938). The Republicans did not fare much better in this era, as Pete Klingman observes in *Neither Dies Nor Surrenders: A History of the Republican Party in Florida, 1867–1970* (Gainesville, 1984). Instead Democrats ruled the state, as seen in William T. Cash, *History of the Democratic Party in Florida* (Tallahassee, 1936).

The Gilded Age governors have received little study. Ruby Leach Carson looks at "William Dunnington Bloxham: The Years to the Governorship, *FHQ*, 27 (January 1949) Kenneth Ray Johnson wrote, "The Administration of William Dunnington Bloxham," (M.A., thesis, Florida State University, 1959). George B. Church, Jr., examines *The Life of Henry Laurens Mitchell, Florida's Sixteenth Governor* (New York, 1978).

Additional articles focus on specific incidents of the era: Peter Klingman, "Inside the Ring: Bisbee-Lee Correspondence, February-April, 1880," *FHQ*, 57 (October 1978), regarding Republican policies during that election year; Judy Nicholas Etemadi, " 'A Love-Mad Man': Senator Charles W. Jones of Florida," *FHQ*, 56 (October 1977), describing the mental aberrations of a two-term United States senator during the 1880s; Albert Hubbard Roberts, "Wilkinson Call, Soldier and Senator," *FHQ*, 12 (April 1934), reviewing Call's senatorial career; and "The Senatorial Deadlock of 1897," *Apalachee* 3 (1948), on the U.S. senatorial race ending Call's career.

The ineffectual first efforts to regulate the rapidly expanding, land-grabbing railroads are described by Durward Long in a two-part article, "Florida's First

Railroad Commission, 1887–1891," *FHQ*, 42 (October 1963 and January 1964). Arnold Marc Pavlovsky, " 'We Busted Because We Failed': Florida's Politics, 1880–1908" (Ph.D. diss., Princeton University, 1973), describes the character of Florida politics responding to state needs.

In contrast to the Gilded Age, Progressive Era Florida has received greater scholarly attention. Besides Woodward, already noted, Dewey W. Grantham, *Southern Progressivism: The Reconciliation of Progress and Tradition* (Knoxville, 1983), notes Florida's limited contribution to the progressive scene. More significant is the analysis by David R. Colburn and Richard K. Scher, *Florida's Gubernatorial Politics in the Twentieth Century* (Gainesville, 1980). Important biographies include Samuel Proctor, *Napoleon Bonaparte Broward, Florida's Fighting Democrat* (Gainesville, 1950); Wayne Flynt, *Duncan Upshaw Fletcher, Dixie's Reluctant Progressive* (Tallahassee, 1971); Stephen Kerber, "Park Trammell of Florida: A Political Biography" (Ph.D. Diss., University of Florida, 1979), a portion of which is published in "Park Trammell and the Florida Democratic Senatorial Primary of 1916," *FHQ* 58 (January 1980); and Wayne Flynt, *Cracker Messiah: Governor Sidney J. Catts of Florida* (Baton Rouge, 1977). Catts has attracted considerable historical attention, as seen in Dorothy Lord, "Sidney J. Catts and the Gubernatorial Election of 1916," *Apalachee* 6 (1967); Wayne Flynt, "Sidney J. Catts: The Road to Power," *FHQ*, 49 (October 1970); and Warren A. Jennings, "Sidney J. Catts and the Democratic Presidential Primary of 1920," *FHQ*, 39 (January 1961). The reason, of course, was Catts's demagoguery and anti-Catholicism, which also have been studied in Robert B. Rackleff, "Anti-Catholicism and the Florida Legislature, 1911–1919," *FHQ*, 50 (April 1972); David P. Page, "Bishop Michael J. Curley and Anti-Catholic Nativism in Florida," *FHQ*, 45 (October 1966); and Wayne Flynt, ed., "William V. Knott and the Gubernatorial Campaign of 1916," *FHQ*, 51 (April 1973).

Other Progressive Era political studies include George F. Pearce, "'Laying the Sins of the L & N at Mr. Blount's Feet': William Alexander Blount's U.S. Senatorial Campaign, 1910–1911," *FHQ*, 63 (July 1984); Emily Howard Atkins, "The 1913 Campaign for Child Labor Reform in Florida," *FHQ*, 35 (January, 1957); A. Elizabeth Taylor, "The Woman Suffrage Movement in Florida," *FHQ*, 35 (July 1957); Kenneth R. Johnson, "The Woman Suffrage Movement in Florida" (Ph.D. Diss., Florida State University, 1966), part of which was published as "Florida Women Get the Vote," *FHQ*, 48 (January 1970); and James B. Crooks, "Jacksonville in the Progressive Era: Political Responses to Urban Growth," *FHQ*, 65 (July 1986); and Ric A. Kabat, " 'Everybody Votes for Gilchrist': The Florida Gubernatorial Campaign of 1908," *FHQ* 67 (October 1988). Elliott Mackle, "Cyrus Teed and the Lee County Election of 1906," *FHQ*, 57 (July 1978), looks at a religious prophet and utopian politics.

Shifting from political history, Florida experienced the Spanish-American War probably more intensely than any other state. William J. Schellings, "The Role of Florida in the Spanish-American War, 1898" (Ph.D. diss., University of Florida,

1958), led to a series of articles including "Florida and the Cuban Revolution, 1895–1898," *FHQ*, 39 (October 1960); "The Advent of the Spanish-American War in Florida, 1898," *FHQ*, 39 (April 1961); "Florida Volunteers in the War with Spain, 1898," *FHQ*, 40 (July 1961); "Key West and the Spanish-American War," *Tequesta* 20 (1960); and "Soldiers in Miami," *Tequesta* 17 (1957). Other articles include Samuel Proctor, "Filibustering aboard the Three Friends," *Mid-America* 38 (1958); Richard V. Rickenbach, "Filibustering with the Dauntless," *FHQ*, 28 (April 1950); Donna Thomas, "'Camp Hell': Miami during the Spanish-American War," *FHQ*, 57 (October 1978); Clayton D. Roth, Jr., "150 Years of Defense Activity in Key West," *Tequesta* 30 (1970); Gerald E. Poyo, "Tampa Cigarmakers and the Struggle for Cuban Independence," *Tampa Bay History* 7 (Fall-Winter, 1985); William Joe Webb, "The Spanish-American War and United States Army Shipping," *American Neptune* 40 (August 1980); Ruby Leach Carson, "Florida, Promoter of Cuban Liberty," *FHQ*, 19 (January 1941); Gustavo J. Goday, "Jose Alejandro Huau: A Cuban Patriot in Jacksonville Politics," *FHQ*, 53 (October 1975); and Julian M. Pleasants, "Frederic Remington in Florida," *FHQ*, 56 (July 1977). Poyo's article was an outgrowth of "Cuban Emigré Communities in the United States and the Independence of Their Homeland" (Ph.D. diss., University of Florida, 1983), in which chapter 6 treats Florida.

The coming of war accentuated the Cuban emigré experience in Florida and drew attention to ethnic groups settling in the state during these years. The major work is George E. Pozzetta and Gary Mormino, *The Immigrant World of Ybor City: Italians and Their Latin Neighbors, 1885–1985* (Urbana and Chicago, 1987). Pozzetta and Mormino also collaborated on "The Cradle of Mutual Aid: Immigrant Cooperative Societies in Ybor City," *Tampa Bay History* 7 (Fall–Winter 1985), while Pozzetta also wrote "Foreign Colonies in South Florida, 1865–1910," *Tequesta* 34 (1974); "Foreigners in Florida: A Study in Immigration Promotion, 1865–1910," *FHQ*, 53 (October 1974); and "Immigrants and Radicals in Tampa, Florida," *FHQ*, 57 (January 1979). Mormino wrote, "'We Worked Hard and Took Care of Our Own': Oral History and the Italians in Tampa," *Labor History*, 23 (Summer 1982). Other authors on the Latin ethnic experience include Durward Long, "An Immigrant Cooperative Medicine Program in the South, 1887–1963," *Journal of Southern History* 31 (November 1965); Louis A. Perez, Jr., "Reminiscences of a Lector: Cubans in Tampa: From Exiles to Immigrants, 1891–1901," *FHQ*, 57 (October 1978); and Jose Rivera Muniz, "Les Cubanos in Tampa," *Revista Bimestre Cuban* 74 (Havana, 1958). In addition, Pozzetta and Harry A. Kersey, Jr., "Yama to Colony: A Japanese Presence in South Florida," *Tequesta* 36 (1976), looks at an attempt to recruit Japanese immigrants. Jerrell H. Shofner and Linda V. Ellsworth, eds., *Ethnic Minorities in Gulf Coast Society: Proceedings of the Gulf Coast History and Humanities Conference*, VIII (Pensacola, 1979), contains articles on Greeks, Jews, Cubans, and other Tampa immigrants in this era. Raymond A. Mohl, "Black Immigrants: Bahamians in Early Twentieth-

Century Miami" *FHQ*, 65 (January 1987), examines West Indian immigration.

The immigrant experience frequently was linked with conflict, the protection of basic worker rights, and the rise of organized labor in Florida. George E. Pozzetta, "A Padrone Looks at Florida: Labor Recruiting and the Florida East Coast Railway," *FHQ*, 53 (July 1975), reflects an early stage of the immigrant work experience. Harry S. Marks, "Labor Problems of the Florida East Coast Railway Extension from Homestead to Key West, 1905–1907," *Tequesta* 32 (1972), chronicles a growing demand for worker rights.

Tampa became a center for labor strife in Durward Long, "Labor Relations in the Tampa Cigar Industry, 1885–1911," *Labor History* 12 (Fall 1971); "La Resistancia: Tampa's Immigrant Labor Union," *Labor History* 5 (Spring 1965); and "The Open-Closed Shop Battle in Tampa's Cigar Industry, 1919–1921," *FHQ* 47 (October 1968). Pozzetta contributed, "'Alerta Tabaqueros!' Tampa's Striking Cigar Workers," *Tampa Bay History* 3 (Fall–Winter, 1981), and Gary Mormino, "Tampa and the New Urban South: The Weight Strike of 1899," *FHQ*, 60 (January 1982). John Conrad Appel links "The Unionization of the Florida Cigar Makers and the Coming of War with Spain," in *Hispanic American History Review* 36 (1956).

For other parts of the state, David Sowell examines "Racial Patterns of Labor in Postbellum Florida: Gainesville, 1870–1900," *FHQ*, 63 (April 1985). Wayne Flynt describes "Pensacola Labor Problems and Political Radicalism, 1908," *FHQ*, 43 (April 1965), and at the end of the era, "Florida Labor and Political Radicals, 1919–1920," *Labor History* 9 (Winter 1968).

A harsher form of labor is seen in N. Gordon Caper, "The Convict-Lease System in Florida, 1866–1923" (Ph.D. diss., Florida State University, 1964); and Jerrell Shofner, "Mary Grace Quackenbos, a Visitor Florida Did Not Want," *FHQ*, 58 (January 1980), and "Forced Labor in the Florida Forests, 1880–1950," *Journal of Forest History* 25 (January 1981).

Among traditional institutions in Florida, the church ranked among the more important. Traditional churches chronicled include Edward Earl Joiner, *A History of Florida Baptists* (Jacksonville, 1970); Jack Dalton, "A History of Florida Baptists" (Ph.D. diss., University of Florida, 1952); Joseph D. Cushman, Jr., *A Goodly Heritage: The Episcopal Church in Florida, 1821–1892* (Gainesville, 1965), and *The Sound of Bells: The Episcopal Church in South Florida, 1892–1969* (Gainesville, 1976); Michael J. McNally, *Catholicism in South Florida, 1868–1968* (Gainesville, 1984); William Erle Brooks, ed., *From Saddlebags to Satellites: A History of Florida Methodism* (Maitland, Fla., 1969); and Cooper C. Kirk, "A History of the Southern Presbyterian Church in Florida, 1821–1891" (Ph.D. diss., Florida State University, 1966). Rufus B. Spain, *At Ease in Zion: A Social History of Southern Baptists, 1865–1900* (Nashville, 1967), includes references to Florida's Southern Baptists.

Less traditional in the Florida religious community were the lives examined by Jane Quinn, "Nuns in Ybor City: The Sisters of St. Joseph and the Immigrant Community," *Tampa Bay History* 5 (Spring–Summer, 1983); and Harry A.

Kersey and Donald E. Pullease, "Bishop William Crane Gray's Mission to the Seminole Indians in Florida, 1893–1914," *Historical Magazine of the Protestant Episcopal Church* (September 1973). Joe M. Richardson, " 'The Nest of Vile Fanatics': William N. Sheats and the Orange Park School," *FHQ*, 64 (April 1986) describes an American Missionary Association attempt to maintain a racially integrated school in Clay County. Fringe religious groups seeking haven in Florida are seen in Russell H. Anderson, "The Shaker Community in Florida," *FHQ*, 38 (July 1959); Lori Robinson and Bill DeYoung, "Socialism in the Sunshine: The Roots of Ruskin, Florida," *Tampa Bay History* 4 (Spring–Summer, 1982); and R. Lyn Rainard, "Conflict Inside the Earth: Koreshan Unity in Lee County," *Tampa Bay History* 3 (Spring–Summer, 1981).

An area in which major change took place in Florida during the Gilded Age and Progressive Era was education. In public education, Arthur O. White, *One Hundred Years of State Leadership in Florida Public Education* (Tallahassee, (1979), looks at the various state commissioners of education in the era. Nita Katharine Pyburn, "William N. Sheats and the Florida High Schools," *Florida Educators* (Tallahassee, 1959), examines one prominent commissioner. Pyburn also wrote *The History of the Development of a Single System of Education in Florida, 1822–1903* (Tallahassee, 1954). Robert L. Mitchell, "Legislative Provisions and Their Effects on Negro Public Education in Florida, 1869–1947" (Ph.D. diss., Florida State University, 1970), is superficial. Robert G. Stakenos, David B. Mock, and Kenneth M. Eaddy, *Educating Hand and Mind: A History of Vocation Education in Florida* (New York, 1984), begins in this era.

At the postsecondary level, Alfred H. Adams, "A History of Public Higher Education in Florida, 1821–1961" (Ed.D. diss., Florida State University, 1962), has two useful chapters. Samuel Proctor, "The University of Florida: Its Early Years, 1853–1906" (Ph.D. diss., University of Florida, 1956), portrays the beginning of the Gainesville institution. Proctor, "The South Florida Military Institute (Bartow): A Parent of the University of Florida," *FHQ*, 32 (July 1953), looks at an antecedent. Leedell W. Neyland, "State-Supported Higher Education among Negroes in the State of Florida," *FHQ*, 43 (October 1964), examines the origins of Florida A&M University. C. L. Crow, "Florida University (1883)," *FHQ*, 15 (October, 1936), describes a bold attempt to establish a statewide university that never came to fruition. Jack C. Lane, "Liberal Arts on the Florida Frontier: The Founding of Rollins College, 1885–1890," *FHQ*, 59 (October 1980), chronicles the beginning of an early private college.

Medical history also has received scholarly attention, partly because of the developments within medical science during these years and partly from the importance of epidemics which periodically threatened the people of subtropical Florida. *The Journal of the Florida Medical Association* (hereafter cited as *JFMA*), publishes an annual historical issue. For Pensacola, Elizabeth Vickers describes "Pensacola's Early Hospitals," *JFMA*, 68 (August 1981), and with F. Norman Vickers, "Notations of Pensacola's Medical History, 1873–1923," *JFMA*, 61 (January 1974). George F. Pearce, "Torments of

Pestilence: Yellow Fever Epidemics in Pensacola," *FHQ*, 56 (April 1978), covers all of the nineteenth century. For Jacksonville, Webster Merrit, *A History of Medicine in Jacksonville and Duval County* (Gainesville, 1949); Richard A. Martin, *A Century of Service: St. Luke's Hospital, 1873–1973* (Jacksonville, 1973); and Margaret C. Fairlie, "The Yellow Fever Epidemic of 1888 in Jacksonville," *FHQ*, 19 (October 1940), are useful. For Miami, William Straight, M.D., chronicles "James M. Jackson, Jr.: Miami's First Physician," *JFMA*, 59 (August 1972), reprinted in *Tequesta* 33 (1973). Straight also wrote "The Yellow Jack," *JFMA*, 58 (August 1971); "Florida and the Spanish Flu," *JFMA*, 68 (August 1981); and "Camp Miami, 1898," *JFMA*, 74 (July 1987).

The most prominent physician of the era and Florida's first state health officer was Dr. Joseph Yates Porter. Wilson T. Sowder, M.D., "Joseph Yates Porter, M.D.," *JFMA*, 54 (August 1967), and Frederick Eberson, "Yellow Fever Fighters: Dr. Joseph Y. Porter and Dr. Isaac Hulse," *JFMA*, 59 (August 1982), are introductions. Albert V. Hardy and Mary Pynchon, *Millstones and Milestones: Florida's Public Health from 1889* (Jacksonville, 1965), is superficial. So is Mary M. Paylor, "A History of Nursing Education in Florida from 1893 to 1970" (Ph.D. diss., Florida State University, 1975). Joy S. Richmond, "Notes on the History of Leprosy in Florida to 1921," *JFMA*, 63 (August 1976), counts 129 cases with most of them in Key West. David T. Courtwright, "The Hidden Epidemic: Opiate Addiction and Cocaine in the South, 1860–1920," *Journal of Southern History* 49 (February 1983), includes data on Jacksonville.

Less has been written about journalism in this era. Thomas S. Graham, "Charles H. Jones, 1848–1913, Editor and Progressive Democrat" (Ph.D. diss., University of Florida, 1973), and "Charles H. Jones: Florida's Leading Gilded Age Editor-Politician," *FHQ*, 59 (July 1980), assays the impact of a major journalist of the era. Joel Webb Eastman, "Claude L'Engle, Florida Muckraker," *FHQ*, 45 (January 1967), portrays a progressive. Ruby Andrews Myers, "Newspaper Pioneering on the Florida East Coast, 1891–1895," *Tequesta* 43 (1983), examines the Miami area. George Green examines "The Florida Press and the Democratic Presidential Primary of 1912," *FHQ*, 44 (January 1966); and C. Peter Ripley, "Intervention and Reaction: Florida's Newspapers and the United States Entry into World War I," *FHQ*, 49 (January 1971).

As Florida moved from frontier toward settled society, one characteristic of the shift was the growing diversity of its culture, from low life to high achievement. Everyday life could be quite mundane, as in Isidor Cohen, *Historical Sketches and Sidelights of Miami, Florida* (Miami, 1925); John Sewell, *Memoirs and History of Miami, Florida* (Miami, 1933); J. K. Dorn, "Recollections of Early Miami," *Tequesta* 9 (1949); Will Davenport, "Growing Up, Sort Of, in Miami, 1909–1915," *Tequesta*, 40 (1980); and Ethan V. Blackman, *Miami and Dade County, Florida* (Miami, 1921). Sewell's work, replete with 200 photographs and interesting commentary by historian Arva Parks, has been reissued under the title *Miami Memoirs* (Miami, 1987). An overview of one community's popular culture is seen in James B. Crooks, "Leisure Time in Jacksonville: 1900 to the First World War," *Journal of Regional Culture* 4 (Spring–Summer, 1984). A city's low life is described by James R. McGovern, "'Sporting Life on the Line': Prostitution in Progressive Era Pensacola," *FHQ*, 53 (October 1975), and Lillian Gilkes, *Cora Crane: A Biography of Mrs. Stephen Crane* (Bloomington, Ind., 1960). Crane was a Jacksonville madam. Paul S. George, "A Cyclone Hits Miami, Carrie Nation's Visit to 'The Wicked City,' " *FHQ*, 58 (October 1979), describes a reaction to one life-style. Sports were important in Bess Beatty, "Baseball: Jacksonville's Gilded Age Craze," *Apalachee* 8 (1978), and James W. Covington, "The Chicago Cubs Come to Tampa," *Tampa Bay History* 8 (Spring–Summer, 1986). Alice Stickland, "Florida's Golden Age of Racing," *FHQ*, 45 (January 1967), describes auto racing on the beaches at Daytona. Kay Tapley, "Camping and Cruising along the Suncoast in 1899," *Tampa Bay History* 2 (Fall–Winter, 1980), chronicles another sport. Joe M. Richardson, "The Florida Excursion of President Chester A. Arthur," *Tequesta* 24 (1960), reports the impact of a visiting dignitary upon Floridians.

At the turn of the century, moving pictures came to Florida, followed by filmmakers. Richard Alan Nelson examines that history in *Florida and the Motion Picture Industry, 1898–1980*, 2 vols. (New York, 1982), and "Palm Trees, Public Relations and Promoters: Boosting Florida as a Motion Picture Empire, 1910–1930," *FHQ*, 61 (April 1983). As the era progressed, the environment became important to some people. Oliver Orr, "T. Gilbert Pearson, Young Ornithologist in Florida," *FHQ*, 62 (October 1953), describes the effort of an Alachua County bird-watcher. Emily Perry Dieterich, "Birds of a Feather: The Coconut Grove Audubon Society, 1915–1917," *Tequesta* 45 (1985), reports on the origins of one environmental group.

For more sophisticated Floridians, theater, music and architecture became important art forms. Jack L. Bilbo, "Economy and Culture: The Boom-and-Bust Theatres of Pensacola, Florida, 1821–1917" (Ph.D. diss., Texas Tech University, 1982), links cultural growth with economic prosperity. Grier M. Williams, "A History of Music in Jacksonville, Florida, from 1822 to 1922" (Ph.D. diss., Florida State University, 1962), is informative. Gloria Jahoda, *The Road to Samarkind: Frederick Delius and His Music* (New York, 1969), and William Randel, "Frederick Delius in America," *Virginia Magazine of History and Biography* 79 (July 1971), describe that artist's life in Florida during the 1880s. Robert C. Broward, *The Architecture of Henry John Klutho: The Prairie School in Jacksonville* (Jacksonville, 1984), focuses on the work of a disciple of Frank Lloyd Wright.

As Florida developed, policing communities became important. Paul S. George, "Criminal Justice in Miami, 1896–1930" (Ph.D. diss., Florida State University, 1975), examines this topic as do a series of his articles, "The Evolution of Miami and Dade County's Judiciary, 1896–1920," *Tequesta* 37 (1976); "Traffic Control in Early Miami," *Tequesta* 37 (1977); "Policing Miami's Black Community, 1896–1930," *FHQ*, 57 (April 1979); and "Miami's City Marshal and Law Enforcement in a New Community, 1896–1907," *Tequesta* 44 (1984).

Meanwhile the impact of war in 1898 and again in 1917–1918 led to increasing military involvement of the state with the federal government. George C. Bittle, "In Defense of Florida: The Organized Florida Militia from 1821 to 1920" (Ph.D. diss., Florida State University, 1965), examines the forerunner of the National Guard. Robert Hawk, *Florida's Army* (Englewood, Fla., 1986), details the history of Florida's National Guard with material on the period covered by this essay. James R. McGovern, "Pensacola, Florida: A Military City in the New South," *FHQ*, 59 (July 1980), examines the growing military influence. George F. Pearce, *The U.S. Navy in Pensacola: From Sailing Ship to Naval Aviation, 1825–1930* (Pensacola, 1980), traces the growth of the navy there.

This chapter's many citations suggest that much has been written about Florida history during the Gilded Age and Progressive Era. Yet much remains undone. Our knowledge of the habits and attitudes, the traditions and precedents, the laws and values, the history and politics of this earlier period sheds light and offers perspective on today and tomorrow's Florida.

# 10

# SUN-BOUND HIGHWAYS: THE GROWTH OF FLORIDA AS AN INDEPENDENT STATE, 1917–1940

GREGORY W. BUSH

FLORIDA'S POPULATION GROWTH was the fastest in the South on the eve of World War I. That pace continued for the next twenty-five years, with population reaching 1,897,414 by 1940. During those years, the state experienced the social, economic, and visual impact of the automobile, a doubling of northern-born migrants, new pressures for social services stimulated by the New Deal and the Great Depression, and a subtle undermining of the racial climate. These changes occurred within a political context of continued dominance by the Democratic Party. The result left most Floridians largely unaware of the scope of the new forces that were inexorably wrenching them from their relatively insulated past.

The secondary literature on this period is, with a few exceptions, sparse or plodding. A highly readable, though not infallible, account is Stetson Kennedy's *Palmetto Country* (New York, 1942). For background on the politics of the 1920s and 1930s, see Charlton Tebeau, *A History of Florida* (Coral Gables, 1971), and James W. Dunn, *The New Deal and Florida Politics* (Ph.D. diss., Florida State University, 1971). Numerous local pictorial books are also valuable for this period, among the best being those of Jerrell Shofner, such as *Jackson County, Florida—A History* (Marianna, Fla., 1985); *Jefferson County* (Tallahassee, 1976); and *Orlando: The City Beautiful* (Tulsa, 1984). See also Linda Ellsworth and Lucius Ellsworth, *Pensacola: The Deep Water City* (Tulsa, 1982); Gary Mormino and Anthony P. Pizzo, *Tampa: The Treasure City* (Tulsa, 1983); Arva Parks, *Miami: The Magic City* (Tulsa, 1981); and James R. Ward, *Old Hickory's Town: An Illustrated History of Jacksonville* (Jacksonville, 1982).

The impact of World War I on Florida has been largely ignored by historians. Five flying schools (out of thirty-five nationwide) were located in Florida, inaugurating the importance of air travel to Florida's future development. As a major ship building city, Jacksonville was the city most strongly affected by the war.

The state's economy, overwhelmingly agricultural on the eve of the war, saw the erosion of the export of phosphates, lumber, and naval stores while demand rose for wartime necessities, fostering, for example, the spread of castor bean production. Citrus production gained little because the concentration process had not yet been invented.

World War I stimulated a widespread movement of people in Florida. Black migration from the Bahamas followed a treaty with Great Britain. Simultaneously, the migration northward by southern-born blacks created fear and anger about lost labor and consumer markets among whites as well as middle-class blacks, as Jerrell Shofner relates in his "Florida and the Black Migration," *Florida Historical Quarterly (FHQ)* 57 (January 1979). See also Charles Garofalo, "Black-White Occupational Distribution in Miami During World War I," *Prologue* 5 (1973).

The anxiety and nationalistic spirit which attended the war reinforced a conservative and moralistic reaction against anything perceived to be alien. The role of the press at the outset of the war is discussed in C. Peter Ripley, "Intervention and Reaction: Florida Newspapers and the United States Entry into World War I," *FHQ*, 49 (January 1971). No scholarship has adequately treated this period of Florida's history. See Thelma Peters, *Biscayne Country* (Miami, 1981), and *Lemon City* (Miami, 1976); Judge Fred H. Davis, "Leon County during the World War," *Tallahassee Historical Society Annual* 3 (1937). Florida also experienced a sharp postwar reaction against labor organizations or other groups perceived to be radical. See Joseph Cafaro, "Tallahassee: Revolution and Red Scare (1917–20)" *Apalachee* 9 (1980–83); Wayne Flynt, "Florida Labor and Political 'Radicalism,' 1919–1920," *Labor History*, 9 (1968).

One partial result of the war saw Prohibition enacted as a constitutional amendment in 1919 after years of political infighting. James Carter has addressed this in "Florida and Rumrunning During Prohibition," *FHQ*, 48 (1969). See also Paul S. George, "Bootleggers, Prohibitionists and Police: The Temperance Movement in Miami," *Tequesta* 39 (1979), and "Criminal Justice in Miami, 1896–1930 (Ph.D. diss., Florida State University, 1975).

Throughout the 1920s and the 1930s, Florida also witnessed continuing racial segregation and white violence against blacks. See David Chalmers, "The Ku Klux Klan in the Sunshine State: The 1920s," *FHQ*, 42 (1964); Paul S. George, "Policing Miami's Black Community, 1896–1930," *FHQ*, 57 (April 1979); and Kenneth Jackson, *The Ku Klux Klan in the Cities 1915–1930* (New York, 1967).

The war brought numerous servicemen to Florida who either stayed or subsequently returned for winter visits, helping to fuel the extraordinary Florida land boom that was in full swing by the early 1920s. For several contemporary accounts see Kenneth Roberts, *Florida* (New York, 1926), and the magazine *Suniland: The Magazine of Florida* published during the 1920s. For a foreign visitor's account see George Kleine, "The Suncoast Viewed through German Eyes," *Tampa Bay History* 3 (1981). For subsequent years see the analysis of Homer Vanderblue, "The Florida Land Boom," *Journal of Land and Public Utility Economics* 3 (May 1927); Theyre H. Weigall, *Boom in Paradise* (New York, 1932); chapter 11 of Frederick Lewis Allen, *Only Yesterday* (New York, 1931); and Kenneth Ballinger, *Miami Millions* (Miami, 1936).

More recent scholarly and popular treatments have been provided by George B. Tindall, "The Bubble in the Sun," *American Heritage* 16 (August, 1965); David Nolan, *Fifty Feet in Paradise: The Booming of Florida* (New York, 1984); John Rothchild, *Up for Grabs: A Trip through Time and Space* (New York, 1985); Paul S. George, "Brokers, Binders, and Builders: Greater Miami's Boom of the Mid–1920's," *FHQ*, 64 (July 1986); Gary Mormino, "1925: The Sun Shines on St. Petersburg," *St. Petersburg Times* (September 27, 1986); Donald Curl, "Boca Raton and the Florida Land Boom of the 1920s," *Tequesta* (1986); Polly Redford, *Billion Dollar Sandbar: A Biography of Miami Beach* (New York, 1970); and Joe McCarthy, "The Man Who Invented Miami Beach," *American Heritage* 27 (December 1975). See also Eun Choi Kyou, "Florida Business Cycles, 1920–1960" (Ph.D. diss., University of Florida, 1964); Gary Malamaud, *Boomtown Communities* (New York, 1984); and Paul S. George, "Passage to the New Eden: Tourism in Miami from Flagler through Everest G. Sewell," *FHQ*, 59 (April, 1981); Donald Curl, "Boca Raton and the Florida Land Boom of the 1920s," *Tequesta* 46 (1986); and Melvin Edward Hughes, Jr., "William J. Howey and His Florida Dreams," *FHQ* 61 (January 1988). The best mine of information for the boom in Miami is Frank Sessa, "The Real Estate Boom in Miami and Its Environs (1923–1926)" (Ph.D. diss., University of Pittsburgh, 1950). See also his article "Miami in 1926," *Tequesta* 16 (1956). For northern reaction to the drain of money into the Florida land boom see Elliott Mackle, "Anti-Florida Propaganda and Counter Measures during the 1920s," *Tequesta* 21 (1961).

Literary studies of the Florida boom are given a good treatment in Mark Bernheim, "Florida: The Permanence of America's Idyll," *Modernist Studies* 4 (1982). Anne Rowe's *The Idea of Florida in the American Literary Imagination* (Baton Rouge, 1986), is an excellent more recent overview of literary treatments of Florida. Ring Lardner saw Florida as "the embodiment of the boom and bust of the American Dream," Rowe relates, a view that comes across clearly in these short stories: "Sun Cured," "Gullibles Travels," and "The Golden Honeymoon." In *The Big Money* (New York, 1936), John Dos Passos expressed his rage at the "Big Men" who succeed in Florida. See also Theodore Dreiser's three articles in *Vanity Fair* (1926).

The architecture of the boom period is covered by Donald Curl in his *Mizener's Florida: America's Resort Architecture* (New York, 1984), and Christina Orr, *Addison Mizener, Architecture of Dreams and Realities* (West Palm Beach, 1977). See also Kathryn Chapman Harwood, *The Lives of Vizcaya: Annals of a Great House* (Miami, 1985), for background on the building of Miami's gaudy palace of James Deering, as well as James T. Maher, *The Twilight of Splendor* (Boston, 1975). See Barbara Baer Capitman, "Rediscovery of Art Deco," *American Preservation* 6 (1978), and Woodrow W. Wilkens, "Coral Gables: 1920s New Town," *Historic Preservation* 30 (1978). See also Metropolitan Dade County office of Community and Economic Development, *From Wilderness to Metropolis* (Miami, 1982), and Addison Mizener's own account, *Florida Architecture* (New York, 1928).

It has all too frequently been posited that the Florida boom ended with the coming of the September 1926 hurricane. But according to Frank Sessa and Paul George, the boom died from other factors: snarled railroad lines, overextended credit, the price cycle, buyer fears spawned by northern banker hostility to money fleeing their banks for dubious Florida real estate and, finally, rumors of intrusive action by the Internal Revenue Service. See also Elliot Mackle, "Two Way Stretch: Some Dichotomies in the Advertising of Florida as the Boom Collapsed," *Tequesta* 31 (1973). Depression hit Florida earlier than much of the country; by 1930 it had the highest unemployment rate in the southeastern United States and the highest per capita debt in the nation. See Emergency Relief Administration, *Unemployment Relief in Florida, July 1932-March 1934* (Jacksonville, 1935).

On the impact of the hurricane itself see Marjory Stoneman Douglas, *Hurricane* (Atlanta, 1958); Joseph Reese, *Florida's Great Hurricane* (Miami, 1926); and L. F. Reardon, *The Florida Hurricane and Disaster* (Miami, 1926). See also Ruth S. Irwin, "Weathering the Storms: The Floyd Wilder Family and the Great Hurricanes of the 1920s," *Tampa Bay History* 5 (1983).

Throughout the 1920s and 1930s, the political landscape of Florida continued to reflect the state's geographical division between the urbanized southeast coast and the northern rural areas. By 1917, the "Anti-corporation movement had lost much of its force," according to Dewey Grantham in *Southern Progressivism* (Knoxville, 1983). Sidney Catts, a former Alabama Baptist preacher and life insurance representative, shrewdly exploited anti-Catholic sentiment and prohibitionist sentiment to become governor in 1916. See Wayne Flynt, *Cracker Messiah: Governor Sidney J. Catts of Florida* (Baton Rouge, 1977), and Robert

B. Rackleff, "Anti-Catholicism and the Florida Legislature, 1911–1919," *FHQ*, 50 (1972).

V. O. Key, Jr., and Alexander Heard in *Southern Politics* (New York, 1984) have characterized Florida politics as consisting of a "multiplicity of state factions, a dispersion of leadership . . . and a discontinuity of lack of persistence in the grouping of voters into factions." (1949 ed.) An indispensable source is David Colburn and Richard Sher, *Florida's Gubernatorial Politics in the Twentieth Century* (Tallahassee, 1980). The standard history of the Democratic party is William T. Cash, *History of the Democratic Party in Florida* (Tallahassee, 1936). For an account of the history of the Republican party see Peter D. Klingman, *Neither Dies nor Surrenders: A History of the Republican Party in Florida 1867–1970* (Gainesville, 1984).

Earlier progressive concerns were fast eroding by 1920. By 1924, the state legislature passed a constitutional amendment forbidding income or inheritance taxes to attract wealthy new residents. See also Victoria H. McDonnell, "Rise of the 'Businessman's Politician': The 1924 Florida Gubernatorial Race," *FHQ* 52 (1973), and her M.A. thesis, "The Businessmen's Politician: A Study of the Administration of John W. Martin, 1925–1929" (University of Florida, 1968). See also Wayne Flynt, "Florida's 1926 Senatorial Primary," *FHQ*, 42 (1963).

Florida turned away from its perennial acceptance of the Democratic party in 1928 and voted for presidential candidate Herbert Hoover over the Catholic governor of New York, Al Smith. See Herbert J. Doherty, Jr., "Florida and the Presidential Election of 1928," *FHQ*, 26 (October 1947). See also David J. Ginzl, "The Politics of Patronage: Florida Republicans during the Hoover Administration," *FHQ*, 61 (1982); James B. Whitfield, *Political and Legal History of Florida* (Atlanta, 1943); Herbert J. Doherty, Jr., "Liberal and Conservative Voting Patterns in Florida" [1928–1948], *Journal of Politics* 14 (1952); and Melvin Edward Hughes, "Florida Preachers and the Election of 1928," *FHQ* 67 (October 1988).

In the winter of 1933 while President-elect Franklin Roosevelt visited Miami, he was the target of an assassination attempt which ultimately killed Chicago's Mayor Anton Cermack. See Nathan Shappee, "Zangara's Attempted Assassination of Franklin D. Roosevelt," *FHQ*, 37 (1958), and Kenneth S. Davis, "Incident in Miami," *American Heritage* 32 (1980).

The Great Depression and the New Deal stimulated tremendous changes in the state's relationship with the federal government. Durward Long, "Key West and the New Deal, 1934–1936," *FHQ*, 46 (January 1968), shows how that city became bankrupt during the depression from a loss of tourism and federal abandonment of the area as a naval post, followed by the centralization of relief efforts stimulated by the New Deal. See also Long's "Workers on Relief 1934–1938 in Key West," *Tequesta* 28 (1968); Garry Boulard, " 'State of Emergency': Key West in the Great Depression," *FHQ* 67 (October 1988); and Vernon M. Leslie, "The Great Depression in Miami Beach," (M.A. thesis, Florida Atlantic University, 1980).

A Brooklyn-born Jew turned Episcopalian, David Sholtz of Daytona Beach, beat former governor John Martin in the gubernatorial race of 1932. His career is rather sketchily covered in Merlin Cox, "David Sholtz: New Deal Governor of Florida," *FHQ*, 43 (October 1964). For other attention on New Deal personalities and programs see Alexander R. Stoesen, "The Senatorial Career of Claude D. Pepper" (Ph.D. diss., University of North Carolina, 1964); Charles B. Lowry, "The PWA in Tampa: A Case Study," *FHQ*, 52 (April 1974); R. Lyn Rainard, "Ready Cash on Easy Terms: Local Responses to the Depression in Lee County," *FHQ*, 64 (January 1986); Marilyn Solee, "The Federal Music Project in Miami, 1935–1939," *Tequesta* 30 (1970); John F. Sweets, "The Civilian Conservation Corps in Florida," *Apalachee* 6 (1963–67); Jerrell Shofner, "Roosevelt's 'Tree Army': The Civilian Conservation Corps in Florida," *FHQ* 65 (April 1987); and Wylie Kilpatrick, "Florida City Debt—A Case Study (1930–1953)," *Journal of Finance* 10 (1955). A useful analysis of government photography can be found in Robert Snyder, "Marion Post and the Farm Security Administration in Florida," *FHQ* 65 (April 1987).

One of the best sources to interpret Florida in the 1930s comes from the books issued by the Federal Writers Project (FWP), directed by Carita Dorsett Corse. These include *Seeing St. Augustine* (1937); *A Guide to Key West* (New York, 1941); *Seeing Fernandia: A Guide to the City and Its Industries* (1940); *The Seminole Indians in Florida* (Tallahassee, 1941) and *Florida, a Guide to the Southernmost State* (New York, 1939). See also Robert Hemenway, "Folklore Field Notes from Zora Neale Hurston," *Black Scholar* 7 (April 1976), which includes some of the notes on a project of Florida Negroes never completed in 1939 and done while Hurston was a member of the FWP.

The impact of new forms of mass communications has just recently begun to interest Florida historians. There is no significant study on the rise of radio in Florida, and several local studies contend over the origin of Florida's first station. See Hampton Dunn, *WDAE, Florida's Pioneer Radio Station* (Tampa, 1972). Older works concentrating on the role of newspapers include William Boiler, "A Study of the Reporting and Interpreting of the League of Nations by a Selected Group of Florida Newspapers" (M.A. thesis, University of Florida, 1958), and Nixon Smiley, *Knights of the Fourth Estate: The Story of the Miami Herald* (Miami, 1975). The promotion of the Florida economy is covered in Martin M. LaGodna, "Agriculture and Advertising: Florida State Bureau of Immigration, 1923–1960," *FHQ*, 46 (1968), and Phillip E. DeBerard, Jr., "Promoting Florida: Some Aspects of the Uses of Advertising and Publicity in the Development of the Sunshine State" (M.A. thesis, University of Florida, 1951). An extended treatment of the statewide motion picture industry can be found in Richard Alan Nelson, *Florida and the Motion Picture Industry, 1898–1980*, (mentioned above). See also Nelson's short account, *Lights! Camera! Florida! Ninety Years of Moviemaking and Television Production in the Sunshine State* (Tampa, 1987), and his articles "High Flyer: Finance and the Silver Screen: The Rise and Fall of the National Film Corporation of America," *Film & History* 13 (1983), and

"Palm Trees, Public Relations, and Promoters: Boosting Florida as a Motion Picture Empire, 1910–1930," *FHQ*, 61 (April 1983).

By the 1920s, the emergence of new technologies of climate control and transportation proved to be of enormous importance in stimulating Florida's fast-paced growth as a tourist haven. On the railroad see Seth Bramson, *Speedway to Sunshine* (Erin, Canada, 1984). Raymond Arsenault has written a stimulating study of a hitherto neglected topic in "The End of the Long Hot Summer: The Air Conditioner and Southern Culture," *Journal of Southern History* 50 (1984). Pan American Airlines began service between Key West and Havana in 1927, while other airlines and routes in service soon followed. See William Lazarus, *Wings in the Sun: The Annals of Aviation in Florida* (Orlando, 1951); Warren Brown, *Florida's Aviation History* (Largo, Fla., 1980); Marilyn Bender and Selig Altschul, *The Chosen Instrument: Juan Trippe, Pan Am* (New York, 1982); C. R. Roseberry, *Glenn Curtiss: Pioneer of Flight* (Garden City, 1972); and Frank Bush, *A Dream of Araby: Glenn Curtiss and the Founding of Opa Locka* (Opa Locka, Fla., 1976).

The pivotal engine of change for Florida in this period, however, was found in the automobile. The opening of the Tamiami Trail in 1928 and the earlier creation of the Dixie Highway and other roadways facilitated the onslaught of northern tourists into Florida in numbers never before seen. See Baynard Kendrick, *Florida Trails to Turnpikes, 1914–1964* (Gainesville, 1964); Paul S. George, "Traffic Control in Early Miami," *Tequesta* 37 (1977); James L. Walker, "Dedication of Tamiami Trail Marker," *Tequesta* 19 (1959); and Doris Davis, "The Tamiami Trail: Muck, Mosquitoes, and Motorists: A Photo Essay," *Tampa Bay History* 1 (1979). New Deal funding was critical in completing the overseas highway to Key West in 1938. See Alice Hopkins, "The Development of the Overseas Highway," *Tequesta* 46 (1986), and Junius E. Dovell, *The State Road Department of Florida* (Gainesville, 1955). There was a curious fascination with speed in the 1920s that was epitomized in the widespread popularity of car racing. Alice Strickland in "Florida's Golden Age of Racing." *FHQ*, 45 (1967) traces the beginnings of race car driving in 1902 up to the 1940s. One result of the rising use of cars is considered in Walter Erickson, "Manslaughter by Automobile in Florida," *University of Florida Law Review* 4 (1951).

On water transportation see Richard J. Sewell "Cross-Florida Barge Canal, 1927–1968," *FHQ*, 46 (1968); Benjamin F. Rogers, "The Florida Ship Canal Project," *FHQ* 36 (1957); George E. Buker, "Tampa's Municipal Wharves," *Tampa Bay History* 5 (1983).

While tourism and agriculture continued to dominate the state's economy, control over the economic and political life of the state began to see new faces of power. Most significant was Alfred I. DuPont's decision in 1926 to live in Florida, which meant that he would infuse the Florida banking industry with millions of his dollars. See the apologetic account by Marguis James, *Alfred I. DuPont, the Family Rebel* (Indianapolis, 1941), and Leon O. Griffith's volume on DuPont's political heir, *Ed Ball: Confusion to the Enemy* (Tampa, 1975). For other accounts on the economic changes besetting the state see Wallace Nelson, "The Economic Development of Florida, 1870–1930" (Ph.D. diss. University of Florida, 1967 or 1962); Mira Wilkins, *Foreign Enterprise in Florida* (Miami, 1979); and Clifton Paisley, "Thirty-Cent Cotton at Lloyd, Florida, 1916–1919," *FHQ*, 49 (January 1971). On state agricultural politics and policies see Martin LaGodna, "The Florida State Department of Agriculture during the Administration of Nathan Mayo" (Ph.D. diss., University of Florida, 1970). See also John McPhee's *Oranges* (New York, 1967); Reinhold Wolff, *Miami: Economic Patterns of a Resort Area* (Coral Gables, 1945); Wylie Kilpatrick, *Manufacturing in Florida* (Gainesville, 1951); Lowell Yoder, *The Consumer Finance Industry in Florida* (Gainesville, 1957); and J. E. Dovell, *History of Banking in Florida* (Orlando, 1955).

Florida's working class continued to find it difficult to organize. For background see Durward Long, "The Open-Closed Shop Battle in Tampa's Cigar Industry, 1919–1921," *FHQ*, (1968). J. Carrington Gramling, "The Development of Florida Labor Law," *Miami Law Quarterly* 7 (1953); N. Gordon Carper, "The Convict Lease System in Florida, 1866–1923" (Ph.D. diss., Florida State University, 1964); M. Dudley Burton, "Florida's Workmen's Compensation, 1935–1950," *Miami Law Quarterly* 5 (1950); and Donald Grubbs, "The Story of Florida's Migrant Farm Workers," *FHQ*, 40 (October 1961). See also Sandra Mohl, "Migrant Farm Workers in America: A Florida Case Study" (M.A. thesis, Florida Atlantic University, 1981). Jerrell Shofner has produced a number of significant studies on labor history, including "Postscript to the Martin Tabert Case: Peonage as Usual in the Florida Turpentine Camps," *FHQ* 60 (1981), and "Forced Labor in the Florida 'Forests,' 1880–1950," *Journal of Forest History* 47 (1981).

On the criminal justice system see Emmett Bashful, *The Florida Supreme Court: A Study in Judicial Selection* (Tallahassee, 1958); Kathleen Pratt, "The Development of the Florida Prison System," (M.A. thesis, Florida State University, 1949); N. Gordon Caper, "The Convict Lease System in Florida, 1866–1923," (Ph.D. diss., Florida State University, 1964); Paul S. George, "Bootleggers, Prohibitionists and Police: The Temperance Movement in Miami, 1896–1920," *Tequesta* 39 (1979); Paul S. George, "Policing Miami's Black Community, 1896–1930," *FHQ*, 57 (April 1979); Paul S. George and William Willbanks, "Reevaluating the Good Ole Days in Dade County: Historical Trends in Dade County Homicides, 1917–1982," *Southern Journal of Criminal Justice* (June 1985); Richard Cofer, "Bootleggers in the Backwoods: Prohibition and the Depression in Hernando County," *Tampa Bay History* 1 (1979); Gordon N. Carper, "Martin Tabert, Martyr of an Era," *FHQ* 52 (1973); Robert P. Ingalls, "The Tampa Flogging Case: Urban Vigilantism," *FHQ*, 56 (1977); Walter Howard, "A Blot on Tampa's History: The 1934 Lynching of Robert Johnson," *Tampa Bay History* 6 (Fall–Winter, 1984); James D. Unnever, Charles E. Frazier, and John C. Henretta, "Race Differences in Criminal Sentencing," *Sociological Quarterly* 2 (1980); Jane Quinn, "Reid v. Barry: The Legal Battle over the 'Best

Location' in Orlando," *FHQ*, (1986); Paul S. George, "The Evolution of Miami and Dade County's Judiciary, 1896–1930," *Tequesta* 36 (1976); Jerrell Shofner, "Murders as Kiss Me Quick: The Underside of International Affairs," *FHQ*, 62 (1984); and Walter T. Howard, "Vigilante Justice and National Reaction: The 1937 Tallahassee Double Lynching," *FHQ* 67 (July 1988).

The religious life of Floridians between the wars can be traced in several sources: Joseph D. Cushman, Jr., *The Sound of Bells: The Episcopal Church in South Florida* (Gainesville, 1976), chapter 14 on Episcopalianism; Rev. Michael McNally, *Catholicism in South Florida, 1868–1968* (Gainesville, 1982); William E. Brooks, ed., *From Saddlebags to Satellites: A History of Florida Methodism* (Nashville, 1969); and Charlton Tebeau, *Synagogue in the Central City: Temple Israel of Greater Miami, 1922–1976* (Coral Gables, 1972). Anti-Semitism of the 1930s is traced in Miami Beach in Polly Redford's *Billion Dollar Sandbar* (New York, 1970).

Several new institutions began operating, including the University of Miami, begun in 1926. See Charlton Tebeau's *The University of Miami: A Golden Anniversary, 1926–1976* (Coral Gables, 1976); Wayne J. Urban, and Arthur O. White, *Florida's Crisis in Public Education: Changing Patterns of Leadership* (Gainesville, 1975); Arthur D. Pollock, "The Evolution of the Organizational Structure of Local Public Education in Florida 1875–1947" (Ph.D. diss., Florida State University, 1968); Samuel Proctor, "History of the University of Florida" (Ph.D. diss., University of Florida, 1956); Samuel Proctor, "William Jennings Bryan and the University of Florida," *FHQ*, 39 (1960); Robert G. Stakenas, David Mock, and Kenneth M. Eaddy, *Educating Hand and Mind: A History of Vocational Education in Florida* (New York, 1984); and Jack Mills, "The Speaking of William J. Bryan in Florida, 1915–1925" (M.A. thesis, University of Florida, 1949). An important force in Florida history was P. K. Yonge, a leading figure in higher education in early twentieth-century Florida. See Ocecie Clubbs, "Philip Keyes Yonge, 1850–1934," *FHQ*, 13 (1935). Longtime Secretary of State R. A. Gray's memoirs are important: *The Power and the Glory* (Tallahassee, 1965). Mary Duncan France's article "A Year of Monkey War: The Anti-Evolution Campaign and the Florida Legislature," *FHQ*, 54 (1975), examines the Florida legislative consideration of several bills prohibiting Darwin's evolutionary theories which conflicted with fundamentalist theology. See also Marian Watkins Black, "The Battle over Uniformity of Textbooks in Florida, 1868–1963," *History of Education Quarterly* 4 (1964), on the battle to make uniform all textbooks in Florida schools. Rackham Holt's *Mary McLeod Bethune: A Biography* (New York, 1969), examines the life of a nationally prominent black educator. See also Theodore Pratt, "Zora Neale Hurston," *FHQ*, 40 (1961); Gwendolyn Mikell, "When Horses Talk: Reflections on Zora Neale Hurston's Haitian Anthropology," *Phylon* 43 (September, 1982); and Satoru Takeuchi, "Dewey in Florida," *Journal of Library History* 1 (1966).

The medical history of Florida, beset by the ever-present mosquitoes and several yellow fever epidemics, can be traced in several places, among those being

John Mulrennan and Wilson Sowder, "Florida Mosquito Control System," *Public Health Reports* 69 (1954); Wilson Sowder, "The Growth of Local Health Units in Florida," *Public Health Reports* 68 (1953); William Straight, M.D., "Jackson Memorial Hospital: A Half Century of Community Service," *The Journal of the Florida Medical Association* 54 (1967); John G. Du Puis, *History of Early Medicine in Dade County* (Miami, 1954); W. H. Y. Smith, "Birth and Early Days of Florida's First County Health Unit (Taylor County, 1930–33)," *Public Health Reports* 68 (1953); and John M. Maclachlan, *Planning Florida's Health Leadership: Health and the People in Florida* (Gainesville, 1954).

The interwar years witnessed a spurt of concern for the environment that later culminated in the creation of the Everglades National Park. An excellent volume on the subject is Nelson Blake, *Land Into Water—Water Into Land: A History of Water Management in Florida* (Tallahassee, 1980). See also the beautifully written history of the Everglades by one of its great champions, Marjorie Stoneman Douglas, *The Everglades: River of Grass* (New York, 1947). Also important are William Robertson, *Everglades: The Park Story* (Miami, 1958); Charlton Tebeau, *Man in the Everglades: 2,000 Years of Human History in the Everglades National Park* (Coral Gables, 1968); Junius E. Dovell, "A History of the Everglades of Florida" (Ph.D. diss., University of North Carolina, 1947); Alexander Stoesen, "Claude Pepper and the Florida Canal Controversy, 1939–1943," *FHQ*, 50 (January 1972); and Lucy Blackman, *The Florida Audubon Society, 1900–1935* (n.p., 1935). Linda D. Vance's "May Man Jennings and Royal Palm State Park," *FHQ*, 55 (1976), examines the first state park.

Few expressed concern for the condition of the natural environment during this period. One who did was Marjorie Kinnan Rawlings. For an examination of her relationship to Florida, see Samuel Bellman, "Marjorie Kinnan Rawlings: A Solitary Sojourner in the Florida Backwoods," *Kansas Quarterly* (1970); Gordon Bigelow, *Frontier Eden: The Literary Career of Marjorie Kinnan Rawlings* (Gainesville, 1966); and John Cech, "Marjorie Kinnan Rawlings's *The Secret River*: A Fairy Tale, a Place, a Life," *Southern Studies* 19 (1980). Rawlings closed her magnificent novel *Cross Creek* (New York, 1942) by seeking a new understanding about the relationship of people to the land and water. The earth could be borrowed, she wrote, but not owned. "We are tenants and not possessors, lovers and not masters." Few Floridians grasped the meaning of her words in the interwar period.

# 11

---

# FLORIDA, FROM 1940 TO THE PRESENT

---

JAMES R. McGOVERN

FLORIDA'S HISTORY AFTER 1940 is mainly characterized by dynamic population growth and urbanization. The state's population at the end of World War II was only 2.2 million; by the end of 1987 it stood at 12 million. From a state ranked twenty-seventh in population in 1940, Florida would become fourth by the late 1980s. Florida's sunshine, coastline, and tropical climate explained those developments, as did the increasing independence and affluence of older Americans. Officially sponsored advertising promotionalism helped consolidate the effect.

The impressive growth and changing character of Florida's population provide the key to its recent history. Before 1940, Florida was basically a rural, southern state with one political party, its land beautiful and resourceful, its population provincial and youthful. By the late 1980s many changes had occurred: the state had some of the nation's largest metropolitan areas; effective two-party politics and a new style of political leadership supportive of business; a cosmopolitan, older, and more Caucasian population, 40 percent of which was born outside the South; a less natural and more man-made environment; and tremendous problems of growth and resource management. Unfortunately, there is no general work on Florida history which even begins to assess these complex changes. Charlton W. Tebeau's *A History of Florida* (Coral Gables, 1980), the basic work, is essentially a political history. Robert B. Marcus and Edward A. Fernald, *Florida: A Geographical Approach* (Dubuque, Iowa, 1975), is a valuable, popularly written, general work covering a wide scope of topics.

The effects of Florida's meteoric growth on its older, more traditional patterns of life in the period 1940 to 1980 are reflected in a number of fine analyses as well as fiction. Ben Green, *Finest Kind: A Celebration of a Florida Fishing Village* (Macon, Ga., 1985), is a remarkably sensitive sociohistorical analysis of the impact of Florida's recent modernization on persons living in one of the state's last fishing villages, Cortez, in Manatee County. A well-documented and researched description of the decline of farming in Leon County in recent times is in Clifton Paisley, *From Cotton to Quail: An Agricultural Chronicle of Leon County, Florida, 1860–1967*, (Gainesville, 1968). Christina Orr-Cahall, "Palm Beach: The Predicament of a Resort," *Historic Preservation* 30 (January 1978), describes and explains effectively the destruction of historic Palm Beach architecture. *The Trouble of It Is* (New York, 1978), is a collection of tales by David M. Newell. The author's regular good people are invariably Florida Crackers who are slowly losing their grip in the face of modernity.

Much of the literature on Florida's environmental conditions and problems is anguished during the period 1940 to 1980, more so with each successive decade. Thomas Barbour's *That Vanishing Eden, a Naturalist's Florida* (Boston, 1944), laments the thirty-year devastation of Florida (1914–1944). June Cleo and Hank Mesouf's *Florida, Polluted Paradise* (New York, 1964), warns in the early 1960s that the Florida of physical beauty and human fulfillment had already succumbed to unregulated commercialism. William R. McCluney, *The Environmental Destruction of South Florida: A Handbook for Citizens* (Coral Gables, 1971), is an alarm and call to arms for the health and survival of South Florida. On Florida's environmental condition since 1960, see also Robert B. Rackelff, *Close to Crisis: Florida's Environmental Problems* (Tallahassee, 1972), and Florida Defenders of the Environment, *Environmental Impact of the Cross-Florida Barge Canal* (Gainesville, 1970). Florida Atlantic University/Florida International University Joint Center for Environmental and Urban Problems, *Growth Management in South Florida: A Guide for Citizen Involvement* (Boca Raton, 1976), is concerned with how to activate citizen involvement in decision making on environmental issues.

Most studies of contemporary Florida are by scholars and commentators who purport to explain the phenomenon of the state's growth and provide analyses of its consequent problems, especially those concerned with land and water management. Stephen H. Flynn's *Florida, Land of Fortune* (Washington, D.C., 1962) is representative of the literature advertising Florida as a land of sun, satisfaction, and golden years. Grace M. Duvall's "The Florida Development Commission and Its Antecedents" (M.A. thesis, University of Miami, 1968) is a needed history of Florida boosterism. T. Stanton Dietrich's *The Urbanization of Florida's Population: An Historical Perspective of County Growth, 1830–1970* (Gainesville, 1978), provides an indispensable statistical survey of Florida's counties based largely on the decennial census of the United States. James F. Burns and Marilyn K. James, *Migration into Florida: 1940–1973* (Gainesville, 1973), gives special consideration to the age groups, places of origin, and location of persons moving to Florida after in-migration. *Urbanization in the South: A Critique and Analysis*, edited by David R. Colburn, George E. Pozzetta, and Richard K. Scher (Gainsville, 1973) is one of the first responses by historians and political scientists in Florida to the impact of the state's increasing urbanization on its life and politics.

Automobile transportation was critical to Florida's post–World War I economic growth. Junius E. Dovell's *The State Road Department of Florida* (Gainesville, 1955), provides the best study, though dated, of the state road department. See also Baynard Kendrick's *Florida Trails to Turnpikes* (Gainesville, 1964). The effects of an important technological breakthrough that facilitated Florida's phenomenal growth are discussed for the South generally in Raymond Arsenault, "The End of the Long Hot Summer: The Air Conditioner and Southern Culture," *Journal of Southern History* 50 (November 1984). A futuristic analysis of Florida's growth is John Naisbitt, *Megatrends* (New York, 1984), which anticipates that Florida, along with California, will become the exclusive megastates of the future. John Naisbitt and Corinne Kuypers-Denlinger's, "Why the Future Belongs to Florida," *Florida Trend* 25 (April 1983), declares that Florida is the bellwether state, surpassing California in the new-information, hi-tech society. An important article among optimists for the future growth in Florida is then- Governor Bob Graham, "How Growth Can Be Managed for the Good of Us All," in *Florida Trend* 26 (June 1983). Tom Ankerson's "Coping with Growth: The Emergence of Environmental Policy in Florida" (M.A. thesis, University of South Florida, 1983) is a quality master's degree thesis which explains how Florida, without an environmental policy as late as 1967, became a leader among states by 1972.

There are several outstanding studies of Florida's land and water management. One of the earliest was Lamar Johnson, *Beyond the Fourth Generation* (Gainesville, 1974). Luther J. Carter, *The Florida Experience: Land and Water Policy in a Growth State* (Baltimore, 1974), is a standard work on the despoilation of Florida's natural environment in the twentieth century. Nelson M. Blake's *Land into Water—Water into Land* (Tallahassee, 1980), is a comprehensive study of the post-1940 period that emphasizes conflicting interests affecting water management. John M. DeGrove, *Land Growth and Politics* (Washington, D.C., 1984) is a careful, authoritative historical treatment of land and water management in several states including Florida, primarily in the 1970s and 1980s.

For a bitter controversy between conservationists and developers over the question of establishing a cross-state waterway, see Benjamin F. Roger's

"The Florida Ship Canal Project," *Florida Historical Quarterly* (*FHQ*), 36 (July 1957). Henry E. Barber, "The Florida Cross-State Barge Canal" (Ph.D. diss., University of Georgia, 1969) examines the first efforts of the Roosevelt administration to effect the project as well as its subsequent revival in 1964. Much of the value of Alexander R. Stoesen's "Claude Pepper and the Florida Canal Controversy, 1939–1943," *FHQ*, 50 (January 1972), is concerned with the effectiveness of conservationist opposition as well as the imbroglio over the canal in 1970–71. George E. Buker's "Engineers vs. Florida's Green Menace," *FHQ*, 60 (April 1982), is a history of Florida's struggle with the water hyacinth in the twentieth century. Frank E. Maloney and Sheldon J. Plager, "Florida's Lakes: Problems in a Water Paradise," *University of Florida Law Review* 13 (Spring 1960), provides a scholarly analysis of Florida's laws affecting public use of the state's freshwater lakes.

Florida's politics and government in the period 1940 to the present have rapidly adjusted to the state's extraordinary growth in population and urbanization. Rural, even pioneering traditions in the Deep South still dominated in 1940. By 1980, urban characteristics dominated—two-party pluralism, reapportionment along urban lines, a large black voting constituency, a governor who could be re-elected, and a legislature which, at last, had adequate staff to devise efficient legislation.

Florida's recent constitutional development has been most successfully discussed by Manning Dauer, including monographs (with Clement Donovan and Gladys Kammerer) *Should Florida Adopt the Proposed Constitution?* (Gainesville, 1968), and *Legislative Power to Revise Constitution, Reorganization of Board of Control, and Other Constitutional Amendments of 1964* (Gainesville, 1964). The basic book on Florida politics, edited by Dauer, is *Florida Politics and Government* (Gainesville, 1980), to which thirty experts contributed articles on various facets of the state's political structure and functions. Anne E. Kelley, *Modern Florida Government* (New York, 1983), though a textbook, is the only comprehensive study of Florida's governmental processes and institutions in the period 1968 to 1978. Two dissertations that were informative when written are Juanita M. Gibson, "The Office of the Governor in Florida" (Ph.D. diss., University of Michigan, 1958), and Daisey Parker, "An Examination of the Florida Executive" (Ph.D. diss., University of Virginia, 1959). Many of the criticisms of Florida government in each dissertation are no longer valid. James M. Dennis, "State Executive Branch Reorganization: The Case of Florida" (Ph.D. diss., University of Florida, 1974), carefully studies reform trends in the executive branch since World War II. *City Managers in Politics, an Analysis of Manager Tenure and Termination* (Gainesville, 1962), by Gladys Kammerer, et al., studies city-manager tenure in ten Florida cities between 1945 and 1962. Allen Morris, "Florida Legislative Committees: Their Growth Since 1822," *FHQ*, 61 (October, 1982) provides a careful, factually sound, chronicle of the evolution of committees in the Florida Legislature, especially useful in recent times. Howard P. Tuckman, ed., *Financing Florida State*

*Government* (Tallahassee, 1979), contains essays by experts on major aspects of Florida's complicated tax structure. Joseph A. Boyd, "A History of the Supreme Court of Florida," *University of Miami Law Review* 35 (1980–1981), is too brief, though the bibliography is helpful.

On Florida politics, Vernon O. Key's classic, *Southern Politics in States and Nation* (New York, 1949), offers reasons for the differences between Florida's factional and unpredictable political patterns and those of other southern states. Manning J. Dauer's "Florida: The Different State," in William C. Havard, ed., *The Changing Politics of the South* (Baton Rouge, 1972), is a perceptive study of Florida's politics. Dauer explains how, despite Florida's large urban population in the 1970s, its citizenry holds negative attitudes toward public institutions and welfare services, the poor quality of many of its schools, its inadequate tax base for higher education, poor prison facilities, and so forth. Jack Bass and Walter Devries, *The Transformation of Southern Politics: Social Change and Political Consequence since 1945* (New York, 1976), contains a helpful summary chapter on changing Florida politics in the 1960s and early 1970s.

For more specialized works, an impressive, comprehensive study is David R. Colburn and Richard K. Scher, *Florida's Gubernatorial Politics in the Twentieth Century* (Tallahassee, 1980). The authors explore the effectiveness of individual governors and concur with Dauer that Florida's politics have been historically conservative. Peter D. Klingman, *Neither Dies Nor Surrenders: A History of the Republican Party in Florida, 1867–1970* (Gainesville, 1984), is more useful for scholars in the period before 1940, though it does include a good critique of Claude Kirk's governorship. William C. Havard and Loren P. Beth, *The Politics of Misrepresentation: Rural-Urban Conflict in the Florida Legislature* (Baton Rouge, 1962), is an excellent study declaring that malapportionment effectively thwarted representative government in Florida. See also James C. Clark, "The 1944 Florida Democratic Senate Primary," *FHQ*, 66 (April 1988).

On individual governors and their administrations, a very brief and uncritical monograph is Millard Caldwell, *The Administration of Millard F. Caldwell as Governor of Florida, 1945–1949* (Tallahassee, 1950). An excellent brief assessment of Fuller Warren's governorship is David R. Colburn and Richard K. Scher, "Florida Historical Gubernatorial Politics: The Fuller Warren Years," *FHQ*, 53 (April 1975). The authors see Warren as "progressive for his times" on some racial issues, and an excellent "salesman" for Florida. Farris Bryant, J. E. Dovell, and David G. Temple, *The Government and Politics of Florida* (Gainesville, 1957), surveys the subject with an emphasis on the modern period, a call for reform. Helen L. Jacobstein, *The Segregation Factor in the Florida Democratic Gubernatorial Primary of 1956* (Gainesville, 1972), contends that the primary vote for incumbent racial moderate LeRoy Collins in 1956 influenced the increasingly moderate racial policy in the state thereafter. The outstanding biography of a political leader in Florida in the period of 1940 to the present is Tom Wagy's *LeRoy Collins of Florida: Spokesman of the New South* (Tuscaloosa, 1985). *Florida across the Threshold: The Administration of Governor LeRoy Collins* (Tallahassee, 1961), provides valuable source data from Collins's speeches, recommendations, and policies on myriad aspects of public policy. Bob Graham's *Workdays: Finding Florida on the Job* (Miami, 1978), reports the findings of candidate for governor Bob Graham as he employs himself in a variety of jobs to meet Floridians and understand their problems.

On prominent political figures of the period who were not governors see Robert A. Gray, *The Power and the Glory: Some Tinsel Also* (Tallahassee, 1965), and *My Story: Fifty Years in the Shadow of the Near Great* (Tallahassee, 1958), the recollections of a political veteran of Tallahassee. Ormund Powers's *E. C., Mr. Speaker, E. C. Rowell* (Webster, Fla., 1977), is an amateurish history but contains valuable information about E. C. Rowell, Speaker of the Florida House in the mid-1960s.

There are several studies on the effects of specific state or federal legislation or programs on Floridians: Jimmie Darrell Phaup's "The Politics of Poverty: Controversy in Three South Florida Migrant Programs" (Ph.D. diss., University of Arizona, 1975); David R. Colburn and Richard Scher, "Aftermath of the Brown Decision: The Politics of Interposition in Florida," *Tequesta* 37 (1977); and Manning J. Dauer, *Florida and the United States Voting Rights Act of 1975* (Gainesville, 1982).

Though economic development is the key to understanding contemporary Florida, there is no single work which attempts to integrate and analyze secondary materials on this subject. Kyou Eun Choi, "Florida Business Cycles, 1920–1960" (Ph.D. diss., University of Florida, 1964), provides helpful information on Florida's economy to 1960. J. E. Dovell's *History of Banking in Florida* (Orlando, 1955), is indispensable in explaining the remarkable growth in Florida's banking. Dovell's *History of Banking in Florida: First Supplement, 1954–1963* (Orlando, 1964), is an update of the previous book. For a later period see John W. Budino, *History of Banking in Florida, 1964–1975* (Orlando, 1976). Baynard Kendrick's *Florida Trails to Turnpikes: 1914–1964* (Gainesville, 1964), establishes a parallel between Florida's economic growth and the growth of the state's road system. There is no history of Florida's railroads, though Seth H. Bramson's *Speedway to Sunshine: The Story of the Florida East Coast Railway* (Erin, Ontario, 1984), is a beginning and is beautifully illustrated. Phillip E. DeBerard, Jr., "Promoting Florida: Some Aspects of the Uses of Advertising and Publicity in the Development of the Sunshine State" (M.A. thesis, University of Florida, 1951), focuses on an important subject which deserves more careful treatment.

Florida's most important entrepreneur in the post–World War II period as well as the "grey eminence" behind its politics was Ed Ball, who administered the duPont estates in Florida: the Florida East Coast Railroad, the Florida National Bank, the St. Joe Paper Company, and thousands of acres of land in the state. Neither of the current biographies of Ed Ball is an acceptable historical work. *Ed Ball: Confusion to the Enemy* (Tampa, 1975), by Leon Odell Griffith, is journalistic and anecdotal and *Confusion to the Enemy: A Biography of Edward*

*Ball* (New York, 1976), by Raymond K. Mason and Virginia Harrison, is a flattering portrait by a personal friend and business associate. John D. Gates's *The DuPont Family* (Garden City, N.Y., 1979) provides a popular work by an informed insider which is especially contributive in the post–1940 period in relating controversies between Ball and his critics within the DuPont family. For an excellent, comprehensive discussion of Senator Claude Pepper's clash with Ed Ball over the latter's ownership and operation of the Florida East Coast Railway, see Alexander R. Stoesen, "Road from Receivership: Claude Pepper, the Dupont Trust, and the Florida East Coast Railway," *FHQ*, 52 (October 1973). Lee Butcher's *Florida's Power Structure: Who's Part of It and Why* (Tampa, 1976), describes, though it does not effectively document, the existence of a power elite in Florida in the mid–1970s.

There are some excellent studies of specific industries in Florida. Leonard E. Zehnder's *Florida's Disney World: Promises and Problems* (Tallahassee, 1975), recounts the history of the planning, building, and operation of Disney World as well as its impact on the economy and people of Central Florida. A good brief history of the land purchases which made Florida's Disneyland possible is in "Disney Creates a Magic Kingdom in Orlando," *Florida Trend* 26 (June 1983). Fred Blakey, *The Florida Phosphate Industry: A History of the Development and Use of a Vital Mineral* (Cambridge, 1973), provides a thorough, though mainly technical discussion of that industry from 1940 to 1970, its most productive period. One of Florida's smaller industries is discussed in Clarence Babcock's *Florida Petroleum Exploration, Production and Prospects* (Tallahassee, 1966). Charles D. Benson and William B. Faherty, *Moonport: A History of Apollo Launch Facilities and Operations* (Washington, D.C., 1978), is an authoritative study of the planning, construction, and operations of NASA's Apollo launch facilities from the origins of Cape Canaveral in 1957 to the launch of Apollo 17 in 1972. A similar but earlier study is Annie Mary Hartsfield, ed., *NASA Impact on Brevard County: Summary Report* (Tallahassee, 1966). Tom Wolfe's *The Right Stuff* (New York, 1979), focuses dramatically on the lives of the astronauts on the Cape during their training there.

Felix Muehlner's *Florida's Foreign Trade* (Gainesville, 1964), is concerned with the impact of foreign trade on the economy of Florida and the value and volume of exports and imports into the state in 1960. Florida Department of Commerce, *A Guide to Florida International Business and Investment Opportunities* (Tallahassee, 1978), is a scholarly book with promotional intent, designed to acquaint foreign businessmen with growing business opportunities in Florida. William G. Tyler and Charles A. Wheeler, *Florida's International Trade and Its Impact on the State Economy* (Gainesville, 1978), establishes that nearly three-fourths of Florida's exports are to the Caribbean and Latin America. Mira Wilkins, "Venezuelan Investment in Florida: 1979," *Latin American Research Review* 16 (1981), examines the extensive Venezuelan investments in Florida's agricultural land, banking, office building, and shopping centers mostly in Dade County in recent times.

There is little on labor in Florida since 1940. Ben Green, "If We'd Stuck Together," *Southern Exposure* 10 (May–June 1982) describes initiatives to organize mullet fishermen into a union in the period from the 1930s until 1958. A distressing revelation of forced labor and peonage among black turpentine and lumber camp workers which persisted in Florida until the 1950s is found in Jerrell H. Shofner, "Forced Labor in the Florida Forests, 1880–1950," *Journal of Forest History* 25 (January 1981). Shofner's "The Legacy of Racial Slavery: Free Enterprise and Forced Labor in the Florida in the 1940s," *Journal of Southern History* 67 (August 1981), illustrates the persistence of racially inspired involuntary servitude foisted on blacks by exploitatory white businessmen and landowners and their willing accomplices among county sheriffs and local police. Sandra M. Mohl's "Migrant Farmworkers in America: A Florida Case Study" (M.A. thesis, Florida Atlantic University, 1981) is an exposé of the plight of the migrant farmworkers in Florida from 1960 to 1980. For a well-researched article on one of the longest and most violent labor disputes in recent American labor history, see Barton Attman, "In the Public Interest? Ed Ball and the FEC Railway War," *FHQ*, 64 (July 1985).

Florida's agricultural economy and history in the twentieth century has been greatly influenced by Commissioner of Agriculture Nathan Mayo, who served this post for thirty-seven years (1923–60). For an evaluation of Mayo's career, see Martin M. LaGodna, "The Florida State Department of Agriculture during the Administration of Nathan Mayo" (Ph.D. diss., University of Florida, 1970). See also Martin LaGodna, "Greens, Grist, and Guernseys: Development of the Florida State Agricultural Marketing System," *FHQ*, 53 (October 1974), which chronicles Florida's innovative and successful programs to assist farmers through farmers' markets. A more detailed analysis of how effectively the state's Farmers' Markets served producers and buyers is in Stanley E. Rosenberger's "A History of the Florida Vegetable Industry and State Farmers' Markets for Vegetables" (Ph.D. diss., University of Florida, 1962). Henry F. Swanson, *Countdown for Agriculture in Orange County* (Orlando, 1975), effectively documents the post–1940 impact of urbanization on agriculture in Orange County. James T. Hopkins, *50 Years of Citrus* (Gainesville, 1960), is a history of the Florida Citrus Exchange (1909–59), a federated marketing cooperative virtually synonymous with the Florida citrus industry.

Joe A. Akerman's *Florida Cowman: A History of Florida Cattle Raising* (Kissimmee, Fla., 1976), provides an excellent description of a major industry in Florida as late as the 1950s. See also Alto Adams, Jr., *A Cattleman's Backcountry Florida* (Gainesville, 1985).

There are a large number of histories of Florida counties of varying quality for recent times. Among the best are Jerrell H. Shofner, *History of Apopka and Northwest Orange County, Florida* (Apopka, Fla., 1982), and Shofner's *History of Jefferson County* (Tallahassee, 1976). Richard Martin, *Consolidation: Jacksonville–Duval County* (Jacksonville, 1968), explains the merger of city and county government of Jacksonville and Duval County.

On education in Florida since 1940, there are several good histories, especially on higher education. Doak S. Campbell, *A University in Transition* (Tallahassee, 1964), narrates the development and remarkable growth of Florida State University from 1941 to 1957 (FSU was known as Florida State College for Women until 1947) from the viewpoint of the president of the institution during that period. Russell M. Cooper and Margaret B. Fisher, *The Vision of a Contemporary University* (Tampa, 1982), offers an apt description of the transition of the University of South Florida from an innovative new institution with bold academic plans in the 1960s to a traditional center of academe modeled on the University of Florida in the 1970s. Daniel L. Schaffer's *From Scratch Pads and Dreams: A Ten-Year History of the University of North Florida* (Jacksonville, 1982), provides a carefully researched history of one of Florida's newer, public universities. Leedell W. Neyland and John W. Riley, *The History of Florida Agricultural and Mechanical University* (Gainesville, 1963), is descriptively adequate, but interpretively sparse.

On Florida's private universities, see James W. Covington and C. Herbert Laub, *The Story of the University of Tampa: A Quarter Century of Progress from 1930–1955* (Tampa, 1955). A much more valuable contribution is Gilbert R. Lycan's *Stetson University: The First 100 Years* (DeLand, Fla., 1983). Charlton W. Tebeau's *The University of Miami: A Golden Anniversary, 1926–1976* (Coral Gables, 1976), is a readable and scholarly account by one of Florida's premier historians. Ralph D. Bald, *A History of Jacksonville University: The First Twenty-Five Years, 1934–1959* (Jacksonville, 1959), provides more of an account than an interpretation. Rackham Holt, *Mary McLeod Bethune: A Biography* (Garden City, N.Y., 1964), is a highly laudatory, undocumented life of the remarkable black educator and founder of Bethune-Cookman College. The best review of Mrs. Bethune's ideas is in Barbara G. Blackwell, "The Advocacies and Ideological Commitments of a Black Educator: Mary McLeod Bethune, 1875–1955" (Ph.D. diss., University of Conn., 1978). B. L. Perry, Jr.'s "Black Colleges and Universities in Florida," *Journal of Black Studies* 6 (September 1975), offers a brief history and rationale for the role of Florida's black colleges and universities by Florida A&M's president.

There is no careful systematic account, let alone an analysis, of public education in Florida, grades Kindergarten through 12. The best study is probably Arthur O. White's *One Hundred Years of State Leadership in Florida Public Education* (Tallahassee, 1979), which explores public education from the vantage of the state superintendents of public instruction, now commissioners of education. Further information on reactionary groups attempting to influence school policy is in Daniel R. Campbell, "Right-Wing Extremists and the Sarasota Schools," *Tampa Bay History* 6 (Spring–Summer 1984). Arthur O. White's *Florida's Crisis in Public Education: Changing Patterns of Leadership* (Gainesville, 1975), provides a scholarly treatment of the disturbing conditions which produced the Florida teacher strike (1968) and the resulting changes in the state's educational leadership. See also Kathleen P. Lyons, "Walkout: A History of the 1968 Florida Teachers' Strike" (M.A. thesis, Florida State University, 1975). Two studies of public school segregation worth examining are William L. Greer's "The Problem of Segregation in Florida Schools and Society" (M.A. thesis, Stetson University, 1955), and Joseph Aaron Tomberlin's "The Negro and Florida's System of Education" (Ph.D. diss., Florida State University, 1967).

An acceptable survey of Florida's health and social services to 1980 may be found in Lewis Bowman and Philip L. Smith, "Health and Social Services" in Manning J. Dauer, ed., *Florida's Politics and Government* (Gainesville, 1980).

Since Florida has a larger percentage of persons aged 65 and older than any other state, it is fitting that literature on this subject is abundant and serviceable. Gordon F. Streib contributes a useful summary essay on Florida's elderly, "The Aged," in Dauer, ed., *Florida's Politics and Government*. There are also several valuable statistical abstracts on older Floridians. These reports are published by established gerontology centers at the University of Florida, Florida State University, University of South Florida, and the University of Miami. Published volumes include John Kraft and Carter C. Osterbind, editors, *Older People in Florida* (Gainesville, 1979, 1981), and Charles Longino, *A Statistical Profile of Older Floridians* (Coral Gables, 1983). Concern for Florida's older population has been shown in a series of publications that resulted from the Southern Conference on Gerontology sponsored for twenty-seven years by the University of Florida. Proceedings are published by University Presses of Florida, Gainesville. Maria D. Vesperi, *City of Green Benches: Growing Old in a New Downtown* (Ithaca and London, 1985), provides a perceptive study of St. Petersburg, Florida. *Old Homes—New Families: Shared Living for the Elderly* (New York, 1984), by Gordon F. Streib, W. Edward Folts, and Mary Anne Hilker, is a study of small group homes for the elderly. An excellent recent article on an important aspect of the life of the aging in Florida is James L. Franke, "Citizen Input and Aging Policy: The Case of Florida," *Research on Aging* 7 (1985). The following dissertations also have special merit: William H. Haas, "The Social Ties between a Retirement Village and the Surrounding Community" (Ph.D. diss., University of Florida, 1980), and Raymond C. Matura, "The Politics of Aging in Florida: A Case Study of the Silver-Haired Legislature" (Ph.D. diss., University of Florida, 1982).

John J. Schwab, et al., *Social Order and Mental Health* (New York, 1979), investigates the effects of change, primarily since World War II, on the mental health of persons in Alachua County, Florida, with implications for all of Florida. Paul S. George, *Visions, Accomplishments, Challenges: Mount Sinai Medical Center of Greater Miami, 1949–1984* (Miami Beach, 1985), is the only professionally researched history of a Florida hospital.

Although there is no secondary account on law enforcement or prison policy in Florida for the contemporary period, a useful discussion of some of the state's problems in these areas may be found in *The Final Report of the Governor's Adult Corrections Reform Plan* (Tallahassee, 1973), and *Corrections Overcrowding Task Force* (Tallahassee, 1984). Frank Murphy, as told to Thomas Helm, *The*

*Frank Murphy Story* (New York, 1968), is a harrowing account of the inhumanity in Florida's state prison in the post–World War II period. Nathanial Lundrigan's "Development of the Florida Schools for Male Youthful Offenders, 1889–1969" (Ph.D. diss., Florida State University, 1975), is a historical narrative on Florida schools for juvenile offenders. William Wilbanks' *Murder in Miami: An Analysis of Homicide Patterns and Trends in Dade County, 1917–1983* (Lanaham, Md., 1984), is largely concerned with homicide in Dade County in 1980. Paul S. George co-authors the one chapter that supplies genuine historical perspective. According to the authors, boom and bust cycles and large numbers of transients contribute importantly to crime in Miami, past and present, though the Miami riot of 1980 and drug wars were new factors contributing to the homicide rate in 1980.

Blacks and women, two groups of Floridians who realized significant advancement in this period, are treated elsewhere in this study. Helen Halley, "A Historical Functional Approach to the Study of the Greek Community of Tarpon Springs" (Ph.D. diss., Columbia University, 1952) is a thorough study of this ethnic group, its place in the overall community, and the factors that have produced this effect.

An excellent summary of bibliographical material on the subject of Cubans in Miami is in Raymond A. Mohl's "Cubans in Miami: A Preliminary Bibliography," *Immigration History Newsletter* 16 (May 1984). Based on interviews and questionnaires with Cuban exiles to Florida from 1959 to 1962, Richard F. Fagan, Richard A. Brody, and Thomas J. O'Leary, *Cubans in Exile: Disaffection and the Revolution* (Stanford, 1968), is concerned with why Cubans left their home country in the early years of the Castro revolution. Juan M. Clark, "The Exodus from Revolutionary Cuba (1959–1974): A Sociological Analysis" (Ph.D. diss., University of Florida, 1975), is a well-researched study of Cuban migrants, legal and illegal, to the United States between 1959 and 1974. *Psycho-Social Dynamics in Miami* (Coral Gables, 1969), investigates the impact of the large 1960s Cuban migration to Miami on other population groups in the Miami area. "Que Pasa Miami? A Survey of Cultural Attitudes," by Sam Jacobs, *Miami Herald*, July 2–6, 1978, is a useful five-part article on attitudes of blacks, Latins, and white non-Latins on the effects of the meeting of cultures in South Florida in the 1960s and 1970s. Thomas D. Boswell and James R. Curtis, *The Cuban-American Experience: Culture, Images and Perspectives* (Totowa, N.J., 1983) is the first comprehensive, balanced survey on the Cuban-American experience that incorporates previous written materials on the subject. Clyde B. McCoy and Diana H. Gonzales, *Cuban Immigration and Immigrants in Florida and the United States: Implications for Immigration Policy* (Gainesville, 1985), provides a useful summary of literature that profiles the 125,000 Mariel refugees to the United States in 1980, demythologizing their image as a marginal and criminal population. Nancy E. Erwin's "The Importance of Neighborhoods for Cuban–Americans in Greater Miami" (Ph.D. diss., University of Florida, 1984), is an interesting comparative study of two Cuban-American communities (one assimilation, one expansion in the Miami-Dade area). Kenneth L. Wilson and W. Allen Martin, "Ethnic Enclaves: A Comparison of Cuban and Black Economics in Miami," *American Journal of Sociology* 87 (July 1982), explains the greater financial success of Cubans over blacks in Miami.

J. Anthony Paredes and Kay Lenihan, "Native American Population in the Southeastern States: 1960–70," *Florida Anthropologist* 32 (June 1973), uses census material to locate nearly seven-thousand native Americans in various counties of Florida. The study emphasizes that a growing number live in cities and that the Indian population as a whole is growing in the Southeast. Light T. Covington's "The Seminoles and Selective Service in World War II," *Florida Anthropologist* 32 (June 1979), establishes that Seminoles were not required to register for selective service in World War II largely because they were few in number and thought to be illiterate. Lucius F. Ellsworth and Jane E. Dysart, "West Florida's Forgotten People: The Creek Indians from 1830 until 1970," *FHQ*, 60 (April 1981), describes the reemergence of Creek Indians as a publicly identifiable group (possibly numbering 6,000 in 1970) in West Florida.

There are several good studies of Florida and Floridians in the arts and literature since 1940. Janette C. Gardner's *An Annotated Bibliography of Florida Fiction 1801–1980* (St. Petersburg, 1983), provides information on hundreds of fictional works on Florida in recent times. Ernest Hemingway lived in Key West from 1928 to 1940. His life there influenced the content of his novels, particularly *To Have and Have Not* (New York, 1965). James McLendon, *Papa Hemingway in Key West* (Miami, 1972), and Sharon Well's *Sloppy Joe's Bar: The First Fifty Years* (Key West, 1983), provide interesting information about Hemingway, his circle of literary visitors, and his fondness for Joe Russell's bar in Key West. Samuel I. Bellmam's *Marjorie Kinnan Rawlings* (New York, 1974), is a study which recommends reconsideration of Mrs. Rawlings as a major American literary figure. The best biography of the author of *The Yearling* is still, however, Gordon Bigelow's *Frontier Eden: The Literary Career of Marjorie Kinnan Rawlings* (Gainesville, 1966). *The Selected Letters of Marjorie Kinnan Rawlings* (Gainesville, 1983), edited by Gordon E. Bigelow and Laura V. Monti, contains nearly two hundred of Mrs. Rawlings's letters. They delineate her personality and reveal the contribution of the rural north Florida environment to her literary success.

Zora Neale Hurston's *Dust Tracks on a Road* (Philadelphia, 1942), is a moving autobiography of one of Florida's outstanding writers. *Mules and Men* (Bloomington, Ind., 1935), contains her penetrating description of Negro folktales and community life. See also Zora Neale Hurston, *Dust Tracks on the Road*, edited and introduced by Robert Hemenway (Urbana, 1985), which restores three chapters that were heavily revised or deleted from the original autobiography. An outstanding interpretation of Hurston's literary contributions is Robert E. Hemenway's *Zora Neale Hurston: A Literary Biography* (Urbana, 1977). Rita T. Schmidt's "With My Sword in My Hand: The Politics of Race and

Sea in the Fiction of Zora Neale Hurston" (Ph.D. diss., University of Pittsburgh, 1983), is a feminist interpretation of Hurston.

A gifted University of Florida professor's essays, articles, and vignettes dealing with the Florida scene in the 1960s and 1970s is in Harry Crews' *Florida Frenzy* (Gainesville, 1982). Many of the mystery novels of John D. MacDonald, set in Ft. Lauderdale, are recommended for descriptions of contemporary social life. His *Condominium* (Greenwich, Conn., 1975) is a commentary on grasping land development and the shoddy construction of a condominium on the Gulf Coast. Theodore Pratt's *Florida Roundabout* (New York, 1959), is a collection of essays and short stories deploring Florida's modernization by one if its best known novelists. Alistair Cooke's *Letters from America* (London, 1951), records observations of a winter trip to Florida by the acute English observer and social commentator.

There is remarkably little history on the subjects of Florida in World War II or the impact of the large military presence on life in Florida in recent times. Perhaps the most comprehensive effort in this regard is a chapter in James R. McGovern, *The Emergence of a City in the Modern South: Pensacola, 1900–1945* (De Leon Springs, Fla., 1976). See also Ben F. Rogers, "Florida in World War II: Tourists and Citrus," *FHQ* 39 (July 1960), and Leon O. Prior, "Nazi Invasion of Florida!" *FHQ*, 49 (October 1970). Robert D. Billinger, Jr., "With the Wehrmacht in Florida: The German POW Faculty at Camp Blanding, 1942–46," *FHQ*, 58 (October 1979), describes Florida's experience with more than four-thousand German prisoners of war held at Camp Blanding during World War II. James R. McGovern's *Black Eagle: The Life of General Daniel "Chappie" James, Jr.* (Tuscaloosa, 1985), describes the brilliant career of the military's first black, four-star general, who was born in Pensacola in 1920.

The history of religion in Florida in recent times is surely one of the neglected areas. The best work on this subject as well as the most pertinent to the contemporary period is Michael J. McNally, *Catholicism in South Florida 1868–1968* (Gainesville, 1982). The author concerns himself with broad questions affecting Catholicism in Florida, the impact of Vatican II, the effects of differences between American and Cuban Catholics, and the Church's relation to black Catholics and black Floridians. Other studies of religion in Florida are more concerned with organizational and parochial issues. These include William E. Brooks, ed., *From Saddlebags to Satellites: A History of Florida Methodism* (Maitland, Fla., 1969), and Joseph D. Cushman, Jr., *The Sound of Bells: The Episcopal Church in South Florida, 1892–1969* (Gainesville, 1976). Paul S. George, *An Enduring Covenant: Temple Emanu-El of Greater Miami, 1938–1988* (Miami Beach, 1988), chronicles the development of one of the most prominent conservative synagogues in Florida and the United States. Louis Ferm's "Billy Graham in Florida," *FHQ*, 60 (October 1981) establishes the popularity of that major evangelist in Florida.

A review of literature useful for an understanding of the history of Florida in the period 1940 to 1980 reveals that its strengths are in those areas where

Floridians have most needed to adapt to new environmental and demographic challenges; hence there are many works concerned with land and water management, with marked urban characteristics, and with urban-related social issues, civil rights for blacks, the plural culture of Miami, and problems of the elderly. The older, rural culture and economy, the period of the 1950s in general, the cultural staples—religion, public education, family life, and traditional women—have not fared as well. Clearly, a new and comprehensive text with social and cultural components is a major priority.

# 12

# BLACK FLORIDIANS

## JOE M. RICHARDSON AND MAXINE D. JONES

WHEN PEDRO MENENDEZ de Aviles put ashore in Florida in 1565, he brought slaves to work on his defenses, but slavery never became deeply entrenched in Spanish Florida. It became far more significant as a haven for slaves escaping from the British colonies. An excellent starting point for studying blacks in Spanish Florida is J. Leitch Wright, *Anglo-Spanish Rivalry in North America* (Athens, Ga., 1971); Jane Landers, "Spanish Sanctuary: Fugitives in Florida, 1687–1790," *Florida Historical Quarterly* (*FHQ*), 62 (January 1984); and Kenneth Wiggins Porter, *The Negro of the American Frontier* (New York, 1971).

Florida continued to be a sanctuary for runaways until it became a British possession in 1763. At this time blacks became more significant as plantation laborers. Then when the Revolutionary War began, loyalist planters fled there with their slaves. J. Leitch Wright, Jr., treats blacks during this period in *Florida in the American Revolution* (Gainesville, 1975); "Lord Dunmore's Loyalist Asylum in the Floridas," *FHQ*, 49 (April 1971), and "Blacks in British East Florida," *FHQ*, 54 (April 1976). Charles L. Mowat, *East Florida as a British Province,*

*1763–1783* (Berkeley, 1943), shows that by 1783 more than 2,500 slaves had been transferred to Florida from South Carolina alone.

At the end of the Revolutionary War, Florida reverted to Spain and again became a haven for runaways. Kenneth W. Porter in "Negroes and the East Florida Annexation Plot, 1811–1813," *Journal of Negro History* 36 (July 1951), suggests that the large number of escaped slaves in Florida was partially responsible for the unsuccessful annexation plot of 1811 and the First Seminole War. Black resistance significantly contributed to American failure in both instances. J. Leitch Wright's "A Note on the First Seminole War as Seen by the Indians, Negroes, and their British Advisors," *Journal of Southern History* 34 (November 1968), illustrates the close relationships between blacks, Indians and the British during the War of 1812.

The United States's acquisition of Florida in 1821 did not end the runaway slave problem. Vast unsettled areas, combined with the often close relationships between blacks and the Seminole Indians, made Florida an attractive refuge for local slaves and those from nearby states. These blacks of all categories frequently identified with Indian interests and collaborated with them during the Seminole Wars. The outstanding authority on blacks and the Seminoles is Kenneth W. Porter, who has written a score of articles on the subject, many of which have been conveniently collected into his *The Negro and the Frontier* (New York, 1971). J. Leitch Wright's *The Only Land They Knew: The Tragic Story of the American Indians in the Old South* (New York, 1981), includes an excellent chapter on general Indian-black relations.

Abolitionist Joshua R. Giddings, *The Exiles of Florida* . . . (Columbus, Ohio, 1858), describes the experiences of slaves who had escaped to Florida and state and national efforts to return them. Daniel F. Littlefield in *Africans and Seminoles: From Removal to Emancipation* (Westport, Conn., 1977), examines slavery, acculturation, and black citizenship rights. A useful supplement to Littlefield is Edwin C. McReynolds, *The Seminoles* (Norman, Okla., 1957).

Slavery in Florida has been adequately, if not definitively, treated. The basic work is Julia Floyd Smith, *Slavery and Plantation Growth in Antebellum Florida 1821–1860* (Gainesville, 1973). Older, but still valuable is Ulrich B. Phillips and James G. Glunt, eds., *Florida Plantation Records of George Noble Jones* (St. Louis, 1927). Susan Bradford Eppes, *The Negro of the South* (Chicago, 1925), is a romantic view of the "peculiar institution" by a member of a prominent slaveholding family. See also Margaret T. Ordonez, "Plantation Self-Sufficiency in Leon County, Florida: 1824–1860," *FHQ*, 60 (April 1982), and Michael G. Schene, "Sugar along the Manatee: Mayor Robert Gamble, Jr., and the Development of Gamble Plantation," *Tequesta* 41 (1981).

Black testimony about slavery in Florida can be found in George P. Rawick, *The American Slave*, vol. 17 (Westport, Conn., 1972), and Gary Mormino, "Florida Slave Narratives," *FHQ* 66 (April 1988). Larry Rivers's two articles, "Dignity and Importance: Slavery in Jefferson County, Florida, 1827–1860," *FHQ*, 61 (April 1983) and "Slavery in Microcosm: Leon County, Florida, 1824 to 1860," *Journal of Negro History* 66 (Fall 1981), offer a local perspective. Studies that treat city slavery include Harry P. Owens, "Appalachicola before 1861" (Ph.D. diss., Florida State University, 1966); Bertram H. Groene, *Antebellum Tallahassee* (Tallahassee, 1971); and Ernest F. Dibble, *Antebellum Pensacola and Military Presence* (Pensacola, 1974). An excellent treatment of slave religion is Robert L. Hall, " 'Do, Lord, Remember Me': Religion and Cultural Change among Blacks in Florida, 1565–1906" (Ph.D. diss., Florida State University, 1984). Information on Zephaniah Kingsley, a Florida planter who flaunted white mores of the period with his views on miscegenation, slavery, and black ability can be found in Philip S. May, "Zephaniah Kingsley, Non-Conformist," *FHQ*, 23 (January 1945) and Faye L. Glover, "Zephaniah Kingsley: Nonconformist, Slave Trader, Patriarch," (M.A. thesis, Atlanta University, 1970).

Much remains to be done on black resistance in Florida. Ray Grande, "Slave Unrest in Florida," *FHQ*, 55 (July 1976), is a brief introduction. Joe M. Richardson, ed., *Trial and Imprisonment of Jonathan Walker at Pensacola, Florida, for Aiding Slaves to Escape from Bondage* (Gainesville, 1974), discusses the attempt of a white northerner to assist slaves and the resulting white hostility. The domestic slave trade is treated in Julia F. Smith, "Slave Trading in Antebellum Florida," *FHQ*, 50 (January 1972). Because of its sparse settlement and long coast line, Florida was an ideal location for foreign and illegal trade in slaves. An enlightening article on the Cuban trade is Dorothy Dodd, "The Schooner Emperor: An Incident of the Illegal Slave Trade in Florida," *FHQ*, 13 (January 1935). Frances J. Stafford, "Illegal Importations: Enforcement of the Slave Trade Laws along the Florida Coast, 1810–1828," *FHQ*, 46 (October 1967), traces the United States's unsuccessful efforts to enforce slave trade laws. On the other hand, Kenneth F. Kiple, "The Case against Nineteenth-Century Cuba-Florida Slave Trade," *FHQ*, 49 (April 1971), tries to prove that the extensive contraband slave trade between Cuba and Florida is largely a myth.

Although free blacks never numbered more than one-thousand in antebellum Florida, their plight has attracted some historical attention. Julie Ann Lisenby, "The Free Negro in Antebellum Florida" (M.A. thesis, Florida State University, 1967), is the most thorough study. Other useful sources include Peter D. Klingman, "A Florida Slave Sale," *FHQ*, 52 (July 1973); Robert J. Walker, Jr., "Free Negroes in Florida to 1864" (M.S. thesis, Florida Agricultural and Mechanical University, 1955); Herbert J. Doherty, Jr., ed., "A Free Negro Purchases His Daughter," *FHQ*, 29 (July 1950); Rosalind Parker, "The Proctors—Antonio, George, and John," *Apalachee* (1946); and Russell Garvin, "The Free Negro in Florida before the Civil War," *FHQ*, 46 (July 1967). Free blacks were seldom welcome in Florida after it was acquired by the United States, as indicated in Ruth Barr and Modeste Hargis, "Voluntary Exile of Free Negroes of Pensacola," *FHQ*, 17 (July 1938).

Since Florida played a minor role in the Civil War, the state during that period has attracted relatively little attention. John E. Johns, *Florida During the Civil War* (Gainesville, 1963), contains a brief discussion of planters and slaves. Gerald Schwartz, ed., *A Woman Doctor's Civil War: Esther Hill Hawks's Diary* (Columbia, S.C., 1984), and Franke Fennell, "Blacks in Jacksonville, 1840–1865" (M.A. thesis, Florida State University, 1978), discuss black soldiers and contrabands in Jacksonville. The major engagement in which black troops were involved was the Battle of Olustee. The battle is detailed in Johns, *Florida during the Civil War*, and David Coles, " 'A Fight, a Licking, and a Footrace': The 1864 Florida Campaign and the Battle of Olustee" (M.A. thesis, Florida State University, 1985).

Reconstruction is perhaps the most exciting period in Florida history for blacks. They became free, founded their own institutions, secured an education, bought land, and exerted considerable political influence for a few years. William Watson Davis, *The Civil War and Reconstruction in Florida* (New York, 1913), for years the standard study, has been supplanted by Jerrell H. Shofner's *Nor Is It Over Yet: Florida in the Era of Reconstruction, 1863–1877* (Gainesville, 1974), and Joe M. Richardson, *The Negro in the Reconstruction of Florida, 1865–1877* (Tallahassee, 1965). A study by a black contemporary, and surprisingly favorable to white Floridians, is John Wallace, *Carpet Bag Rule in Florida: The Inside Workings of the Reconstruction of Civil Government in Florida after the Close of the Civil War* (Jacksonville, 1888). A useful white memoir is Ellen Call Long, *Florida Breezes; or, Florida, New and Old* (Jacksonville, 1883; facsimile reprint, Gainesville, 1962). For the view of an unabashed romantic and unreconstructed white see Susan Bradford Eppes, *Through Some Eventful Years* (Macon, Ga., 1926).

Obviously former slaves needed some assistance in adjusting to freedom, which was partially provided by the Freedmen's Bureau created in 1865. George R. Bentley's *A History of the Freedmen's Bureau* (Philadelphia, 1955), contains considerable information about Florida. See also Joe M. Richardson, "An Evaluation of the Freedmen's Bureau in Florida," *FHQ*, 41 (January 1963). One of the greatest adjustments both blacks and whites had to make was to a free labor system. An excellent study of the decline of agriculture in North Florida and how it affected former slaves is Clifton Paisley, *From Cotton to Quail: An Agricultural Chronicle of Leon County, Florida, 1860–1967* (Gainesville, 1968). Edward K. Eckerts's "Contract Labor in Florida during Reconstruction," *FHQ*, 47 (July 1968), shows that the new system too often resulted in debt peonage for blacks. Blacks did not accept such repression without resistance. They occasionally tried to improve their position by forming unions and striking, as indicated by Jerrell Shofner in "Militant Negro Laborers in Reconstruction Florida," *Journal of Southern History* 39 (August 1973), and "The Labor League of Jacksonville: A Negro Union and White Strike-breakers," *FHQ*, 50 (January 1972).

Among the positive aspects of Reconstruction was the creation of schools and the formation of black churches. Joe M. Richardson, "Christian Abolitionism:

The American Missionary Association and the Florida Negro," *Journal of Negro Education* 40 (Winter 1971), traces the activities of the major northern benevolent society for blacks. Bruce Rosen, "The Influence of the Peabody Fund on Education in Florida," *FHQ*, 55 (January 1977), notes that the Peabody Fund largely ignored black education. See also Murray D. Laurie, "Union Academy: A Freedmen's Bureau School in Gainesville, Florida," *FHQ*, 65 (October 1986). The best treatment of the black church is Robert L. Hall's dissertation mentioned previously. Also useful is Hall's "Tallahassee's Black Churches, 1865–1885," *FHQ*, 58 (October 1979). There is some discussion of the black family and black social life in Richardson's *The Negro in the Reconstruction of Florida*, but neither subject has yet received adequate treatment.

When the Civil War ended, President Andrew Johnson's reconstruction policy left political power in white hands. The Florida legislature passed a series of harsh, discriminatory laws subordinating blacks. The laws are discussed in Joe M. Richardson, "Florida Black Codes," *FHQ*, 47 (April 1969). In 1867 Congress passed legislation mandating black suffrage. From 1868 to 1876 blacks played a significant role in Florida politics. Black participation in the Constitutional Convention of 1868 is treated in Jerrell H. Shofner, "The Constitutional Convention of 1868," *FHQ*, 41 (April 1963), and Richard L. Hume, "Membership of the Florida Constitutional Convention of 1868: A Case Study of Republican Factionalism in the Reconstruction South," *FHQ*, 51 (July 1972). Naturally blacks were most prominent in the Republican party, as ably discussed in Peter D. Klingman, *Neither Dies Nor Surrenders: A History of the Republican Party in Florida, 1867–1970* (Gainesville, 1984). See also John A. Meador, "Florida Political Parties, 1865–1877" (Ph.D. diss., University of Florida, 1964).

General studies of Reconstruction in Florida deal with black politicians in varying degrees. Peter D. Klingman traces the life and times of Florida's only black United States representative in *Josiah Walls: Florida's Black Congressman* (Gainesville, 1976). Joe M. Richardson, "Jonathan C. Gibbs: Florida's Only Negro Cabinet Member," *FHQ*, 42 (April 1964), notes the outstanding, though brief, career of Gibbs. The career of a powerful politician and church leader in Leon County is sketched by Dorothy Dodd, "'Bishop' Pearce and the Reconstruction of Leon County," *Apalachee* (1946). Bess Beatty describes the views and activities of a black poet, politician, and newspaper editor in "John Willis Menard: A Progressive Black in Post–Civil War Florida," *FHQ*, 59 (October 1980). Information on other black politicians may be found in Emma L. Thronbrough, *T. Thomas Fortune: Militant Journalist* (Chicago, 1972). Black political power was circumscribed by both fraud and intimidation. Ralph L. Peek, "Lawlessness and the Restoration of Order in Florida, 1868–1871," (Ph.D. diss., University of Florida, 1965), depicts the violence during these troubled years and federal efforts to protect blacks. Parts of Peek's dissertation have been elaborated in articles; see especially "Curbing of Voter Intimidation in Florida," *FHQ*, 43 (April 1965), and "Election of 1870 and the End of Reconstruction in Florida," *FHQ*, 45 (April 1967). The election of 1876 marked the end of significant black political power in the state. For a thorough analysis of that election consult Jerrell H. Shofner's *Nor Is It Over Yet* and "Fraud and Intimidation in the Florida Election of 1876," *FHQ*, 42 (April 1964).

The Gilded Age was a tragic one for Florida blacks. They lost much of what had been gained during Reconstruction. They could expect discrimination, segregation, and disfranchisement. Edward C. Williamson, *Florida Politics in the Gilded Age, 1877–1893* (Gainesville, 1976), gives some attention to declining black political influence. Arnold M. Pavlovsky, "We Busted because We Failed: Florida Politics, 1880–1908" (Ph.D. diss., Princeton University, 1974), details white determination to maintain supremacy. See also Jesse J. Jackson, "Republicans and Florida Elections and Election Cases, 1877–1891" (Ph.D. diss., Florida State University, 1974). An overwhelming fear of Republican and black resurgence caused Florida to be the first ex-confederate state to disfranchise blacks. Despite disfranchisement, blacks retained some political influence in a few areas, as illustrated in Edward N. Akin, "When a Minority Becomes a Majority: Black Jacksonville Politics, 1887–1907," *FHQ*, 53 (October 1974). Barbara Ann Richardson, "A History of Blacks in Jacksonville, Florida, 1860–1895: A Socioeconomic Study" (Ph.D. diss., Carnegie-Mellon University, 1975), discusses politics as well as other aspects of black life. A general treatment of the rise of segregation and discrimination and the black response may be found in Wali Rashash Kharif, "The Refinement of Racial Segregation after the Civil War" (Ph.D. diss., Florida State University, 1983).

Generally blacks remained landless, unskilled laborers during the late nineteenth century. Jerrell H. Shofner depicts peonage labor in "Forced Labor in the Florida Forests, 1880–1950," *Journal of Forest History* 25 (January 1981). Susan Hamburger, "On the Land for Life: Black Tenant Farmers on Tall Timbers Plantation," *FHQ*, 66 (October 1987), focuses on black tenant farming on a former plantation in Leon County in the late nineteenth century. Blacks also made up a disproportionate share of convict workers. N. Gordon Carper, "The Convict Lease System in Florida, 1866–1923" (Ph.D. diss., Florida State University, 1964), traces the brutal lease system from its origin until the state legislature prohibited county leasing. Disfranchisement, segregation, and economic subordination did not end violence against blacks. Edward C. Williamson, "Black Belt Political Crisis: The Savage-James Lynching, 1882," *FHQ*, 45 (April 1967), illustrates that race relations were always volatile and that murder was easily provoked. Joseph B. Capponi, a black attorney and school principal in St. Augustine, published his response to the black condition in *Ham and Dixie: A Just, Simple and Original Discussion of the Southern Problem* (St. Augustine, 1895).

Some gains were made by Black Floridians in the Gilded Age. Blacks continued to pursue education and support their churches and fraternal societies, and a few were able to purchase land and businesses. Sharon Wells, *Forgotten Legacy: Blacks in Nineteenth-Century Key West* (Key West, 1982) lists names of black business people. The career of outstanding newspaper editor Matthew M.

Lewey is sketched in I. Garland Penn, *The Afro-American Press and Its Editors* (Springfield, Mass., 1891). The early life in Jacksonville of an outstanding black poet, educator, song writer, diplomat and civil rights leader is described in James Weldon Johnson, *Along This Way: The Autobiography of James Weldon Johnson* (New York, 1933). A splendid biography of this remarkable man is Eugene Levy, *James Weldon Johnson: Black Leader, Black Voice* (Chicago, 1975). Blacks' continuing pursuit of education is traced in Bonnie K. Edwards, "Negro Education in Florida: 1865–1900" (M.A. thesis, Florida State University, 1970), and Harry A. Kersey, Jr., "St. Augustine School: Seventy-five years of Negro Parochial Education in Gainesville, Florida," *FHQ*, 51 (July 1972). Barbara F. Agresti, "Household and Family in the Postbellum South: Walton County, Florida, 1870–1885" (Ph.D. diss., University of Florida, 1976), analyzed the unpublished federal census schedules and concluded that despite numerous hardships the black family was strengthened considerably during this period.

Conditions of blacks did not improve with the turn of the century. Donald H. Brogaw, "Status of Negroes in a Southern Port City in the Progressive Era: Pensacola, 1896–1920," *FHQ*, 51 (January 1973), details the decline of the economic and social status of Pensacola's black middle class. In Miami, blacks suffered from segregation, violence, police intimidation, and a double standard for black and white criminals, as illustrated by Paul S. George, "Policing Miami's Black Community, 1896–1930" *FHQ*, 57 (April 1979). See also George's "Criminal Justice in Miami: 1896–1930," (Ph.D. diss., Florida State University, 1975). Blacks often vigorously opposed humiliating class legislation. August Meier and Elliott Rudwick, "Negro Boycotts of Segregated Streetcars in Florida, 1901–1905," *South Atlantic Quarterly* 69 (Autumn 1970), indicates that black boycotts for a time prevented the segregation of streetcars in Jacksonville and Pensacola, but ultimately the protests failed. In "Custom, Law, and History: The Enduring Influence of Florida's 'Black Code'," *FHQ*, 55 (January 1977), Jerrell H. Shofner claims that Jim Crow laws of the 1880s went beyond the black codes of Reconstruction in separating the races. Racial segregation was more extensive in 1900 than in 1865.

In politics blacks were only an issue to be used against candidates. Arthur O. White, "Race, Politics and Education: The Sheats-Holloway Election Controversy, 1903–1904," *FHQ*, 53 (January 1975), shows how race was used against Superintendent of Public Instruction William N. Sheats. Two Wayne Flynt biographies, *Duncan Upshaw Fletcher: Dixie's Reluctant Progressive* (Tallahassee, 1971), and *Cracker Messiah: Governor Sidney J. Catts of Florida* (Baton Rouge, 1977), illustrate that blacks were not a serious factor in state politics. They still attended Republican state conventions to help select presidential candidates, but as George N. Greene, "Republicans, Bull Moose, and Negroes in Florida, 1912," *FHQ*, 43 (October 1964), demonstrates, national Republicans often advocated a "lily white" position in the South, which limited black influence. No wonder many black Floridians wanted to leave their homes. Jerrell H. Shofner, "Florida and the Black Migration," *FHQ*, 57 (January 1979), contends that the largest proportional migrations of blacks from the entire South occurred from West Florida, Tampa, and Jacksonville.

Black powerlessness can also be seen in their economic position and the continuing violence against them. Although the state had stopped leasing prisoners in 1919 and had prohibited county leasing in 1923, employers continued to hold indebted workers almost as slaves, according to Jerrell H. Shofner, "Postscript to the Martin Tabert Case: Peonage as Usual in the Florida Turpentine Camps," *FHQ*, 60 (October 1981). See also N. Gordon Carper, "Slavery Revisited: Peonage in the South," *Phylon* 37 (March 1976). White supremacy was constantly reinforced by violence against blacks. Shofner suggested in "Judge Herbert Rider and the Lynching at La Bell," *FHQ*, 59 (January 1981), that the mob ruled in Florida during the 1920s. John L. Wilson, "Days of Fear: A Lynching in St. Petersburg," *Tampa Bay History* 5 (Fall–Winter 1983) discusses the 1914 murder of John Evans. A 1934 lynching which received nationwide attention is ably treated in James R. McGovern and Walter T. Howard, "Private Justice and National Concern: The Lynching of Claude Neal," *The Historian* 42 (August 1981), and James R. McGovern, *The Anatomy of a Lynching, the Killing of Claude Neal* (Baton Rouge, 1982). Lynching in the 1920s was accompanied by renewed Klan activity. David Chalmers, "The Ku Klux Klan in the Sunshine State: The 1920s," *FHQ*, 42 (January 1964), depicts Klan violence.

In the face of great obstacles, blacks struggled to improve their status and gained some success, especially in education. In an incisive monograph Barbara R. Cotton, *The Lamplighters: Black Farm and Home Demonstration Agents, 1915–1965* (Washington, D.C., 1982) discusses how black agents, who were underpaid and often discriminated against, took "improved methods of farming and home economics to rural and urban dwellers." A readable account of the state's only publicly supported predominately black university is Leedell W. Neyland and John W. Riley, *The History of Florida Agricultural and Mechanical University* (Gainesville, 1963). Black educators organized the Florida State Teachers' Association in 1890. The FSTA is briefly traced until it merged with the Florida Education Association in 1966 in Gilbert L. Porter and Leedell W. Neyland, *The History of the Florida State Teachers' Association* (Washington, D.C., 1977).

Black education was not equally funded, and many white educators and politicians thought black education should be primarily vocational. The struggle over what type of education blacks should receive is treated in Neyland and Riley's *History of Florida Agricultural and Mechanical University* and Raymond Wolters, *The New Negro on Campus: Black College Rebellions of the 1920s* (Princeton, 1975). Information on black population, housing, health, social agencies, employment, churches, schools, business, and fraternal organizations in Tampa in the 1920s may be found in Arthur Raper, J. H. McGrew, and Benjamin Mays, *A Study of Negro Life in Tampa: Made at the Request of the Tampa Urban League and the Tampa Young Men's Christian Association* (Tampa, 1927).

There is no general study of Florida blacks during the Great Depression, but several works should be consulted. Enoch D. Davis, *On the Bethel Trail* (St. Petersburg, 1979), provides glimpses of black life both before and during the 1930s. Unemployment problems are noted in Edward D. Davis, "A Study of the Incidence and Effects of Unemployment in the Case of Five Hundred Negro Families of Tampa, Florida," *The Quarterly Journal* 4 (October 1935). Joseph A. Mannard, "Black Company Town: A Peculiar Institution in Pierce, Florida," *Tampa Bay History* 1 (Spring–Summer 1979), describes life in a small town. Education is discussed in D. E. Williams, "A Perspective of Florida Negro Schools," *The Quarterly Journal* 2 (November 1932), and Anna May Cleek, "The Development of Negro Education as an Integral Part of Public Education of Florida" (M.A. thesis, University of Cincinnati, 1933). Publications by two Florida educators are especially useful. John Irving E. Scott presents a personal account of the 1930s and 1940s of a man intimately involved with Florida education, including the struggle for equal salaries for black teachers, in *The Education of Black People in Florida* (Philadelphia, 1974). D. E. Williams, *A Brief Review of the Growth and Improvement of Education for Negroes in Florida, 1927–1962* (Atlanta, 1963), is written by a longtime state agent for black schools.

Much can be learned from biographies of important Floridians of the period. Lottie Clark, "Negro Women Leaders of Florida" (M.S. thesis, Florida State College for Women, 1942), gives interesting sketches of several black women. Leedell W. Neyland, *Twelve Black Floridians* (Tallahassee, 1970), is aimed at junior and senior high school readers but contains characterization of significant people who lived in Florida from 1866 to the present. Ray Charles and David Ritz's *Brother Ray* (New York, 1978), traces Ray Charles's early life in Greenville and several other Florida cities. There are several studies of Mary McLeod Bethune, outstanding educator and leader, who founded the Daytona Normal and Industrial School for Girls (later Bethune-Cookman College) in 1904 and became president of Bethune-Cookman College in 1932. Clarence G. Newsome, "Mary McLeod Bethune in Religious Perspective: A Seminal Essay" (Ph.D. diss., Duke University, 1982), claimed of Bethune that more than anyone between Booker T. Washington and Martin Luther King, Jr., "she stood at the helm of the Negroes' struggle for racial justice." A popular biography is Rackham Holt, *Mary McLeod Bethune: A Biography* (Garden City, N.Y., 1964). Consult also Jesse Walter Dees, *The College Built on Prayer: Mary McLeod Bethune* (Daytona Beach, 1953).

Some of the most exciting information about one aspect of Florida life comes from Zora Neale Hurston, who was born in the all-black town of Eatonville in 1901. Hurston knew the Florida locale well, and depicted both the landscape and the people with color and precision. *Mules and Men* (Philadelphia, 1935), is based largely on folklore collections from Florida. Although a novel, *Their Eyes Were Watching God* (Philadelphia, 1937), contains interesting characters that are obviously based on Hurston's Eatonville experience, autobiographical material is found in *Dust Tracks on a Road* (Philadelphia, 1942). Hurston's skill and enigmatic personality have stimulated several studies of the author and her works. A sensitive, thoughtful biography that attempts to unravel the puzzles of Zora Neale Hurston is Robert E. Hemenway, *Zora Neale Hurston: A Literary Biography* (Urbana, 1967). See also Theodore Pratt, "Zora Neale Hurston," *FHQ*, 40 (July 1961); Joyce O. Jenkins, "To Make a Woman Black: A Critical Analysis of the Women Characters in the Fiction and Folklore of Zora Neale Hurston" (Ph.D. diss., Bowling Green State University, 1978); and Alice Walker, ed., *I Love Myself When I am Laughing. . . And Then Again When I am Looking Mean and Impressive* (Old Westbury, N.Y., 1979).

A majority of the publications about black Floridians since World War II focuses on three issues: the increasing black role in politics, school desegregation, and the civil rights movement. Among the number of studies tracing the rise in black registration after decades of disfranchisement are Charles D. Farris, "The Reenfranchisement of Negroes in Florida," *Journal of Negro History* 39 (October 1954); William G. Carleton and Hugh D. Price, "America's Newest Voter: A Florida Case Study," *Antioch Review* 14 (December 1954); and Hugh D. Price, *The Negro and Southern Politics: A Chapter of Florida History* (New York, 1957). Annie Mary Hartsfield and Elston R. Roady, *Florida Votes, 1920–1962* (Tallahassee, 1963), clearly traces the increase of black registration, most of it in the Democratic party. Roy A. Jackson, "Registration and Party Affiliation: A Case Study of Black Floridians" (Ph.D. diss., Howard University, 1982), shows that registration remained primarily Democratic.

State politicians were still cautious about courting the black vote as late as 1956 for fear that it would alienate white voters. Discussions of this factor are found in Elston E. Roady, "The Expansion of Negro Suffrage in Florida," *Journal of Negro Education* 26 (Winter 1957); Helen L. Jacobstein, *The Segregation Factor in the Florida Gubernatorial Primary of 1956* (Gainesville, 1972); and David R. Colburn and Richard K. Scher, *Florida Gubernatorial Politics in the Twentieth Century* (Tallahassee, 1980). William G. Carleton, "Negro Politics in Florida: Another Middle-Class Revolution in the Making," *The South Atlantic Quarterly* 57 (Autumn 1958), suggests that black political power was relegated mostly to middle-class blacks and that they were still in the position of having to deliver the vote to white candidates. Blacks, however, were slow in gaining power on the local level, as seen in Gary Mormino, "Tampa: From Hell Hole to the Good Life" in Richard M. Bernard and Bradley R. Rice, eds., *Sun Belt Cities: Politics and Growth Since World War II* (Austin, 1983). Examinations of the black power structure in Orlando and Miami include John T. Washington, "Power in the Black Subcommunity of Orlando" (Ph.D. diss., University of Florida, 1977), and Natalie M. Davis, "Blacks in Miami and Detroit: Communities in Contrast" (Ph.D. diss., University of North Carolina at Chapel Hill, 1976).

One of the first serious attempts to desegregate Florida schools came in 1949, when Virgil D. Hawkins and several other blacks applied to the University of Florida Law School. The complex story of Hawkins's numerous lawsuits is untangled in Algia R. Cooper, "Brown v. Board of Education and Virgil Darnell Hawkins: Twenty-Eight Years and Six Petitions to Justice," *Journal of Negro History* 64 (Winter 1979), and Samuel Selkow, "Hawkins, the United States Supreme Court and Justice," *Journal of Negro Education*, 31 (Winter 1962). The broader struggle for desegregation came after the Brown case in 1954. The starting point for studying desegregation is Joseph A. Tomberlin, "The Negro and Florida's System of Education: The Aftermath of the Brown Case," (Ph.D. diss., Florida State University, 1967), and Tomberlin, "Florida and the School Desegregation Issue, 1954–59: A Summary Review," *Journal of Negro Education* 43 (Fall 1974). Tomberlin points out that the Brown decision was implemented only at black insistence. For the next several years progress reports were published, including that of Charles U. Smith and A. S. Parks, "Desegregation in Florida—A Progress Report," *Quarterly Review of Higher Education among Negroes* 25 (January 1957).

Florida fortunately escaped much of the turmoil that developed in other southern states. Robert H. Ackerman, "The Triumph of Modernization in Florida Thought and Politics: A Study of the Race Issue from 1954 to 1960" (Ph.D. diss., American University, 1967) attributes this, in part, to the state's high level of prosperity, which it hoped to maintain, and to moderate leadership. Perhaps the most significant factor in the desegregation struggle was the leadership of Governor LeRoy Collins. A thoughtful treatment of Collins's leadership is Thomas R. Wagy, *Governor LeRoy Collins of Florida: Spokesman of the New South* (University, Ala., 1985). David R. Colburn and Richard K. Scher, "Aftermath of the Brown Decision: The Politics of Interposition in Florida," *Tequesta* 37 (1977), ably traces the failure to stay desegregation. Collins's increasingly enlightened racial views are depicted in Sandra L. Fanning, "A Study of Changes in Racial Attitudes as Revealed in Selected Speeches of Leroy Collins, 1955–1965" (M.A. thesis, University of South Florida, 1969). Other material for the Collins years can be found in Allen Morris, ed., *Florida across the Threshold: The Administration of Governor Leroy Collins, January 4, 1955–January 3, 1961* (Tallahassee, 1961). Although Collins helped avoid the inflammatory rhetoric and massive resistance of other states, little desegregation occurred during his administration. Studies of the slow attempts to integrate public schools include James W. Jackson, "A History of School Desegregation in Lee County, Florida" (Ph.D. diss., University of Miami; 1970), Thomas D. Milligan, "An Investigation of Public School Desegregation in Polk County, Florida" (Ph.D. diss., George Peabody College for Teachers, 1967); and Carleton B. Bryant, "With More than Deliberate Speed: A Historical Study of Six Major Issues in Secondary Education in Palm Beach County, Florida, 1954–1972, From a Black Perspective" (Ph.D. diss., Florida Atlantic University, 1975). Everett A. Abney, "The Status of Florida's Black School Principals," *Journal of Negro Education* 43 (Winter 1974), notes the impact of desegregation on black school officials. White flight replaced residential segregation as a stumbling block to school desegregation. This issue is treated in Michael Giles, Douglas S. Galtin, and

Everett F. Cataldo, "The Impact of Busing on White Flight [in Florida]," *Social Science Quarterly* 55 (September 1974).

After the Brown decision Florida began to build black junior colleges. Carol L. Zion, "The Desegregation of a Public Junior College: A Case Study of Its Negro Faculty" (Ph.D. diss., Florida State University, 1965), claims that with integration many black faculty lost their positions. Black students gradually increased in number in Florida's white colleges, but life there was not always easy. Jomills H. Braddock likened their position to that of colonials in "Colonialism, Education and Black Students: A Social-Psychological Analysis" (Ph.D. diss., Florida State University, 1973). At nearly all predominantly white schools blacks formed student unions as support systems. James L. Palcic, "The History of the Black Student Union at Florida State University, 1968–1978" (Ph.D. diss., Florida State University, 1979), concludes that the BSU at Florida State broadened the curriculum and forced the hiring of black faculty and recruitment of black students. John Egerton, *The Black Public Colleges: Integration and Disintegration* (Nashville, 1971) deals with the impact of desegregation on black colleges. George E. Curry, *Jake Gaither: America's Most Famous Black Coach* (New York, 1977), not only describes the career of the legendary gentleman and coach but also tells the reader about segregation, black education, and desegregation.

In the Civil Rights struggle of the 1950s and 1960s, several cities in Florida played significant roles. Tallahassee experienced early civil rights activity. A readable study of Tallahassee is Glenda Alice Rabby, "Out of the Past: The Civil Rights Movement in Tallahassee, Florida" (Ph.D. diss., Florida State University, 1984). Gregory B. Padgett, "C. K. Steele and the Tallahassee Bus Boycott" (M.A. thesis, Florida State University, 1977), concentrates on a major figure in the Florida civil rights movement. Also useful are Charles U. Smith and Lewis M. Killian, *The Tallahassee Bus Protest* (New York, 1958), and Robert M. White, "The Tallahassee Sit-ins and Core: A Nonviolent Revolutionary Submovement" (Ph.D. diss., Florida State University, 1964). Susan Hamburger, "The 1968 Tallahassee Riots following the Assassination of Martin Luther King," *Apalachee* 9 (1984), describes that disorder. An excellent brief treatment of Tampa is Steven F. Lawson, "From Sit-in to Race Riot: Businessmen, Blacks and the Pursuit of Moderation in Tampa, 1960–1967," in Elizabeth Jacoway and David R. Colburn, eds., *Southern Businessmen and Desegregation* (Baton Rouge, 1982). Moderation, however, did not prevent violence, as indicated in Gayle E. Davis, "Riot in Tampa" (M.A. thesis, University of South Florida, 1976), and "Civil Rights Protest in Tampa: Oral Memoirs of Conflict and Accommodation," *Tampa Bay History* 1 (Spring–Summer 1979). Douglas L. Fleming, "Toward Integration: The Course of Race Relations in St. Petersburg, 1868 to 1963" (M.A. thesis, University of South Florida, 1973), is a limited but useful study of that city. Consult also Darryl Paulson, "Stay Out, the Water's Fine: Desegregating Municipal Swimming in St. Petersburg, Florida," *Tampa Bay History* 4 (Fall–Winter 1982), and Darryl Paulson and

Janet Stiff, "An Empty Victory: The St. Petersburg Sanitation Strike, 1968," *FHQ*, 57 (April 1979).

Historic St. Augustine was the scene of considerable disorder in 1963–64. Student sit-ins began in 1961, and the struggle culminated during Easter week, 1964. Martin Luther King, Jr., said that St. Augustine was the most lawless city he had worked in. David R. Colburn, "The St. Augustine Business Community: Desegregation, 1963–64," in *Southern Businessmen and Desegregation*, concluded that unlike businessmen in several Florida cities, St. Augustine businessmen played no positive role. *Racial and Civil Disorder in St. Augustine: Report of the Legislative Investigating Committee* (Tallahassee, 1965), is helpful to researchers. Information on race relations, economics, and social conditions of Miami blacks is found in United States Commission on Civil Rights, *Confronting Racial Isolation in Miami: A Report of the United States* (Washington, D.C., 1982). A black perspective is seen in Manning Marable, "The Fire This Time: The Miami Rebellion, May 1980," *The Black Scholar* 11 (July-August 1980). Charlotte Downey-Anderson, "The 'Coggins Affair': Desegregation and Mores in Madison County, Florida," *FHQ*, 59 (April 1981) shows the rigidity of racial customs in a rural county. David Dukes, *I Have Never Lived in America* (New York, 1978), is the memoirs of a civil rights activist in North Florida. Edward D. Davis, *A Half Century of Struggle for Freedom in Florida* (Orlando, 1981), is an account by a participant. Enoch D. Davis, *On the Bethel Trail* (St. Petersburg, 1979), concentrates on the 1950s and 1960s.

One of the goals of blacks in the civil rights movement was to secure equal justice. Margaret Vandiver analyzed black-white sentences between 1924 and 1966 in "Race, Clemency and Executions in Florida: 1924–1966" (M.A. thesis, Florida State University, 1983). Although race was less significant than she anticipated, Vandiver found that the defendants' and victims' race influenced decisions to execute or grant clemency. Jeffrey Lichson, *David Charles: The Story of the Quincy Five* (Tallahassee, 1974), illustrates the difficulty of blacks in court. William Bradford Huie, *Ruby McCollum, Woman in the Suwannee Jail* (New York, 1956), is a story of interracial sex, murder, and race relations in Suwannee County. The study by Steven F. Lawson, David R. Colburn, and Darryl Paulson, "Groveland: Florida's Little Scottsboro," *FHQ*, 65 (July 1986), demonstrates that Florida's courts and sheriffs could, as late as the 1950s, assure the same injustice to blacks earlier served by vigilantes and lynch law. Sociologists have long argued that the appointment of black policemen was an effective contribution to justice and respect for the law. Several cities had a few black policemen in the 1940s, but it remained for the civil rights movement to force many areas to accept their first black officials. James A. Ball, "A Study of Negro Policemen in Selected Florida Municipalities" (M.S. thesis, Florida State University, 1954), treats black policemen in West Palm Beach, Belle Glade, and Tallahassee. Most black policemen at this time patrolled only in black sections. Brian C. Hennessy, "The Racial Integration of Urban Police Departments in the South: Case Studies of Three North Florida Cities" (M.A. thesis, Florida

State University, 1974), deals with policemen in Tallahassee, Jacksonville, and Pensacola.

At the same time that black Floridians were fighting for their civil rights they were struggling, often unsuccessfully, for economic security. As already noted, Jerrell H. Shofner has shown that dismantling the convict lease system did not end peonage. Pete Daniel, *The Shadow of Slavery: Peonage in the South, 1901–1969* (Urbana, 1972), uses Florida examples. Sara Harris and Robert F. Allen, *The Quiet Revolution: The Story of a Small Miracle in American Life* (New York, 1978), treats migrant workers as does Jimmie D. Phaup, "The Politics of Poverty: Controversy in Three South Florida Migrant Programs" (Ph.D. diss., University of Arizona, 1975). Mark Lane, *Arcadia* (New York, 1970), is about the poisoning of seven black children, but also notes economic conditions. Not all rural blacks were poverty-stricken, migrant workers. William J. Simmons, "Johnson's Crossing, an Institutional Analysis of a Rural Black Community" (Ph.D. diss., University of Florida, 1981), discussed home ownership in a rural Northeast Florida black community. A good study of black housing, economics, family, and the transition of females to womanhood is Molly Crocker Dougherty, *Becoming a Woman in a Rural Black Culture* (New York, 1978).

The greatest extremes of black poverty and prosperity are found in cities, since blacks are heavily concentrated in metropolitan areas. Migration to the cities has been especially rapid since the 1940s. Eugene G. Sherman, "Urbanization and Florida's Negro Population: A Case Study" (Ph.D. diss., Purdue University, 1968), assesses the impact of urbanization on Florida's black population. George Kirkham, *Signal Zero* (Philadelphia, 1976), graphically depicts the crime and squalor in Jacksonville. Unfortunately, little has been written about the numerous blacks who have succeeded admirably in business, the professions, and the general work force, but Paul M. Decker, "A Study of Job Opportunities in the State of Florida for Negro College Graduates," *Journal of Negro Education* 29 (Winter 1960), shows that court rulings concerning racial integration were beginning to improve employment opportunities for blacks. Useful studies of black housing include William A. Stacey, *Black Home Ownership: A Sociological Case Study of Metropolitan Jacksonville* (New York, 1972), and Reinhold P. Wolff, *Negro Housing in the Miami Area: Effects of the Postwar Building Boom* (Coral Gables, 1951).

There is no general study of black Floridians, but in the last two decades considerable effort has been made to uncover black history. Professional historians have begun to include blacks in local and state studies. Jerrell H. Shofner, *History of Jefferson County* (Tallahassee, 1976), is an example. Space constraints prevent inclusion of many useful publications in this essay, but two things are clear. Much research remains to be done, yet there is a surprisingly large body of material available on the exciting history of black Floridians.

# 13

# WOMEN IN
# FLORIDA HISTORY

LINDA VANCE

FLORIDA'S WOMEN MADE significant and lasting contributions to the development of the state, for it was they who were the civilizers and community builders, the ones who organized and maintained Florida's first hospitals, libraries, schools, orphanages, charities, museums, parks, symphonies, churches, and other social institutions. Women also gave impetus to and lobbied tirelessly for most of the state's progressive legislation—its child labor laws, pure food and drug laws, conservation and wildlife protection measures, its educational, welfare and penal reforms, and its public health programs.

But women and their achievements appear only sparingly in the state's conventional historical literature. To find Florida's women one must eventually turn to the women themselves, to their own writings, diaries, reminiscences, correspondence, organization and club minutes, directories, yearbooks, and other such sources. Works such as Charlton Tebeau's and Ruby Leach Carson's *Florida from Indian Trail to Space Age* (Delray Beach, Fla., 1965); Ellwood Nance's *The East Coast of Florida* (Delray Beach, Fla., 1962); D. B. McKay's *Pioneer Florida* (Tampa, 1959); Harry G. Cutler's *History of Florida, Past and Present*

(New York, 1923); George M. Chapin's *Florida, 1513–1913, past, present, and future* (Chicago, 1914); William T. Cash's *The Story of Florida* (New York, 1938); Homer Edward Moyer's *Who's Who and What to See in Florida* (St. Petersburg, 1935); Charles L. Trinkner's *Florida Lives* (Hopkinsville, Ky., 1966); and Henry S. Marks, *Who Was Who in Florida* (Huntsville, Ala., 1973), all include information on women. The best books providing short biographical sketches of prominent women are Lucy Blackman's classic two-volume work *The Women of Florida* (Jacksonville, 1940), which covers women who were active prior to the 1940s, and Eloise Cozen's five-volume *Florida Women of Distinction* (Daytona Beach, 1956–1973), which features short sketches of women who made their marks after 1940. See also Gary Mormino and Milly St. Julien, *Women in Florida History* (Tampa, 1988), a brochure that accompanies a slide presentation on Florida's women.

City and county histories are good sources for ferreting out information on specific women. Examples are Mary Barr Munroe's "Pioneer Women of Dade County" *Tequesta* 3 (July 1943); Eve Bacon's *Orlando, a Centennial History, 1875–1975* (Orlando, 1977); Gussie Rudderman's *Gainesville Women of Vision* (n.p., 1981); Leora Sutton's "Women in Pensacola, 1765–1965" (unpub. ms., 1977); Ellen Babb and Milly St. Julien's, "Public and Private Lives, Women in St. Petersburg at the Turn of the Century," *Tampa Bay History* 8 (Spring–Summer 1986); Cathy Slusser's "Women of Tampa Bay: A Photo Essay," *Tampa Bay History* (Fall 1983); Caroline Avice's "A Few Women of Old St. Augustine" (unpub. ms., 1937); Pleasant Gold's *History of St. Augustine* (St. Augustine, 1928); Clara Hayden's *A Century of Tallahassee Girls as Viewed From the Leaves of Their Diaries* (Atlanta, n.d.); and Derna de Pamphilis, editor, *Profiles: An Appreciation of Martin County Women* (Stuart, Fla., 1976). Additionally, American Mothers Committee, *Mothers of Achievement in American History, 1776–1976* (Rutland, Vt., 1976), and Edward James's three-volume *Notable American Women, 1607–1950* (Cambridge, Mass., 1971), include a few nationally prominent Florida women.

With the exception of archaeological and anthropological monographs, there is no substantive work pertaining to Florida's Indian women, although several articles do exist. They include Tom Knott's *Indian Princesses and Soldiers* (Yankeetown, Fla., 1974), T. Frederick Davis's "Milly Francis and Duncan McKrimmon," *Florida Historical Quarterly (FHQ)*, 21 (January 1943); D. Elderdice's "Pocahontas of Florida" *Mentor* (February 1928); and B. Gonciar's "Indian Princess of Florida: Ulehlah, Daughter of Ucita, Chief of the Hirrihiqua Tribe," *Hobbies* (October 1948). Twentieth-century Anglo women worked to improve the lot of the Seminole Indians, and much information about Seminole women can be garnered by reading what these women wrote. Mary Barr Munroe's "The Seminole Women of Florida," *Tequesta* 41 (1981), is a reprint of an article that was first published at the turn of the century. August Burghard's *Watchie-Esta-Hutrie* (Ft. Lauderdale, 1968), tells the story of Ivy Stranahan's labors among the Indians. Minnie Moore Willson, the most outspoken defender of the Indians, wrote extensively about the Seminoles. Useful are her "Tales from an Old Bandanna Mammy," *Florida Magazine* (1903); *The Seminoles of Florida* (Philadelphia, 1896); and *The Birds of the Everglades and Their Neighbors, the Seminole Indians* (Tampa, 1920). The story of deaconess Harriet Bedell, who devoted much of her life to the Seminoles, can be found in William Hartley and Ellen Hartley's *A Woman Set Apart* (New York, 1963), and in "Reverend Harriet Bedell," *Naples Now* (1979). Harry A. Kersey, Jr., in "Educating the Seminole Indians of Florida, 1879–1970," *FHQ* (July 1970), discusses the efforts of Willson, Stranahan, and others and some of the state's feminine organizations that promoted Seminole welfare. Pat Cunningham and Cooper Kirk's "The Seminoles Today: An Oral History Interview with Betty Mae Jumper," *Broward Legacy* (Winter–Spring 1981), recounts the modern-day life of a Seminole woman.

Apache women who lived briefly in Florida are treated in two essays: Omega East's "Apache Prisoners in Fort Marion, 1886–87," *El Escribano* 6 (January 1969), and Luis Arana and Eugenia B. Arana, "The Wives of Geronimo," *El Escribano* 10 (July 1973).

Little has been written about women who lived in Florida during the two Spanish eras, but the following works are helpful: Jane Landers' "Women in East Florida, 1784–1821" (unpub. ms., 1980); Luís Rafael Arana's "A Bitter Pill of the Widow Cendoya," *El Escribano* 9 (April 1972); Jack Holmes's *Do It! Don't Do It! Spanish Laws on Sex and Marriage* (Pensacola, 1982); Susan Fatio L'Engle's *Notes of My Family and Recollections of My Early Life* (Jacksonville, 1887); and Amy Bushnell's unpublished manuscript "Women of the Parallel Politics: Spanish and Hispanized Indian, in Seventeenth-Century Florida" (1986).

Italian and Cuban women are treated in Gary Mormino and George Pozzetta's "Immigrant Women in Tampa: The Italian Experience, 1890–1930," *FHQ*, 61 (January 1983), and in Helen Smith's "Immigrant Women in Ybor City, 1900" (unpub. ms., 1982). The Ruby Diamond manuscript collection listed at the University of Florida library contains correspondence between female members of a pioneer St. Augustine Jewish family.

Prominent black women, such as Eartha M. M. White, Zora Neale Hurston, and Mary McLeod Bethune, are covered in such works as Leedell Neyland's *Twelve Black Floridians* (Tallahassee, 1970); Robert E. Hemenway's *Zora Neale Hurston: A Literary Biography* (Urbana, 1977); Louise Beauchamp's "Zora Neale Hurston and the Mural of Florida History" *Apalachee* 9 (1980); Margaret Wilson's "Zora Neale Hurston: Author and Folklorist," *Negro History Bulletin* 4 (1982); Theodore Pratt's "Zora Neale Hurston," *FHQ*, 40 (July 1961); Rackham Holt's *Mary McLeod Methune: A Biography* (Garden City, N.Y., 1964); and Elaine Smith's "Mary McLeod Bethune and the National Youth Administration," in *Clio Was a Woman: Studies in the History of American Women*, edited by Mabel D. Deutrich and Virginia C. Purdy (Washington, D.C., 1980). The pamphlet "Pioneer Women of East Florida" *African Methodist*

*Church, 1532* (n.d.), describes the accomplishments of a group of black church women; Samuel Proctor in "Yankee Schoolmarms in Postwar Florida," *Journal of Negro History* 44 (1959), recounts the experience of white women teaching in freedmen's schools after the Civil War; and Carrie Elliot writes about an ex-slave woman in "Aunt Memory at the Fair," *Tallahassee Historical Society Annual* 2 (1935).

Several valuable contemporary accounts of life in nineteenth-century Florida were written by women. The most significant of these accounts are Ellen Call Long's *Florida Breezes: or, Florida, New and Old* (Jacksonville, 1883; facsimile reprint, Gainesville, 1962), *Negro Witchcraft* (unpub. ms., 1893), and "Princesse Achille Murat: A Biographical Sketch," *FHQ*, 2 (July 1909); Susan Bradford Eppes's *Through Some Eventful Years, 1926* (facsimile reprint, Gainesville, 1967), and *The Negro of the Old South* (Chicago, 1925); Mary Elizabeth Dickinson's *Dickinson and His Men: Reminiscences of the [Civil] War in Florida, 1890* (facsimile reprint, Gainesville, 1962); and Margaret Fleming Biddle's *Hibernia, The Unreturning Tide* (New York, 1947). Bertram Groene's "Lizzie Brown's Tallahassee," *FHQ*, 48 (October 1969), describes life in Tallahassee in the 1850s, and the trials and tribulations of a woman managing a plantation alone are recounted in Ellen Hodges and Steve Kerber's "Children of Honor: Letters of Winston and Octavia Stephens, 1861–62," *FHQ*, (July 1977), and their "Rogues and Black-Hearted Scamps: Letters of Winston and Octavia Stephens, 1862–63," *FHQ*, (July 1978). The story of the colorful and winsome nineteenth-century belle, Ellen Adair White, is treated in Margaret A. Uhler's " 'Florida White': Southern Belle," *FHQ*, (January 1977), and Eliza Horn, *The Diary of Eliza Horn, Way Key, East Florida, 1867–69* (Jacksonville, 1937), tells one girl's story of life on a Florida key during Reconstruction.

During the 1880s and 1890s, several women wrote travel guides and descriptive narratives about the state. Among the best are Helen Ingram's *Florida. Beauties of the East Coast*, (Jacksonville, 1893), and Helen K. Ingram *Tourists' and Settlers' Guide to Florida* (Jacksonville, 1895); Jane Griffings's *Letters from Florida* (Lancaster, N.H., 1883); Helen G. Warner's *Home Life in Florida* (Louisville, 1889); Eunice Beecher's *Letters from Florida* (New York, 1879); Margaret DeLand's *Florida Days* (Boston, 1889); Abbie M. Brook's *Petals Plucked from Sunny Climes, 1880* (facsimile reprint, Gainesville, 1976); Harriet Beecher Stowe's *Palmetto Leaves, 1873* (facsimile reprint, Gainesville, 1968), and her "Our Florida Plantation," *Atlantic Monthly* (1879).

Women's history as well as local history would be much poorer without the reminiscences of pioneer women. Included in this genre are Ruth Robbins Beardley's *Pioneer in the Everglades* (Ft. Pierce, Fla., n.d.); Mrs. Charles Gibson's *Pioneering in Hillsborough County, Florida* (n.p., 1972); Ruby Leach Carson's "Her [Julia Tuttle's] Faith Brought the Railroad to Miami," *Florida Living Magazine* (August 1956); Thelma Peters's *Memoirs of Estell DesRocher Zumwalt: A Miami Pioneer* (Miami, 1974), and her *Miami 1909, with Excerpts from Fannie Clemons' Diary* (Miami, 1985); Kenneth Hooker's *Susan*

*Huntington Hooker, a [Miami] Memoir* (New York, 1952); Emily L. Bell's *My Pioneer Days in [Ft. Pierce] Florida* (Miami, 1928); Adelaide H. Reed's "[Bradenton] Florida Pioneer," *FHQ*, 37 (October 1958); Edna M. Harvey's "My Life in South Florida" *Tequesta* 43 (1983); Mary D. Conrad's "Homesteading in [Lemon City] Florida during the 1890s" *Tequesta* 17 (1957); Judith Wade's "Margaret Elizabeth Daniel Lee: Pinellas Pioneer," *Tampa Bay History* 3 (Spring 1981); Charlotte Niedhauk's "Pioneering on Elliot Key, 1934–35" *Tequesta* 29 (1969); Lula M. Pallicer's "Pioneer New River Schoolgirl," *Broward Legacy* (Summer 1982); and Morning E. McDaniel's "Memoirs of a Pioneer [Ft. Myers] Girl," *Tampa Bay History* 5 (Fall 1983). The life of Swedish pioneers in the Orlando area as told from the pages of a young girl's diary is found in Jean Yothers and Paul W. Wehr's "Diary of Kena Fries," *FHQ*, (January 1984).

Florida's women first gained public recognition through their formal associations, such as local women's clubs, the Women's Christian Temperance Union, and others. The histories, yearbooks, minutes, and directories yield some of the richest material on the state's women. In this vein one should examine Lucy W. Blackman's *The Florida Federation of Women's Clubs, 1895–1939* (Jacksonville, 1939); Estella L. Crow's *History of the Miami Woman's Club, 1900–1955* (Miami, 1957); *The Woman's Club of Jacksonville: Golden Jubilee, 1897–1947* (Jacksonville, 1947); *The Florida Bulletin* (1921–1926) and *The Florida Clubwoman* (1927 to date), both official organs of the Florida Federation of Women's Clubs; Gertrude Kent's "Housekeeper's Club of Coconut Grove," *Update* 4 (April 1977); Thelma Peters's "A Home for the Working Girl" *Update* 4 (April 1977); Ida DeGarmo's *Life Story of Minnie E. Neal, President of the Women's Christian Temperance Union, Florida* (n.p., 1936); *Annual Meeting of the Women's Christian Temperance Union of Florida* (Jacksonville, 1884); Nell S. Murfree's *History of Martha Reid Chapter, No. 19, United Daughters of the Confederacy* (n.p., 1971); Cathryn G. Lancaster's *Early Years of the Florida Division of the United Daughters of the Confederacy, 1896–1921* (Winter Park, Fla., 1983); Mrs. Townes R. Leigh's *History of the Florida Division of the United Daughters of the Confederacy* (n.p., 1927); May Mann Jennings's "Women [Club] Work in Florida," *Florida Magazine* (April 1922); Letty M. Fifield's *History of Jacksonville YWCA* (Jacksonville, 1950); George B. Utley's "Florida Library Association," *Florida Library Bulletin* 1 (1927); and Lucille N. Lindsay's "Three Areas Enriched by Florida Women from 1900 to 1920," (unpub. ms., 1968).

Literature reflecting the critical involvement of women in environmental matters includes Lucy W. Blackman's *The Florida Audubon Society, 1900–1935* (n.p., 1935); Marjory Stoneman Douglas's *The Everglades, River of Grass* (New York, 1947); Emily P. Dieterich's "Birds of a Feather: The Coconut Grove Audubon Society, 1915–1917" *Tequesta* 45 (1985); Jean E. Little's "The Life and Work of Jeanette T. Connor" (M.A. thesis, Stetson University, 1933); *Jacksonville Garden Club, Founder's Circle Yearbook* (Jacksonville, 1927); Ella G. Alsop's *History of the Florida Federation of Garden Clubs*

(Jacksonville, 1943); Mrs. J. A. Hendley's *Make Florida Worthy of the Name 'Land of Flowers'* (Gainesville, 1916); May Mann Jennings's "Royal Palm State Park," *Mr. Foster's Travel Magazine* (January 1919), and her "Conservation in Florida," *Christian Science Monitor* (October 1925); and Linda Vance's "May Mann Jennings and Royal Palm State Park," *FHQ*, 55 (July 1976).

Public health and medical care were major concerns of women in Florida. The following works have helped to document this interest: L. M. Goggins, "Florida's First Institute for Midwives" *Public Health Nursing* 3 (1934); William M. Straight, M.D., "Pensacola Campaign through a Nurse's Eye," *The Journal of the Florida Medical Association*, 56 (August 1969), and his "Lady Doctor [Eleanor Galt Simmons] of Coconut Grove" *The Journal of the Florida Medical Association* 56 (August 1969); Anna Darrow, "Old Doc Anna," *The Journal of the Florida Medical Association* 61 (1974); Mrs. James DeVito, "Progress of the Woman's Auxiliary of the Florida Medical Association," *The Journal of the Florida Medical Association* 61 (January 1974); Elizabeth D. Vickers, "F. Elizabeth Crowell: Pensacola's Pioneer Nurse," *The Journal of the Florida Medical Association* 70 (August 1983), and her "Francis Elizabeth Crowell: Pioneering Angel of Mercy in Turn of the Century Pensacola," *Pensacola History Illustrated* 1 (1984); Richard A. Martin, *A Century of Service: St. Luke's Hospital, 1873–1973* (Jacksonville, 1973); and Edith Gray, *The History of the Jacksonville Chapter of the American Red Cross, World War I Period* (Jacksonville, n.d.).

In addition to public health and medical matters, women assisted their communities through their churches and synagogues. Helpful here are Presbyterian Church, U.S.A., *Synod of Florida: Women of the Church, a House Not Made with Hands* (Bradenton, 1964); Joe M. Richardson, "'We Are Truly Doing Missionary Work,' Letters from American Missionary Association Teachers in Florida, 1864–1874," *FHQ*, 54 (October 1975); and Jane Quinn, *The Story of a Nun: Jeanie Gordon Brown* (St. Augustine, 1978), and her "Nuns in Ybor City: The Sisters of St. Joseph and the Immigrant Community," *Tampa Bay History* 5 (Spring–Summer, 1983).

From its earliest history women were the state's educators, establishing and staffing many of its pioneer educational institutions. Works which document this involvement include Myra Marshall's "'Mrs. Mathematics': Reminiscences of Broward County," *Broward Legacy* 5 (Winter–Spring, 1982); Lula F. Miller's *Perspectives: Fifty Years of Bartram School, 1934–84* (Jacksonville, 1984); Venila L. Shores's "Florida State College for Women," *Tallahassee Historical Society* 3 (1937); Sister Mary Alberta's "A Study of the Schools Conducted by the Sisters of St. Joseph of the Diocese of St. Augustine, Florida, 1866–1940" (M.A. thesis, University of Florida, 1940); Sister Thomas McGoldrick's "The Contributions of the Sisters of St. Joseph of St. Augustine to Education, 1866–1960" (M.A. thesis, University of Florida, 1961); *Lest We Forget: Silver Anniversary History of the Florida Congress of Parents and Teachers, 1923–1948* (Orlando, 1948); Alice Fry's "Recollections of a Florida Schoolteacher," *FHQ*, 43 (January 1965); Gertrude Kent's "The Coconut Grove

School," *Tequesta*, 31 (1971); and Sarah Lou Hammond's "Anna E. Claires and Kindergarten Education in Florida," in Florida State University Research Council, ed., *Florida Educators* (Tallahassee, 1959).

There is a small but solid body of literature that has traced women's struggle for the franchise and political equality in Florida. It includes Annette Elizabeth Taylor's "The Woman Suffrage Movement in Florida," *FHQ*, 36 (July 1957); Kenneth R. Johnson's "The Women Suffrage Movement in Florida" (M.A. thesis, Florida State University, 1966), and his "Florida Women Get the Vote," *FHQ*, 48 (1970); David L. Lawrence's "The Women's Rights Movement in Florida: From Suffrage to Equal Rights" (M.A. thesis, University of South Florida, 1980); James R. McGovern's "Helen Hunt West: Florida's Pioneer for ERA," *FHQ*, 57 (July 1978); Joan S. Carver's "The First League of Women Voters in Florida: Its Troubled History," *FHQ*, 63 (April 1985), her "Women in Florida Politics, 1928–1978," *Journal of Politics* (August 1979), and her "The Equal Rights Amendment in the Florida Legislature," *FHQ*, 60 (April 1982); Allen Morris's "Florida's First Woman Candidates," *FHQ*, 63 (April 1985); and Evelyn Jean Davis, "The Socialization of Women into Politics: A Case Study of the League of Women Voters" (Ph.D. diss., Florida State University, 1983). For Florida women as lawmakers, see Mary Carolyn Ellis and Joanne V. Hawks, "Creating a Different Pattern: Florida's Women Legislators, 1928–1986," *FHQ*, 66 (July 1987).

Florida's women have always been workers, but these labors are poorly documented. The few works which exist include Works Progress Administration, *Florida. Women's and Professional Division* (Washington, D.C., 193?); U.S. Women's Bureau, *Women in Florida Industries* (Washington, D.C., 1930); Yearbooks of the Florida Federation of Business and Professional Women's Clubs (P. K. Yonge Library, University of Florida, Gainesville); Lucy F. O'Brien's "The Tribune's First Woman Reporter," *Tampa Bay History* 4 (Spring 1982); Bernadette K. Loftin's "A Woman Liberated: Lillian C. West, Editor," *FHQ*, 52 (April 1974); Jean Sneed's "The Florida Newspaper Woman of 1970" (M.A. thesis, University of Florida, 1970); James R. McGovern's "'Sporting Life on Line': Prostitution in Progressive Era Pensacola," *FHQ*, 54 (October 1968); Robert Johnson, "Florida's Female Executives: Climbing on Their Own Merits," *Florida Trend* 19 (December 1976); and "Women in the Law—Introduction," *Florida Bar Journal*, 18 (November 1984).

The most immediate need in the field of Florida women's history is good biographies of the state's most important female citizens. Available to date are Linda Vance's *May Mann Jennings, Florida's Genteel Activist* (Gainesville, 1986); Lillian Gilkes' *Cora Crane: A Biography of Mrs. Stephen Crane* (Bloomington, 1960); Samuel Bellman's *Marjorie Kinnan Rawlings* (New York, 1974); Gordon Bigelow's *Frontier Eden: The Literary Career of Marjorie Kinnan Rawlings* (Gainesville, 1966); Forrest Wilson's *Crusader in Crinoline, the Life of Harriet Beecher Stowe* (Philadelphia, 1941); Johanna Johnston's *Runaway to Heaven:*

*The Story of Harriet Beecher Stowe* (Garden City, N.Y., 1963); and the already noted biographies of Zora Neale Hurston and Mary McLeod Bethune. Thus, there remains much to do, for "the harvest truly is plenteous, but the laborers are few."

# 14

# THE SEMINOLE AND MICCOSUKEE INDIANS OF FLORIDA

JOHN K. MAHON

LIKE THE OTHER tribes of North America, the Florida Indians failed to develop a written language. Lacking written Indian history, the only record of the Florida Indians was set down by white men, and filtered through white culture.

Sources covering large segments of Florida Indian history include: Wyatt Blassingame, *Seminoles of Florida* (Tallahassee, n.d.); James W. Covington, "Seminole Leadership: Changing Substance, 1858–1958," *Tequesta* 40 (1980); Charles H. Fairbanks, *The Florida Seminole People*, Indian Tribal Series, (Phoenix, 1973); Harry A. Kersey, "Educating the Seminole Indians of Florida, 1879–1969," *Florida Historical Quarterly* (*FHQ*), 49 (July 1970); Harry A. Kersey, Jr., "Seminole Indians of Florida," in *Southeastern Indians since Removal*, ed., Walter Williams (Athens, Ga., 1979); Robert Thomas King, "The Florida Seminole Polity, 1858–1978," (Ph.D. diss., University of Florida, 1978); Edwin C. McReynolds, *The Seminoles* (Norman, Okla., 1957); Minnie Moore-Wilson, *The Seminoles of Florida* (New York, 1896); Wilfred T. Neill, *Florida's Seminole Indians* (Silver Springs, Fla., 1952); and Irwin M. Peithman, *The Unconquered Seminole Indians* (St. Petersburg, 1957).

The aboriginal tribes of Indians in Florida were these: Calusa, Tocobago, Apalachee, Timucua (various bands); Potano, Ocali, Utina, Yustega, Saturiwa, Agua Dulce, Acuera, and Ibi. All disappeared leaving a vacuum into which eventually came other bands from southeastern North America, most of them of the Muskogean family. The newcomers were Yamassee, lower Creeks, upper Creeks, Oconee, Chiaha, Tamathli, Tallassees, and Eufalas. The Eufalas brought with them Hichiti, the forebear of the modern Miccosukee language. The others spoke Muskogee. The two tongues are not mutually intelligible, and have been a factor that divided the Indians into two separate groups.

By 1815 there were about five-thousand of the post-aborigine Indians in Florida. Already the various Muskogean bands were becoming known as "Seminolies," taken by some people to mean wild ones, and by others to refer to Indians who wanted to remove themselves from the Creeks. Even when drawing away from the Creeks, they shaped their culture around clans as the Creeks did. Lineage was matriarchal; when a man married he went to live with his wife's clan—he could not marry within his own— and leadership, insofar as it was hereditary, followed the female line. Women owned most of the personal property, which they could keep, moving their husbands out, if found unsuitable. Separation was easy and free of stigma.

Since Seminole men, like the Creeks, attained distinction only through war and hunting, they put their energies into those activities, leaving the women to do the manual labor. Ritual, drawn from the Muskogean culture, regulated day-to-day living. The pivotal ceremony was the annual green corn dance in which the life of the tribe was symbolically renewed and purified. A council of elders sat in judgment on individuals who had violated the mores. The entire tribe then pleaded with supernatural forces to grant them good crops and good hunting and to preserve them from destruction.

During the Second Spanish Period, 1783–1821, the Indians, Seminole and Miccosukee, firmly established themselves in North Florida. The interior of Florida in reality belonged to the Indians. Certain skillful chiefs were able to play the English off against the Spanish and to acquire from English traders the kinds of goods they could not supply themselves. They became possessors of large herds of cattle. Early in the nineteenth century, then, Florida was proving to be an excellent habitat for these Indians.

See Jerald Milanich and Samuel Proctor, eds., *Tecahale: Essays on the Indians of Florida and Southeastern Georgia during the Historic Period* (Gainesville, 1978); Adelaide Bullen, *Florida Indians of Past and Present* (Gainesville, 1965); William C. Sturtevant, "Creek into Seminole," *North American Indians in Historical Perspective*, eds., Eleanor Leacock and Nancy Lurie (New York, 1971); John R. Swanton, *Early History of the Creek Indians and Their Neighbors*, Bureau of American Ethnology (BAE) Bulletin 73, (Washington, D.C., 1922); Swanton, *Religious Beliefs and Medical Practices of the Creek Indians*, 42nd Annual Report, BAE, 1924, 1925, (Washington, D.C., 1928); Swanton, *Social Organization and Social Usages of the Indians of the Creek Confederacy* (Washington, D.C., 1928); Verner W. Crane, *The Southern Frontier, 1670–1732* (Ann Arbor, 1929); Kenneth Wiggins Porter, "The Cowkeeper Dynasty of the Seminole Nation," *FHQ*, 30 (April 1952); Porter, "The Founder of the 'Seminole Nation'—Secoffee or Cowkeeper?" *FHQ*, 27 (April 1949); William C. Sturtevant, "Spanish-Indian Relations in Southeastern North America," *Ethnohistory* 9 (Winter 1962); Mark F. Boyd, ed.,"A Topographical Memoir [of Hugh Young] on East and West Florida with Itineraries of Gen. Jackson's Army, 1918," *FHQ*, 13 (July and October 1934, and January 1935); Henry S. Halbert and T. H. Ball, *The Creek War of 1813 and 1814*, (Chicago, 1895); Frank L. Owsley, Jr., *Struggle for the Borderlands: The Creek War and the Battle of New Orleans, 1812–1815* (Gainesville, 1981); Mark F. Boyd, *Florida Aflame: Background and Onset of the Seminole War, 1835* (Tallahassee, 1951); John K. Mahon, *History of the Second Seminole War, 1835–1842* (Gainesville, 1967); Francis Harper, ed., *The Travels of William Bartram* (New Haven, 1958); Caleb Swann quoted in Henry Schoolcraft, *Historical and Statistical Information Respecting the History, Condition and Prospects of the Indian Tribes of the United States* (Philadelphia, 1851–1857); John M. Goggin, "Source Materials for the Study of the Florida Seminole Indians" (laboratory notes no. 3, Anthropology Department, University of Florida, 1959); William H. Simmons, *Notices of East Florida with an Account of the Seminole Nation of Indians* (Charleston, 1822); Alexander Spoehr, *Camp, Clan and Kin among the Cow Creek Seminoles of Florida*, Field Museum of Natural History, Anthropological Series 33, no. 3 (Chicago, 1941); Spoehr, *Kinship System of the Seminoles of Oklahoma*, Field Museum of Natural History, Anthropological Series 33, no. 2, (Chicago, 1942); Howard F. Cline, *Notes on Colonial Indians and Communities in Florida, 1700–1821;* and Charles H. Fairbanks, *Ethnohistorical Report on the Florida Indians*. Both Cline and Fairbanks are photocopied in *Florida Indians*, vols. 1-3, (New York, 1973, 1974). See also Emma Lila Fundaburk, *Southeastern Indians, Life Portraits: A Catalog of Pictures, 1564–1860* (Luverne, Ala., 1958), and J. Leitch Wright, Jr., *Anglo-Spanish Rivalry in North America* (Athens, Ga., 1971).

Beginning in the 1770s slaves ran away from their masters in the southeastern United States and created settlements adjacent to Indian villages in Florida. Their relationship with the red men was that of peasant to lord in the feudal system; they paid tribute in kind but were not chattel. Many in the United States regarded Florida as part of their natural domain and sought means to acquire it from Spain. To that end the United States government in 1811 supported a revolt in East Florida known as the Patriot War, but as war with England loomed, the Madison administration, unwilling to fight both England and Spain, withdrew its clandestine support.

Once the War of 1812 was over, the United States grew more aggressive again, leading to the First Seminole War in 1817–18. Major General Andrew Jackson arrived in March 1818 to punish the Indians. On 26 March, he crossed the international boundary with 3,500 men, two-thirds of them Creek warriors, willing as usual to side with the white men against other Indians. In less than a month, Jackson destroyed the fighting power of the Seminoles west of the Suwannee River; he then went on to conquer St. Augustine, Pensacola, and St. Marks, the only points actually controlled by Spain.

The Spanish government, certain that it could not hold Florida, transferred it to the United States in 1821 for some not very valuable considerations. Between four and five-thousand Indians were transferred with the land. There were some guarantees for the red men in the transfer treaty, but the United States never honored them. The transfer was the beginning of the end of prosperity for the Florida Indians.

See Charles R. Paine, "The Seminole War of 1817–1818" (M.A. thesis, University of Oklahoma, 1938); Mahon, *The Second Seminole War*; Rembert W. Patrick, *Aristocrat in Uniform: Duncan L. Clinch* (Gainesville, 1963); Robert V. Remini, *Andrew Jackson and the Course of American Empire* (New York, 1977); Thomas S. Woodward, *Reminiscences of the Creek and Muskogee Indians* (Montgomery, 1859; reprinted 1939); J. Leitch Wright, Jr., "A Note on the First Seminole War . . . ," *Journal of Southern History* 34 (November 1968); Rembert W. Patrick, *Florida Fiasco: Rampant Rebels on the Georgia-Florida Border, 1810–1815* (Athens, Ga., 1954); Kenneth Wiggins Porter, "Negroes and the Seminole War, 1817, 1818," *Journal of Negro History* 36 (July 1951); Joshua R. Giddings, *The Exiles of Florida* (1858; facsimile reprint, Gainesville, 1964); Fairbanks, "A Topographical Memoir [of Hugh Young]" (Young was with Andrew Jackson); John Griffin, ed., "Some Comments on the Seminoles in 1818," *Florida Anthropologist* (*F.A.*) 10 (1957); and Virginia Bergman Peters, *The Florida Wars*, (Hamden, Conn., 1979).

United States agents negotiated the Treaty of Moultrie Creek, September 1823, by which they attempted to confine the Indians to 4,032,940 acres of poor land without access to the ocean or the Gulf. Confinement was not successful; so a policy of removal was tried. This conformed to the national policy enacted in 1830 to transplant all Indians dwelling east of the Mississippi River to the west. As before, the red men denied the validity of two removal treaties of 1823 and 1833, and refused to leave their homeland. When violence became frequent, white Floridians demanded immediate removal or else extermination.

Intransigence on both sides resulted in the Second Seminole War, 1835–1842. At the end of seven years the Indian population in Florida stood at around 300; 3,824 Indians had been captured and shipped out and unknown numbers had died. The remaining 300 had been gradually driven into the wetlands of South Florida.

See Clarence E. Carter, ed., *Territorial Papers of the United States: Florida Territory*, vols. 22–25 (Washington, D.C., 1956–1962); Mahon, *The Second Seminole War*; John T. Sprague, *The Origin, Progress and Conclusion of the Florida War* (New York, 1848; facsimile reprint, Gainesville, 1964); George A. McCall, *Letters from the Frontiers* (Philadelphia, 1868; facsimile reprint, Gainesville, 1974); Simmons, *Notices*; Charles Vignoles, *Observations upon the Floridas* (New York, 1823); Frederick Cubberly, "Ft. King," *FHQ*, 5 (Jan. 1927); Charles J. Kappler, *Indian Affairs: Laws and Treaties*, second edition, 2 vols. (Washington, D.C., 1904); Mark F. Boyd, "Horatio S. Dexter and the Events Leading to the Treaty of Moultrie Creek," *F.A.* 11 (September 1958); "A Diary of Joshua Nichols Glenn, St. Augustine in 1823," *FHQ*, 29 (October 1945); *Senate Document 151*, 10 February 1836 and *HR Document 267 and 271* (these three in the 24th Cong., 1st sess. 1836); George E. Buker, *Swamp Sailors* (Gainesville, 1973); Milton Meltzer, *Hunted Like a Wolf: The Story of the Seminole War* (New York, 1972); Peters, *The Florida Wars*; George Walton, *Fearless and Free: The Seminole Indian War* (New York, 1977); John Bemrose, *Reminiscences of the Second Seminole War* (Gainesville, 1966); Myer M. Cohen, *Notices of Florida and the Campaigns* (Charleston, 1836; facsimile reprint, Gainesville, 1966); Ethan Allen Hitchcock, *Fifty Years in Camp and Field . . .* , ed. W. A. Croffut (New York, 1909); Jacob Rhett Motte, *Journey into Wilderness. . .*, ed. James F. Sunderman, (Gainesville, 1953); [Woodburne Potter], *A Late Staff Officer, the War in Florida* (Baltimore, 1836); [W. W. Smith], *A Lieutenant of the Left Wing, Sketch of the Seminole War* (Charleston, 1836); Herbert J. Doherty, Jr., *Richard Keith Call* (Gainesville, 1961); Patrick, *Clinch*; Chester Kieffer, *Maligned General: The Biography of Thomas S. Jesup* (San Rafael, Calif., 1979); William Hartley and Ellen Hartley, *Osceola: The Unconquered Indian* (Hawthorne, 1973); Charles W. Elliott, *Winfield Scott: The Soldier and the Man* (New York, 1937); Holman Hamilton, *Zachary Taylor*, 2 vols. (New York, 1941, 1951); Edward S. Wallace, *General William Jenkins Worth...* (Dallas, 1953); Kenneth Wiggins Porter, several articles on blacks and Seminoles in the *Journal of Negro History* and the *FHQ*; Mahon, *The Second Seminole War*; Michael Paul Duffer, "The Seminole-Black Alliance in Florida..." (M.A. thesis, George Mason University, 1972); and *The Army and Navy Chronicle, 1835–1842*, which replaced *Military and Naval Magazine*, March 1833–August 1835.

During the seven years following the Second Seminole War, increased white pressure for land sent survey teams into places that the Indians considered theirs. Incidents of violence and destruction of property increased, illustrating once again the inability of the two races to live peacefully in close quarters. Actual warfare broke out once more in 1855, continuing intermittently for the next two years. This sporadic conflict is known as the Third Seminole War (1855–58).

See James W. Covington, *The Billy Bowlegs War* (Chuluota, Fla., 1982); Andrew P. Canova, *Life and Adventures in South Florida* (Palatka, Fla., 1885); Logan U. Reavis, *Life and Military Services of General William Selby Harney* (St. Louis, 1878); George Rollie Adams, "General William Selby Harney, Frontier Soldier, 1800–1889" (Ph.D. diss., University of Arizona, 1983); J. O. Parrish, *Battling the Seminoles, Featuring John Akins Scout* (Lakeland, Fla., 1930); John M. Schofield, *Forty-Six Years in the Army* (New York, 1897); Charles H. Coe, *Red Patriots: The Story of the Seminoles* (1898; facsimile reprint, Gainesville, 1974); Sturtevant, "Creek into Seminole"; Loomis L.

Langdon, "Campaigning in the Everglades," *The Helping Hand* 31 (July 1899); Kenneth Wiggins Porter, "Billy Bowlegs in the Seminole Wars," *FHQ*, 55 (January 1967); Ray B. Seley, Jr., "Lt. Hartsuff and the Banana Plants," *Tequesta* 23 (1963); Alexander S. Webb, "Campaigning in Florida in 1855," *Journal of the American Military Service Institution* 45 (November–December 1909); Patricia R. Wickman, "A Trifling Affair: Loomis Lyman Langdon and the Third Seminole War," *FHQ*, 63 (January 1985).

The Civil War scarcely touched the Florida Indians. During this time they made another in a series of radical readjustments necessary to survive under white pressure. They began to cultivate small, widely scattered plots, relying too on hunting and fishing. Now they lived in chickees instead of cabins, and wore loose, cool, but protective, clothing. They became skilled in making and handling large dugout canoes. The processes of survival were carried out by extended family units. Their new life-style was sharply different from the cattle herding and village dwelling of Spanish times. Except for occasional trips to white-run trading posts, they were isolated from white men.

The clan system ordered the lives of both Seminoles and Miccosukees, who shared many similarities. Both lived in similar chickees and wore the same clothing. The principal observable difference between them was language; each still spoke its own tongue.

See Alan K. Craig and Christopher Peebles, "Ethnoecological Change among the Seminoles, 1740–1840," *Geoscience and Man* 5 (10 June 1974); Harry A. Kersey Jr., *Pelts, Plumes, and Hides: White Traders among the Seminole Indians, 1870–1930* (Gainesville, 1975); Frederick A. Ober, "Ten Days with the Seminoles," *Appleton's Journal of Literature, Science and Art* 14, numbers 332, 333 (July and August 1875); Richard H. Pratt, *Battlefield and Classroom*, ed. Robert M. Utley, (New Haven, 1964); Spoehr, *Camp*; Spoehr, *The Florida Seminole Camp*, Field Museum Anthropological Series 33 no. 3, (25 December 1944); William C. Sturtevant, ed., "R. H. Pratt's Report on the Seminoles in 1879," *F.A.* 9 (1956); and MacCauley's report printed as "The Seminole Indians of Florida," BAE Annual Report, 1883–1884, (Washington, D.C., 1887).

Sale of state wetlands beginning in the 1880s reduced Indian hunting and fishing ranges. From 1906 to 1913, the buyers dug canals to drain the northeastern portion of the Everglades, and in 1928 the state built the Tamiami Trail, opening much of the new dry land. Since the Indians had no claims to any land valid under white law, they appeared to be in danger of being dispossessed. To avert this, sympathetic white people formed themselves into Indian aid societies to buy land for the red men. By 1900 they had purchased 23,000 acres; then in 1917 the State set aside 100,000 acres in the Everglades for them. Instead of occupying these areas, the Indians began to move slowly from camps deep in the Everglades to the land beside the Tamiami Trail. The federal government opened three reservations: Dania, 475 acres in 1911; Brighton, 35,779 acres in 1936; and Big Cypress, 42,800 acres in 1937.

By 1900, the Seminole Indians still led a good, independent life, but in spite of reservations, the space they needed was shrinking. To trade with white dealers, the red men relied heavily on egret plumes and alligator hides. After Congress outlawed the killing of egrets, and later also protected alligators, the Indians turned to otter, raccoon, and other marketable skins, but white competitors outdid them there.

Life for the Indians became very difficult during the Great Depression. The Indians put increased effort into cultivating small gardens for food, and some families became tourist attractions at resorts around Miami. Others worked in the fields for agribusinesses, exploiting the rich mucklands uncovered by draining. Bright garments, miniature dugouts, sofkee spoons, and other souvenirs the men and women could make brought in some money. Here again, the Seminoles were undertaking another radical readjustment of their life-style.

After 1885, the federal government began to concern itself with the Florida Indians, in that year placing an agent among them. Agents came and went, the Indians remained poor and behindhand in education and in white relationships. This was the case when Franklin D. Roosevelt became president and inaugurated the New Deal. The latter touched and altered almost every aspect of American life, including Indian affairs. The instrument of change was the Indian Reorganization Act (The Wheeler-Howard Act) passed in 1934. One of its objects was to mandate a framework of tribal government that could articulate effectively with the various state and federal agencies. Such organization was entirely outside the Seminole experience. Such government as they had was unstructured, centered around the clans and around the elders of the tribal council. The clans regulated most aspects of normal living, and could take drastic action when abnormal conditions developed.

See Charles B. Corry, *Hunting and Fishing in Florida*, Second Edition (Boston, 1896); James W. Covington, the following seven citations: "The Brighton Indian Reservation, 1935–1938," *Tequesta* 36 (1976); "The Dania Reservation, 1911–1927," *F.A.* 29 (December 1976); "Federal and State Relations with the Florida Seminoles, 1875–1901," *Tequesta* 32 (1972); "Florida Seminoles, 1900–1920," *FHQ*, 53 (October 1974); "The Seminoles and the Civilian Conservation Corps," *F.A.* 34 (December 1981); "The Seminoles and Selective Service in World War II," *F.A.*, 32 (June 1979); "The Seminole Indians in 1908," *F.A.* 26, (December 1981); Alan Craig and David McJunkin, "Stranahan's: The Last of the Seminole Trading Posts," *F.A.* 24 (June 1971); Lorenzo D. Creel, *Report of Investigation of the Seminole Indians in Florida*, National Archives, BAE records (Washington, D.C., 1911); James L. Glenn, *My Work among the Florida Seminoles*, ed. Harry A. Kersey, Jr., (Gainesville, 1982); Robert F. Greenlee, "Ceremonial Practices of the Modern Seminoles," *Tequesta* 1 (August 1942); and William B. Hartley, *A Woman Set Apart* [Deaconess Bedell], (New York, 1963).

The next twelve titles are by Harry A. Kersey, Jr.: *Pelts, Plumes and Hides* (Gainesville, 1975); "The Case of Tom Tiger's House," *FHQ* 53 (January 1975);

with Mark S. Goldman, "The Dania Indian School, 1927–1936, *Tequesta* 39 (1979); "Federal Schools and Acculturation among the Florida Seminoles, 1927–1954," *FHQ* 59 (October 1980); "Florida Seminoles and the Census of 1900," *FHQ* 60 (October 1981); "Friends of the Seminole Society, 1899–1926," *Tequesta* 34 (1974); "Private Societies and the Maintenance of Seminole Tribal Integrity, 1899–1957," *FHQ* 56 (January 1978); "The Seminole 'Uprising' of 1907," *F.A.* 37 (June 1974); with Donald Pullease, "Bishop William Crane Gray's Mission to the Seminole Indians of Florida, 1893–1914," *Historical Magazine of the Protestant Episcopal Church* 42 (September 1973); "Florida Seminoles in the Depression and New Deal, 1933–1942: An Indian Perspective," *FHQ* 65 (October 1986); and " 'New Red Atlantis': John Collier's encounter with the Florida Seminoles in 1935," *FHQ* 66 (October 1987).

See also Roy Nash, *A Survey of the Seminole Indians of Florida*, 71st Cong. 3rd sess. Sen Doc. 314, (1931); Fred C. Wallace, "The Story of Captain John C. Casey," *FHQ* 41 (October 1962); Patsy West, "The Miami Indian Tourist Attractions...," *F.A.* 24 (December 1981).

Two new activities brought the Seminoles deeper into the white world than they had ever been before. The first of these was cattle raising. In 1934 the federal government sent 500 drought-weakened steers to Florida from the stricken Middle West. Beginning with these, the Indians slowly moved into substantial production of beef, which remains a flourishing business.

The second new activity has been education. The Bureau of Indian Affairs (BIA) opened a day school at Brighton in 1938, and one at Big Cypress in 1940. But the first Seminole to go through high school was obliged to attend the Cherokee Indian School, from which he was graduated in 1945. Because the Indians were barred entry into Florida high schools, none was graduated in Florida until 1957. Since the Florida schools were opened to them, many Seminoles have been graduated and a growing number have entered and gone through college.

In the mid-1950s the BIA finally convinced the Seminole tribe to adopt the sort of political organization called for in the Wheeler-Howard Act of 1934. In 1957 the Seminole tribe, with Bureau aid, adopted a constitution. It provided for a council to control the political life, headed by a chairman and a board to handle business matters.

The Miccosukees, stressing their continuous distinctness, refused to amalgamate with the Seminole tribe. Instead, in 1961, they created their own constitution and received federal recognition as a separate tribe. Nevertheless many Miccosukees live among the Seminoles, are married to Seminoles and are part of the tribe. Ten years after federal recognition, the Miccosukee tribe received the power to draw funds directly rather than through the BIA, enabling them to allocate money at the local level as they see their own needs.

In 1946 Congress created the Indian Claims Commission and invited all tribes who thought the United States had unfairly deprived them to file claims. The Seminoles entered a suit against the nation claiming compensation for lands taken from them by force or by fraud. The Miccosukees, demanding land, not money compensation, refused to be a part to the Seminole suit. Finally, after many hearings, the commission awarded the tribe $16,000,000. But the money has never been paid because the Creeks, the Seminole-blacks in Oklahoma, and the Oklahoma Seminoles claim unacceptable parts of it. Meanwhile, the funds have remained in the U.S. Treasury and with accrued interest reached $20,000,000 by 1978.

In the 1980s, tribal wealth shot upward due to the sale of cigarettes free of state tax and to the operation of bingo halls. The tribe can carry on these enterprises outside state law because the United States Supreme Court has declared that the Indians are on sovereign land, and thus are beyond state control in these two enterprises. The two programs have brought in millions of dollars, most of it retained by the tribe to build gymnasiums, buy heavy machinery, operate a day care center, run a Seminole written language program, and build a police department. The tribe has also purchased 4.5 acres for a small reservation at Immokalee and 8.5 acres for a massive bingo hall and cigarette concession at Tampa. In 1982, when income soared to $5,000,000, the fourteen hundred members of the tribe began to receive $150 twice a month.

The Miccosukees do not share in the money generated by cigarettes and bingo. In 1971, however, the State of Florida paid them $975,000 for land previously taken and never paid for. It also gave them the exclusive use of 189,000 acres in the Everglades in which to hunt and fish without permits. Around three hundred persons are recognized members of the Miccosukee tribe. There are perhaps two hundred Indians in camps along the Tamiami Trail unaffiliated with either tribe. The Trail Indians retain their traditional religion.

At the conclusion of the Third Seminole War in 1858, no more than 150 Indians remained in Florida. In the 1980s their descendents number between 2,000 and 2,500. These figures demonstrate the remarkable ability of the Florida Indians to adapt to radical changes, to survive and multiply.

See Margot Ammidown, "The Seminole Tribe Inc.: Winning and Losing at the White Man's Game," *F.A.* 34 (December 1981); Louis Capron, "Florida's Emerging Seminoles," *F.A.* 12 (November 1969); Robert Carr, "The Brickell Store and the Seminole Indian Trade," *F.A.* 34 (December 1981); James W. Covington, "The Trail Indians of Florida," *FHQ* 58 (September 1965); Covington, "White Control of Seminole Leadership," *F.A.* 18 (September 1965); William C. Emerson, M.D., *The Seminoles* (New York, 1954); Robert F. Greenlee, "Aspects of Social Organization and Material Culture of the Seminole of Big Cypress," *F.A.* 5 (December 1952); Merwyn S. Garbarino, *Big Cypress, a Changing Seminole Community* (New York, 1972); Bennie C. Keel, "An Analysis of Muskogee Kinship," *F.A.* 26 (June 1973); and Harry A. Kersey, Jr., and Ross Greene, "Upgrading Indian Education: A Case Study of the Seminoles," *School Review* (February 1975). The following were also authored by Kersey: "Economic Prospects of the Florida Seminole Indians," *Florida Planning and Development Journal* 20 (December 1969); "The Ahfatchee Day

School," *Teacher's College Record* 72 (September 1970); "The Seminole Indians of the Big Cypress Receive a Three-Phase Program," *Journal of American Indian Education* 10 (October 1970); "Training Teachers in a Seminole Indian School," *Journal of Teacher Education* 22 (April 1971); and "Improving Reading Skills of the Seminole Indian Children," *Journal of American Indian Education* 10 (May 1971). See also Robert T. King, "Clan Affiliation and Leadership among the Twentieth-Century Florida Indians," *FHQ* 55 (October 1976); and William C. Sturtevant, "The Medicine Bundles and Busks of the Florida Seminoles," *F.A.* 7 (May 1954).

# 15

# THE URBANIZATION OF FLORIDA

## RAYMOND A. MOHL

FEW STATES CAN match modern Florida's patterns of population growth and urbanization. By the mid-1980s, Florida was the nation's most rapidly growing large state. With almost twelve million people in 1987 and growing more than twice as fast as the national population, Florida has recently passed Pennsylvania as the fourth most populous state in the nation. Building on tourism, recreation, retirement, and high-tech and service industries, Florida has reaped a large share of the massive post–World War II sunbelt migration. The state has also been on the receiving end of an enormous migration of refugees, exiles, and immigrants from Latin America and the Caribbean.

Not only is Florida increasing rapidly in population, but this population is heavily urbanized as well. Florida's population was 20 percent urban in 1900 and 55 percent urban in 1940. The urban proportion rose substantially each decade thereafter, reaching 80.5 percent in 1970, and 84.3 percent in 1980. Moreover, Florida continues to urbanize at a high rate. Six of the nation's ten fastest growing metropolitan areas are now located in Florida. Demographers have projected Florida's population at over twenty-two million by the time the postwar baby boomers reach retirement age early in the twenty-first century. It is also quite predictable that most of these new Floridians will be urbanites, as metropolitan areas push out their boundaries into rural and undeveloped land to accommodate the newcomers. Florida has become the quintessential urban state of the postindustrial age.

Despite Florida's dramatic urban growth over the past several decades, very little in the way of serious scholarly analysis has focused on this important pattern of statewide urbanization. However, an enormous literature has examined smaller bits and pieces of the Florida urban experience. This literature ranges from scholarly books and articles on individual cities or urban problems to popular local histories and the impressionistic writing of journalists. This essay will provide an initial bibliographical overview of Florida urbanization, surveying some of the most important and useful writings on the subject.

For most of the twentieth century, Florida's urban growth outstripped that of the rest of the South. For the larger context of southern urbanization, see Rupert B. Vance and Nicholas J. Demerath, eds., *The Urban South* (Chapel Hill, 1954), and Dudley L. Poston, Jr., and Robert H. Weller, eds., *The Population of the South: Structure and Change in Social Demographic Context* (Austin, 1981). The place of Florida in the more recent urbanization of the sunbelt can be examined in Carl Abbott, *The New Urban America: Growth and Politics in Sunbelt Cities* (Chapel Hill, 1981; rev. ed., 1987); David R. Goldfield, *Cotton Fields and Skyscrapers: Southern City and Region, 1607–1980* (Baton Rouge, 1982); and James C. Cobb, *Industrialization and Southern Society, 1877–1984* (Lexington, 1984).

The demographic dimension of Florida's changing urban pattern can be researched in the decennial volumes of the U.S. Census and in the *Florida Statistical Abstract* published annually since the 1960s by the University of Florida. The most recent demographic analysis of Florida growth is Raymond Arsenault and Gary Mormino, "From Dixie to Dreamland: Demographic and Cultural Change in Florida, 1880–1980," in Randall M. Miller and George E. Pozzetta, eds., *Shades of the Sunbelt: Essays on Ethnicity and Race in the Urban South* (Westport, Conn., 1988). A good statistical summary of Florida urban growth can be found in T. Stanton Dietrich, *The Urbanization of Florida's Population: An Historical Perspective of County Growth, 1830–1970* (Gainesville, 1978). For additional demographic analysis, see Dietrich, *The Changing Patterns of Florida's Population, 1950–1970* (Tallahassee, 1974); James F. Burns and Marilyn K. James, *Migration into Florida, 1940–1973* (Gainesville, 1973); and Stanley K. Smith, "Florida in the Twentieth Century: A Survey of Demographic Change," *Business and Economic Dimensions* 18 (1982), the lead article of a special issue on demographic change in Florida.

Only a few studies have specifically considered urbanization as a statewide phenomenon in Florida. In 1957, Florida State University researchers produced an unpublished report on the subject for Governor LeRoy Collins: William M. Griffin, "Selected Problems Relating to Urbanization in Florida" (Tallahassee,

1957). In 1973, the University of Florida sponsored a conference on the subject, published in mimeo form: David R. Colburn, et al., eds., *Urbanization in the South: A Critique and Analysis* (Gainesville, 1973). For a briefer analysis, see Sigismond de R. Diettrich, "Florida's Metropolitan Growth," University of Florida *Economic Leaflets* 7 (November 1948). A specific study of black urbanization in Florida can be found in Eugene G. Sherman, Jr., "Urbanization and Florida's Negro Population: A Case Study" (Ph.D. diss., Purdue University, 1968). These are the only studies to consider the general pattern of Florida urbanization. Obviously, much remains to be done, but the student of this subject has an enormous literature of more specific studies upon which to draw for such an investigation.

## MIAMI AND SOUTH FLORIDA

Urbanization has been an especially powerful phenomenon in the Miami metropolitan area, and in South Florida generally. Scholars from a variety of disciplines have been working on this subject for several decades. For general overviews of urbanization in the South Florida area, begin with William W. Jenna, Jr., *Metropolitan Miami: A Demographic Overview* (Coral Gables, 1972); David B. Longbrake and Woodrow W. Nichols, Jr., *Sunshine and Shadow in Metropolitan Miami* (Cambridge, 1976); and Raymond A. Mohl, "Miami: The Ethnic Cauldron," in Richard M. Bernard and Bradley R. Rice, eds., *Sunbelt Cities: Politics and Growth since World War II* (Austin, 1983).

There are no scholarly urban biographies of Miami. Some earlier books on Miami and environs, particularly those written during the 1920s, have a promotional flair: Victor Rainbolt, *The Town That Climate Built: The Story of the Rise of a City in the American Tropics* (Miami, 1924); Rex Beach, *The Miracle of Coral Gables* (Coral Gables, 1926); and T. H. Weigall, *Boom in Paradise* (New York, 1932). Helen Muir, *Miami, U.S.A.* (New York, 1953), has popular appeal but lacks scholarly analysis, as do three books by Thelma Peters: *Lemon City: Pioneering on Biscayne Bay, 1850–1925* (Miami, 1976); *Biscayne Country, 1870–1926* (Miami, 1981); and *Miami, 1909* (Miami, 1984). The most recent account of the city is journalist T. D. Allman's *Miami: City of the Future* (New York, 1987). Allman should be read in conjunction with two other recent Miami books: David Rieff, *Going to Miami: Exiles, Tourists, and Refugees in the New America* (Boston, 1987), and Joan Didion, *Miami* (New York, 1987), both of which deal extensively with the Cuban exile community in the city.

A number of illustrated histories of Miami provide good photographic evidence of the city's growth, development, and change. Especially useful are Arva Moore Parks, *Miami: The Magic City* (Tulsa, 1981); Howard Kleinberg, *Miami: The Way We Were* (Miami, 1985); Bob Kearney, ed., *Mostly Sunny Days: A Miami Herald Salute to South Florida's Heritage* (Miami, 1986). On nearby Fort Lauderdale, see Philip J. Weidling and August Burghard, *Checkered Sunshine: The Story of Fort Lauderdale, 1793–1955* (Gainesville, 1966), a popular narrative, and Stuart B. McIver, *Fort Lauderdale and Broward County* (Woodland

Hills, Calif., 1983), an illustrated history; and Paul S. George, *A Jewel In The Wilderness: Fort Lauderdale from Early Times to 1911* (Fort Lauderdale, 1988). For the northern edge of urbanized South Florida, see Donald W. Curl, *Palm Beach County: An Illustrated History* (Northridge, Calif., 1986).

For the most part, the broad picture of Miami and South Florida history has been neglected, but historians and other social scientists have been exploring varied and more narrow facets of the urban experience in this region of the state. The early establishment and development of Miami has received its share of attention. For the city-building activities of Henry M. Flagler, see Sidney W. Martin, *Florida's Flagler* (Athens, Ga., 1949); Nathan D. Shappee, "Flagler's Undertakings in Miami in 1897," *Tequesta* 19 (1959); David L. Chandler, *Henry Flagler: The Astonishing Life and Times of the Visionary Robber Baron Who Founded Florida* (New York, 1986); and the more recent Edward N. Akin, *Flagler: Rockefeller Partner and Florida Baron* (Kent, Ohio, 1988). On early twentieth-century urban growth and change, see Millicent Todd Bingham, "Miami: A Study in Urban Geography," *Tequesta* 9 (1948); F. Page Wilson, "Miami, from Frontier to Metropolis," *Tequesta* 14 (1954); Frank B. Sessa, "Real Estate Expansion and Boom in Miami and Environs during the 1920s" (Ph.D. diss., University of Pittsburgh, 1950); Stuart B. McIver, *The Greatest Sale on Earth: The Story of the Miami Board of Realtors, 1920–1980* (Miami, 1980); and David Nolan, *Fifty Feet in Paradise: The Booming of Florida* (New York, 1984). Suggestive of the physical growth of Miami is Edward Ridolph, *Biscayne Bay Trolleys: Street Railways of the Miami Area* (Forty Fort, Pa., 1981). For Miami Beach creator Carl Fisher, see Jane Fisher, *Fabulous Hoosier* (New York, 1947). On the postboom era of the 1930s, see Vernon M. Leslie, "The Great Depression in Miami Beach" (M.A. thesis, Florida Atlantic University, 1980).

On the changing economic activities of the Miami metropolitan area, consult Reinhold P. Wolff, *Miami: Economic Pattern of a Resort Area* (Coral Gables, 1945); Atlantic Research Corporation, *Economic Base Study—Metropolitan Miami* (Miami, 1962); Dade County Development Department, *Economic Survey of Metropolitan Miami* (Miami, 1963); Mira Wilkins, *Foreign Enterprise in Florida: The Impact of Non-U.S. Direct Investment* (Miami, 1979); and Raymond A. Mohl, "Changing Economic Patterns in the Miami Metropolitan Area, 1940–1980," *Tequesta* 42 (1982). Since the 1970s, Miami has emerged as an important center of international trade and banking. These developments are surveyed in David A. Heenan, "Global Cities of Tomorrow," *Harvard Business Review* 55 (May–June 1977); Eric Calonius, "Banking's Frontier Town," *Florida Trend* 22 (March 1980); Annetta Miller, "Miami Free Trade Zone," *Florida Trend* 23 (November 1980); Donald E. Baer, "Behind Miami Surge in International Banking," *Caribbean Basin Economic Survey* 7 (January–March 1981); Emmanuel N. Roussakis, "The Edges Come to Miami," *The Bankers Magazine* 164 (May–June 1981); Joe Hice, "Coral Gables: Trade Center for the Americas," *Florida Trend* 23 (February 1981); and Barry B. Levine, "The

Capital of Latin America," *The Wilson Quarterly* (Winter 1985). Jan B. Luytjes, *Economic Impact of Refugees in Dade County* (Miami, 1982) evaluates the role of the newcomers in Miami's changing economy. In addition, such publications as *Miami Economic Research*, published in the 1950s at the University of Miami, the monthly *Florida Trend*, the weekly *South Florida Business Review*, and the "Business Monday" section of the *Miami Herald* all provide good coverage of the changing economic patterns of the Miami metropolitan area.

Miami is one of the few urban areas in the United States to have achieved a powerful metropolitan government (known as Metro) that cuts across municipal boundaries. The best introduction to this complex political development can be found in Public Administration Service, *The Government of Metropolitan Miami* (Chicago, 1954); Reinhold P. Wolff, *Miami Metro: The Road to Urban Unity* (Coral Gables, 1960); Edward Sofen, *The Miami Metropolitan Experiment* (rev. ed., New York, 1966); and Paris Glendening, "The Metropolitan Dade County Government: An Examination of Reform" (Ph.D. diss., Florida State University, 1967). Also useful on this subject are James F. Horan and G. Thomas Taylor, Jr., *Experiments in Metropolitan Government* (New York, 1977); Franklin Parson, *The Story of the First Metropolitan Government in the United States* (Winter Park, 1958); and Gustave Serino, *Miami's Metropolitan Experiment* (Gainesville, 1958).

An enormous periodical literature traces every turn in the battle for Metro. Particularly useful articles are Wendell G. Schaeffer, "Miami Looks at the Problems of Municipal Government," *Public Administration Review* 15 (Winter 1955); Joseph Metzger, "Metro and Its Judicial History," *University of Miami Law Review* 15 (Spring 1961); Edward Sofen, "Problems of Metropolitan Leadership: The Miami Experience," *Midwest Journal of Political Science* 5 (February 1961); Thomas J. Wood, "Dade County: Unbossed, Erratically Led," *Annals of the American Academy of Political and Social Science* 353 (May 1964); John DeGrove, "Metropolitan Dade County: The Unfinished Experiment," *Florida Planning and Development* 21 (July–August 1970); Richard D. Gustely, "The Allocation and Distributional Impacts of Governmental Consolidation: The Dade County Experience," *Urban Affairs Quarterly* 12 (March 1977); and Juanita Greene, "Dade Metro: Turbulent History, Uncertain Future," *Planning* 45 (February 1979). In addition, the *National Municipal Review* (after 1958 called the *National Civic Review*) covered Metro developments closely during the 1950s and 1960s. The most recent overviews of the current state of Metro are Aileen R. Lotz, *Metropolitan Dade County: Two-Tier Government in Action* (Boston, 1984), and Raymond A. Mohl, "Miami's Metropolitan Government: Retrospect and Prospect," *Florida Historical Quarterly (FHQ)*, 63 (July 1984).

There is a considerable and still growing literature on Miami's changing racial and ethnic makeup. For the early Bahamian community in Miami, see Raymond A. Mohl, "Black Immigrants: Bahamians in Early Twentieth-Century Miami," *FHQ*, 65 (January 1987). Other publications on Miami's early black community include Charles Garofalo, "Black-White Occupational Distribution in Miami during World War I," *Prologue* 5 (Summer 1973); Paul S. George, "Colored Town: Miami's Black Community, 1896–1930," *FHQ*, 56 (April 1978); Paul S. George, "Policing Miami's Black Community, 1896–1930," *FHQ*, 57 (April 1979); and Raymond A. Mohl, "Trouble in Paradise: Race and Housing in Miami during the New Deal Era," *Prologue*, 19 (Spring 1987); and Paul S. George and Thomas K. Peterson, "Liberty Square: 1933–1987. The Origins and Evolution of a Public Housing Project," *Tequesta* 48 (1988).

After World War II, Miami's black population grew considerably, creating tensions in the housing market as well as in the political arena and the economic system. Examining some of these issues are: Reinhold P. Wolff and David Gillogly, *Negro Housing in the Miami Area: Effects of the Postwar Housing Boom* (Coral Gables, 1951); Charles Abrams, *Forbidden Neighbors: A Study of Prejudice in Housing* (New York, 1955), which has a chapter on Miami Housing problems in the 1950s; Elizabeth L. Virrick, "New Housing for Negroes in Dade County," in Nathan Glazer and Davis McEntire, eds., *Studies in Housing and Minority Groups* (Berkeley, 1960); Harold M. Rose, "Metropolitan Miami's Changing Negro Population, 1950–1960," *Economic Geography* 40 (July 1964); Warren M. Banner, *An Appraisal of Progress, 1943–1953* (New York, 1953); James W. Morrison, *The Negro in Greater Miami* (Miami, 1962).

On the role of blacks in Miami's more recent history, see National Commission on the Causes and Prevention of Violence, *Miami Report: The Report of the Miami Study Team on Civil Disturbances in Miami, Florida, during the Week of August 5, 1968* (Washington, D.C., 1969); U.S. Commission on Civil Rights, *Confronting Racial Isolation in Miami: a report of the United States Commission on Civil Rights* (Washington, D.C., 1982); H. Jerome Miron, *Prevention and Control of Urban Disorders: Issues for the 1980s* (Washington, D.C., 1980); Bruce Porter and Marvin Dunn, *The Miami Riot of 1980: Crossing the Bounds* (Lexington, Mass., 1984); Manning Marable, "The Fire This Time: The Miami Rebellion, May 1980," *The Black Scholar* 11 (July–August 1980); and Thomas D. Boswell, et al., "Attitudes, Causes and Perceptions: The 1980 Black Riot in Dade County (Miami), Florida," *The Florida Geographer* 20 (October 1986).

On blacks in Miami, the following unpublished theses and dissertations are also useful: David H. Cohn, "The Development and Efficacy of the Negro Police Precinct and Court of the City of Miami" (M.A. thesis, University of Miami, 1951); Arthur E. Chapman, "The History of the Black Police Force and Court in the City of Miami" (D.A. thesis, University of Miami, 1986); and Natalie M. Davis, "Blacks in Miami and Detroit: Communities in Contrast" (Ph.D. diss., University of North Carolina, 1976). For comparisons of blacks in Miami and other Florida cities, see two articles by Morton D. Winsberg, "Changing Distribution of the Black Population: Florida Cities, 1970–1980," *Urban Affairs Quarterly* 18 (1983), and "Flight from the Ghetto: The Migration of Middle-Class and Highly Educated Blacks into White Urban Neighborhoods," *American Journal of Economics and Sociology* 44 (October 1985).

Miami's black population has remained relatively stable compared to other groups in an area that has experienced some dramatic population shifts during the past several decades, primarily stemming from the enormous influx of Cuban exiles. Over a twenty-five-year period after 1959, some 800,000 Cubans left their homeland for the United States, and a large portion of them settled in Miami. By the mid-1980s, Cubans and other Hispanics made up more than 60 percent of the population of the city of Miami and over 43 percent of the population of Metro-Dade County.

Scholars were slow to turn their attention to the Cuban immigration experience, but in the past five years or so there has been a vast outpouring of books and articles on the Cubans in Miami. Three recent books provide a good introduction to the subject: Thomas D. Boswell and James R. Curtis, *The Cuban-American Experience: Culture, Images, and Perspectives* (Totowa, N.J., 1984); Alejandro Portes and Robert L. Bach, *Latin Journey: Cuban and Mexican Immigrants in the United States* (Berkeley, 1985); and Sylvia Pedraza-Bailey, *Political and Economic Migrants in America: Cubans and Mexicans* (Austin, 1985). Richard Fagen, et al., *Cubans in Exile: Disaffection and the Revolution* (Stanford, 1968), offers an analysis of who left Cuba and why, based on extensive survey research and interviewing of early exiles in Miami. Jose Llanes, *Cuban-Americans: Masters of Survival* (Cambridge, 1982), is based on oral histories of Cuban exiles in the United States. On Miami as immigration port, see Raymond A. Mohl, "Miami: American Gateway," in Gail F. Stern, ed., *Freedom's Doors: Immigrant Ports of Entry to the United States* (Philadelphia, 1986).

Much has been written on the social and economic adaptation of the Cubans in their new home in Miami. Sponsored by the University of Miami's Center for Advanced International Studies, *The Cuban Immigration, 1959–1966, and Its Impact on Miami–Dade County, Florida* (Coral Gables, 1967), was a pioneering early study. Other studies that provide important insights are Joe Hall, *The Cuban Refugee in the Public Schools of Dade County* (Miami, 1965); Rafael J. Prohías and Lourdes Casal, *The Cuban Minority in the United States* (Boca Raton, 1973); William Francis Mackey and Von Nieda Beebe, *Bilingual Schools for a Bicultural Community: Miami's Adaptation to the Cuban Refugees* (Rowley, Mass., 1977); F. P. Eichelberger, "The Cubans in Miami: Residential Movements and Ethnic Group Differentiation" (M.A. thesis, University of Cincinnati, 1974); Kathy A. Darasz, "Cuban Refugees in Miami: Patterns of Economic and Political Adjustment" (M.A. thesis, Florida Atlantic University, 1982); Antonio Jorge and Raul Moncarz, "Cubans in South Florida: A Social Science Approach," *Metas* (Fall 1980); Kenneth L. Wilson and Alejandro Portes, "Immigrant Enclaves: An Analysis of the Labor Market Experiences of Cubans in Miami," *American Journal of Sociology* 86 (September 1980); Lourdes Arguelles, "Cuban Miami: The Roots, Development, and Everyday Life of an Emigré Enclave in the U.S. National Security State," *Contemporary Marxism* 5 (Spring 1982); Alejandro Portes, "The Rise of Ethnicity: Determinants of Ethnic Perceptions among Cuban Exiles in Miami," *American Sociological Review* 49 (June 1984); and Herbert

Burkholz, "The Latinization of Miami," *New York Times Magazine* (September 21, 1980). On changing language patterns, consult Melvyn C. Resnick, "Beyond the Ethnic Community: Spanish Language Roles and Maintenance in Miami," *International Journal of the Sociology of Language* 69 (1988). Michael J. McNally, *Catholicism in South Florida, 1868–1968* (Gainesville, 1984), devotes considerable space to the response of the Catholic Church to the Cuban newcomers in Miami. On Cuban Jews, see Seymour B. Liebman, "Cuban Jewish Community in South Florida," in Morris Fine and Milton Himmelfarb, eds., *American Jewish Yearbook* (New York, 1969).

In the past decade, the Cubans have begun to alter significantly the character of urban politics in the Miami metropolitan area. This subject is discussed in Paul S. Salter and Robert C. Mings, "The Projected Impact of Cuban Settlement on Voting Patterns in Metropolitan Miami, Florida," *Professional Geographer* 24 (May 1972); Max Azicri, "The Politics of Exile: Trends and Dynamics of Political Change Among Cuban-Americans," *Cuban Studies* 11–12 (July 1981–January 1982); Max Azicri, "Cultural and Political Change among Cuban-Americans (1958–1982)," *Revista/Review Interamericana* 12 (Summer 1982); Raymond A. Mohl, "Race Ethnicity and Urban Politics in the Miami Metropolitan Area," *Florida Environmental and Urban Issues* 9 (April 1982); "The Politics of Ethnicity in Contemporary Miami," *Migration World* 14 (1986); Christopher L. Warren, et al., "Minority Mobilization in an International City: Rivalry and Conflict in Miami," *PS* 19 (Summer 1986); Christopher L. Warren and John F. Stack, Jr., "Immigration and the Politics of Ethnicity and Class in Metropolitan Miami," in John F. Stack, Jr., ed., *The Primordial Challenge: Ethnicity in the Contemporary World* (Westport, Conn., 1986); Mohl, "Ethnic Politics in Miami, 1960–1986, in Miller and Pozzetta, eds., *Shades of the Sunbelt*; and two articles by Gerald R. Webster and Roberta Haven Webster: "Ethnic Bloc Voting in Miami," *The Florida Geographer* 20 (October 1986), and "Ethnicity and Voting in the Miami-Dade County SMSA," *Urban Geography* 8 (January– February 1987).

For additional bibliographical guides through the thickets of Cuban exile history, see Lourdes Casal and Andres R. Hernandez, "Cubans in the U.S.: A Survey of the Literature," *Cuban Studies/Estudios Cubanos* 5 (July 1975); Esther B. Gonzalez, *Annotated Bibliography on Cubans in the United States, 1960–1976* (Miami, 1977); Raymond A. Mohl, "Cubans in Miami: A Preliminary Bibliography," *Immigration History Newsletter* 16 (May 1984); and Lyn MacCorkle, *Cubans in the United States: A Bibliography for Research in the Social and Behavioral Sciences, 1960–1983* (Westport, Conn., 1984).

Miami's Cuban newcomers have been joined since the mid-1970s by a growing population of Haitian exiles and immigrants, perhaps as many as 100,000 in the metropolitan area. On the Haitian experience, Jake C. Miller, *The Plight of Haitian Refugees* (New York, 1984) is a good beginning, although the book has a weak research base. More specifically on the Miami experience are Thomas Boswell's two articles: "The New Haitian Diaspora: Florida's

Most Recent Residents," *Caribbean Review* 11 (Winter 1982), and "In the Eye of the Storm: The Context of Haitian Migration to Miami, Florida," *Southeastern Geographer* 23 (November 1983). The chief interpreter of the recent Haitian experience in Miami is Alex Stepick, an anthropologist who has written a number of published studies and mimeographed reports, mostly based on survey research and fieldwork. For a sampling of Stepick's work, see *Haitian Refugees in the U.S.* (London, 1982); "Haitian Boat People: A Study in the Conflicting Forces Shaping U.S. Immigration Policy," *Law and Contemporary Problems* 45 (Spring 1982); "The New Haitian Exodus: The Flight from Terror and Poverty," *Caribbean Review* 11 (Winter 1982); *The Haitian Informal Sector in Miami* (Miami, 1984); *The Business Community of Little Haiti* (Miami, 1984), and with Alejandro Portes, "Flight into Despair: A Profile of Recent Haitian Refugees in South Florida," *International Migration Review* 20 (Summer 1986). Other important studies of the Miami Haitians are Kimberly J. Zlokoski, "The Effects of Length of Residence and Stage Migration on the Demographic Characteristics of a Haitian Community in Miami, Florida" (M.A. thesis, University of Miami, 1980); Yetta Deckelbaum, "Little Haiti: The Evolution of a Community" (M.A. thesis, Florida Atlantic University, 1983); Robert A. Ladner, et al., *Demography, Social Status, Housing and Social Needs of the Haitian Population of Edison–Little River* (Miami, 1983); Kristine Rosenthal, "In the Shadow of Miami: Haitian Sojourn," *Working Papers Magazine* 9 (September–October 1982); and Bryan O. Walsh, "Haitians in Miami," *Migration Today* 7 (September 1979). For a bibliographic guide to a growing literature on the Haitians, see Raymond A. Mohl, "The New Immigration: A Preliminary Bibliography," *Immigration History Newsletter* 17 (May 1985).

There are several studies of the interrelationships of racial and ethnic groups in Miami. On competition for residential space, for example, see Morton D. Winsberg, "Housing Segregation of a Predominantly Middle-Class Population: Residential Patterns Developed by the Cuban Immigration into Miami, 1950–74," *American Journal of Economics and Sociology* 38 (October 1979); Benigno E. Aguirre, et al., "The Residential Patterning of Latin American and Other Ethnic Populations in Metropolitan Miami," *Latin American Research Review* 15 (1980); Morton D. Winsberg, "Ethnic Competition for Residential Space in Miami, Florida, 1970–80," *American Journal of Economics and Sociology* 42 (July 1983). Both blacks and Cubans are analyzed in an early University of Miami study, *Psycho-Social Dynamics in Miami* (Coral Gables, 1969), as well as in the more recent thesis by Patrick O'Hare, "Racial and Ethnic Conflict in Miami, 1960–1985" (M.A. thesis, Florida Atlantic University, 1987). For differing economic experiences of Cubans and blacks, see Kenneth L. Wilson and W. Allen Martin, "Ethnic Enclaves: A Comparison of the Cuban and Black Economies in Miami," *American Journal of Sociology* 88 (July 1982). Several useful studies focus on both the Cubans and Haitians, drawing comparisons and contrasts: Metro-Dade County, *Social and Economic Problems among Cuban and Haitian Entrant Groups in Dade County, Florida* (Miami, 1981); Raymond

A. Mohl, "An Ethnic 'Boiling Pot': Cubans and Haitians in Miami," *Journal of Ethnic Studies* 13 (Summer 1985); Mohl, "The New Caribbean Immigration," *Journal of American Ethnic History* 5 (Spring 1986); and Anthony P. Maingot, "Ethnic Bargaining and the Noncitizen: Cubans and Haitians in Miami," in Stack, ed., *The Primordial Challenge*.

On crime and criminal justice, see Paul S. George, "Criminal Justice in Miami, 1896–1930" (Ph.D. diss., Florida State University, 1975); William Wilbanks, *Murder in Miami: An Analysis of Homicide Patterns and Trends in Dade County (Miami) Florida, 1917–1983* (Lanham, Md., 1984); Dewey W. Knight, Jr., and Hall Tennis, "Minorities and Justice in Greater Miami: A View from the Metro-Courthouse," *Urban Resources* 2 (Spring 1985). A somewhat different approach to the subject is offered in journalist Edna Buchanan's *The Corpse Had a Familiar Face: Covering Miami, America's Hottest Beat* (New York, 1987). For a related issue, see Metro-Dade County, *Needs Assessment Study: Terrorism in Dade County* (Miami, 1979). On organized crime in the postwar era, see Henning Heldt, "Miami: Heaven or Honky-Tonk?" in Robert S. Allen, ed., *Our Fair City* (New York, 1947). Two books by journalist Hank Messick focus on crime in Miami: *Syndicate in the Sun* (New York, 1968), which deals with traditional organized crime operations, and *Of Grass and Snow: The Secret Criminal Elite* (Englewood Cliffs, N.J., 1979), which examines the illegal drug trade in Miami.

On urban planning in Miami, a good starting point is Metro-Dade County, *Comprehensive Development Master Plan for Metropolitan Dade County* (Miami, 1979). Two good graduate theses on Miami planning are Carmen J. Cavezza, "The Revitalization of Miami, Florida's Central Business District" (M.A. thesis, University of Miami, 1969), and Constance M. Rogier, "The Comprehensive Development Master Plan: A Study of Environmental Politics" (Ph.D. diss., University of Pittsburgh, 1982). Miami's architectural history is traced in Metro-Dade County, *From Wilderness to Metropolis: The History and Architecture of Dade County, Florida, 1825–1940* (Miami, 1982); Laura Cerwinske, *Tropical Deco: The Architecture and Design of Old Miami Beach* (New York, 1981); and Hap Hutton, *Tropical Splendor: An Architectural History of Florida* (New York, 1987). Luther J. Carter, *The Florida Experience: Land and Water Policy in a Growth State* (Baltimore, 1974), deals in part with environmental issues in the Miami area, as does William Ross McCluney, *The Environmental Destruction of South Florida* (Coral Gables, 1971). For educational history, begin with Asterie Baker Provenzo and Eugene F. Provenzo, Jr., *Education on the Forgotten Frontier: A Centennial History of the Founding of the Dade County Public Schools* (Miami, 1985).

## TAMPA BAY AREA

A useful starting place for the study of Tampa is Gary R. Mormino, "Tampa: From Hell Hole to the Good Life," in Richard M. Bernard and Bradley R. Rice, eds., *Sunbelt Cities: Politics and Growth since World War II* (Austin, 1983). See also Durwood Long's articles, "The Making of Modern Tampa," *FHQ*, 69 (April 1971), and "The Historical Beginnings of Ybor City and Modern Tampa," *FHQ*, 45 (July 1966); and Gary R. Mormino, "Tampa and the New Urban South," *FHQ*, 60 (January 1982). For a brief, heavily illustrated overview, consult Gary R. Mormino and Anthony P. Pizzo, *Tampa: The Treasure City* (Tulsa, 1983), which also contains a good bibliography. Walter P. Fuller, *St. Petersburg and Its People* (St. Petersburg, 1972), provides a good beginning for investigation of this nearby Tampa Bay area city.

Unlike most other Florida cities, Tampa was a center for working-class immigrants from the late nineteenth century. The best and most innovative study of Tampa's varied social and ethnic history is Gary R. Mormino and George E. Pozzetta, *The Immigrant World of Ybor City: Italians and Their Latin Neighbors in Tampa, 1885–1985* (Urbana, 1987). A model study placed within the larger context of American urban and ethnic history, this book has an extensive bibliography. For a sampling of important articles on Tampa's ethnic and labor history, the following might be investigated fruitfully: Louis A. Perez, Jr., "Cubans in Tampa: From Exiles to Immigrants, 1892–1901," *FHQ*, 57 (October 1978); George E. Pozzetta, "Immigrants and Radicals in Tampa, Florida," *FHQ*, 57 (January 1979); Susan D. Greenbaum, "Afro-Cubans in Exile: Tampa, Florida, 1886–1984," *Cuban Studies/Estudios Cubanos* 15 (Winter 1985); Greenbaum, *Afro-Cubans in Ybor City: A Centennial History* (Tampa, 1986); Joan Marie Steffy, "The Cuban Immigrants of Tampa, Florida: 1886–1898" (M.A. thesis, University of South Florida, 1975); Durwood Long, "La Resistencia: Tampa's Immigrant Labor Union," *Labor History* 6 (Fall 1965); Durwood Long, "Labor Relations in the Tampa Cigar Industry, 1919–21," *FHQ*, 47 (October 1968); George E. Pozzetta, "Italians and the Tampa General Strike of 1910," in George E. Pozzetta, ed., *Pane E Lavoro: The Italian Working Class* (Toronto, 1980); Gerald E. Poyo, "Tampa Cigarmakers and the Struggle for Cuban Independence," *Tampa Bay History* 7 (Fall–Winter 1985). For a good collection of articles entitled "A Centennial History of Ybor City," see *Tampa Bay History* 7 (Fall–Winter 1985); Robert P. Ingalls, "Lynching and Establishment Violence in Tampa, 1858–1935," *Journal of Southern History* 53 (November 1987). On Tampa's more recent history, see Steven F. Lawson, "From Sit-in to Race Riot: Businessmen, Blacks, and the Pursuit of Moderation in Tampa, 1960–1967," in Elizabeth Jacoway and David R. Colburn, eds., *Southern Businessmen and Desegregation* (Baton Rouge, 1982).

## FLORIDA'S OTHER URBAN/METROPOLITAN AREAS

A growing scholarly literature has begun to sketch out the urban history of Jacksonville. James Robertson Ward, *Old Hickory's Town: An Illustrated History of Jacksonville* (Jacksonville, 1982), provides a solid introduction to the city's history. Richard A. Martin, *The City Makers* (Jacksonville, 1972), is a history of Jacksonville in the mid-nineteenth century as reflected in the biography of one of the city's pioneer boosters, James J. Daniel. Important articles on early Jacksonville include James B. Crooks, "Changing Face of Jacksonville, Florida, 1900–1910," *FHQ*, 62 (April 1984) and Crooks, "Jacksonville in the Progressive Era: Political Responses to Urban Growth," *FHQ*, 65 (July 1986). On blacks in late-nineteenth-century Jacksonville, the standard work is Barbara A. Richardson, "A History of Blacks in Jacksonville, Florida, 1860–1895" (Ph.D. diss., Carnegie-Mellon University, 1975). Consult as well, Edward N. Akin, "When a Minority Becomes the Majority: Blacks in Jacksonville Politics, 1887–1907," *FHQ*, 53 (October 1974), and, on Jacksonville and Pensacola, August Meier and Elliott Rudwick, "Negro Boycotts of Segregated Streetcars in Florida, 1901–1905," *South Atlantic Quarterly* 69 (Autumn 1970). For the city's more recent history, an important study is Richard Martin, *Consolidation: Jacksonville, Duval County. The Dynamics of Urban Political Reform* (Jacksonville, 1968), which offers a detailed history of the politics of the 1967 city-county consolidation in Jacksonville. For the impact of consolidation on blacks, see two articles by Lee Sloan and Robert M. French: "Race and Governmental Consolidation in Jacksonville," *Negro Educational Review* (April–July 1970), and "Black Rule in the Urban South?" *Transaction* 9 (November–December 1971). J. Edwin Benton and Darwin Gamble, "City/County Consolidation and Economies of Scale," *Social Science Quarterly* 65 (March 1984), concludes that consolidation did not reduce municipal taxes and spending.

In the late nineteenth century, Key West was Florida's largest city. Key West was also ethnically diverse, with white and black immigrants from the Bahamas and a large number of Cuban exiles. For the blacks, see Sharon Wells, *Forgotten Legacy: Blacks in Nineteenth-Century Key West* (Key West, 1982). A number of sources discuss the Key West Cubans, including Elmer T. Clark, *The Latin Immigrant in the South* (Nashville, 1924), and McNally, *Catholicism in South Florida, 1868–1968*. Several articles by Gerald E. Poyo provide comparative coverage of early Cubans in Key West and Tampa: "Key West and the Cuban Ten Years War," *FHQ*, 57 (April 1979); "Cuban Patriots in Key West, 1878–1886: Guardians of the Separatist Ideal," *FHQ*, 61 (July 1982); "Cuban Communities in the United States: Toward an Overview of the Nineteenth Century Experience," in Miren Uriarte-Gastón and Jorge Cañas-Martinez, eds., *Cubans in the United States* (Boston, 1984); "The Impact of Cuban and Spanish Workers on Labor Organizing in Florida, 1870–1900," *Journal of American Ethnic History* 5 (Spring 1986); and "Evolution of Cuban Separatist Thought in the Emigrant Communities of the United States, 1848–1895," *Hispanic American Historical Review* 66 (August 1986). Other Key West studies include: Donald Gordon Lester, "Key West during the Civil War" (M.A. thesis, University of Miami, 1949), and Durwood Long, "Key West and the New Deal, 1934–1936," *FHQ*, 46 (January 1968).

Less studied is Pensacola, but the literature is expanding. A scholarly introduction to the city can be found in James R. McGovern, *The Emergence of a City in the Modern South: Pensacola, 1900–1945* (DeLeon Springs, Fla., 1976), which discusses the city's economic, political, and social history, but emphasizes the importance of the U.S. Naval Air Station for Pensacola's metropolitan growth. This point is also elaborated in James R. McGovern, "Pensacola, Florida: A Military City in the New South," *FHQ*, 59 (July 1980). For additional material on Pensacola, see Wayne Flynt, "Pensacola Labor Problems and Political Radicalism, 1908" *FHQ*, 43 (April 1965), and Donald M. Bragaw, "Status of Negroes in a Southern Port City in the Progressive Era: Pensacola, 1896–1920," *FHQ*, 51 (January 1973). Linda Ellsworth and Lucius Ellsworth, *Pensacola: The Deep Water City* (Tulsa, 1982), provides a brief, illustrated overview of the city's history.

The nation's oldest city, St. Augustine, has also received some attention from recent scholars. Jean Parker Waterbury, ed., *The Oldest City: St. Augustine, Saga of Survival* (St. Augustine, 1983), is a collection of scholarly articles on the city's history, chronologically organized. On the colonial period, see Kathleen Deagan, *Spanish St. Augustine: The Archaeology of a Colonial Creole Community* (New York, 1983). Thomas Graham, *The Awakening of St. Augustine: The Anderson Family and the Oldest City, 1821–1924* (St. Augustine, 1978), provides an urban history context. The city's more recent history is examined in David R. Colburn, *Racial Change and Community Crisis: St. Augustine, Florida, 1877–1980* (New York, 1985). For photographic evidence of urban change and development, consult Karen Harven, *St. Augustine and St. Johns County: A Pictorial History* (Virginia Beach, 1980).

Relatively little of a scholarly nature has been written about Orlando. The chief overview, also illustrated, is Jerrell H. Shofner, *Orlando: The City Beautiful* (Tulsa, 1984), but see also Eve Bacon, *Orlando: A Centennial History*, 2 vols. (Chuluota, Fla., 1975). Some recent issues are considered in Debnath Mookherjee, "The Impact of Urban Growth on Land Use in the Urban Fringe of Orlando, Florida," *Southeastern Geographer* 11 (1962) and Richard E. Fogelsong, "Central Florida's High-Tech Challenge," *Rollins Alumni Record* (Winter 1986). On the state capital, a useful monograph is Bertram H. Greene, *Antebellum Tallahassee* (Tallahassee, 1971). Little has been written on the growth of Florida retirement communities, but see the chapter on Sun City, Florida, in Frances Fitzgerald, *Cities on a Hill: A Journey through Contemporary American Cultures* (New York, 1986).

As the previous pages suggest, a voluminous literature on Florida urban topics already exists. Additional material can be ferreted out of Florida local and regional journals such as *Tequesta, Tampa Bay History, El Escribano, Apalachee*, and *Spanish River Papers*. For more contemporary observations on the Florida urban scene, consult *Florida Trend* and the monthly city magazines: *Miami/South Florida Magazine, Miami Mensual, Jacksonville Magazine, Tampa Bay Magazine*, and *Orlando Magazine*. A comprehensive and effective overview of the urbanization of Florida—one that fits together all of the pieces over a long span of time—remains to be written. Those who might take on such a task will be able to draw upon the literature cited here as well as the enormous range of sources traditionally used by urban historians, including published state and municipal documents and reports, photographic records, oral histories, newspapers, and the materials available in local archives and historical societies. Good hunting!

*PART TWO*

---

# *ARCHIVES AND SOURCES*

# 16

# THE P. K. YONGE LIBRARY OF FLORIDA HISTORY

## ELIZABETH ALEXANDER

| | |
|---|---|
| Street address: | 404 Library West |
| | University of Florida |
| | Gainesville, Florida 32611 |
| Telephone: | (904) 392–0319 |
| Days and hours: | Monday–Friday, 8:00 A.M. to 5:00 P.M. |

THE P. K. YONGE Library of Florida History is a collection of Floridiana spanning five centuries and consists of books, manuscripts, newspapers, periodicals, maps, and microfilm. The nucleus of this research library was given in 1945 to the University of Florida by Julien C. Yonge of Pensacola, and the library named it in honor of his father, Philip K. Yonge, a twenty-year member of the state Board of Control and the state Plant Board, and a major force behind the growth of higher education in Florida. This already extensive collection of Floridiana grew quickly in subsequent years.

The P. K. Yonge Library of Florida History supports teaching and research through the Ph.D. level in Florida history and provides reference service to all qualified researchers. Holdings reveal 22,850 book titles, 3,000 Hollinger manuscript boxes, 2,400 maps, and 8,500 reels of microfilm. All materials are maintained in a closed stack area. Manuscripts, together with colonial documentation, newspapers, rare books, and maps are the unique primary sources which constitute the greatest asset of the P. K. Yonge Library of Florida History. In 1977, G. K. Hall published in four volumes the *Catalog of the P. K. Yonge Library of Florida History*.

Holdings include both primary and secondary source materials pertinent to all aspects of Florida's history: exploration and voyages to 1565, the Huguenot colony, the First Spanish Period, the English colony, the American Revolution, the Second Spanish Period, the First Seminole War, cession to the United States, the Second and Third Seminole Wars, territorial and early statehood, Civil War and Reconstruction, Cuba and the Spanish-American War, twentieth-century Florida. Support for these chronological periods of the state's history is found in broad subject areas: description and travel, religion, politics and government, land records, agriculture, archaeology, fiction concerning Florida's history, biographies, and the histories of those border states (Louisiana, Alabama, Georgia, North and South Carolina, Virginia, Mississippi) that are essential in researching Florida's early history. Colonial Latin American histories are available to the researcher as well as an impressive county and local history section. Since the early 1950s all theses and dissertations concerning the history of the state have been acquired.

In Spanish exploration to 1565, research is possible using memoirs and biographies of discoverers, collections of printed document sources, bibliographies, and printed general histories as well as histories of early Spanish missions. Particularly useful is the thirty-three-volume set of printed documents of voyages and discoveries from the collection of Fernandez Navarrete. Pilot guides and historical maps and charts should assist the scholar in his research.

The French impact on Florida was quite brief. The history of the Huguenot colony, 1562–65, finds support in documentation on microfilm from the Bibliotheque Nationale and the Archives Diplomatiques in Paris, and many printed sources of the sixteenth century published in France. Researching this three-year period of Florida's history requires the use of Spanish documentation for the complete picture. Manuscript maps and illustrations and engravings of the French in Florida as well as histories of French voyages and biographies of those early explorers and colonists are held by the Yonge Library.

The largest collection of primary documentation held by the Yonge Library is that of Spain's control and ownership of the Floridas, 1565–1764 and 1784–1821. Copies of this documentation consist of microfilm and photostats purchased from the Archivo General de Indias in Seville, Spain and the Library of Congress. In an attempt to make this vast documentation available to researchers, a Spanish Florida Borderlands Program was begun in 1974. To date, calendars have been completed for the Stetson Collection, photostats dating from 1512 to 1783, the East Florida Papers, 1784–1821, and the Papeles Procedentes de Cuba, records of Spain's colonies in North America, 1760–1821. Complete legajos of the First Spanish Period are currently being researched and foliated in the Archivo General de Indias, and will be microfilmed for the P. K. Yonge Library of Florida History. These legajos are from five major sections within the Archivo: justicia, escribania de camera, contratacion, contaduria, and Santo Domingo. As each legajo is acquired from Spain, calendars are being maintained. Indexes are available to Spanish manuscript collections held by the Yonge Library of the following late–nineteenth- and twentieth-century historians: Woodbury Lowery, Joseph B. Lockey, Jeanette Thurber Connor, and Buckingham Smith. Microfilm from the Library of Congress and original documents held by the Yonge Library of the papers of Vicente Sebastian Pintado have been calendared, as well as the Spanish dominion papers of the Mississippi Provincial Archives. This documentation is supported by historic maps and charts covering those dates of Spanish control as well as printed histories, bibliographies, microfilm of early newspapers, land grant records, and parish records.

Spain ceded the Floridas to Great Britain in 1763 and two decades of British rule followed. Primary documentation from the Public Record Office, Great Britain, Public Archives of Canada, and the British Museum in London are the basic research sources for this period. Both the papers of General Gage and General Haldimand provide the military and diplomatic information needed for research, and papers from Fulham Palace in London the religious information. Complementing the microfilm of official documentation is the Joseph B. Lockey manuscript collection consisting of photostat and transcriptions from the Public Record Office, U.S. State Department, the New York Public Library, the New York Historical Society, and the Georgia Department of Archives. Indexes to this collection are available. Research is enhanced with British maps of the period, printed histories, American loyalist materials, as well as newspapers on microfilm from the Carolinas, Virginia, Georgia, and Florida.

In researching the three Seminole Wars, 1817–1818, 1835–1842, and 1855–1858, the basic book collection is supported by nineteenth-century maps, microfilm primarily from records held by the U.S. National Archives, and newspapers from South Carolina, Georgia, and Florida. Strengthening research possibilities are the manuscript materials in the Yonge Library. Papers of Colonel William Davenport and papers of twentieth-century historians Louis Capron, Major Edward Keenan and T. O. Brown are essential in revealing all aspects of the wars. Manuscript holdings include personal narratives, correspondence, diaries, letterbooks, Indian captive narratives, and ledgers. All are extensive.

For the territorial and early statehood period, 1821–1861, sources are primarily official documentation of both the U.S. government and of the state of Florida. The legislative records of Florida are extensive and complete and are complimented by ordinances of Andrew Jackson, compilations of public acts, constitutions, governors' letterbooks, and laws and statutes. Federal documentation as it relates to Florida consists of the American State Papers, U.S. Census Office records and those of the U.S. General Land Office. The official documentation supports investigation into plantation life and travels within the territory. Newspapers from South Carolina, Georgia, and Florida are available for research, and the early map collection is good. One unique manuscript collection is that of David Levy Yulee, Florida's U.S. senator, 1845–51. Both Andrew Jackson manuscripts and land and plantation manuscripts provide insight into this period of the state's history.

Sources for the history of the Civil War and Reconstruction, 1861–77, rest primarily on regimental and military histories, official records, and microfilm of military service records from the U.S. Adjutant General's Office. Important official correspondence, letters to and from are on microfilm from both the U.S. Navy Department and the U.S. War Department. All facets of the Civil War and Reconstruction are accessible in personal narratives, letterbooks, diaries, correspondence, and major manuscript collections. The Winston Stephens papers, papers of Samuel A. Swann, Chandler C. Yonge, David Levy Yulee, and Lt. Governor William H. Gleason provide insight into the social and economic life of the period, blockade running, the Freedman's Bureau, slavery, railroads, and battles. Both printed sources of travels in the Confederacy and newspapers on microfilm from Georgia, South Carolina, and Florida are good research materials for this era. Excellent maps of this period exist and help identify regional historic areas.

The Spanish-American War (1898) sources for investigation include the regimental and military histories and the compiled service records from the U.S. Adjutant General's Office. Several excellent dissertations have been completed on this war, and Florida newspapers provide a wealth of day-by-day reporting. Personal narratives and diaries contribute to an in-depth study, as do the large holdings of photographs. Periodical literature on this period is voluminous.

Holdings treating the twentieth century include papers of Florida governors: Napoleon B. Broward, Millard F. Caldwell, Spessard L. Holland, and William S. Jennings; papers of United States Senators and Representatives: Charles O. Andrews, Spessard L. Holland, Scott Loftin, Charles Bennett, Lex Green, Joseph Hendrick, Sid Herlong, D. R. Matthews, J. Hardin Peterson, Dwight L. Rodgers, Paul G. Rodgers, and Thomas A. Yon. Major manuscript collections of members of Florida's senate and house are available. All offer vast research potential for the subject of politics and government. Five manuscript collections on the Everglades, three collections concerning the citrus industry, and two collections on integration are just a few subject areas available to the researcher. Three large manuscript collections on the barge canal exist to access its history through three centuries.

Research is supported in all subject areas by theses and dissertations, biographies, and official Florida documents. The Yonge Library holds microfilm of both metropolitan and county newspapers published throughout the state. All titles through the recent past have been filmed.

In 1985 the P. K. Yonge Library of Florida History initiated a series of publications designed to access primary source materials on Florida's history. Research Publication 1 was *The Florida Situado: Quantifying the First Eighty Years, 1571–1651* (Gainesville, 1985), by Dr. Engel Sluiter.

# 17

# FLORIDA STATE ARCHIVES

PAUL S. GEORGE

| | |
|---|---|
| Street Address: | R. A. Gray Archives |
| | Library and Museum Building |
| | 500 South Bronough Street |
| | Tallahassee, Florida 32301–0250 |
| Telephone: | (904) 487–2073 |
| Days and hours: | Monday–Friday, 8:00 A.M. to 5:00 P.M. |

IN 1967, MORE than 120 years after Florida became a state, the legislature finally created a state archives. In 1976, the State Archives was combined with the state's records management program to form the Bureau of Archives and Records Management within the Division of Library and Information Services. In the same year, the Florida State Archives moved to the new R. A. Gray Building.

The Florida State Archives administers a large collection of materials that relate to the state's history. Material on virtually any subject in Florida history can be found there. The archival collection is comprised of the following areas:

*1. Public Records Collection.* It represents the largest segment of the archives. These records were created by the departments and agencies of the state government in the course of their work and were selected for permanent retention in the archives because of their historical nature. The records are generally arranged in their original order under the agency that created them. Public records in the archives include acts of the legislature from 1821 to the present; records of Florida's governors, and various boards and commissions, court records, and selected local records. Many of the records of Florida before 1821 are located in the Library of Congress.

*2. Local Government Records.* An invaluable resource for studying local history, this segment includes resolutions and ordinances of county legislatures, county tax rolls, deeds, marriage and probate records, and school board minutes.

*3. Manuscript Collections.* These holdings are composed of a variety of collections from private citizens, organizations, businesses, and other segments of Florida society. They include family letters, diaries, business records, and other materials of Floridians.

*4. Florida Photographic Collection.* The collection consists of more than 700,000 images of Florida people and places from the mid-1800s to the present. Photographic copies, lithographs, maps, photographs, and other visual artifacts are included in the collection.

Several important collections of photographs have been obtained from across Florida. More than fifteen-thousand prints and negatives from the photographer William Fishbaugh portray Miami and Coral Gables in the 1920s and 1930s while twenty-five thousand negatives by Gordon Spottswood and his son record life in Jacksonville from the era of World War I through the 1960s. Patrons can acquire copies, either prints or negatives, of most items in the Florida Photographic Collection at a nominal cost.

*5. Genealogical Resources.* The collection consists of more than five-thousand volumes of informational resources such as family records, county histories, and U.S. Census records.

*6. Congressional Papers.* The archives contain a significant collection of papers of Floridians who served in the United States Congress. For instance, the complete papers of Congressman Don Fuqua, who represented a district in northwest Florida for many years, fill five-hundred cubic feet of space.

The Florida State Archives continues to add valuable new materials to its collection. In 1987, for instance, the archives obtained records of Florida servicemen dating from 1826. The historical documents include photographs of Florida troops from the 1890s to modern times, as well as Civil War vouchers for the Eighth Florida Regiment.

Copy services are available to all patrons. In addition to photocopies, the archives can provide copies of most types of records in its collections.

# 18

---

# THE STATE LIBRARY
# OF FLORIDA

---

BARBARA E. MATTICK

| | |
|---|---|
| Street Address: | R. A. Gray Building |
| | 500 South Bronough Street |
| | Tallahassee, Florida 32301–8021 |
| Telephone: | (904) 487–2651 |
| Days and hours: | Monday–Friday, 8:00 A.M. to 5:00 P.M., closed state holidays |

IN 1845, FLORIDA'S first state legislative council authorized the secretary of state to collect all of the state's books and maps and to establish three libraries: executive, legislative, and judicial. In spite of this early initiative, no real provision was made for a library until 1925, when the legislature created the State Library, an independent agency outside of the Department of State. This act was implemented on March 26, 1927, with the appointment of a state Library Board and the first State Librarian, William T. Cash. The new librarian was given charge of the original library collections, which held approximately twenty-five hundred titles, mostly United States and Florida government documents. He immediately began to collect additional materials through gifts, purchase, or exchange. The Works Progress Administration, through the Historical Records Survey, added greatly to the collection in the 1930s, and in 1940–41, Dorothy Dodd was hired as State Archivist.

In 1949, the State Library was moved to the state supreme court building. Dorothy Dodd became the State Librarian after Cash's death in 1952 and held that position until her retirement in 1965. During her tenure she was instrumental in building the State Library's influence and collections, with particular impact on what is now the Florida Collection.

In 1969, the State Library again came under the authority of the secretary of state when it became a division within the Department of State. In 1976, the State Library was moved to a facility specifically designed for it, the R. A. Gray Building. For the first time, the Florida Collection was housed in its own carefully controlled area, fittingly named the Dorothy Dodd Room.

The state and federal documents, which were the majority of items originally gathered in 1845, are now housed in the Documents Collection. The Florida Collection staff works very closely with other staff to coordinate research in both collections. The Florida Collection specializes in materials other than government documents covering all aspects of Florida's past, present, and future. Researchers will find information on a wide range of topics, including wildlife, business, agriculture, archaeology, the arts, Florida fiction, education, and government, as well as history. This information is in a variety of formats: books, pamphlets, maps, broadsides, clippings, pictures, and micromaterials. Although primarily intended to serve state employees on state business and public libraries throughout the state, the collection is open to patrons from the general public and is used by them regularly.

The Florida Collection is a research collection. No materials circulate. Duplicate books may be sent out of state on interlibrary loan. An unusual feature of the Florida Collection is its open book stacks. Limited photocopying is provided by the staff depending upon the condition of the desired material.

The book collection is significant in its depth and scope and includes many rare items. Materials from the late sixteenth century to the latest publications provide a broad view of Florida over three centuries. It is complimented by many subcollections of primary materials. One of the oldest of these is the Florida map collection, which contains approximately eight-hundred pieces. Original maps date from the sixteenth century to the present. Some photostats are also included. Original and photostatic reproductions of Florida city bird's-eye views are also part of the map collection.

The Florida Collection has a broadside collection of approximately two-hundred pieces, believed to be the largest collection of Florida broadsides in existence. Items date primarily from the nineteenth and twentieth centuries.

Manuscripts have been a part of the Florida Collection since its inception. Included in this collection are diaries, letters, and other personal papers; research notes; and ledgers, account books, and other business records. Most pieces date from the nineteenth and twentieth centuries; many date from the antebellum period. Major selections from this collection are the Ives, McCoy, Murat, Gavin, and Sawyer papers. The Ives Papers (1860–65, 1 diary, 5 folders) include Civil War letters and a photoreproduction of a Civil War diary. The Samuel Duff McCoy Papers (1922–25, 1955, 2 folders) are concerned with a journalist's investigation of the Martin Tabert murder which had resulted from cruelty in the Florida convict lease system. The Achille Murat Papers (1827–50, 2 boxes) deal with the Republican party in Florida and Wakulla County church records. The Albert P. and Albert H. Sawyer Papers (1891–1912, 5 boxes) are concerned with the Florida coastline canal, canal building, and land development on the lower east coast of Florida.

Diaries included in the manuscript collection are those of Florida's first governor, William D. Mosely (1850); the Seton/Fleming family (1850–54, 1867); and Thomas S. Jesup (October 1, 1836–May 30, 1837).

The Florida Collection houses Florida newspapers dating primarily from the nineteenth and early twentieth centuries. Most are microfilmed (133 reels), but some are original copies. Approximately five-hundred titles are included in this collection.

Other microfilmed materials of special interest are: original papers of the Spanish Land Grants (39 reels); Florida Military Post returns, 1800–1916 (115 reels); historical information relating to military posts and other installations, 1700–1900 (8 reels); originals of the Territorial Papers, Florida Series, October 13, 1777-September 9, 1824 (11 reels); and Leon County Court Minutes, March 14, 1824 to September 19, 1833 (1 reel).

Ephemera is another large part of the collection. Pamphlets, invitations, official programs, tickets, and promotional brochures fill twelve legal-sized drawers and two archival boxes.

Other major collections unique to the Florida Collection are: World War II military camp newspapers, city directories, political campaign literature, and church records. The military camp newspapers, including thirty-one titles, provide valuable insight into the everyday life of the military personnel who were scattered throughout the state during World War II. Besides giving glimpses of personal lives, they show the impact of the war on Florida.

The Florida Collection maintains the most complete set of back and current Florida city directories in existence. Some cities are covered from the early twentieth century. These materials are valuable sources for local information, historical preservation research, and the tracking of individuals or businesses.

The Political Campaign Literature Collection, filling two legal-sized file drawers, contains campaign material issued for candidates for statewide offices. Most date from the twentieth century, with emphasis since the 1940s.

The Florida Collection maintains an extensive collection of church minutes from most of the major Protestant denominations. Because many of the minutes date from the early nineteenth century, they are useful for researching church development, social and theological issues, and prominent church individuals. The most notable church records are the working papers of a survey of churches throughout the state, an invaluable source of historical information on individual congregations. The surveys often provide dates of founding, ministers' names, and an inventory of the church's records in existence at the time of the survey. These records are arranged by county and sometimes are further broken down by denominations. Even though the survey was never compiled into a published work, the painstakingly gathered information is preserved in the Florida Collection. The Historical Records Survey yielded ninety-six bound volumes of Works Progress Administration typescripts of writings which are not necessarily related to churches. These include diaries, memoirs, letters, documents, and other items of historic interest.

The Florida Collection is a rich source for such primary materials. The uniqueness of some and the accessibility of all, combined with the readily available supportive secondary works, make the collection a vital information center for all scholars concerned with the state of Florida.

# 19

## THE FLORIDA HISTORICAL SOCIETY LIBRARY

PAUL EUGEN CAMP

| | |
|---|---|
| Street address: | University of South Florida Library |
| | 4204 Fowler Avenue |
| | Tampa, Florida 33620 |
| Telephone: | (813) 974–3815 |
| Days and hours: | Monday–Fridays, 8:00 A.M. to 5:00 P.M. |

ESTABLISHED IN 1856 in St. Augustine, the Florida Historical Society quickly accumulated a useful collection of books, documents, and relics relating to the state's history. Over the years, the society's library has operated out of several locations. In 1962, it moved to the recently opened University of South Florida Library in Tampa. It has remained there, and is housed in the Special Collections Department of the university's main library. The Florida Historical

Society Library is open for research use by any interested person. Major Florida manuscript holdings of the Florida Historical Society include:

*El Destino Plantation Papers* (1795–1908, 1 cu. ft.). These papers relate to the operations of El Destino and Chemonie plantations in Jefferson County, Florida. The bulk of the papers deal with the operations of the plantations. Most of the papers date from the antebellum period. Many of them were published as *Florida Plantation Records from the Papers of George Noble Jones*, edited by U. B. Phillips and J. D. Glunt (St. Louis, 1927).

*Love Family Papers*, (1947, .5 cu. ft.). Manuscript and working papers for "Love Family of Gadsden County, Florida Descendants of Alexander Love Who Lived 'On the side of the Water Called Drownding Creek—Three Miles Above Betts Bridge,' Bladen County, North Carolina, and also other Allied Families" were compiled by Mrs. Pearl Trogden Love in 1947.

*Richard Keith Call Papers* (1819–1911, 2 cu. ft. plus a four-hundred-page journal). Correspondence and other papers of R. K. Call (1792–1862), a territorial governor of Florida, deal with politics, affairs of state and family affairs. The collection includes the 400-page "Journal of R.K. Call," which contains much relating to Call's service with Andrew Jackson in the Creek War and Call's military activities in the Second Seminole War (1835–42). Included in the collection are many letters and papers of Ellen Call Long, Call's daughter and author of *Florida Breezes*.

*Abram Morris Taylor Papers* (1888–1940, 4 cu. ft.). Taylor was state senator from St. Johns County, 1925–31, as well as a person very actively involved in a myriad of community-related affairs. The collection consists of correspondence, business documents, and printed ephemera, together with ledgers and other record books. It provides a wealth of material relating to St. Augustine during the Flagler era.

*Francis P. Fleming Papers* (1812–1908, 2 cu. ft.). Fleming (1841–1908) was the fifteenth governor of Florida (1889–93). He was also a Confederate officer, serving with the Second Florida Regiment. The collection includes four letterbooks covering the period 1901–08, but little relative to his term as governor. It also houses material dating from the Civil War, including twenty-nine muster rolls and other documents relating to the Second Florida Regiment (1862–63).

*Holmes Family Papers* (1826–1921, .5 cu. ft.). These papers are primarily business documents relating to the operations (lumbering activities and land transactions) of the antebellum Florida firm of Palmer and Ferris. Also included are correspondence and other papers of the Holmes family.

*Greenslade Papers* (1764–1898, 4 cu. ft.). These papers relate to the operations of the Indian trading firm of Panton, Leslie and Company and its successor, John Forbes and Company. Much of the collection consists of correspondence addressed to John Innerarity, who headed the Pensacola office of John Forbes and Company.

*Cruzat Papers* (1775–1847, 1.5 cu. ft.). These additional papers relate to the operations of the Panton, Leslie and Company and John Forbes and Company in the Spanish Floridas and southern United States.

*Herbert Jackson Drane Papers* (1922–39, .5 cu. ft.). The Drane Papers include correspondence relative to activities of Drane, a state political figure of the early 1900s, concerning Florida history, particularly Second Seminole War sites.

*F. R. Blankenship Papers* (1943–46, 1 cu. ft.). The collection relates to Blankenship's service as post engineer at Camp Gordon Johnston in Franklin County, Florida, during World War II. Materials include camp publications as well as photographs of the camp.

*Martha M. Reid Papers* (1860–1908, .5 cu. ft.). The collection consists primarily of letters between Mrs. Reid, widow of Florida territorial governor Robert Raymond Reid, and various correspondents during her service as matron at a military hospital in Virginia during the Civil War. Many of the letters are from her son Raymond, who served with the Second Florida Regiment until his death in action in April 1864.

*Pleasant Woodson White Papers* (1839–94, 1 cu. ft.). The bulk of the collection consists of official correspondence (1861–65) relating to White's service as chief of the Confederate Commissary Department in Florida during the Civil War. Much of this correspondence relates to the gathering and shipment of cattle for the Confederate army. The collection also includes family correspondence, and four letterbooks covering the period 1863–94.

*Letterbook of Governor John Milton of Florida* (1861–63, 720 pages). The official letterbook contains copies of letters written by Florida's Civil War governor, John Milton. It is accompanied by a photocopy of a continuation of the letterbook covering 1864, the original of which is in the State Archives of Florida, Tallahassee.

*Sunny South Farms Record Books* (1903–05, 7 ledgers). These are operational records of Sunny South Farms, Ft. Ogden, Florida, a citrus grove operated by Russell and Company.

*A. S. Baldwin Weather Journal* (1844–46, 1 volume). This journal of weather observations was taken at Jacksonville, Florida, for the period January 1844 to December 1846.

*New Ross Plantation Journal* (1829–33, 1 volume). This journal of operations on Judge Farquhar Bethune's New Ross Plantation, located near Jacksonville, Florida, covers the period from July 1829 to July 1833. It records daily work assignments and activities of the hands, crop information, and weather observations.

*Joseph H. Day Diary* (1877, 1 volume). This diary of a journey from Augusta, Georgia, to the Miami area from May 1, 1877, to June 13, 1877, contains useful observations on the Miami region.

*E. J. Leman Diary* (1878–79, 86 pages). This diary records a lady's tour of the South from January 19, 1878, to April 14, 1879. Much of her time was spent in St. Augustine, Florida. The diary is illustrated with contemporary photographs.

*John Wolcott Phelps Journal* (1838, 1842, 146 pages). This journal was kept by Phelps, who was an army officer during the removal of the Cherokees from North Carolina. Phelps had earlier served in the Second Seminole War, and the journal contains several references to events in Florida.

*John Pickell Journals* (1831, 2 volumes, 43 pages total). Included are parts four and five of a journal kept by Pickell while an army lieutenant engaged in surveying the route of a projected canal across East Florida. Part four covers May to August, 1831 (19 pages). The first three parts are not present.

*Thomas F. Russell Journal* (1907–08, 71 pages). The journal is an account of a hunting trip in Lee County, Florida.

*Hester Perrine Walker Account* (1885). This account of the Indian Key Massacre (August 7, 1840) was written in 1885 by Mrs. Walker, the daughter of noted botanist Henry Perrine, the best known victim of the massacre.

*David A. Watt Papers* (1890–1901, 223 pages total). The collection consists of a 180-page typescript entitled "Letty, Betty & Jo," which is an unpublished account of life in Florida and the St. Petersburg area, 1884–1889. The typescript is accompanied by correspondence relating to it, and by five manuscript accounts of a series of sailing trips along the southwest Florida coast during the period 1890 to 1901. The five accounts total 43 pages and are accompanied by contemporary snapshot photographs.

*Thomas S. Williams Day Book* (1845–72, 1 volume). The account book kept by Mr. Day in Florida, this volume was used as source material by Marjorie Kinnan Rawlings for her novel *The Yearling* (New York, 1938).

*Judson House Register* (1860–62, 1 volume folio). This is the register of guests at the Judson House, the leading hotel in Jacksonville, which was destroyed during the Civil War.

# 20

# SPECIAL COLLECTIONS, THE FLORIDA STATE UNIVERSITY LIBRARY

SUSAN HAMBURGER

| | |
|---|---|
| Mailing address: | The Robert Manning Strozier Library<br>The Florida State University<br>Tallahassee, Florida 32306–2047 |
| Telephone: | (904) 644–3271, 3219 |
| Days and hours: | Monday–Thursday, 9:00 A.M. to 6:00 P.M.; Friday 9:00 A.M. to 5:00 P.M.; closed weekends and all university holidays. |

EARLY ON, THE library began to build an impressive Floridiana collection, which is part of its Special Collections Department. By 1940, it possessed 337 volumes, among them such rare Floridiana as Godfrey's *An Authentic Narrative of the Seminole War, and of the Miraculous Escape of Mrs. Mary Godfrey, and Her Four Female Children* (Providence, 1836); Johns' *The Life and Sufferings of Mrs. Jane Johns*, 1837; Aurelia Robbins's *A True and Authentic Account of the Indian War in Florida*, 1836; William Bartram's *Travels through North and*

*South Carolina, Georgia, East and West Florida*, 1792; and Sidney A. Kimber's *A Relation, or Journal, of a Late Expedition to the Gates of St. Augustine, on Florida*, 1744.

Many of the original sources in the manuscript collection encompass local, regional, and southern history. A large span of time periods in Florida's history—from the Spanish colonial period to the twentieth century—are represented. Topical collections range from Civil War, railroads, and politics, to literature.

A small collection of early Florida records are contained in the collection. The Shelburne papers (82 items) contain British East and West Florida records. Dr. Mark F. Boyd donated photocopies of original Spanish manuscripts from the Archivos General de Indias, Seville, Spain, (845 items) dealing with the Spanish period in Florida history. An original copy of the Forbes Plat Book contains printed forms and maps outlining land holdings surveyed from 1852–56 in middle Florida. The Panton, Leslie and Company (which evolved into John Forbes and Company) originally purchased 1,250,000 acres from the Indians between 1804–11.

By far the largest source of antebellum, rural information is the Leon County plantation records for El Destino and Chemonie (16 items), Pine Hill (843 items), and Lester plantations (3 items), complemented by materials in the Elliot (2 items), Gamble (8 items), Winthrop (4,082 items), Bird and Ulmer (55 items), Bradford (194 items), Yarbrough (18 items), and Hollingsworth (520 items) papers.

Besides these antebellum records, scholars will find research materials on the Civil War, particularly the Confederacy, in diaries and letters among the Hugh Black (67 items), Fairbanks (2,017 items), Thomas (895 items), Gramling (2 items), Inglis (1 item), Love-Scarborough (137 items), Shaw (17 items), Willson (1 item), and Parkhill (39 items) papers. Music scholars will note two bound volumes of piano music owned by Susan Branch of Live Oak Plantation, Leon County, daughter of Territorial Governor John Branch.

Collections dealing with slavery constitute a small portion of the manuscript holdings. Many of the aforementioned plantation records contain information about slaves. A collection specifically about the conditions of slaves from 1830 to 1861 contains passes and permits to travel and live alone in St. Augustine (96 items). A slave bill of sale from Jackson County in 1848 documents the transactions between John Brett, Jr., and William Daniel.

Diaries often depict an individual's reaction to local, regional, or state events as well as personal affairs. William Randolph Beverly Hackley, attorney for the southern district of Florida, wrote three diaries (in the Goulding Collection) about people, events, weather, and conditions affecting life on the Florida Keys while living in Key West from 1830–57. Frank Hatheway's diary contains observations on his travels, Tallahassee activities, and his health from 1845 to 1848. John S. Winthrop's six diaries from 1889 to 1920 record his activities in Tallahassee, the local social scene, and weather and crop information on his two plantations, Barrow Place and Betton Hill.

Following the Civil War, many social, fraternal, service, and veterans organizations formed. The records of the In-As-Much Circle of the Florida Branch of the International Order of the King's Daughters and Sons (1894–1966, 3,412 items) reveal the Tallahassee group's charitable activities, including the establishment of the town's first hospital. While this group looked forward, the United Confederate Veterans, Florida Division (1889–1938, 194 items) looked backward to the war, seeking money for monuments and pensions as reflected in their minutes, records, and publications.

Merchants, particularly in Tallahassee and Leon County, kept store account books which record the goods, prices and methods of payment in towns and rural areas. The researcher can find rich sources of information in the account books of L. E. Bradley (1927–61, 18 items), R. F. Van Brunt (1902–11, 2 items), James M. Williams (1849–53, 3 items), and William P. Slusser (1860–63, 1 item). Some of Slusser's personal papers (1859–77, 10 items) document the purchase of the land for his store and a later auction sale of his goods. Other unidentified account books (1843–63, 5 items) are included in the Tallahassee Merchant Account Books collection. Two store account books from the Metcalf, Georgia/Northeast Leon County, Florida, area from 1929 to 1939 record purchases of dry goods, food, seed, wagons, and *guano* (fertilizer).

One of the largest industries in the North Florida/South Georgia area is timbering. The lumber industry records of the West Yellow Pine Company (1898–1916, 32,870 items) of Madison, Florida, and Olympia, Georgia, and the Rosasco family (1916–63, 5,238 items) of Pensacola contain materials detailing their businesses. The Rosasco and Leonard Papers (1913–50, 36,359 items) deal with naval stores, another timber industry product. The William Foster Hankins Papers (1923–65, 1,564 items) consists of research material on the lumber and timber industry in Florida. One of the unprocessed collections, the German-American Lumber Company Papers (1899–1918, 437 items), contains letter files and ledger books.

Equally as important to Florida as the lumber industry were the railroads. The Flagler Enterprises Papers (1884–1917, 2,929 items) include documents detailing the construction of railroad bridges, engineering specifications and blueprints, maps, land deeds, and plats for Henry M. Flagler's Florida East Coast Railway (F.E.C.). Carlton J. Corliss worked for the F.E.C. from 1904 to 1914 as Chief Clerk for the Key West Extension. His scrapbooks contain correspondence, articles, and pamphlets relating to the F.E.C. The papers of Jerry Carter, longtime public service commissioner, (1923–66, 40,968 items) are Interstate Commerce Commission finance dockets for Florida railroads. Antebellum railroads are represented by John D. Gray's 1836 letter concerning the St. Joseph–Lake Wimico Railroad and eight documents from the Florida Railroad Company (1855–60) construction from Fernandina to Cedar Key.

Banks played an important and controversial role in Florida's history. One holograph letter by the secretary of the Bank of Florida refers to the financial difficulties Florida banks experienced in 1844. The largest collection of bank records will be found in the Lewis Bank Papers (1854–1957, 3,296 items). The records include cash books, collection registers, daybooks, draft registers, ledgers, letterpress books, remittance registers, and other miscellaneous records for this Tallahassee institution. Examples of the bank notes and currency used in antebellum, Confederate, and postbellum Florida can be located within numerous collections.

A researcher wishing to see examples of business letterheads of Florida companies from 1879 to 1896 will find forty-nine samples ranging from hotels, livery, newspapers, real estate, factories, and citrus groves, to druggists.

Two collections of original material deal with Indians in Florida. In 1853 Florida governor Thomas Brown responded to a letter from a Georgia cavalry captain, William B. Cone, denying his offer to fight the Indians. A little more than 100 years later the Miccosukee tribe of the Seminole Indians were concerned about their rights, which are highlighted in a collection of ten letters from 1957 to 1959.

The Everglades, while the home of the Seminoles, is also the site of the Everglades National Park. The Everglades National Park Commission Papers (1946, 4 items) includes the minutes of the first meeting and a letter to property owners indicating the commission's intention to establish the park. Drainage of the Everglades and other areas of South Florida is discussed in forty-five letters written between 1911 and 1912 by Fred C. Elliot, the chief engineer and secretary of the Internal Improvement Fund. Much of Elliot's papers (1935–62, 1,548 items) deal with the Everglades. Governor Spessard Holland's papers contain eighteen letters of personal correspondence concerning the Everglades National Park in 1971.

The microfilm reels contain fifteen notebooks of correspondence, memorabilia, addresses, and articles written by Edwin B. Browning of Madison County about education in Florida from 1941 to 1973. Another collection concerned with education is the Doak Campbell Papers (1962–67) on the Governor's Committee on Quality Education (98 items) and the Governor's Conference on Education (11 items) and projects, programs, and correspondence related to national educational concerns. Within J. Valma Keen's collection are scrapbooks (1942–63, 3 items) that include clippings, letters, programs, and photographs about education in Florida. Dorothy L. Hoffman (1903–85) taught at Florida State University from 1927 to 1974. Many of her papers (2,427 items) from 1942–74 deal with FSU and the Department of Modern Languages.

The largest collection on the motion picture industry in Florida is the Richard Alan Nelson Collection (4,437 items) of photocopies of newspaper articles from 1898 to 1980. Kent Theatres in Tallahassee donated 5,521 items to the Cinema Promotional Materials collection of press books, records, taped radio commercials, and videotapes advertising films shown in the Florida Theater, Tallahassee, from 1957 to 1976.

Collections specific to Tallahassee's development cover a wide range of topics. Besides the aforementioned merchants' account books, the manuscripts collection contains seven Tallahassee city tax books from 1879 to 1887. The Tallahassee Pecan Company Records (1913–37, 131 items) are the business records of this real estate company, which bought up five-thousand acres north of Tallahassee to sell five-acre lots of pecan trees. The Frank D. Moor Collection (1884–1975 1,823 items) contains papers and records of some of the various business enterprises and service organizations in Tallahassee with which Moore was involved in his long and fruitful life.

State politics is represented by the papers of former governors, senators, and other government officials. Photocopies of personal, business, and gubernatorial papers (117 items) of former governor Albert Waller Gilchrist from 1876 to 1929 were donated. The papers of Spessard Lindsey Holland (1941–71, 21,626 items) consist of personal correspondence, campaign material, and memorabilia. The Fuller Warren Papers (1927–73, 60,900 items) cover the former governor's public, including his 1948 and 1956 campaigns, and private life. Warren's controversy with Senator Estes Kefauver's Crime Committee is well documented. Senator Duncan Upshaw Fletcher received 186 letters from numerous presidents, senators, government officials, Florida governors, and other prominent people between 1909 and 1943. Robert A. Gray served as Florida secretary of state from 1930 to 1961; he compiled fifteen scrapbooks of his life and career from 1901 to 1969. Allen Morris, newspaperman and clerk of the house, donated his extensive collection (1861–1967, 16,084 items) of personal and professional records, newspaper columns, and research materials on Florida politics. Malcolm Johnson, former editor of the *Tallahassee Democrat*, wrote about Florida politics, politicians, and environmental concerns. Included among the 9,604 items are various politicians' campaign materials, Johnson's columns, personal correspondence, subject files, and memorabilia from 1940 to 1978.

The most extensive political collection is the Mildred and Claude Pepper Library. Over 700,000 items and still growing, the Pepper Papers (1910–present) contain the official and personal papers, recordings, photographs, and memorabilia of the late Congressman Claude Pepper and his wife Mildred. Pepper's career in politics began in 1929.

# 21

# SPECIAL COLLECTIONS, UNIVERSITY OF SOUTH FLORIDA LIBRARY

PAUL EUGEN CAMP

Street address:     University of South Florida
                    4204 Fowler Avenue
                    Tampa, Florida 33620
Telephone:          (813) 974–2731
Days and hours:     Monday–Friday, 8:00 A.M. to 5:00 P.M.

FROM ITS INCEPTION in 1962, the Special Collections Department aimed at developing a comprehensive collection of Florida materials. The primary focus of its development has been on materials dealing with the history of the Tampa Bay area.

The Special Collections Department is located on the fourth floor of the University of South Florida's main library building in Tampa. The department has a staff of five, including two professional librarians. Its collections are housed in a closed stack area, and materials are retrieved on request by the staff or for use in a supervised reading room. Selective photocopying is permitted in most cases. Photography is permitted in the department for persons having photographic equipment; alternatively, arrangements may be made for photographs through the University's photographic services unit.

The archival holdings of the department total approximately 1,250 cubic feet, with an additional 471 cubic feet for the University of South Florida Archives. The collections range in date from the late eighteenth century to the present, with the bulk of the holdings falling within the period 1880 to 1970. In 1982, the Department was designated as the ultimate home for the personal research collections of Florida historians Hampton Dunn and Tony Pizzo. Much of the latter's materials relate to Ybor City, Tampa's historic Latin community.

*Jose Luis Avellanal Papers* (1915–1981, 82 cu. ft.). These papers document the life and career of Lt. General Jose Luis Avellanal-Jiminez. Much of the collection relates to Avellanal's activities in his native Tampa. General Avellanal pursued careers in medicine and law, was founder of Tampa's Pan American Federation and of the Cuban Legion of Honor, and was active in several other orders of chivalry.

*Jose Ramon Avellanal Papers* (1885–1938, 15 cu. ft.). Jose Ramon Avellanal (1869–1927) was one of Tampa's most respected physicians and founded one of the city's first public health services. For many years, he was a leading figure in Ybor City, Tampa's Latin immigrant community. His business interests included cigar manufacturing, health services, and a chain of drugstores, and ranged from New York to Cuba. The collection consists of nine cubic feet of papers generated by Dr. Avellanal plus six cubic feet of papers relating to his estate. The major groups of documents comprising the collection are correspondence files (1895–1927); files on his clinic, El Bien Publico (1904–27), records relating to his drugstore operations (1909–38), and records of his Public Welfare Company (1924–27).

*Margaret Louis Chapman Papers* (1951–71, 3.5 cu. ft.). Included are correspondence and other papers of Margaret L. Chapman (1916–81). A longtime executive secretary of the Florida Historical Society, she was active in Florida history circles, and much of the collection consists of correspondence on the history of the state with academic scholars and other researchers. The bulk of the papers date from the period 1963 to 1970.

*Papers of Governor LeRoy Collins* (1950–85, 258 cu. ft.). These papers relate to the career of (Thomas) LeRoy Collins, thirty-third governor of Florida (January 1955–January 1961). Following his term, Governor Collins served as president of the National Association of Broadcasters, and was first director of the federal Community Relations Service under President Lyndon B. Johnson. The collection includes the files related to Collins's unsuccessful senatorial campaign in 1968. In addition to 258 cubic feet of papers, the collection contains 44 linear feet of sound recordings, films, and videotapes, with much of this material dating from the 1968 campaign.

*Louis de la Parte, Jr., Papers* (1965–73, 10 cu. ft.). Included are papers relating to Mr. de la Parte's career in the Florida legislature. De la Parte represented Hillsborough County in the Florida House (1962–65) and represented District 22 (including Hillsborough County) in the Florida Senate (1967–74). He served as senate president pro tempore in 1973 and 1974.

*John W. Egerton Papers* (1955–65, 2.5 cu. ft.). Egerton served as editor of the University's news bureau from 1960 to 1965. This collection consists of a three-hundred-page manuscript with supporting research files. Entitled "The Controversy: One Man's View of Politics in the Making of a University," (Tampa, ca. 1965), Egerton's unpublished study examines the impact of the controversial Johns Committee (the Florida Legislative Investigation Committee) investigation of the University of South Florida in a McCarthy-like hunt for communists and homosexuals in the early 1960s.

*Cody Fowler Papers* (1959–68, 3 cu. ft.). The papers of Fowler (1893–1978) relate to his service as chairman of Tampa's Bi-Racial Committee (1959–64) and with the city's Commission on Community Relations (1964–67). A prominent white attorney, Fowler played a major role in facilitating nonviolent racial integration in Tampa during the turbulent Civil Rights era of the 1960s.

*Florence Irene Fritz Papers* (1930–69, 3 cu. ft.). Included are correspondence and other documents of southwest Florida publisher, author, and historian Florence Fritz, including material relating to her work as a welfare worker in Lee County, Florida, during the depression era. Much of the collection focuses on her publications, including the Fort Myers tourist magazine *Hello Stranger!* and historical books on Lee County and the surrounding area.

*George S. Gandy Papers* (1892–1941, 1 cu. ft.). Florida real estate developer and businessman George Gandy (1851–1946) is best known as the builder of Gandy Bridge (1922–24), the first bridge to span Tampa Bay. The collection consists of records relating to Gandy's enterprises, with extensive files relating to the construction and operation of Gandy Bridge.

*Papers of Congressman Sam M. Gibbons* (1954–79, 147 cu. ft.). These papers document the career of Tampan Sam M. Gibbons in the U.S. House of Representatives from 1962 to 1979. The collection also contains some material relating to Gibbons's legislative career in the Florida House of Representatives (1953–57) and Florida Senate (1959–62). The Gibbons Papers are currently under seal, and may be used only with written authorization from Congressman Gibbons.

*Dr. Stephen Gyland Papers* (1952–60, 1.5 cu. ft.). Included are correspondence and other documents of Tampa physician Stephen Gyland (1893–1960). Dr. Gyland was a pioneer in the study and treatment of functional hypoglycemia.

*Baynard Hardwick Kendrick Papers* (1915–70, 10.5 cu. ft.). Kendrick (1894–1977) was a nationally known writer of detective novels, at least twenty of which utilize Florida settings. Kendrick was also a respected Florida historian. He wrote several book-length historical works, the best known of which is an official history of the state Road Department, *Florida Trails to Turnpikes* (Gainesville, 1964). The collection includes manuscripts of most of his novels and historical writings, including an unpublished history of the Florida lumbering industry.

*Papers of Father Jerome, O.S.B.*, (1912–66, 3 cu. ft.). Father Jerome Wisniewski, O.S.B., was a horticulturalist, poet, writer, and Florida historian. He resided at St. Leo Abbey in San Antonio, Florida, from 1908 until his death. Included in the collection are correspondence, material relating to his publications, and much material relative to his Florida history research.

*Records of the Tampa Italian Club* (1912–42, 6 cu. ft.). Included are membership records of Tampa's Unione Italiana, for decades the social center of Tampa's large Italian immigrant community. The records provide such information as names, ages, and birthplaces of members, dues paid, and other membership data.

*Records of the Marti-Maceo Club* (1900–64, 6.5 cu. ft.). La Union Marti-Maceo is a mutual aid society formed by Afro-Cuban cigar workers around the turn of the century to provide medical and social benefits for its members. In 1984 the Marti-Maceo Club placed its archives, consisting of membership and financial records, meeting minutes, and other operational records of the organization, on permanent loan to the USF Special Collections Department.

*H. Lee Moffit Papers* (1974–84, 50 cu. ft.). These are papers relating to the legislative career of Tampa attorney H. Lee Moffit, who began his service career in the Florida house in 1974.

*Elwood C. Nance Papers* (ca. 1930–65, 5 cu. ft.). Educator, author, and historian, Nance (1900–65) was the author of several books related to Florida history. From 1945 to 1957 Dr. Nance was president of the University of Tampa. The collection includes correspondence files, manuscripts and research for his publications, and other materials relating to his activities in Florida and as a military chaplain during World War II.

*O'Brien Papers* (1931–65, 10 cu. ft.). This collection consists of the papers of Lucy Fulghum O'Brien, with some papers of her husband, Michael J. O'Brien. A prominent Tampan, Mrs. O'Brien was one of Tampa's first newspaperwomen. The collection contains correspondence files, including extensive correspondence with Tampa artist Jack Wilson, manuscripts and other materials relating to Mrs. O'Brien's writings, and manuscripts of Mr. O'Brien's short stories, as well as much material relevant to Tampa local history.

*Progress Village Records* (1958–70, 3 cu. ft.). These records relate to the planning and construction of Progress Village, Tampa's first low-income housing project. The collection contains correspondence files, working papers, construction plans, and a variety of other records. The great bulk of the papers dates from the period 1959 to 1960.

*Herbert S. Phillips Papers* (1871–1962, 9 cu. ft.). Phillips (1870–1962) was a Tampa educator and attorney. He served as State's Attorney for Florida's sixth Judicial Circuit from 1900 to 1913, and as U.S. District Attorney for the southern district of Florida from 1913 to 1921 and from 1936 to 1953. The collection contains correspondence, speeches, and legal cases dating from 1896 to 1962. Particularly interesting are the materials relating to Mr. Phillips's work in the cause of racial segregation (1954–62), to which he was committed.

*Sanchez y Haya Papers* (1926–53, 1.5 cu. ft.). Included are legal papers and correspondence relating to the Tampa cigar manufacturing firm of Sanchez y Haya and the Sanchez estate.

*Robert W. and Helen S. Saunders Papers* (1921–84, 19 cu. ft.). These papers relate to the careers of Mr. and Mrs. Saunders, officers of the NAACP during the Civil Rights era in Florida. Mr. Saunders served as Florida field director for the NAACP from 1952 to 1966. In the mid-70s he became Director of the Hillsborough County Equal Employment Opportunity Office. Mrs. Saunders was also a leader in the Civil Rights struggle, serving in various posts with the Tampa Branch of the NAACP, including that of president. The vast bulk of the papers date from the period 1952 to 1980.

*T. Terrell Sessums Papers* (1961–74, 67.5 cu. ft.). Papers relating to Mr. Sessum's career in the Florida House of Representatives (1963–74). Mr. Sessums was Speaker pro tempore in 1969 and 1970, and Speaker of the House in 1973 and 1974.

*Simmons Family Papers* (1772–1943, 2 cu. ft.). Included are correspondence, business, and legal papers relating to the Simmons family of North Carolina and Florida primarily in the nineteenth century.

*David Elmer Smiley Papers* (1918–27, 1 cu. ft.). Smiley (1879–1960) was a newspaper editor, publisher, and owner.

*St. Petersburg, Florida, Public School No. 83 Records* (1890–1933, 1 cu. ft.). Included are early records of the first public school in St. Petersburg, established in 1890. The core of the collection is four original school record books covering the period 1890 to 1900. The collection includes a record book for the year 1932–33, together with numerous teachers' reports and printed school ephemera. Also present is a manuscript by Olin King, the school's first principal, giving the history of the school, written in 1894–95. The records include pupil information, attendance data, records of subjects studied and texts used, and so forth.

*Jack Wilson Papers* (1864–1965, 2 cu. ft., plus oversized materials). Papers include correspondence, miscellaneous papers, and art work relating to the career of Tampa artist and book illustrator Jack Wilson (1913–65), together with a small amount of earlier material relating to the Wilson family.

*Records of the Work Projects Administration in Tampa* (1938–43, 18 cu. ft.). This collection consists mostly of working papers and drafts of projected publications generated by the Federal Writers Project in Tampa, though significant materials relating to other branches of the Works Progress Administration (W.P.A.) are also present. Although the great bulk of the materials relates to Tampa, some W.P.A. materials treating other parts of Florida are also part of the collection. In addition to publication drafts and research papers, the collection contains some records, such as worker's time sheets and staff schedules, relating to the administrative aspects of the Florida W.P.A. The collection is particularly strong in research materials relating to the history of Tampa and Ybor City during the 1930s and early 1940s.

*Walter P. Fuller Papers* (1890–1973, 15 cu. ft.). Included are correspondence, business papers, and other materials relating to Mr. Fuller's activities as a real estate developer during the Florida boom and later.

*Ku Klux Klan Minutes* (1927–28, 38 pp.) These minutes record meetings of the Palm Beach Klavern of the Ku Klux Klan, covering the period January 27, 1927, to June 19, 1928.

*James McKay Receipt Book* (1850–68, 149 leaves). Receipts for sums paid by prominent Tampa cattleman and ship owner Captain James McKay cover purchases of cattle and other goods and services. Each receipt is signed by the recipient, and most include a description of the goods sold.

*Tampa Cattle Shipment Record Book* (1880, 48 pp.). This is a record of cattle shipped from Ballast Point (Tampa) for five months in 1880. Each entry records marks and brands of the cattle comprising the shipment, the shipper, the name of the ship and the name of the ship's master.

*Tampa Customs House Record Book* (1887–93, 94 pp.). This is a record of seizures of contraband found on ships entering the Port of Tampa from September 22, 1887, to July 6, 1893. Entries include such information as the type of contraband and the name of the ship on which it was found.

# 22

# SOURCES FOR THE STUDY OF WEST FLORIDA PREHISTORY, HISTORY, AND CULTURE

## JAMES A. SERVIES

THE MAJOR DEPOSITORY for materials relating to the history of the Florida panhandle—embracing Bay, Calhoun, Escambia, Gulf, Holmes, Jackson, Okaloosa, Santa Rosa, Walton, and Washington counties—is the John C. Pace Library of The University of West Florida. An extensive collection of local imprints, 1821 to date, is available, together with a wide variety of printed materials touching the archaeology and history of the region. Resources include files of county newspapers, many of them unique; microfilmed documents from foreign archives; original manuscripts, including family papers and business records of West Florida interest; and printed materials touching adjacent portions of the Gulf Coast.

### *JOHN C. PACE LIBRARY, SPECIAL COLLECTIONS DEPARTMENT*

Street address:     11,000 University Parkway
                            Pensacola, Florida

Mailing address:    The University of West Florida
                            Pensacola, Florida 32514-5750

Telephone:              (904) 474–2710
Days and hours:         Monday–Friday, 8:00 A.M. to 4:30 P.M.; Saturday, 8:00 A.M.
                        to noon

All materials are available to researchers either by visiting the library's Special Collections Department or by correspondence. Microfilm readers and printers are available; photocopy equipment is also available at a modest charge. A limited number of study facilities are available for extended research.

Comprehensive finding aids to the library's resources are available to users. The library's *Guide to the Manuscripts & Special Collections* (Pensacola, 1979), has been supplemented by detailed inventories of individual manuscript collections. *A Bibliography of West Florida*, compiled by James A. Servies (3rd ed., Pensacola, 1982, 3 vols.; supplement, 1982, 1 vol.), is a chronological guide to the printed literature of the region, 1535–1981. Included are local imprints; works in all subject fields touching the life of West Florida; printed documentary sources concerning its exploration and early history; guides to manuscript collections of regional interest; pertinent state, federal and local documents; and articles in periodicals and scholarly journals. The *Bibliography* is indexed in detail: supplements are issued in five-year intervals.

A "Bibliography of Florida, 1500–1945," an expansion of the *Bibliography of West Florida*, is being compiled by Mr. and Mrs. James A. Servies; inquiries should be addressed to them at 1305 Lansing Dr., Pensacola, FL 32504.

The library's cataloged holdings are included in the OCLC computerized database. As a member of the Florida Center for Library Automation, The University of West Florida also participates in the statewide network and is a member of the Research Libraries Information Network (RLIN). A variety of local and commercial databases are available to scholars.

The special resources of the John C. Pace Library, The University of West Florida, include printed materials touching the historic British West Florida region, embracing portions of the present states of Alabama, Mississippi, and Louisiana. Special collections are available for the study of regional maps, photographs, and printed ephemera; emphasis is placed on documentary sources relating to the chief exploitive activities in the region—lumbering and fishing—and papers relating to the social life and origins of its people.

Major collections of historical manuscripts in The University of West Florida library include: the business papers, letterbooks, and ledgers of the Alger-Sullivan Lumber Company, 1800–1957, one of the largest firms in the State and founder of Century, Florida; papers of the Axelson-Newton families of Walton and Escambia counties; the legal and family papers of the Blount family of Pensacola, especially William Alexander Blount (1851–1921), the first Floridian to serve as president of the American Bar Association, and his sons, Fernando Moreno Blount (1882–1966) and Alexander Clement Blount (1889–1978), both prominent Pensacola lawyers and civic leaders; general papers, correspondence, and medical records of Herbert Lee Bryans, M.D. (1889–1961), president of the American Medical Association, 1935, and president of the Florida State Board of Health, 1941–57; the personal, political and selected official papers of Florida Governor Sidney J. Catts (1863–1936); correspondence and legal and educational papers of Harold Bryan Crosby, judge of the First Judicial Circuit of Florida and founder and first president of the University of West Florida; the Fred O. Howe Papers, including business records of his ship brokerage firm, ca. 1890–1940, and the Pensacola division of the Louisville and Nashville Railroad, ca. 1929–48; the Innerarity-Hulse Papers, 1793–1915, including correspondence and business records of the Pensacola-based Indian trading firms Panton, Leslie and Company and John Forbes and Company, the papers of Dr. Isaac Hulse, Surgeon of the Pensacola Navy Yard, and legal papers touching titles to the Forbes lands near Apalachicola; the Thomas A. Johnson Papers, a onetime Chairman of the Florida State Road Department; the personal and political papers of U.S. Senator Charles W. Jones (1834–97) and his son, John Bryne Jones (1866–1954), Pensacola civic leader and city manager; diaries, family papers, and correspondence of Frank C. Horton and his wife, Esther Landrum Horton, of Mobile, Alabama, and Pensacola, ca. 1888–1910; the McLaughlin family papers, including the corporate and financial records of the several railroad companies established by Elwood McLaughlin and other members of the family, 1868–1962; the scrapbooks, correspondence, and miscellaneous papers collected by Miss B. A. Murphy (d. 1967), of Pensacola; the Panton, Leslie Papers, including microfilm and photocopies of manuscripts from numerous repositories throughout the world, relating to that firm and to John Forbes and Company, 1739–1847, assembled by Dr. William S. Coker; the Rolfs family papers, including papers relating to the German-American Lumber Company; the Rosasco family papers, including the reports of the Bay Point Mill Company, of Bagdad, the business and social papers of William S. Rosasco (1855–1931) and his family, of Milton and Pensacola, and correspondence of the Rosasco Brothers firm of Pensacola and Genoa, Italy; the watercolor and pencil sketches of George Washington Sully (1816–70), depicting scenes along the Gulf Coast, ca. 1820–49; the archives of The University of West Florida, 1964–84; family papers and printed materials reflecting activities of Thomas Campbell Watson (1844–1918) and his family; legal and personal papers of William H. Watson (1876–1967), Pensacola attorney, including the correspondence of Timothy W. Bludworth (1821–64), from Civil War battlefields in Tennessee and Virginia, and papers relating to the Baker family of Surry County, Virginia, and West Florida; correspondence, legal papers, and business records of the Yonge family, 1781–1934, with emphasis on legal affairs and land speculation in territorial Florida. The papers and correspondence of longtime United States Congressman Robert L. F. Sikes, formerly on deposit with the University of West Florida, have been transferred to Congressman Sikes's office. Inquiries should be addressed to him, in care of the Robert L. F. Sikes Public Library, 805 Highway 90 E., Crestview, Florida, 32536.

The documentary, archival, and artifactual sources for the study of West Florida history are available in many other specialized agencies in the region. The more important depositories include:

## HISTORIC PENSACOLA PRESERVATION BOARD

| | |
|---|---|
| Street address: | 205 East Zaragoza Street<br>Pensacola, Florida |
| Mailing address: | P. O. Box 308<br>Pensacola, Florida 32592 |
| Telephone: | (904) 444–8905 |
| Days and hours: | Monday–Saturday, 10:00 A.M. to 4:30 P.M. |

A research library and collection of artifacts recovered from the historic district are maintained; special emphasis is placed on maps, photographs, and documentary records touching the historic structures, individuals, businesses, and agencies associated with the Pensacola Historic District.

## T. T. WENTWORTH, JR., FLORIDA STATE MUSEUM

| | |
|---|---|
| Street address: | 330 South Jefferson Street<br>Pensacola, Florida 32501 |
| Telephone: | (904) 444–8586 |
| Days and hours: | Monday–Saturday, 10:30 A.M. to 4:30 P.M.; Sunday, 1:00 P.M.<br>to 4:30 P.M. |

The historical collections of the T. T. Wentworth, Jr., Museum have recently been donated to the state and are administered by the Historic Pensacola Preservation Board. Resources include local imprints, general books and newspapers, archaeological materials primarily of West Florida interest, photographs and works of art, Indian relics, documents from foreign archives, family correspondence, and business records.

## THE HISTORICAL SOCIETY MUSEUM

| | |
|---|---|
| Street address: | 115 Westview Avenue<br>Valparaiso, Florida 32580 |
| Mailing address | Historical Society of Okaloosa, and Walton Counties, Inc.<br>Same |
| Telephone: | (904) 678–2615 |
| Days and hours: | Tuesday–Saturday, 11:00 A.M. to 4:00 P.M.; Sunday, 2:30 P.M.<br>to 5 P.M. |

Resources now consist of over twenty-five thousand items, including printed materials, artifacts, family papers, genealogical files, audiovisual materials, and business records. Of special interest are the collections of farm, household, and industrial implements derived from the heartland communities in West Florida. The Museum is open to the public from 11:00 A.M. to 4:00 P.M., Tuesday through Saturday; 2:30 to 5:00 P.M., Sunday.

## THE NAVAL AVIATION MUSEUM

Mailing address:        U.S. Naval Air Station
                        Pensacola, Florida 32508

Telephone:              (904) 452–3604

Days and hours:         Monday–Sunday, 9:00 A.M. to 5:00 P.M.

A small research library is maintained together with audiovisual resources and log books of early aviators.

## THE PENSACOLA HISTORICAL MUSEUM

Street address:         405 South Adams Street
                        Pensacola, Florida 32501

Telephone:              (904) 433–1559

Days and hours:         Monday–Saturday, 9:00 A.M. to 4:30 P.M.

A major depository for West Florida materials, both printed and three-dimensional, is the Lelia Abercrombie Historical Library, featuring genealogical files relating to Escambia and Santa Rosa county families and printed works reflecting Pensacola history from the late eighteenth century until the present day. Many artifacts, including prehistoric and historic Indian relics, are also preserved.

The museum also offers over fifty-thousand photographs and glass-plate negatives by local photographers, ca. 1860–1940, oral history tapes, and ephemera illustrating the social and economic life of the community since Reconstruction.

Major individual collections include the account books, correspondence, and business papers, ca. 1790–1915, of Dr. G. O. Brosnaham, artifacts and general works relating to Christ Church, ca. 1790–1955; the family papers and business correspondence of John A. Kirkpatrick, ca. 1885–1903; deeds, corporate papers and business records of J. S. Leonard, ca. 1868–1915; the Stephen Russell Mallory Collection, including correspondence of members of the family, ca. 1858–96, and biographical notes by the late Miss Occie Clubbs; the Saltmarsh Family Collections, including scrapbooks with notes touching the social life of Pensacola, ca. 1900–12; business records of the Southern States Lumber Company, ca. 1890–1930; and the genealogical notes and papers of Ella Rupert Wright.

The museum has sponsored a variety of historical publications and is the publisher of *Pensacola History Illustrated*.

### THE TEMPLE MOUND MUSEUM

| | |
|---|---|
| Street address: | 139 Miracle Strip Parkway<br>Fort Walton Beach, Florida |
| Mailing address: | P.O. Box 1449<br>Fort Walton Beach, Florida 32548 |
| Telephone: | (904) 243–6521 |
| Days and hours: | Tuesday–Saturday, 10:00 A.M. to 4:00 P.M.; Sunday, 1:00 P.M.<br>to 4:00 P.M. |

A small research library is maintained, together with audio-visual materials, maps, and a research collection of over five-thousand items of cultural materials of Indian origin.

### COURTHOUSES OF WEST FLORIDA

The historian, genealogist, and specialist will find extensive resources relating to West Florida counties among the retrospective records preserved in the court-houses.

*Bay County.* Clerk of the Circuit Court, 300 E. 4th Street, Panama City, Florida 32401; telephone (904) 763–9061. Records include Deed books and mortgages from 1885; marriages, civil and criminal cases, military discharges, incorporations, and county commission minutes from 1913.

*Escambia County.* Clerk of the Circuit and County courts, Judicial Center, 190 Governmental Center, Pensacola, Florida 32501–5796; telephone (904) 436-5240. Included are wills and probate records from 1821; circuit and county court cases from 1804; and deeds, marriage records, business transactions from 1821; naturalization files, 1885–1903; voter registrations, from 1912; and administrative papers of the county from 1875.

*Holmes County.* Clerk of the Court, 201 N. Oklahoma Street, Bonifay, Florida 32425; telephone (904) 547–3656. County records available on microfilm from the early 1900's include deeds, mortgages, probates, civil and criminal dockets, and minutes of the county commission.

*Jackson County.* Clerk of the Court, P.O. Drawer 510, Marianna, Florida 32446; telephone (904) 482–3354. Included are deed books from 1848; tax records from 1895; original tax books (fragmentary, ca. 1860–99), wills and estates, from 1836; county and circuit records from 1848; and marriages from 1848.

Records transferred to the State Library include tax books, 1820–42; census records, 1825–62; court records (scattered, ca. 1828–94); contracts and bonds, 1827–58; treasurer's reports and accounts, 1823–35.

*Okaloosa County.* Clerk of the Circuit Court, Courthouse, Crestview, Florida 32536; telephone (904) 682–2711. Included are complete files of county records from its formation in 1915.

*Santa Rosa County*. Clerk of the Courts, P.O. Box 472, Milton, Florida 32572; telephone (904) 623–3639. Official records include deeds, marriages, probates, and miscellaneous court records. Name indexes are contained in most of the volumes.

*Walton County*. Clerk of the Circuit and County Court, 100 East Nelson Avenue, P.O. Box 1260, DeFuniak Springs, Florida 32433; telephone (904) 892–3134. Included are complete files of marriages from 1885; probate records from 1882; deeds from ca. 1880; and some county newspapers from 1910.

*Washington County*. Clerk of the Circuit Court, P.O. Box 647, 201 W. Jackson Avenue, Chipley, Florida 32428–0647; telephone (904) 638–0281. Included are county records from ca. 1885.

# 23

# MANUSCRIPT COLLECTIONS IN DUVAL COUNTY

## DANIEL SCHAFER

WITH TWO THRIVING historical societies in Jacksonville, as well as two universities and a multicampus junior college, it is disappointing to learn that there are few significant collections of historical manuscripts available to local researchers. While manuscripts concerning Northeast Florida can be found at the P. K. Yonge Library of Florida History at the University of Florida and elsewhere, few can be found in Duval County. Those that are available are located at the Thomas G. Carpenter Library at the University of North Florida, the Florida Room at the Haydon Burns Public Library, the Beaches Historical Society Library, and the Jacksonville Historical Society holdings at Jacksonville University.

### *EARTHA M. M. WHITE AND JOHN E. MATHEWS, JR., COLLECTIONS, UNIVERSITY OF NORTH FLORIDA*

Street address:     4567 St. Johns Bluff Boulevard South
                    Jacksonville, Florida 32216

Mailing address:        P.O. Box 17074
                        Jacksonville, Florida 32216


Telephone:              (904) 646–2618

Days and hours:         By appointment only.

The collections of greatest importance in Duval County are those of Eartha
M. M. White, and the John E. Mathews, Jr. Eartha White, born in Jacksonville
in 1878, became one of the most respected black citizens in the city's history.
Teacher, social worker, real estate broker, opera singer, and philanthropist, Ms.
White was also the founder of a "colored" orphanage, two "old folks homes,"
and the Clara White Mission. Avidly interested in Afro-American history and
culture, Ms. White collected manuscripts, documents, photographs, newspaper
clippings, notes, and memorabilia throughout her lifetime that are preserved in
this collection. Its strength is the more than one-thousand photographs of persons
and institutions in Jacksonville's black community. There are also several boxes
of photographs of religious and labor groups in the South taken by R. Lee
Thomas, an itinerant black photographer from Mound Bayou, Mississippi.

John E. Mathews, Jr., born in Jacksonville in 1920, was a leading member
of Florida's House of Representatives and Senate from 1956 to 1970 and an
unsuccessful candidate for governor. He was instrumental in reapportionment,
the writing of a new state constitution, and expansion of the Florida State
University System. Manuscripts in this extensive collection detail Mathews's
early life, family members, college days, military experience, legal career, and
his activities in the Florida legislature. There are numerous photographs, some
memorabilia, and an extensive collection of papers relevant to the career of John
E. Mathews, Sr., a Florida Supreme Court justice.

## BEACHES AREA HISTORICAL SOCIETY

Street address:         415 Pablo Avenue
                        Jacksonville Beach, Florida 32250

Mailing address:        P.O. Box 50646
                        Jacksonville Beach, Florida 32240

Telephone:              (904) 246–0093

Days and hours:         By appointment only.

Holdings at the Beaches Area Historical Society are primarily limited to
newspapers, scrapbooks, and photographs of life at Jacksonville's beaches.
There is an 1889 register from the Murray Hall Hotel, Pablo Beach, Florida
(now Jacksonville Beach), and a manuscript collection donated by Ernest Porter,
founder of the Jacksonville Beaches Life Saving Corporation.

## *HAYDEN BURNS PUBLIC LIBRARY*

| | |
|---|---|
| Street address: | 122 North Ocean Street<br>Jacksonville, Florida 32202 |
| Telephone: | (904) 630–2413 |
| Days and hours: | Monday, 10:00 A.M. to 8:00 P.M.; Tuesday-Thursday, 10:00 A.M. to 5:30 P.M.; Friday–Saturday, 10:00 A.M. to 6:00 P.M.; Sunday (September to May only), 1:00 P.M. to 5:00 P.M. |

The Florida Room at the Haydon Burns Public Library has Duval County's largest collection of historical materials related to Florida. The collection consists primarily of printed materials, including city law books from 1868, city council minutes, and rare books and maps. Manuscript collections include Patrick Egan's accounts of the Civil War in Florida (Egan was a member of the Third Rhode Island Heavy Artillery), and the 1864 diary of Lieutenant Cyrus W. Brown, of the Third Regiment of United States colored troops. The diary of General Harvey Brown, with commentary by his daughter Emily Brown, contains information on East Florida from 1821 to 1828 and from 1835 to 1837. The papers of Mrs. Charles Gobert are concerned with land holdings and property sales in East Florida prior to the Civil War. The final collection, the Personal Record of Howard P. Wright, contains documents and testimonials to Wright's career as an FBI agent, mostly concerning events outside Florida from 1915 to 1930. There is also a volume of correspondence and minutes of meetings of the Kirby-Smith Camp, Sons of Confederate Veterans.

## *THE JACKSONVILLE HISTORICAL SOCIETY, JACKSONVILLE UNIVERSITY LIBRARY*

| | |
|---|---|
| Street address: | 2800 North University Boulevard<br>Jacksonville, Florida 32211 |
| Telephone: | (904) 744–3962 |
| Days and hours: | By appointment only. |

The Jacksonville Historical Society maintains its library holdings at the Jacksonville University Library. The collection consists mainly of printed materials and photographs, with only a few manuscript materials. A typewritten manuscript by Calvin Robinson entitled "An account of some of my experiences in Florida during the rise and progress of the Late rebellion," contains priceless eyewitness observations of Jacksonville during the Civil War. Miscellaneous manuscripts, photographs, and scrapbooks pertaining to the life of Jacksonville architect Mellen Clark Greeley can be found in the collection. There is an 1870 diary by Mary Ann Bigelow, information related to the Emily Broward chapter of the Children of the Confederacy, and six folders of materials concerning the lumber industry in Northeast Florida (compiled by Addie Welch Crosby). A manuscript by Soloman M. Brash explores the history of Congregation Ahaveth Chesed. Ernest LeBaron has compiled a history of his grandfather, surveyor and engineer John Francis LeBaron, which includes a manuscript diary of 1869.

# 24

# HISTORICAL COLLECTIONS IN VOLUSIA COUNTY

THOMAS W. TAYLOR

LARGELY UNKNOWN, VOLUSIA County is a storehouse of remarkable historical information. Several collections of national importance are located there as well as the sources for research material of state and regional significance.

## *MARY MCLEOD BETHUNE FOUNDATION*

Street address:      Carl S. Swisher Library
                     Bethune–Cookman College
                     640 Second Avenue
                     Daytona Beach, Florida 32014

Telephone:           (904) 255–1401

Days and hours:      By appointment only.

Perhaps the most important of the nationally significant collections is the depository of the papers of Mary McLeod Bethune, located at the headquarters of the Mary McLeod Bethune Foundation in her historic home on the campus of Bethune-Cookman College in Daytona Beach. This unique collection includes letters, diaries, photographs, and artifacts which belonged to this black luminary. This library also includes documents on the founding and history of Bethune-Cookman College.

### THE HALIFAX HISTORICAL SOCIETY MUSEUM

| | |
|---|---|
| Street address: | 252 South Beach Street |
| | Daytona Beach, Florida 32014 |
| Telephone: | (904) 255–6976 |
| Days and hours: | Tuesday–Saturday, 10:00 A.M. to 4:00 P.M. |

This museum contains an interesting and unique collection of information concerning the early history of automobile racing. Assembled through a period of many years by Lawson Diggett, it includes documents from Daytona Beach and the world's other great race tracks. Diggett also collected information on local history, and his huge 1930s model of the Daytona Beach boardwalk is a masterpiece. Other Diggett models are interesting examples of what we would today call "folk art," and reflect the life and times of Central Florida in the early twentieth century.

Of regional and local significance, the Halifax Historical Society Museum collections include an eight-hundred-year-old Timucuan canoe and many other Indian artifacts, as well as files and artifacts relating to Indigo and sugar plantations in the British period and in the Second Spanish period. The Charles Bockelman collection contains information on the eighteenth century King's Road and the Second Seminole War of the 1830s. The museum's archives include a remarkable newspaper collection for the area which, with a few gaps, goes back to 1883. Ten thousand photographs and thousands of early post cards document the visual appearance of the Halifax area during the past century, and files and notes on the area's early families prepared by noted historians Ianthe Bond Hebel, Copeland Smith, and others represent a wealth of information yet to be tapped. Numerous important artifacts, including the bell from the first steam locomotive to enter Daytona and the Bible belonging to Matthias Day, the city's founder, are among the items on display at the museum.

### VOLUSIA COUNTY LIBRARIES

The various libraries throughout the county also have information on local history.

*The DuPont-Ball Library.* Stetson University, 421 North Boulevard, DeLand, Florida 32720; telephone (904) 734–4121, extension 220. This library contains the Florida Baptist Archives, information relating to Stetson University, and early newspapers of DeLand and Volusia County.

*The Brannon Memorial Library*. 105 South Riverside Drive, New Smyrna Beach, Florida 32069; telephone (904) 428–2572. This library contains files on the local history of New Smyrna Beach and books on the ill-fated colony of New Smyrna established by Dr. Andrew Turnbull in 1769.

*The Ormond Beach Public Library*. 30 South Beach Street, Ormond Beach, Florida 32074; telephone (904) 673–0163. This library houses photographs and books by local authors treating the early history of Ormond Beach.

# 25

---

# HISTORICAL COLLECTIONS IN ST. AUGUSTINE

---

## WILLIAM R. ADAMS

AS THE OLDEST continuously inhabited settlement of European origin in the United States, the diminutive city of St. Augustine occupies a position of unparalleled significance in U.S. and Florida history. Throughout the colonial period (1565–1821), Spain administered its territorial claims in the southeastern United States from St. Augustine. During the hiatus of British control (1764–84), the city served as the capital of British East Florida. Accordingly, the historical documentation pertaining to the city transcends local and state importance.

### *THE ARCHIVES OF THE DIOCESE OF ST. AUGUSTINE*

| | |
|---|---|
| Street address: | 11625 Old St. Augustine Road<br>Mandarin, Florida 32241 |
| Mailing address: | P.O. Box 24000<br>Jacksonville, Florida 32241 |
| Telephone: | (904) 262–3200 |
| Days and hours: | Monday–Friday, 8:30 A.M. to 4:30 P.M. |

The parish records, containing the baptismal, marriage, and death certificates and records maintained by the church from 1594 to 1821, are housed in the archives of the Diocese of St. Augustine. The diocesan archives also contains correspondence and other records relating to parish and diocesan activity.

## THE ST. AUGUSTINE HISTORICAL SOCIETY

| | |
|---|---|
| Street address: | 271 Charlotte Street<br>St. Augustine, Florida 32084 |
| Telephone: | (904) 824–2872 |
| Days and hours: | Monday–Friday, 9:00 A.M. to 5:00 P.M. |

The St. Augustine Historical Society, organized in 1885, contains manuscripts, documentary materials, and published works dealing with St. Augustine. Its microfilm holdings of collections from the Spanish archives emulate those found at the P. K. Yonge Library of Florida history. Records pertaining to property ownership and description in the city of St. Augustine, including block and lot cards, inventories, deeds, tax assessor's inventories, various maps from the colonial period to the present, and the individual property information compiled in the 1978–81 comprehensive survey of sites and properties are found at the society's library. The society's extensive holdings include miscellaneous files and photographs on individual sites and buildings, subject files, and a comprehensive collection of serial and published secondary works pertaining to the city's history. The society now serves as custodian for municipal and county records. Especially vital are the nineteenth-century records maintained by St. Johns County, which served for much of that time as the seat of local government for most of East Florida.

## HISTORIC ST. AUGUSTINE PRESERVATION BOARD

| | |
|---|---|
| Street address: | Government House<br>St. George and Cathedral Streets<br>St. Augustine, Florida 32084 |
| Telephone: | (904) 825–5033 |
| Days and hours: | By appointment |

The Historic St. Augustine Preservation Board, an agency of the State of Florida, possesses a well-organized collection of maps for the city, and the individual Florida Master Site file forms for more than 2,300 historic sites and buildings in the city. The board has sponsored the archaeological investigations that have been proceeding since the early 1960s and has many of the records assembled from that work.

## THE NATIONAL PARK SERVICE

Street address:            Castillo de San Marcos
                           One Castillo Drive
                           St. Augustine, Florida 32084

Telephone:                 (904) 829–6506

Days and hours:            Monday–Friday, 9:00 A.M. to 4:00 P.M.

The National Park Service office maintains a collection of documents designed to support interpretative and preservation activities at the site. Its microfilm holdings are extracted from materials contained in the Spanish documents collection at the P. K. Yonge Library of Florida History. Some records from the U.S. Army Corps of Engineers Jacksonville District Office have been gathered in the research files of the Castillo.

## HEADQUARTERS OF THE ADJUTANT GENERAL OF THE STATE OF FLORIDA

Street address:            Marine and St. Francis Streets
                           St. Augustine, Florida 32085

Mailing address:           Department of Military Affairs
                           P.O. Box 1008
                           St. Augustine, Florida 32085

Telephone:                 (904) 824–8461

Days and hours:            Monday–Friday, 8:00 A.M. to 5:00 P.M.

The holdings include incomplete muster rolls from the Indian wars (1835–42 and 1852–56) and lists of Confederate and Union troops from Florida. Organized muster rolls for the Florida militia are found for the 1896–1918 period as well as for personnel enlisted in the Florida National Guard since 1898. Particularly interesting are the service records for the approximately forty-thousand men who served during World War I.

# 26

# COLLECTIONS IN HILLSBOROUGH COUNTY

PAUL EUGEN CAMP

## *HILLSBOROUGH COUNTY HISTORICAL COMMISSION*

| | |
|---|---|
| Mailing address: | Museum and Research Room, Second Floor<br>Hillsborough County Courthouse<br>Tampa, Florida 33602 |
| Telephone: | (813) 272–5919 |
| Days and hours: | Monday–Friday, 10:00 A.M. to 4:00 P.M. |

THE HILLSBOROUGH COUNTY Historical Commission provides a museum of local and state historical items. It also maintains a research and genealogical library specializing in Florida and southeastern United States census records. Florida manuscript holdings of the Hillsborough County Historical Commission include:

*Carlton Family Records* (from 1775, 1 folder). Records relating to the Carlton family were compiled by Mrs. John Branch. These materials deal with the

Carlton and allied families in North Carolina, Georgia, and Florida.

*George T. Davis Papers* (1934, 1 folder). Holdings include photographs, sound tapes, newspaper items, biographical information, and other materials relating to Mr. Davis, builder of the Davis Causeway (later renamed Courtney Campbell Causeway) across Tampa Bay. The collection contains information relative to the Davis family and to the building of the causeway.

## CITY OF TAMPA ARCHIVES AND RECORDS CENTER

| | |
|---|---|
| Street address: | 1104 East Twiggs Street |
| | Tampa, Florida 33602 |
| Telephone: | (813) 223–8030 |
| Days and hours: | Monday–Friday, 8:00 A.M. to 4:00 P.M. |

The city's archival and records collections contain the official records of Tampa's municipal government. The collection includes very extensive microfilm holdings. Additionally, those city records which are considered to have permanent historical value are housed in the City Archives, and are being microfilmed to ensure their preservation. The archival collection contains the original minute books of the city, dating back to the late 1800s. The collection also includes records of the Town of Fort Brooke and the City of West Tampa, municipalities that now comprise part of the city of Tampa.

## SPECIAL COLLECTIONS DEPARTMENT

| | |
|---|---|
| Street address: | Tampa/Hillsborough County Public Library |
| | 900 North Ashley Street |
| | Tampa, Florida 33602 |
| Mailing address: | Same |
| Telephone: | (813)223–8865 |
| Days and hours: | Monday–Thursday, 9:00 A.M. to 9:00 P.M.; Friday, 9:00 A.M. to 6:00 P.M.; Saturday, 9:00 A.M. to 5:00 P.M. |

The Special Collections Department of the Tampa Public Library houses the library's Florida materials, local history collection, and genealogy collection, as well as a variety of rare or special books. The Department's holdings are particularly strong in original photographic materials portraying the Tampa area from the late nineteenth century to the 1960s. Manuscript holdings include:

*Burgert Brothers Photographic Registers* (1885–1962, 14 ledgers). Manuscript registers recording photographic work done by Burgert Brothers, Tampa's leading commercial photographers during the late nineteenth and first half of the twentieth centuries. The original registers serve as a key to the Burgert Brothers' negative archive of over forty-thousand photographic negatives, which is also housed in the Special Collections Department.

*Document Relating to the Establishment of Georgia* (1732?, 92 pp.). This is a manuscript entitled "Some Account of the Designs of the Trustees for Establishing Colonys in America," apparently written in London, circa 1732, for the Trustees for Establishing the Colony of Georgia in America. The document relates to planning for the establishment of the colony of Georgia. It relates to Florida only in that the territory that became Georgia was viewed by the Spanish as part of Florida.

*City of Tampa Major Street Plan* (1941, 192 pp.). The typescript entitled "Report on Major Street Plan for City of Tampa, Florida," was prepared by the Simmons-Sheldrick Company and dated Jacksonville, 7/25/1941. It is illustrated with original photographs of the streets discussed. The report examines Tampa's road net in detail, identifying problem areas and recommending solutions.

### MERL KELCE LIBRARY, UNIVERSITY OF TAMPA

| | |
|---|---|
| Street address: | 401 West Kennedy Boulevard |
| | Tampa, Florida 33505 |
| Telephone: | (813) 253–3333, ext. 464 |
| Days and hours: | Monday–Thursday, 8:00 A.M. to 12:00 midnight; Friday, 8:00 A.M. to 5:00 P.M.; Saturday, 1:00 P.M. to 5:00 P.M.; Sunday, 1:00 P.M. to 12:00 midnight; closed holidays and when school is not in session. |

*William C. Cramer Papers* (1954–70, 43 cu. ft.). The Cramer Collection contains correspondence and other papers relating to U.S. Representative William C. Cramer's sixteen-year career in Congress. A longtime resident of St. Petersburg, Cramer served as a Florida congressman from 1954 to 1970.

*Paul Danahy Collection* (1953–74, 10.5 cu. ft.). The collection, named for its donor Judge Paul Danahy, includes correspondence, reports, publications, and other materials relating to governmental consolidation attempts in Hillsborough County.

**27**

---

# BROWARD COUNTY HISTORICAL COLLECTIONS

---

## RODNEY E. DILLON, JR.

BROWARD COUNTY HAS, in the past decade, experienced a notable awakening of interest in local history. This phenomenon has been manifested in the creation of numerous local historical societies, increased historic preservation efforts, the appearance of several historical publications, and the development of two principal archives.

### *BROWARD COUNTY HISTORICAL COMMISSION*

| | |
|---|---|
| Street address: | 100 South New River Drive, East |
| | Fort Lauderdale, Florida 33301 |
| Telephone: | (305) 765–5872 |
| Days and hours: | Monday–Friday, 8:00 A.M. to 4:30 P.M. |

The Broward County Historical Commission was created by county ordinance in 1972 and given broad responsibilities for preserving and promoting interest in Broward County's history. It has conducted public functions which promote historical interest, issued publications, designated and assisted in the preservation of historic sites, and assisted in the creation and work of historical and history-related societies. It has also a comprehensive research archives for the county and the surrounding area.

The earliest known documents pertaining to the land which today is Broward County are maps from the first Spanish and British periods outlining Florida's Atlantic coastal features. Twenty-three of these maps are among the over five-hundred maps, charts, and plats in the Historical Commission's map collection. Among these early maps are the 1507 Tabula Terra Nova and the 1631 America Septemtrionalis, first to identify New River (R. Novo) by its present name.

The second Spanish and early territorial periods, during which the first non-Indian settlement in present-day Broward County flourished, are represented by microfilms of the Monroe County (of which today's Broward County was then a part) Deed Books A and B, 1824–38 (2 rolls), the *Key West Gazette*, 1831–32 (1 roll), and the *Key West Inquirer*, 1834–36 (1 roll). Additional information on the New River Settlement from circa 1788 to 1836 can be found in documents located in the commission's vertical files. These papers deal with several of the early settlers, most notably the Lewis and Cooley families.

The Second Seminole War marked the end of the New River Settlement and brought United States forces into the southeastern Florida wilderness. The Historical Commission's collection of National Archives microfilm for the Seminole War period is one of the largest and most comprehensive in southern Florida. This collection includes selections from *Letters Received by the Office of the Adjutant General, 1836–42* (27 rolls); *Letters Sent by the Office of Indian Affairs, Florida Superintendency and Seminole Agency Emigration, 1824–50* (7 rolls); *Memoir of Reconnaissances with Maps during the Florida Campaign, 1854–58* (2 rolls); and one roll each of *Fort Lauderdale Post Returns, 1839–42; Letters Relating to the Navy and Marine Corps in the Florida War*; and *Letters Received by the Topographical Bureau of the War Department, 1838–54*.

Valuable information on the Second Seminole War is available in several newspapers on microfilm in the Historical Commission archives. The *Charleston Mercury* and the *Charleston Courier* for 1836 (2 rolls each) reported extensively on activities in Florida during the early stages of the war. The *Army and Navy Chronicle*, 1835–42 (2 rolls) thoroughly documents the army's drive into southern Florida in 1837–38 and subsequent operations in the Everglades.

Other nongovernment microfilms from the Seminole War period include James A. Robertson's *Calendar of Manuscripts in the Indian Office*, and W. P. Rowles's *Incidents and Observations in Florida in 1836*, both contained on one roll, and the *Lauderdale Family Papers, 1812–1909* (3 rolls). The Lauderdale papers contain a variety of letters and other documents relating to Major William Lauderdale, the Tennessee volunteer officer who led the first troops into present Broward County in 1838, and for whom the post, and later the city, of Fort Lauderdale were named. Two additional microfilms of Seminole

War officers' papers are the *Nathan S. Jarvis Diary, 1837–39*, from the library of the American Academy of Medicine (1 roll), and the *John Rogers Vinton Papers, 1836–42*, from Duke University (1 roll). Jarvis was a surgeon with the army in Florida, and Vinton commanded Fort Lauderdale for a short time in 1841.

The period between the end of the Seminole Wars and the 1890s was a relatively inactive one in Broward County. Fortunately, the few activities that did take place were well documented, including the establishment of a House of Refuge for shipwrecked sailors and the visits of several explorers and sportsmen. From this period, the Historical Commission has the field notes and maps produced by the first government surveys of the region: those of George MacKay (1845) and Marcellus A. Williams (1870). Microfilm of the *Annual Reports of the United States Life Saving Service, 1876–1914* (1 roll), and an original logbook from the Fort Lauderdale House of Refuge are also on file in the commission archives, as is a copy of Lake Worth area pioneer Charles W. Pierce's memoirs of his travels throughout southeastern Florida from the 1870s to the 1890s.

The modern settlement of Broward County dates from the last decade of the nineteenth century. Newspaper holdings covering this period of settlement begin with *The Tropical Sun* of Juno and West Palm Beach, 1891–1915 (9 rolls), the first newspaper published in southeast Florida. Since all of present Broward County before 1909, and most before 1915, lay in Dade County, the *Miami Daily Metropolis*, 1897–1915 (35 rolls) and the *Weekly Miami Metropolis*, 1904–1917 (11 rolls) contain a good deal of information on the region, as well as extensive coverage of the Everglades drainage project. Jacksonville's *Florida Times-Union*, the state's largest paper of the period, also contains scattered Broward County area references. Issues in the commission archives include January–March 1900 (1 roll) and January–February 1908 (1 roll).

*Dade County Plat Books A and B, 1–5*, and *8–15* (4 rolls) cover the period from 1892 to 1923. The drainage period is represented by a 1915 pamphlet entitled *Back to Broward* (1 roll), and by the 1910 *Dade County Census Population Schedules* (1 roll), which contain listings for Fort Lauderdale, Dania, and Hallandale. Miscellaneous personal papers, political literature, letters, and photographs in the Napoleon Bonaparte Broward Collection provide a good deal of information on Florida's nineteenth governor, particularly his activities in south Florida.

The *Fort Lauderdale Sentinel*, 1913–25 (10 rolls) and the *Fort Lauderdale Herald*, 1919–23 (3 rolls) are the earliest newspapers printed in Broward County, and span the period from the pioneer days of 1910–19 to the Florida "land boom." The great increase in population and economic activity just prior to and during the boom resulted in a tremendous surge of newspaper publishing, which is reflected in the Historical Commission's microfilm holdings of the *Hollywood Reporter*, 1922 (1 roll), the *Miami Herald*, 1924 and 1925 (31 rolls), and the *Fort Lauderdale Morning Sun*, February-May 1926 (2 rolls). The 267 rolls of the *Fort Lauderdale News* begin in 1925, at the peak of the boom, and continue through 1958. This large collection is being updated annually. A microfilm copy of the personal papers of Fort Lauderdale architect Francis Abreu (1 roll) also provides information on a significant aspect of boomtime Broward County.

The collapse of the land boom, the Great Depression, World War II, and the postwar population explosion are well documented in the Historical Commission archives. In addition to the *Fort Lauderdale News*, newspapers covering this period include the *Hollywood Herald*, 1931–50 (7 rolls) and the *Fort Lauderdale Times*, 1940–42 (9 rolls).

Oral history interviews cover a period from the early 1900s to the 1980s. Broward County's relatively recent development has provided a unique opportunity to capture the memories of many of its founders and pioneers on tape. At present, the oral history collection includes 114 interviews on 147 cassette tapes. Forty-seven of these have been transcribed.

Major personal manuscript collections of twentieth-century material include personal and business papers, clippings, and photos. The Robert H. Gore Collection, including microfilm (2 rolls) and photographs, traces the career of the newspaper editor who became one of the most powerful forces in Broward County's political and economic life from the 1930s to the 1970s. An important supplement to the county's engineering records are the papers of Herbert C. Davis, who served as county engineer from 1915 to 1924 and from 1932 to 1957. His papers detail the construction of several major roads and highways. Another major collection is that of Easter Lily Gates, county elections supervisor from 1928 to 1968. Her collection, not yet cataloged, contains a number of scrapbooks, photo albums, correspondence, and political literature.

Although it contains images from earlier periods, the Historical Commission's photo collection (4 file drawers) concentrates on the period from the 1920s to the present. Additional specialized photographic collections include over eight-hundred slides, mostly views of historic structures photographed in the late 1970s, and nine-hundred aerial photographs covering the entire county, and taken, for the most part, during the 1960s, when rapid residential and commercial development literally changed the face of the county.

Broward County city directories in the Historical Commission collection cover Fort Lauderdale, 1918–75 (except for several years during the Depression when no directories were published); Hollywood 1940–41, 1946–53, 1955–58, and 1960–73, and Pompano 1955–64, 1966–71, 1973, 1976–77, and 1980.

Combined with twenty-four drawers of vertical files containing miscellaneous pamphlets and clippings, Xerox copies of numerous rare, out-of-print publications, a full set of the Florida State Master Site File for Broward County, and a library of over six-hundred volumes, these archival collections provide a wealthy source of material for research on the history of Broward County and the surrounding southeast Florida region.

The Historical Commission's office is open to the general public. Staff members will assist researchers, and photocopies are available at fifteen cents a copy.

## *FORT LAUDERDALE HISTORICAL SOCIETY*

| | |
|---|---|
| Street address: | 219 Southwest Second Avenue |
| | Ft. Lauderdale, Florida |
| Mailing address: | P.O. Box 14043 |
| | Fort Lauderdale, Florida 33302 |
| Telephone: | (305) 463–4431 |
| Archive days and hours: | Monday–Friday, 10:00 A.M. to 4:00 P.M.; closed legal holidays |
| Museum days and hours: | Monday–Saturday, 10:00 A.M. to 4:00 P.M.; Sundays, 10:00 A.M. to 1:00 P.M. |

Founded in 1962 for the purpose of collecting, preserving, and interpreting the history of Fort Lauderdale and the surrounding area, the Fort Lauderdale Historical Society is the oldest and largest historical society in Broward County. Its holdings focus on the city of Fort Lauderdale, but also contain information on Broward County and Florida history as a whole. The society operates the Fort Lauderdale Historical Museum and maintains an excellent research collection, including a two-thousand-volume library and extensive archives.

Information on the early exploration and settlement of the Fort Lauderdale area, including military activities of the Second and Third Seminole Wars, can be found in the Historical Society's collection of 275 maps. Other original documents from the Seminole War period include miscellaneous newspapers, such as *The Metropolitan* (Georgetown, Washington, D.C.), January 29, 1836, and *Niles National Register* (Baltimore), November 11, 1839. The oldest original document directly relating to Fort Lauderdale in the society's collection is a March 22, 1838, letter from sutler William Tucker at "Camp Lauderdale near Cape Florida" to his brother George in Massachusetts.

Also particularly relevant to Fort Lauderdale's nineteenth-century history are the 4,800 compiled "Beachcomber" columns written by *Fort Lauderdale Daily News* columnist Wesley W. Stout (14 manuscript boxes). Published between 1952 and 1971, Stout's columns trace the progress of his research on many historical subjects. A file card index accompanies this collection. Thirteen additional manuscript boxes contain Stout's research notes and typed abstracts of newspapers relating to Florida and Broward County. These abstracts cover the years 1836–71, 1877–83, and 1884–1960, and include papers from several Florida communities.

Also covering the period of early settlement is one of the society's largest and finest collections, the Stranahan Collection (52 manuscript boxes). Frank Stranahan, who came to the New River in 1893 to operate the ferry on the county road, is popularly regarded as the founder of modern Fort Lauderdale. The collection includes papers, correspondence, documents, ledgers, clippings, and photographs. It also contains background material on both the Stranahan and Cromartie families, but focuses on the lives of Frank and Ivy Stranahan (his wife) and their many endeavors in Fort Lauderdale from 1893 to 1971.

Recollections from Mrs. Stranahan and other early Fort Lauderdale pioneers can be found in the Historical Society's oral history archives, which contains 245 cassette and reel-to-reel tapes, and fifty typed transcriptions. Of particular note are several interviews recorded during the late 1950s and early 1960s with residents who had arrived in the 1890s and 1900s.

Several documents in the society's collection provide information on Fort Lauderdale's first years following incorporation in 1911. Among these are miscellaneous original newspapers, including a rare copy of the *Fort Lauderdale Sentinel*'s April 7, 1911, issue reporting the town's incorporation. A 1911 business directory entitled *Historical and Progressive Review of Miami, Fort Lauderdale and Other Sections in Dade County, Florida*, presents concise sketches of the new municipality's leading commercial establishments, as well as extensive information on the Everglades drainage project and the south Florida drainage canal system then being constructed.

The Historical Society's collection of city directories includes the full run from 1918 through 1981. Early issues contain listings not only for Fort Lauderdale, but for adjacent Broward County towns, and even for the agricultural communities at the southern end of Lake Okeechobee. These city directories are complemented by a set of forty-five Fort Lauderdale telephone directories dating from 1922 to the present.

A wealth of information from the 1920s, particularly on the real estate boom of mid-decade, in the Society's archives, includes excellent collections of architectural and engineering drawings.

Ninety reels of rare film footage, many from the 1920s, make up one of the Historical Society's most unique collections. Film subjects include aerial views of the developing city taken by real estate promoters during the Florida land boom and scenes of devastation photographed immediately after the September 18, 1926, hurricane. The 1926 hurricane is also the subject of over thirty tapes in the oral history collection, several souvenir photo booklets, and three excellent panoramic photographs of the city.

The physical growth of Broward County during the land boom and at other intervals throughout the first half of the twentieth century is documented in the Historical Society's collection of Sanborn Fire Insurance Maps, including those for Fort Lauderdale in 1912, 1914, 1918, 1924, 1928, 1936, and 1955; Pompano for 1939; Dania for 1924 and 1934; and Hollywood for 1926.

The society's archives contain valuable material on the early years of Port Everglades, which opened in 1928, including photographs, newspaper articles, correspondence, and reports.

An interesting aspect of Broward County's Depression era—the effect of that economic collapse and resulting New Deal programs on the Seminole Indians—is the subject of the James L. Glenn Collection (1 file drawer) of photographs and manuscripts. Glenn served as special commissioner to the Seminoles from 1931 to 1935.

With approximately 220,000 images, the Historical Society's photographic collection is one of the largest in the state. The bulk of these photographs, numbering almost 200,000, were donated to the society by local photographer Gene Hyde, and document various aspects of Fort Lauderdale life from the 1930s to the 1970s. The remainder of the photographic collection covers the range of Fort Lauderdale and Broward County history from the nineteenth century to the present. Of particular note are the society's collection of 4,600 slides and the collection of 2,600 postcards, many dating from the decade 1910–19.

The Depression and economic revival experienced by South Florida from the 1930s to the 1960s also forms the setting for a collection of architectural drawings and blueprints donated by architect Courtney Stewart (3 drawers).

Several small, short-lived newspapers appeared in Broward County in the late 1930s and early 1940s. They contain valuable information and viewpoints not available from major newspapers. Among the smaller papers in the Historical Society's collections are scattered issues of *The Free Press, Fort Lauderdale Greetings*, and the black paper *Fort Lauderdale Colored Bulletin*.

Collections relating to World War II, a period during which Fort Lauderdale became a major training center for the armed forces, include over forty oral history tapes, photographs, and a bound volume of the air station newspaper, *The Avenger*, spanning the years 1944 and 1945.

A collection constantly growing in value is the newspaper clipping file kept by the Society's first director, Florence C. Hardy (100 boxes).

The Historical Society archives are open to the public, with staff members available to assist researchers. Photocopying service at 15 cents per page is also available. The society maintains full darkroom facilities, and prints can be purchased of any negatives in the photographic collection.

# 28

---

# SOURCES IN
# DADE COUNTY

---

## REBECCA A. SMITH

DADE COUNTY IS fortunate to have several major and minor collections of research materials relating to state and local Florida history. Each repository has its own focus and strengths. The proximity of these varied, complementary, and rich holdings provide historians with opportunities for a "field day" pursuing their research.

### *CHARLTON W. TEBEAU LIBRARY OF FLORIDA HISTORY*
### *HISTORICAL MUSEUM OF SOUTHERN FLORIDA*

Street address:          101 West Flagler Street
                         Miami, Florida 33130

Telephone:               (305) 375–1492

Days and hours:          Monday–Friday, 10:00 A.M. to 4:30 P.M.; First and third Sat-
                         urdays of the month, 12:30 P.M. to 4:30 P.M.; appointments
                         recommended

In 1940, the Historical Association of Southern Florida (HASF) was founded as a private, nonprofit organization dedicated to the history of the lower third of the state of Florida. HASF opened a museum and research collection in 1962, obtained accreditation in 1979, and moved to its present facilities in the Metro-Dade Cultural Center in 1984. HASF is now one of the largest and most sophisticated historical museums in the southeastern United States.

HASF's collections contain a wide variety of materials that can be studied by researchers. The Research Center houses the written and graphic collections of HASF, in particular the Charlton W. Tebeau Library of Florida History and the Woodrow W. Wilkins Archives of Architectural Records.

Three-dimensional objects, approximately ten-thousand artifacts, range from extensive finds from archaeological digs in Dade County to household utensils and tourist souvenirs.

The prints and photographs collections exceed five-hundred-thousand images, mainly still photographs of southeast Florida. Prints date from the 1590s, photographs from 1883 to the present. About ten-thousand of the most popular photos, with most of the very small collections, are in the Photo Reference Files; folders of pictures in these files are arranged by place and/or subject, using headings established by the Library of Congress Prints and Photographs Division. These files contain many images by William Fishbaugh and Richard B. Hoit, as well as many by amateurs. Other photographic holdings include the work of: Ralph Munroe (1883–ca. 1915, 670 views); Claude C. Matlack (1918–40, ca. 8,000 prints of Miami Beach and southeast Florida); Annette and Rudi Rada (1950s–1960s, ca. 5,000 images of building interiors and exteriors); Miami Beach Visitor and Convention Authority (1910s–1980, ca. 30,000 images of Miami beach); *Coral Gables Times Guide* (mainly 1960s, ca. 6,000 prints); *Miami Herald* (early 1900s, ca. 3,000 prints and negatives); and *Miami News* (1970s, ca. 400,000 negatives; 1900s–1960s, ca. 2,000 images).

Prints vary from early engravings and nineteenth–century woodcuts from magazines to twentieth-century posters. The "crown jewel" is a complete set of the double elephant folio edition of John James Audubon's *Birds of America*. The collection of over six-thousand postcards spans the entire state, and is arranged by place and subject. Illustrated books, periodicals, and pamphlets pertaining to South Florida are also available.

Manuscript holdings range from the nineteenth century to the present, total approximately 400 linear feet, and include diaries, letters, papers, and company records. Developers' papers and records include: Julia Tuttle (1889–98, 1954, 3 linear inches); Carl Fisher (1896–1939, 7 linear feet); George Merrick (1928–42, 4 linear feet); James Franklin Jaudon (1908–38, 8 linear feet); and the Greater Miami Chamber of Commerce (1919–65, 7 linear feet). R. V. Waters's papers (1922–65, 8 linear feet) pertain to aviation and the proposed development of Islandia, now Biscayne National Park. Family papers include: the Perrine family (1741–1975, 6 linear inches); the Santini family (1849–1920, 4 linear feet); the Apthorp family (1856–99, 6 linear inches); and the Gilpin family (1903–17, 4 linear inches). Organizational records include the Audubon Society of Coconut Grove (1915–22, 3 linear inches), Friends of the Everglades (1970–74, 3 linear feet), and the Miami Conservatory of Music (1926–38, 5 linear feet). Historians and authors are also represented, for example, Charlton Tebeau (1 linear foot), Jean Taylor (ca. 1970–86, 20 linear feet), and Ellen and William Hartley (1966–77, 17 linear feet).

The Woodrow W. Wilkins Archives of Architectural Records, part of the Research Center, contains architectural drawings of buildings in Dade County. Most significant are the Walter De Garmo drawings (245 sets totalling 2,000 sheets) of mainly Mediterranean revival structures dating from the 1910s.

Printed resources on Florida and South Florida are also available, including about 4,000 books; magazines; journals; 1,200 maps; Dade County city directories, early 1900–70s; and fire insurance maps. As a museum research center books, periodicals, and pamphlets pertaining to museum and historical society operations also are available. This literature covers topics as varied and useful to historians as conservation of objects, procedures for conducting oral history programs, management of volunteer programs, and the design and construction exhibitions.

### FLORIDA COLLECTION, MIAMI-DADE PUBLIC LIBRARY

Street address:          101 West Flagler Street
                         Miami, Florida 33130

Telephone:               (305) 375–2665

Days and hours:          Monday–Saturday, 9:00 A.M. to 6:00 P.M.; Thursday, 9:00
                         A.M. to 9:00 P.M.; Sunday, 1:00 P.M. to 6:00 P.M., Octo-
                         ber–May

The Main Library is located in the attractive Metro-Dade Cultural Center. It functions as the research library for the system. Two of its departments are of special interest to Florida historians—the Florida Collection and the Genealogy Collection.

The Florida Collection contains extensive holdings (over 5,500 volumes) of reference and circulating books on state and local topics. The rare books collections include first editions, such as Catesby's natural history; autographed Floridiana; dime novels with Florida settings; Spanish-American War volumes; and nineteenth-century government documents. The library is a depository for state and federal documents. Reference books include Dade County city directories from 1904 to the present.

Newspapers are the Florida Collection's specialty. Microfilm runs of state, local and Bahamian newspapers comprise a valuable research source. These include: the *Miami Herald* (1904–present), *Miami News* (1896–present), *Key West Citizen* (1926–present), *Fort Myers News Press* (1916–31), *Florida Times Union* (1882–present), *Miami Review* (1926–present), various Tampa papers (1855–91), *Tampa Morning Tribune* (1890–present), *Miami Times* (1948–present), *Homestead Enterprise* (1914–31), *South Florida Banner* (1912–14), *Diario Las Americas* (1956–present), *Coral Gables Times* (1961–77), *Coral Gables*

*Riviera* (1926–46 with issues missing), *Miami Tribune* (1924–35, with issues missing), *San Mateo Item* (1908–11), and *Illustrated Daily Tab* (1925–26). Bahamas and South Carolina newspapers regularly reported Southeast Florida news; these holdings include: *Charleston Daily Courier* (1852–73), *Bahamas Gazette, Argus and Herald* (1784–1851), *Nassau Guardian* (1849–1932), *Nassau Times* (1874–94), Nassau *Royal Gazette* (1804–1837), and *Royal Gazette/South Carolina Gazette/Charleston Gazette* (1732–82). From 1962 to 1979, the Florida Collection systematically filed newspaper clippings from the local papers by subject and microfilmed the files. Beginning in 1980, staff have been computer-indexing six local newspapers; this index is available in the Florida Collection and several other libraries around the state. The Agnew Welch scrapbooks contain clippings on local history, arranged by subject, from the 1930s to the 1950s.

The Romer collection, one of the Florida Collection's prize possessions, contains 17,500 photographs by Gleason Waite Romer of Greater Miami from 1925 to 1961, with some earlier copy work. A computer-generated subject index to the images provides access to each item; prints are arranged by negative number.

The Genealogy Collection, next to the Florida Collection, contains books and microfilm of state as well as national interest. A complete microfilm set of the national census records for all states, 1790–1910, can be perused here; one would have to go to Atlanta to find another.

The media history center in the basement of the library houses the WTVJ film archives, which consists of news film from 1949 to 1978 made by Florida's oldest television station.

## SPECIAL COLLECTIONS, OTTO G. RICHTER LIBRARY

| | |
|---|---|
| Mailing address: | University of Miami<br>Post Office Box 248214<br>Coral Gables, Florida 33124 |
| Telephone: | (305) 284–3247 |
| Days and hours: | Monday–Friday, 9:00 A.M. to 4:00 P.M., by appointment |

The institution's Florida Collection, Special Collections, and University Archives contain the materials most likely to interest students of Floridiana; all three collections are administered by Special Collections on the eighth floor of the library.

The publications holdings include over 13,500 Floridiana titles, about 450 Floridiana periodicals, and 2,436 books written by university faculty. The Library is also a depository for government documents.

The vast Cuban and Caribbean publications holdings remind us of Florida's Spanish origins and long-term connections with the Caribbean. For detailed information on holdings, see the *Catalog of the Cuban and Caribbean Library of the University of Miami* (Boston, 1977). Of special note is the extensive collection of Cuban immigrant periodicals dating from 1959 to the present. Written, edited, or published by Cubans in exile in the United States, these issues record culture and events affecting recent state and local history.

The archives and manuscripts collections of interest to Florida historians include: the papers of Marjory Stoneman Douglas (ca. 1900–present, exceeding 12 cubic feet, partially arranged); Minnie Moore-Wilson Papers (1859–1937, 22.25 cubic feet), especially concerning Seminoles; August Seymour Houghton Papers on the conservation of Florida wildlife (1938–48, 11 cubic feet); Florida East Coast Railway, mainly Model Land Company records, (1910–66, 51 cubic feet, unarranged); Effie Knowles Papers on Seminoles (1950–68, 1 cubic foot); Florida Power and Light newspaper clippings (1926–40, 57 cubic feet); Florida Philharmonic Orchestra records (1965–82, 35 cubic feet); and the Florida Chapter of the American Association of University Women (1946–79, 18 cubic feet). The Truth About Cuba Committee records (1961–75, 77.34 linear feet) are the records of the first nonprofit Cuban exile organization.

The Mark F. Boyd collection (1794–1968, 23 cubic feet) contains eight-thousand books, maps, drawings, papers, translations, and other primary material pertaining to Florida history, especially for the Spanish periods, the British period, and the Seminole Wars. The Boyd maps fill fifteen map case drawers, date from 1514 to circa 1785, include originals and reproductions, and are especially strong for Pensacola, St. Augustine, and the Caribbean.

Boom era developer N. B. T. Roney's collection of 31 maps of Florida and the Caribbean date from 1644 to 1860 and are also notable. Bernhardt Muller's architectural drawings (approximately 650 sheets) document 1920s Opa Locka structures based on an Arabian Knights theme. The 386 drawings by landscape architect William Lyem Phillips include the grounds of Bok Tower, the Tallahassee capitol entrance, and Fairchild Tropical Garden. The Cuban exile poster collection contains over 600 posters about or by Cuban immigrants and events. Over 500 postcards and 1,000 photographs of Cuba are also available.

Smaller libraries and archives in Dade County are briefly noted below.

## BLACK ARCHIVES, HISTORY AND RESEARCH FOUNDATION OF SOUTH FLORIDA, INC

Street address:        Joseph Caleb Community Complex
                       5400 N.W. 22 Avenue
                       Miami, Florida 33142

Telephone:             (305) 638–6064

Days and hours:        By appointment only.

Founded in 1977, the Black Archives manuscripts collections include Marion Shannon's papers on black schools and Theodore Gibson's papers (ca. 4,000 leaves on 1 microfilm reel). Gibson was a clergyman, leader in the civil rights movement, and City of Miami commissioner. Photographs and memorabilia relating to blacks in greater Miami are also available.

## *CUBAN EXILE HISTORY AND ARCHIVES PROJECT*

Street address:          Latin American and Caribbean Center
                         Florida International University
                         Tamiami Campus, Miami, Florida 33199

Telephone:               (305) 554–2895

Days and hours:          By appointment only.

Founded in 1985, this repository is expanding rapidly; its materials, which pertain to Cuban-Americans, include manuscripts, historical documents, ephemera, and oral history interviews, with holdings exceeding 150 linear feet.

Other repositories whose collections focus on the institution hosting them include Fairchild Tropical Garden, Temple Israel of Greater Miami, and Vizcaya. These collections contain a wide variety of written and photographic sources.

# 29

# MONROE COUNTY, MAY HILL RUSSELL LIBRARY

WRIGHT LANGLEY

| | |
|---|---|
| Street address: | 700 Fleming Street |
| | Key West, Florida 33040 |
| Telephone: | (305) 294–8488 |
| Days and hours: | Monday–Saturday, 9 A.M. to 5 P.M. |

DOCUMENTS AND RECORDS tracing the broad cultural influences of Bahamians, Cubans, English and other nationalities who in the early 1800s began settling the southernmost island of Key West are preserved in the rich collections of the May Hill Russell Library. The history department is recognized as having one of the best regional collections in Florida. It has three microfilm readers which can reproduce copies. Copies of photographs can also be ordered.

In addition to large special collections of microfilm, such as those containing federal court records relating to the wrecking or salvaging industry and other admiralty records, 1828 to 1911, the library has a vast number of microfilm reels of official Monroe County records and local and state newspapers. It also has over 5,000 black and white photographs and some color slides and postcards on the history of Key West and the Florida Keys, along with maps and Sanborn insurance maps. Eighteenth– and nineteenth-century burial records indicating in most instances the name, date of death, and cause are listed on IBM cards and accompanied by copies of pages from the Key West Cemetery sexton's log. The latest inventory indicates the department also has 3,000 books, 1,245 reels of microfilm, and 75 oral history video and cassette tapes.

Just ninety miles from Havana, Cuba, the island of Key West has from its beginnings attracted Cubans fleeing Spanish oppression. Documents and rare books in the collection of the Cuban Consulate in Key West and San Carlos Institute were microfilmed. These records not only relate to the Key West's Cuban-American population, but they are significant to an understanding of the commercial history of South Florida and Cuba, Cuban diplomatic history, and United States–Cuban relations. These 63 reels of microfilm represent 120 boxes of documents, 24 bound registers, and 85 printed titles.

Gerald Poyo and Jane Garner, *The Inventory of the Records of the Consulate* (Austin, Texas, 1983) identifies the material as: "registers; shipping—both air and sea—and other commercial documents; legal documents; correspondence, cablegrams, birth, baptismal, marriage, death records; naturalization office inventories; reports, pamphlets, official instructions and bulletins; clippings; minutes; printed materials; photographs." The records are arranged in six sections:

Section 1: "Despachos de Buques y Aviones. Diligencias Commercials" contains a variety of documents certified by the consul that relate to maritime and commercial matters, including passenger and crew lists of private and commercial vessels departing Key West for Cuba, 1929–60.

Section 2: "Correspondencia" contains official consular correspondence and communications.

Section 3: "Diligencias Consulares" contains registers of documents issued covering 1903–29; a civil registry of Cubans in Key West (registers of birth, marriage, and death records including passports and visas issued); and a variety of unusual maritime documents.

Section 4: "Archivo Consular" contains documentation of the internal operations of the consular office—personnel salary receipts, inventories, and annual reports between the years 1917 and 1961.

Section 5: "Practicas Consulares" contains official communications, circulars, instructions, and information from the Cuban Ministry of State to the foreign service. Communications and circulars date as early as 1908, with most of the material post–1930.

Section 6: "Miscelanea" contains material relating to the San Carlos Institute and documentation on the construction of the Jose Marti monument in Bayview Park in Key West.

Printed material includes five titles relating to Key West history and eighty others that are primarily Cuban government documents. Many of the titles existed in no more than one library in the United States and often had not been previously microfilmed.

Key West became the adopted home of many Bahamian fishermen and wreckers working in the area. There are over one-hundred microfilm reels of Bahamian records of marriages, wills, census, property conveyance, slave registry, land grants, and miscellaneous documents.

Official Bahamas records include microfilm of the government's "Old Series" dating back to 1764, with documents relating to deeds, conveyances, and land grants up through the early 1820s. Those searching for their Bahamian roots will find over sixty reels on births, deaths, and marriages, each covering varying periods beginning in 1850. These records are supplemented by reels of newspapers—*Bahamas Gazette* (1784–86), *Royal Gazette* (1804–15), *Bahama Argus* (1831–35), *Nassau Times* (1874–94), *Nassau Guardian* (1894–1925) and *Bahama Herald* (1849–63).

Other newspapers include almost all of the issues of the island's primary newspaper, which continues today—*The Key West Citizen*. Microfilm reels of this newspaper and its predecessors extend from the early 1900s. There are also scattered copies of other short-lived local newspapers.

The newspaper collection on microfilm contains *Pensacola Gazette* (1824–58), *Charleston Mercury* (1822–28), *Charleston Courier* (1816–28), St. Augustine newspapers including *Gazette* and *Florida Herald* and *The News* from the early 1800s, *Miami Metropolis* (1897–1922), and *Ft. Myers Press* (1884–1914).

Those pursuing research on the United States Navy will find some one-hundred reels of letters received by the secretary of navy from captains (1821–29) and miscellaneous documents on the Gulf Blockading Squadron during the Civil War and the U.S. military posts at Key West and Ft. Jefferson.

# 30

# BLACK ARCHIVES RESEARCH CENTER AND MUSEUM OF FLORIDA A&M UNIVERSITY

PAUL S. GEORGE

| | |
|---|---|
| Mailing address: | Florida A&M University<br>P.O. Box 809<br>Tallahassee, Florida 32307 |
| Telephone: | (904) 599–3020 |
| Days and hours: | 9:00 A.M. to 4:00 P.M. weekdays; other times by request |

THE BLACK ARCHIVES Research Center and Museum is located in the Carnegie Library Building, the oldest structure on the campus of Florida A&M University (1907). The Black Archives was established by an act of the Florida legislature in 1971, and began operating in 1977. The archives's collection reflects black presence and participation in southern, national, and even world history. Holdings and services include artifacts, manuscripts, art works, oral history tapes, meeting and research rooms, and a mobile touring museum. James N. Eaton, founder and archivist-curator of the Black Archives, has labored diligently to build the collection.

Eaton's success is evident in an archival collection that consists of more than 500,000 letters, papers, correspondences, photographs, films, rare maps and books. It is especially deep in materials pertaining to the antebellum, Civil War, and Reconstruction eras. Of particular interest to Florida history researchers are the public and private papers of each of the presidents of Florida A&M University from 1888 to the present. The archives also contain large collections of papers from other black colleges and universities, especially Florida Memorial College; Civil War records of black Floridians; and a vast collection of material on black education and race relations in the South.

The archives also offer researchers the papers, photographs, and other artifacts of more than one hundred individuals and organizations—many reaching beyond the confines of Florida. Florida-related materials include the Jake Gaither films and tapes on football in America; the Cannonball Adderly Collection (selected items); the Floy Britt Collection of photographs on the 4–H in Florida; official records of the National Negro Home Demonstration Agent Association; and memorabilia of the 54th Colored Regiment, United States Army.

# 31

# THE HENRY MORRISON FLAGLER MUSEUM ARCHIVES

J. KENNETH JONES AND JOAN RUNKEL

Street address:    Whitehall Mansion
                   Cocoanut Row
                   Palm Beach, Florida

Telephone:         (407) 655–2833

Days and hours:    By appointment only.

ESTABLISHED IN 1960, the Henry Morrison Flagler Museum Archives is a primary source of information for Henry Morrison Flagler's development of Florida, with the emphasis on the construction of the Key West Extension Railway. It includes graphs and blueprints. A major portion is at present not indexed and is not available for research; it is pertinent mainly for engineering and construction details.

Other categories included in the archives are: hotels and business enterprises developed by Henry Morrison Flagler, including photographs; papers and memorabilia related to Henry Morrison Flagler and family; original architectural drawings by Carrere and Hastings for construction of Henry M. Flagler's mansion in Palm Beach, Florida ("Whitehall"); and miscellaneous articles and photographs pertaining to other Florida cities.

The chronological limits of the collection are approximately 1860–1935.

**32**

# SMALL ARCHIVES AND PRIVATE HOLDINGS IN FLORIDA

PATRICIA R. WICKMAN

BECAUSE OF THE youth of Florida's libraries, historical societies, and museums, much primary material has been, and still is, held at the local level by municipal agencies, individuals, and small, independent organizations. Large, official, state-sponsored, centralized repositories are still in the minority in Florida.

In general, researchers must direct their interests in specific historical topics toward several types of repositories, the occurrences of which are not, unfortunately, standardized across the state.

As a consequence, history shoppers rarely will find everything they want at the documentary "supermarkets," such as the P. K. Yonge Library of Florida History at the University of Florida or the University of South Florida's Special Collections. They still will have to seek out the small, single-source purveyors of local history and the individually held discrete-topic collections.

This situation has become especially evident in recent decades as history researchers have begun to examine nontraditional (i.e. nonlinear) documents. Individuals as keepers of communities' oral traditions, for example, folk craftsmen and storytellers and musicians; photographic collections; as well as material culture holdings and historic sites—all are finally being viewed as valuable informational sources that are critical to the assembly of a total historical picture.

The following, then, is a delineation of some of the lesser-known and nontraditional information repositories which are currently available to researchers in the field of Florida history. They include only those portions of their holdings which will be of interest to researchers of Florida history and are primary materials which are unlikely to be available from other sources.

## ALACHUA COUNTY

### MRS. CHRISTOPHER MATHESON COLLECTION

Street address:          526 Southeast 1st Avenue
                         Gainesville, Florida 32601

Telephone:               (904) 372–7122

Days and hours:          By appointment only.

The Judge Augustus Steele Collection includes the 1873 ancestral home in which Mrs. Matheson still resides, as well as numerous personal documents, photographs, and memorabilia. Judge Steele (1792–1864) was a pioneer settler at Fort Brooke (Tampa), newspaper editor at Magnolia (near St. Marks), the first Hillsborough County judge, a state legislator, and a municipal official at Cedar Key.

### DR. ROBERT S. THOMSON COLLECTION

Street address:          Department of English
                         Turlington Hall
                         University of Florida
                         Gainesville, Florida 32611

Telephone:               (904) 392–1060

Days and hours:          By appointment only.

Holdings include Dr. Alton Morris, Dr. Edwin Kirkland, and Dr. Francis Hayes Collections, as well as later student collections from the 1940s and 1950s. These include oral narratives, folktales, legends, superstitions, folk medicines, songs and ballads, and proverbs, all specifically Florida materials. The collections are composed of several hundred untranscribed tape recordings and approximately five cubic feet of supporting documents.

### FLORIDA STATE MUSEUM, JAMES A. FORD LIBRARY

Street address:          Museum Road
                         Gainesville, Florida 32611

Telephone:              (904) 392–1721
Days and hours:         Monday–Friday, 8:00 A.M. to 5:00 P.M.; restricted access

Holdings include the Charles H. Fairbanks Collection of personal and academic papers and field notes; the Ripley P. Bullen Collection of personal correspondence and field notes; and the Florida Park Service Collection of archaeological records (pre-1952). Other primary documents include archival materials relating to Florida State Museum (FSM)–sponsored archaeological research projects headed by William H. Sears, E. Thomas Hemmings, and others. Total size of the above primary documents collection is approximately thirty cubic feet. In addition to these archives, the FSM also holds within its artifact collections the materials recovered from some of these and many other archaeological sites around Florida.

## *UNIVERSITY OF FLORIDA ORAL HISTORY PROJECT*

Street address:         Dr. Samuel Proctor, Director
                        Museum of Florida History
                        Museum Road
                        Gainesville, Florida 32611
Telephone:              (904) 392–1721
Days and hours:         Monday–Friday, 8:00 A.M. to 5:00 P.M.; by request

The Oral History Project archive is the largest central repository of oral history collections in the state. The project encompasses a total of 2,995 tape recordings covering 2,477 separate interviews, of which 1,696 have been transcribed (including 781 final drafts). The interviews fall into four broad categories: Indian projects, local history, Floridiana, and miscellany. The Indian groups included in the collection are: Catawa (S.C.); Cherokee (N.C.); Choctaw (Fla. and Miss.); Creek (Ala. and Okla.); Lumbee (Md., D.C., N.C.); Rappahannock (Va.); and Seminole (Fla.). Of these, 92 percent have been transcribed. The local history interviews cover twenty-two Florida counties and account for 710 tape recordings, of which 48 percent have been transcribed.

The Floridiana collection covers such statewide topics as: civil rights (St. Augustine), Confederate veterans, corps of engineers, blacks, community colleges, constitutional revision, personalities, Republicans, Florida Bicentennial Commission, citrus, education, WRUF Radio, Suwanee River, Park Trammell, Ray Washington's "Cracker Florida," University of Florida, J. Hillis Miller Health Center, and the University of Florida College of Law.

The Oral History Project holds an additional collection of approximately 350 sound recordings of music, guest lectures on the University of Florida campus, radio programs, poetry readings, and class lectures. In addition, the project contains 123 video tape recordings covering the University of Florida, Alachua County, Clearwater, rural blacks, the history of the naval stores industry in Florida and Georgia, southeastern Indians, as well as video tapes of the Michael

Gannon television interview program "Conversations" for the period 1985–present. Finally, the Oral History Project also owns a substantial collection of slides and photographs relating to southeastern Indians.

## BAKER COUNTY

### BAKER COUNTY HISTORICAL SOCIETY

Street address:        Old Baker County Jail Building
                       McIver Street
                       Macclenny, Florida

Mailing address:       P.O. Box 856
                       Macclenny, Florida 32063

Days and hours:        Tuesday and Thursday, 2:00 P.M. to 7:00 P.M.; other times by
                       prior arrangement only

Holdings include the Colonel Mace Harris Collection and the Lois Knabb Coleman Collection of genealogical materials, with emphasis on Baker County and the immediate area. Collections include videotapes of oral history interviews focusing on individual residents and local history topics, family histories, and compilations of Baker County death notices and marriage records covering the late nineteenth century through the present.

## CITRUS COUNTY

### CRYSTAL RIVER PUBLIC LIBRARY

Street address:        8619 West Crystal Street
                       Crystal River, Florida 32629

Telephone:             (904) 795–3716

Days and hours:        Monday–Thursday, 9:00 A.M. to 9:00 P.M., Friday–Saturday,
                       9:00 A.M. to 6:00 P.M.

Holdings include the United States Nuclear Regulatory Commission Collection. The library is the official depository for documents pertaining to Florida Power Corporation's nuclear plant at Crystal River.

## DADE COUNTY

### JAY I. KISLAK FOUNDATION COLLECTIONS AND GALLERY

Street address:        7900 Miami Lakes Drive West
                       Miami Lakes, Florida 33016

Telephone:             (305) 364–4100

Days and hours:        Monday–Friday, 11:00 A.M. to 2:00 P.M.; other hours by appointment

The Jay I. Kislak Foundation collections consist generally of books, documents, manuscripts, maps, artwork, and three-dimensional artifacts relative to the history of Florida, the circum-Caribbean, and New Spain in the colonial era—in all, approximately two-thousand items.

The Floridiana Collection (the majority of the materials) consists of about eight-hundred paper artifacts. These are rare, primary documents and contemporaneous published materials relative to sixteenth-, seventeenth-, eighteenth-, and early nineteenth-century Florida. The Americana Collection (about 700 items), also contains numerous rare materials concerning Christopher Columbus, Spanish claims and discoveries in the New World, the British in the Caribbean, and the colonial era in United States history. This is an excellent archive for Florida scholars. A small number of the items are on permanent exhibit in the Foundation's Gallery (same location), and the rest are available there to researchers upon request.

## HAMILTON COUNTY

### *FLORIDA FOLKLIFE PROGRAM*

Street address:        Stephen Foster State Folk Culture Center
                       U.S. Highway 41 and State Road 136
                       White Springs, Florida

Mailing address:       P.O. Box 265
                       White Springs, Florida 32096

Telephone:             (904) 397–2192

Days and hours:        Monday–Friday, 8:00 A.M. to 5:00 P.M., access by request

Materials in this archive document all aspects of current (twentieth-century) Florida folklore and folklife. Types of documents include: 17,000 color slides; 5,000 black-and-white photographs; 1,500 reel-to-reel recordings; 600 audio cassettes; 100 video cassettes (mainly programs produced by the agency to document discrete topics); 20 square feet of vertical files (primarily compiled news clippings arranged by subject and topic); and 10 square feet of vertical files, including transcripts of the audio recordings listed above (both reel-to-reel and cassette), the WPA/Stetson Kennedy Collection of personal field notes from the 1930s, the Thelma Bolton Collection of Florida folklore, and the WPA Federal Writers' Project on Florida Folklore Collection (approximately 3,000 pages).

## MANATEE COUNTY

### *MANATEE COUNTY HISTORICAL RECORDS LIBRARY*

Street address:        1405 Fourth Avenue West
                       Bradenton, Florida 34205

Mailing address:       Office of the Clerk of the Circuit Court
                       P.O. Box 1000
                       Bradenton, Florida 33506

Telephone:             (813) 749–1800

Days and hours:        Monday–Friday, 8:30 A.M. to 5:00 P.M.

The principal collection includes all official county records from 1856 to the present. In addition, the archive acts as repository for the Manatee County Historical Society's photographic collection, which includes approximately five-thousand photographs reproduced from the collections of various local individuals over a period of fifteen years.

# 33

## ARCHIVES OUTSIDE OF FLORIDA

B. CARLYLE RAMSEY

ANY STUDENT OF Florida history might wish to examine the collections of several out-of-state libraries or repositories. A nearby collection rich in Florida archival manuscript sources from the colonial period to the present resides at the Georgia Historical Society in Savannah. It is also an invaluable repository for genealogical studies. The Georgia Department of Archives and History also contains several manuscript collections and other documents pertinent to Florida history. These items range from Creek Indian letters, talks, and treaties to documents on Spanish and British East and West Florida.

Three collections in South Carolina are helpful, especially for the student who is conducting research on Florida in the seventeenth and eighteenth centuries. The University of South Carolina's "Caroliniana" collection in Columbia houses a very impressive holding in genealogical and document sources for one researching families who migrated from the Carolinas to Florida, particularly north Florida. Such families include Gadsden, Glass, Heyward, McMaster, Miller, Oates, Pinckney, Robinson, Searcy, Shepard, and Thompson. In addition, there is an ample number of letters dealing with the antebellum and Civil War periods.

One might be particularly interested in Dr. S. B. Shepherd's account of the Union army's occupation and burning of Jacksonville, Florida, in 1862–63. There is also an impressive collection of travelogues on Florida. Near the University of South Carolina library stands the South Carolina State Library, which has an adequate collection on Florida and the Carolinas in the sixteenth and seventeenth centuries.

Located in historic Charleston, the South Carolina Historical Society's repository is also worth the serious scholar's review. The collection includes colonial records of Spanish Florida, John Harris Woodruff's narratives, and the *Charleston Book*, edited by William G. Simms with a new introduction by David Moltke Hansen (Spartenburg, S.C., 1973).

The University of North Carolina at Chapel Hill is also a valuable repository for scholars who are interested in colonial as well as subsequent periods. The Perkins collection at Duke University in Durham contains over one-thousand books and other materials on Florida, especially the colonial period. Both of these university libraries include small collections on Miami.

The William L. Clements Library, University of Michigan, has holdings on colonial Florida which may prove useful and informative for both the Spanish and British periods. The Library of Congress in Washington, D.C., offers a superb manuscript collection for the Spanish and British colonial periods as well as for Territorial Florida and the era of early statehood.

# APPENDIX I

---

# CHRONOLOGY OF FLORIDA HISTORY

---

| | |
|---|---|
| ca. 9000 B.C. | Florida's first inhabitants arrive; they were part of the "Indians" who crossed a land bridge from Siberia to Alaska in the late Ice Age. |
| 5000 B.C. | First quasi-permanent settlements appear in Florida. |
| A.D. 1500 | Spanish treasure ships begin journeying through the Straits of Florida on their return voyage to Spain. |
| 1513 | In the first recorded visit by a European, Juan Ponce de Leon comes to a land he names "Pascua Florida" because he visits it in the period of Spain's "Feast of Flowers." |
| 1516–65 | Several Spanish expeditions, including that of Hernando de Soto, visit Florida. |
| 1562 | Jean Ribault brings a French expedition to the St. Johns River. |
| 1564 | Rene de Goulaine de Laudonniere, with more than three-hundred settlers almost all of whom were French Huguenots, establishes Fort Caroline on the St. Johns River. |
| 1565 | Admiral Pedro Menendez de Aviles establishes St. Augustine, destroys Fort Caroline, and eliminates the French presence in Florida. |
| 1566 | Beginning of intensive effort by Jesuit and Franciscan friars to convert Indians to Christianity. |

| 1586 | British sea dog Sir Francis Drake sacks and burns St. Augustine. |
|------|------------------------------------------------------------------|
| 1600–76 | Spanish missions and outposts spread into northwest Florida. |
| 1672–98 | Because of continued threats to the security of St. Augustine, the Spanish construct the impregnable Castillo de San Marcos at the entrance to St. Augustine harbor. |
| 1698 | Reestablishment of Pensacola as a military garrison. |
| 1702–03 | The British launch raids upon St. Augustine and other Spanish settlements. |
| 1719 | The French temporarily control Pensacola. |
| 1740 | Under the leadership of James Oglethorpe, the British invade Florida from Georgia but fail to reduce the fort and capture St. Augustine. |
| 1763 | Florida becomes a British colony following the Seven Years War. |
| 1763–84 | England's administration of Florida includes its division into the colonies of East and West Florida. |
| 1776–80 | Tories pour into the Floridas, which remain loyal to Great Britain during the American Revolution. |
| 1781 | Spaniards capture Pensacola from the British. |
| 1783 | Florida is returned to Spain by the British in exchange for the Bahamas. |
| 1785–1821 | Spain's grip over Florida grows weaker as Americans, British, and Indians raise havoc in the colony. |
| 1818 | Andrew Jackson eliminates the Indian menace to American settlements north of Florida in the First Seminole War. |
| 1819–21 | Negotiations between Spain and the United States lead to the Adams-Onís Treaty, which cedes Florida to the latter. |
| 1821 | As military governor of Florida, Andrew Jackson receives the colony from Spanish authorities for the United States. |
| 1822 | Florida becomes a territory of the United States; William P. Duval appointed first governor; legislative council also appointed. |
| 1824 | Tallahassee becomes the capital of the territory of Florida. |
| 1830s | Florida's first railroad begins operating. |
| 1835–42 | The Second Seminole War rages throughout parts of Florida. |
| 1838–39 | In anticipation of statehood, Florida creates a constitution. |
| 1840 | Territorial population reaches 54,477. |
| 1845 | Florida enters the United States as the twenty-seventh state. |
| 1850 | Florida's population reaches 87,445. |
| 1855 | First Internal Improvement Act, which uses swamp, overflowed land, and other land ceded to the state by federal government to furnish impetus for a system of railroad and canal transportation. |
| 1861 | Florida secedes from the Union; joins Confederate States of America soon after. |
| 1861–65 | 15,000 Floridians serve in Confederate armies; the state is a major supplier of salt, beef, and bacon to Confederacy. |
| 1864 | Confederate defeat of Union forces at Olustee in largest battle of Civil War in Florida. |
| 1867 | Beginning of Radical Reconstruction, with federal military occupation of Florida and the South. |

| 1868 | Approval of new constitution restores civil government. |
| 1877 | Restoration of white Democratic rule. |
| 1881 | Hamilton Disston, Philadelphia industrialist, purchases four million acres of swamp land at twenty-five cents an acre in an effort to convert it into agriculturally productive farmland and the site of new communities. |
| 1884 | Henry Plant's railroad steams into Tampa, opening the area to development. |
| 1886 | Henry M. Flagler begins constructing a railroad and hotel system on the east coast. |
| 1888 | First commercial shipment of recently discovered phosphate. |
| 1894–95 | Two great freezes devastate citrus and other agricultural crops. |
| 1896 | Flagler's Florida East Coast Railway enters Miami, creating a city overnight. |
| 1898 | Spanish-American war leads to creation of embarkation camps at Tampa, Miami, and Jacksonville. |
| 1901 | Fire destroys Jacksonville. |
| 1905 | Construction begins on Florida East Coast Railway's Overseas Railroad, which crosses the Keys to Key West. |
| 1905 | Everglades Reclamation begins under leadership of Governor Napoleon Bonaparte Broward. |
| 1906 | Hurricane results in death of hundreds of laborers on Overseas Railroad. |
| 1913 | Florida East Coast Railway enters Key West. |
| 1914 | First regularly scheduled commercial airline begins operating between two cities in United States, St. Petersburg and Tampa. |
| 1917–18 | Florida hosts American soldiers, especially aviators, in several training camps. |
| 1922 | WDAE Tampa, Florida's first radio station, begins operating. |
| 1923 | Leasing of convicts to lumber companies and other commercial interests abolished. |
| 1924–25 | Great real estate boom sweeps south Florida and other parts of the state. |
| 1926 | Boom busts. |
| | Killer hurricane brings death and destruction to southern Florida. |
| 1927 | Pan American Airways begins operations in Key West. |
| 1928 | Another devastating hurricane brings death to nearly two-thousand persons on southeastern shores of Lake Okeechobee. |
| 1930 | Eastern Air Transport inaugurates service between Miami and New York. |
| 1931 | Pari-mutuel wagering at horse and dog tracks legalized. |
| 1934 | Constitutional amendment exempts homesteads from taxation up to $5,000. |
| 1935 | Hurricane devastates part of Florida Keys; about four-hundred persons killed; Overseas Railroad destroyed. |
| 1937 | Payment of a poll tax as a prerequisite to voting abolished. |
| 1941–45 | Florida serves as huge training camp for hundreds of thousands of men and women in the armed forces. |

| | |
|---|---|
| 1942 | German submarines spotted off the southeastern coast of Florida; four German saboteurs who land near Ponte Vedra are apprehended quickly. |
| 1946 | Statewide building boom follows end of World War II; veterans crowd into colleges. |
| 1947 | Florida State University and University of Florida become co-educational. |
| 1949 | WTVJ Miami begins operations as Florida's first broadcast television station. |
| 1950 | Kefauver Crime Investigating Committee conducts hearings into organized crime in Miami and South Florida. |
| 1955 | Legislature authorizes state turnpike system. |
| 1956 | Leroy Collins becomes first chief executive re-elected to a successive term. |
| 1957 | Legislature adopts an "Interposition" resolution denying that the U.S. Supreme Court had the right to "enact" law, as the legislators defied the high court's ruling in *Brown vs. Board of Education* of Topeka (1954). |
| 1958 | Explorer I, America's first earth satellite, sent aloft from Cape Canaveral. |
| 1959 | Fidel Castro takes power in Cuba, catalyzing a massive Cuban migration to Miami and southern Florida. |
| | Orchard Villa Elementary in Dade County becomes first previously all-white public school in State to admit blacks. |
| 1960 | With a population of 4,951,560, Florida becomes tenth largest state. |
| | Utilizing lunch counter sit-ins, blacks demonstrate against segregation. |
| 1961 | Alan Shepard becomes first American in space after blasting off from Cape Canaveral. |
| | Ill-fated Bay of Pigs invasion snuffs out Cuban refugees' hopes of an early return to homeland. |
| 1962 | Cuban missile crisis brings threat of war close to home. |
| 1964 | Violence accompanies desegregation efforts in Jacksonville and St. Augustine. |
| | Florida Atlantic University opens in Boca Raton. |
| 1965 | Board of Regents takes over policymaking for Florida's institutions of higher learning. |
| | "Freedom flights" from Cuba begin; in next seven years, airlifts bring 262,000 Cubans to Miami. |
| 1966 | Claude Kirk becomes first Republican to win election as governor since 1872. |
| 1968 | Voters approve three amendments which combined give Florida virtually new constitution. |
| | Republican national convention held on Miami Beach. |
| | Statewide teacher walkout. |
| | Edward Gurney becomes first Republican ever elected to U.S. Senate by popular vote. |
| 1969 | First moon landing following blastoff from Cape Kennedy. |

| 1971 | The crown jewel of Florida tourism, Disneyworld, opens near Orlando. |
| 1974 | Reubin O. Askew becomes the first governor to be elected to successive four-year terms. |
| 1977 | Snow falls as far south as Miami on one frigid day in January. |
| 1980 | The "Mariel Boatlift," a chaotic flotilla of small boats, delivers 120,000 Cubans to Florida. |
| | Liberty City riots bring death and wholesale devastation to parts of Dade County. |
| 1981 | The space shuttle blasts off from the Kennedy Space Center, heralding a new age in space travel. |
| 1982 | Legislature establishes single-member districts for house and senate, thus placing itself for the first time on a completely one man, one vote basis. |
| | Florida Senate rejects Equal Rights Amendment. |
| 1983, 1985 | Devastating freezes ruin citrus groves in central Florida. |
| 1986 | Space shuttle Challenger explodes soon after lift-off from Cape Canaveral, killing its seven-person crew. |
| 1987 | With twelve million inhabitants, Florida passes Pennsylvania as the fourth most populous state. |

---

# SELECTED LIST OF ORGANIZATIONS, INSTITUTIONS, AND REPOSITORIES WITH SPECIAL INTERESTS IN FLORIDA HISTORY

---

Black Archives, History and Research Foundation of South Florida, Inc.
Dorothy J. Fields, Founder
Joseph Caleb Community Complex
5400 N.W. 22 Avenue
Miami, Florida 33142

Black Archives Research Center and Museum
James N. Eaton, Director
P.O. Box 809
Florida A&M University
Tallahassee, Florida 32307

Broward County Historical Commission
Rodney Dillon, Historian
100 S. New River Drive, East
Fort Lauderdale, Florida 33301

Bureau of Florida Folklife Programs
Ormond Loomis, Director
P.O. Box 265
White Springs, Florida 32096

City of Coral Gables Planning Department
Historic Preservation Division
Ellen Uguccioni, Historic Landmark Officer
305 Biltmore Way
Coral Gables, Florida 33114

Dade Heritage Trust
Roberta DiPietro, Executive Director
190 S.E. 12 Terrace
Miami, Florida 33131

Division of Historical Resources
George W. Percy, Director
R. A. Gray Building
500 South Bronough
Tallahassee, Florida 32399–0250

Florida Historical Confederation
Andrew Brian, Chairman
University of South Florida Library
Tampa, Florida 33620

Florida Historical Society
Paul S. George, President
University of South Florida Library
Tampa, Florida 33620

Florida State University
Robert Manning Strozier Library, Special Collection
Tallahassee, Florida 32306-2047

Florida Trust for Historic Preservation
P.O. Box 11206
Tallahassee, Florida 32302

Fort Lauderdale Historical Society
Dan Hobby, Executive Director
219 S.W. 2nd Avenue, P.O. Box 14043
Fort Lauderdale, Florida 33301

Halifax Historical Society
252 S. Beach Street P.O. Box 2686
Daytona Beach, Florida 32015

Historical Association of Southern Florida
Randy F. Nimnicht, Executive Director
Rebecca Smith, Research Librarian
101 W. Flagler Street
Miami, Florida 33130

Historic Broward County Preservation Board
Diana McTique, Chairman
Paul S. George, Director
600 Sagamore Road
Ft. Lauderdale, Florida 33301

Historic Florida Keys Preservation Board
Wright Langley, Director
500 Whitehead Street
Key West, Florida 33040

Historic Palm Beach County Preservation Board
John P. Johnson, Executive Director
Town Hall
North Federal Highway
Boca Raton, Florida 33432

Historic Pensacola Preservation Board and West Florida Museum of History
James W. Moody, Director
205 E. Zaragoza Street
Pensacola, Florida 32501

Historic St. Augustine Preservation Board
Hector Miron, Director
P.O. Box 1987
St. Augustine, Florida 32084–1987

Historic Tallahassee Preservation Board
Kevin McGorty, Director
329 N. Meridian Road
Tallahassee, Florida 32301

Historic Tampa–Hillsborough Preservation Board
Stephanie Ferrell, Director
425 W. Kennedy Boulevard
Tampa, Florida 33606

Jacksonville Historical Society
J. J. Daniel, President
4985 Moreven Road
Jacksonville, Florida 32210

Jacksonville Public Library, Hayden Burns Branch
Carol Harris, Curator, Florida and Genealogy Collection
122 N. Ocean Street
Jacksonville, Florida 32202

Manatee County Historical Commission
Cathy Slusser, Coordinator
604 15th Street, East
Manatee, Florida 33508

Metro-Dade Historic Preservation Division
Office of Community and Economic Development
Ivan A. Rodriguez, Director
Warner Place, Suite 101
111 S.W. 5th Avenue
Miami, Florida 33130

Miami-Dade Public Library, Florida Room
Samuel Boldrick, Librarian

101 W. Flagler Street
Miami, Florida 33130

Miami Pioneers Club
Arthur E. Chapman, President
250 N.W. North River Drive
Miami, Florida 33128

Pensacola Historical Society and Museum
Norman Simmons, Curator
405 S. Adams Street
Pensacola, Florida 32501

Street Augustine Historical Society
Page Edwards, Jr., Director
271 Charlotte Street
St. Augustine, Florida 32084

St. Lucie Historical Society
414 Seaway Drive
Fort Pierce, Florida 33449

Seminole Tribal Historical Society
Joe Dan Osceola, President
5791 S. State Road 7
Fort Lauderdale, Florida 33314

State Library of Florida, Florida Collection
R. A. Gray Building
500 South Bronough Street
Tallahassee, Florida 32399–0250

University of Miami, Otto G. Richter Library
Helen C. Purdy, Head, Archives and Special Collections
P.O. Box 248214
Coral Gables, Florida 33124

University of South Florida Library, Special Collections
Vacancy in Directorship
Tampa, Florida 33620

John C. Pace Library
The University of West Florida
Dean DeBolt, Librarian
Pensacola, Florida 32514

P. K. Yonge Library of Florida History
University of Florida
Elizabeth Alexander, Librarian
404 Library West
Gainesville, Florida 32611

# INDEX

# ABOUT THE CONTRIBUTORS

WILLIAM R. ADAMS is president of a public history consulting firm. He holds an M.A. in history from the University of Minnesota, and a Ph.D. in the same discipline from The Florida State University. A former Executive Director of the Florida Bicentennial Commission and the Historic St. Augustine Preservation Board, Adams has written articles for the *Florida Historical Quarterly* and several historic preservation journals.

ELIZABETH ALEXANDER is the Librarian and Chairman of the P. K. Yonge Library of Florida History, and the Florida History Bibliographer for the University of Florida Libraries. She received her Bachelor's degree from The Florida State University, and her Master of Library Science degree from the University of North Carolina, Chapel Hill. She is the co-author of *A Bibliography and Subject Index of Publications Issued by Official Florida Agencies* and *A Guide to the Major Manuscript Collections of the P. K. Yonge Library of Florida History*.

GREGORY W. BUSH is Assistant Professor of History, University of Miami. He earned a B.A. degree from Colgate University and his Ph.D. in history from Columbia University. Bush is Associate Editor of *Film and History*, and (with Dan Curry and Paul George) produced the film *Patriotic Parades: Wartime Miami, 1898–1945*. He was the founder of the Louis Wolfson II Media History Center, Inc., which is located in Miami.

AMY TURNER BUSHNELL is Assistant Professor of History, University of South Alabama. She holds an M.A. in Latin American studies and a Ph.D. in Latin American history from the University of Florida. Bushnell is the author of *The King's Coffin: Proprietors of the Spanish Florida Treasury, 1565–1702*, as well as many articles on early Florida.

PAUL EUGEN CAMP is a librarian in the Special Collections Department of the University of South Florida Library. Camp received his B.A. in English from the University of South Florida, and an M.S. in Library Science from The Florida State University. He has served as Executive Secretary of the Florida Historical Society and has contributed articles to *The Tampa Bay History* and *Broward Legacy*.

WILLIAM S. COKER is Professor and Chairman of the Department of History, University of West Florida. He holds an M.A. from the University of Southern Mississippi and a Ph.D. in history from the University of Oklahoma. A prolific scholar, Coker is the co-author (with Thomas D. Watson) of *Indian Traders of the Southeastern Spanish Borderlands: Panton, Leslie & Company and John Forbes & Company, 1783–1847*, and *The Siege of Pensacola, 1781*.

JAMES B. CROOKS is Professor of history at the University of North Florida. He holds master's and Ph.D. degrees in history from The Johns Hopkins University. Crooks has authored *Politics and Progress: The Rise of Urban Progressivism in Baltimore, 1895–1914*, as well as articles on Jacksonville.

RODNEY E. DILLON, JR., is Special Projects Coordinator, Broward County Historical Commission. He earned a B.A. in history from Florida Atlantic University and an M.A. from the University of Florida. Formerly Research Historian for the Fort Lauderdale Historical Society, Dillon has published articles in the *Florida Historical Quarterly*, *Tampa Bay History*, and the *Broward Legacy*, among other journals.

HERBERT J. DOHERTY, JR., is Professor of History and Social Sciences, University of Florida. He earned his B.A. and M.A. from the University of Florida and a Ph.D. in history from the University of North Carolina, Chapel Hill. Doherty is the author of *The Whigs of Florida, 1845–1854*, *Richard Keith Call: Southern Unionist*, and thirty articles on Florida.

ROBIN F. A. FABEL is Associate Professor of History at Auburn University. He received his B.A. and M.A. from Oxford University and a Ph.D. from Auburn University. Fabel has written widely on British Florida. His publications include *Bombast and Broadsides: The Lives of George Johnstone* and *The Economy of British West Florida, 1763–1781*.

MICHAEL V. GANNON is Professor of History at the University of Florida. Gannon holds degrees from the Catholic University of America and from the University de Louvain in Belgium. He earned his Ph.D. in history from the University of Florida. A Prolific scholar, Gannon's publications include *Rebel Bishop: The Life and Era of Augustin Verot* and *The Cross in the Sand*. Gannon has served as Associate Dean of Arts and Sciences, University of Florida, and he is presently Director of the Early Contact Period Study Program.

PAUL S. GEORGE is Director of the Historic Broward County Preservation Board and an adjunct instructor in history at the University of Miami and Florida Atlantic University. He received his M.A. and Ph.D. from The Florida State University. George is President of the Florida Historical Society. He has authored *Florida Yesterday and Today* as well as articles in the *Florida Historical Quarterly, Journal of Southern Criminal Justice*, and *Tequesta*, among others.

SUSAN HAMBURGER is Associate University Librarian in the Special Collections Department, Robert Manning Strozier Library, The Florida State University, Tallahassee. She holds an M.A. in history from The Florida State University and a Master of Library Science from Rutgers–The State University of New Jersey. She has authored articles and book reviews that have appeared in the *Florida Historical Quarterly*, *Southern Historian*, and *Library Journal*.

SIR JACK D. L. HOLMES received his M.A. from the University of Florida and Ph.D. in Latin American studies at the University of Texas. Sole author of twelve books and over one hundred journal and paper articles, Holmes was knighted by the Spanish government for his work in the history of Spanish West Florida. His *Gayoso: The Life of a Spanish Governor in the Mississippi Valley, 1789–1799* won the Louisiana Literary Award for the Best Book of 1965.

J. KENNETH JONES is Assistant Director of the Henry Morrison Flagler Museum in Palm Beach. He attended the State University of New York and graduated from the Ringling School of Art in Sarasota. Earlier, Jones served as Curator of Decorative Arts and Cultural History, the Charleston Museum.

MAXINE D. JONES is Assistant Professor of History, The Florida State University. She holds master's and Ph.D. degrees from the above institution. She has published articles on black history in several journals.

WRIGHT LANGLEY is Director of the Historic Florida Keys Preservation Board. He holds a Bachelor of Fine Arts degree in illustrative photography from Rochester Institute of Technology and an M.S. in journalism from Boston University. Langley is the coauthor of six photo-histories, four of them on Key West and the Florida Keys.

JOHN K. MAHON is Professor Emeritus of History at the University of Florida. He earned a B.A. from Swarthmore College and a Ph.D. in history from the University of California at Los Angeles. Mahon's many publications include *History of the Second Seminole War, The War of 1812*, and *History of the Militia and the National Guard*.

BARBARA E. MATTICK holds the position of Historic Sites Specialist in the State of Florida's Division of Historical Resources. Formerly she was Research Librarian for the Florida Collection of the State Library of Florida. She earned her master's in history and a Master of Library Science from The Florida State University.

JAMES R. MCGOVERN is Professor of History at the University of West Florida. He holds M.A. and Ph.D. degrees in history from the University of Pennsylvania. McGovern's books on Florida history include *Anatomy of a Lynching: The Killing of Claude Neal* and *Black Eagle: A Biography of General Daniel "Chappie" James*.

JERALD T. MILANICH is Curator of Archaeology at the Florida State Museum. He received his Ph.D. in anthropology from the University of Florida, specializing in the archaeology and ethnohistory of the Indians of the southeastern United States. Milanich is the author and editor of numerous articles and books, including *Florida Archaeology* (with Charles Fairbanks), and *The Early Southeast, a Sourcebook* (edited). He is currently President of the Southeastern Archaeological Conference.

RAYMOND A. MOHL is Professor of History and Chairman of the Department at Florida Atlantic University. He is a graduate of Hamilton College and holds a Ph.D. in history from New York University. He is the author of several books, including *Poverty in New York, 1783–1825* and *The Making of Urban America*. Mohl is also editor of the *Journal of Urban History*.

SAMUEL PROCTOR holds three degrees from the University of Florida, including the Doctor of Philosophy in history. A prolific scholar and inspirational teacher, he is Julien C. Yonge Professor of Florida History and Distinguished Service Professor, University of Florida. Proctor is the author and editor of numerous articles and monographs, including *Napoleon Bonaparte Broward, Florida's Fighting Democrat*. He has served as editor of the *Florida Historical Quarterly* since 1963.

B. CARLYLE RAMSEY is Dean of Instruction and Student Development at Danville Community College in Virginia. He holds master's and Ph.D. degrees in history from The Florida State University. Ramsey has published widely in the areas of history and higher education, with articles appearing in the *Georgia Historical Quarterly* and *Community College Frontiers*.

JOE M. RICHARDSON is Professor of History at The Florida State University. He holds M.A. and Ph.D. degrees in history from The Florida State University. He has written four books on black history and numerous articles that have appeared in such publications as the *Journal of Negro History*, *Florida Historical Quarterly*, and the *Missouri Historical Review*. A sterling teacher, Richardson has directed twenty theses and eleven dissertations to completion.

JOAN RUNKEL is curator of the Henry Morrison Flagler Museum, Palm Beach. She graduated from Northwest Institute of Medical Technology in Minneapolis. She has worked at the museum since 1978.

DANIEL SCHAFER is Professor of History, University of North Florida. He holds a B.S. degree from the University of North Dakota and a Ph.D. in history from the University of Minnesota. Schafer has authored *From Scratch Pads and Dreams: A Ten Year History of the University of North Florida* and co-authored a book on Jacksonville during the Civil War. His articles have appeared in numerous history journals, including the *Florida Historical Quarterly* and *El Escribano* (The Journal of the St. Augustine Historical Society).

JAMES A. SERVIES was head of the University of West Florida Libraries until his recent retirement. Holder of the Ph.D. and M.A. degrees from the University of Chicago, Servies has produced a prodigious amount of book-length bibliographic studies, including *A Bibliography of John Marshall*, *The Siege of Pensacola, 1781: A Bibliography* and *A Bibliography of West Florida, 1535–1971*. He continues to pursue research in the bibliography and history of West Florida.

REBECCA A. SMITH is Curator of Research Materials, Historical Association of Southern Florida, Miami. She holds a Master of Library Science from The Florida State University. Smith has served as photo editor for *Miami, the Magic City* and *One Hundred Years on Biscayne Bay, 1887–1987*.

THOMAS W. TAYLOR is a park ranger for the National Parks Services at the Castillo de San Marcos, St. Augustine. He holds an M.A. in history from the University of North Carolina, Greensboro. Taylor served as Executive Director of The Halifax Historical Society. His articles have appeared in several journals.

LINDA VANCE is a public historian living in Austin, Texas. Holder of a B.S. in History from the University of Houston and a Ph.D. in the same discipline from the University of Florida, Vance is the author of *May Mann Jennings, Florida's Genteel Activist* and several articles. She has enjoyed recent success with screenwriting.

PATRICIA R. WICKMAN is Director of Art Collections for the Kislak Organization and the Jay I. Kislak Foundation, Miami, Florida. She holds a B.A. in history, with high honors, and an M.A. in the same discipline from the University of Florida. Wickman has served as Senior Curator for the State of Florida's Museum of Florida History. She has written articles that have appeared in, among other journals, the *Florida Historical Quarterly*.